Confronting Death

Luis Moris
Editor

Murray Stein
Consulting Editor

CHIRON PUBLICATIONS • ASHEVILLE, NORTH CAROLINA

www.ChironPublications.com

Front cover painting by Diane Stanley
Interior design by Danijela Mijailovic
Cover design by Diane Stanley
Printed primarily in the United States of America.

ISBN 978-1-68503-499-3 paperback
ISBN 978-1-68503-500-6 hardcover
ISBN 978-1-68503-503-7 electronic
ISBN 978-1-68503-501-3 limited edition paperback
ISBN 978-1-68503-502-0 limited edition hardcover

Library of Congress Cataloging-in-Publication Data Pending

*This book is dedicated to
all its authors. For their courage
to confront death.*

*And to Gaby, who was forced
to confront death all too soon.*

Table of Contents

Jung's Confrontation with Death

An Introduction

Luis Moris

Whatever you do, if you do it sincerely, will eventually become the bridge to your wholeness, a good ship that carries you through the darkness of your second birth, which seems to be death to the outside.

C. G. Jung. A letter from 1945.

My main reason for wanting to create this book is the lack of any book of its kind. Despite the centrality of death in our lives and in our work as Jungian analysts, there is a surprising lack of literature about how Jungians understand death, how we work with death, how we prepare, if we do, for death. Even though there have been more published works on the subject following the publication of Jung's *Red Book* in 2009,[1] there remains much more for us — — Jungian

---

[1] This is probably due to the fact that *The Red Book* is filled with figures that Jung's "I" calls the dead. *The Red Book* is divided into three different books: *Liber Novus, Liber Secundus* and *Scrutinies*. All three books describe scenes of death and encounters with the dead, but the two most relevant books in relation to the dead are *Liber Secundus,* where Jung's "I" is asked to "deliver" the dead, and *Scrutinies*, where Philemon teaches the dead seven sermons, a section of the book also known as *Sermones*. *Sermones*, "a psychological cosmology cast in the form of a Gnostic creation myth" (Shamdasani, 2020, p. 50), was the culmination, as it were, of a series of paranormal experiences Jung had in January of 1916. Whereas *Liber Novus* and *Liber Secundus* took years for their completion, *Sermones* was written in the space of three evenings (Jung, 1963/1995, p. 216), and according to Christine Maillard, professor of German culture and literature

analysts, scholars, and students — to explore on the topic of death. Carl Gustav Jung (1875–1961) himself hoped that analysts would research this area. When setting out topics for further research in his address on the founding of the C. G. Jung Institute in Zürich in 1948, he said: "The investigation of pre- and post-mortal phenomena … are particularly important because of the relativisation of space and time that accompanies them" (Jung, 1948/1977a, para. 1138). Sonu Shamdasani, editor of *The Red Book*, writes that Jung "would have been quite disappointed" (Shamdasani, 2008, p. 24) had he witnessed the institute's lack of subsequent research on this theme.

Jung was consistent, throughout his life, in not wanting to engage in metaphysical questions since he was a psychologist, a scientist. Indeed, "Jung often presents himself as a metaphysical skeptic" (Main, 2022, p. 103), typically stating, for example, that one "cannot grasp anything metaphysical, one can only do so psychologically" (Jung, 1929/1968b, para. 73). The type of questions that arise in relation to death are inherently metaphysical, so that a purely rational psychology cannot even address them. Jung, however, particularly with the theoretical developments after his near-death experience in 1944, elaborated a psychology that allows us not only to approach metaphysical questions but also to work with them. In fact, I would argue that because of Jung's emphasis on taking inner experiences as psychological facts, which on occasion can even hint at the reality of an afterlife (1963/1995, p. 332), Jungian analysis can be understood as a psychotherapeutic approach that not only welcomes death into the analytical room but actually has as an aim to integrate it with life. For Jung, "not

___
at the University of Strasbourg and author of essays and books on Jung's *Red Book*, *Sermones* is the first stone, the germ, from which the entire psychology of Jung would be built (Maillard, 1993, p. 32). Following Maillard's statement, one could argue that the dead are central in the creation of Jung's psychology.

only [his] own dreams, but also occasionally the dreams of others, helped to shape, revise, or confirm [his] views on a life after death" (p. 336). The unconscious, which is "limitless, unknowable, without time and space, just as the so-called 'hereafter' is described" (Jung & Jaffé, 2023, p. 152), was understood by Jung as a possible "precursor to a post-mortal existence" (p. 152). Accordingly, he stated that "If I cannot come up with any evidence for an afterlife with my logical reasoning and intellect, I am dependent on intuitive hints and suggestions from the unconscious, including dreams, and feel justified in taking them more or less seriously" (p. 154).

Jungian analysis is today one of the few places where the post-secular individual who cannot adhere to the purely religious or purely scientific perspectives on life can find a space in which the *experience* of life after death, whether it is through a dream, a synchronistic event, a fantasy, or a near-death experience, can be taken seriously: reexperienced, thought through, challenged, tested. Indeed, since the "dead appear to exist in a sphere to which we are connected through our inner world of images" (Jung & Jaffé, 2023, p. 152), analysis can be seen as a portal for experiencing death. Jung stated that "a man should be able to say he has done his best to form a conception of life after death" (1963/1995, p. 333). As the following section shows, Jung's confrontation with death was constant, from childhood to old age, as he himself wrestled with this "age-old heritage of humanity: an archetype, rich in secret life, which seeks to add itself to our own individual life in order to make it whole" (p. 333).

The mystery of death in the life of Jung

The mystery that death brings to life was a lifelong preoccupation for Jung. Is there life after death? Are ghosts real? How do we understand apparitions? These were some of the questions that Jung tried (really tried) to answer throughout his life. It is no exaggeration that Jung's life was, from birth until death, surrounded by the theme of death. Not only was he born in a family where it was common to speak to the spirits of the dead, as his mother and maternal grandfather claimed to do (Ellenberger, 1970; Charet, 1993; Jaffé, 1997, among others), but he also grew up in an environment where "paranormal experiences were virtually commonplace in Jung's family" (Main, 2004, p. 66). Growing up as the son of a pastor, Jung saw how dead bodies were brought to his home and witnessed funerals led by his father in the nearby cemetery (Jung, 1963/1995, pp. 22–24). Jung also experienced apparitions. For instance, remembering his childhood, he writes that "One night I saw coming from [my mother's] door a faintly luminous, indefinite figure whose head detached itself from the neck and floated along in front of it, in the air, like a little moon. Immediately another head was produced and again detached itself. This process was repeated six or seven times" (pp. 33–34).[2] These sorts of experiences were not considered impossible by the youthful Jung, since he writes that "there were dreams which foresaw the death of certain persons, clocks which stopped at the moment of death, glasses which shattered at the

_____

[2] Jung claimed to have experienced ghosts on different occasions. For instance, in *Memories, Dreams, Reflections* he writes about "a case of haunting" that he experienced in Bollingen during the winter of 1923–1924 (1963/1995, pp. 255–258). In addition, in 1920, after staying in a cottage in Buckinghamshire, England, he claimed that he "was convinced the house was haunted" (1950/1977b, para. 775). Jung claimed to have seen "the head of an old woman, and the right eye, wide open, glared at [him]. The left half of the face was missing below the eye. The sight of it was so sudden and unexpected that [he] leapt out of the bed with one bound, lit the candle, and spent the rest of the night in an armchair" (para. 774). Jung also claimed that his house in Küsnacht had been haunted in 1916 and that not only he but others in the house experienced it (1963/1995, p. 215).

critical moment. All these things had been taken for granted in the world of my childhood" (p. 121).

As an adolescent Jung attended spiritual séances organized by his mother, where his cousin Helene Preiswerk was the medium. Shamdasani writes that "from the transcripts, it is clear that [Jung] appears to have initially accepted communications from figures such as his paternal and maternal grandfathers through Helene Preiswerk as veridical" (2008, p. 15). The séances, however, were stopped when she was found trying to fabricate the apparitions. The observation and analysis of these séances with his cousin became Jung's doctoral thesis. During the second semester at university, Jung read a book about the beginnings of the 19th-century movement of spiritualism, which made him conclude that "the phenomena described in the book were in principle much the same as the stories I had heard again and again in the country since my earliest childhood. The material, without a doubt, was authentic" (1963/1995, p. 119).[3]

In his second Zofingia lecture, "Some Thoughts on Psychology," delivered in 1897, Jung aimed "to establish the immortality of the soul" (Shamdasani, 2003, p. 200), as he stated that the "soul does not represent a force in a material form, and ... subsists outside the concepts of space and time. Thus, sufficient reason exists for us to postulate the immortality of the soul" (Jung, 1897/1983, p. 32). In *Memories, Dreams, Reflections* (1963/1995), when remembering this period of his life, he wrote: "why, after all, should there not be ghosts? How did we know something was

---

[3] In 1925 Jung claimed that during his student years he "thought that after all there might be ghosts" (1989/2012a, p. 5). At university Jung "courageously schooled himself, intensively studying occult literature" (Oeri, 1970, p. 187), as he read virtually all that was available to him at the time on the topic of spiritualism (Jung, 1963, p. 120).

'impossible'? ... For myself I found such possibilities extremely interesting and attractive. They added another dimension to my life; the world gained depth and background" (p. 120). By 1905, being a psychiatrist at the Burghölzli Clinic in Zürich, Jung claimed to have studied eight mediums (1905/1977c, para. 724).

Later, in 1916, Jung stated that his house was haunted by spirits of the dead that needed answers from him (1963/1995, p. 215). Arguably, one of the most relevant sections of *The Red Book* is in *Scrutinies*, where Philemon teaches the dead "because these dead ended their lives too early. These were seekers and therefore still hover over their graves. Their lives were incomplete ... [so he] must teach them, so that their life may be fulfilled and they can enter into death" (2009/2012b, p. 514). The latter, Shamdasani argues, is the basis for Jung's myth of death, what he calls Jung's "private cosmology" (Shamdasani, 2008, p. 20), which in part consists of giving answers to the dead, because it "seemed the dead only knew what they knew when they died" (p. 20). Shamdasani claims that the dead in *The Red Book* are "the ancestors. It is the dead. This is no mere metaphor. This is no cipher for the unconscious or something like that. When [Jung] talks about the dead he means the dead" (Hillman & Shamdasani, 2013, p. 2).[4] Toward the end of his life

---

[4] Besides Shamdasani, other scholars have also argued that the dead in *The Red Book* can be understood as real dead. For instance, James Hillman writes that in *The Red Book* "Jung calls attention to the one deep, missing part of our culture, which is the realm of the dead. The realm not just of your personal ancestors but the realm of the dead, the weight of human history" (Hillman & Shamdasani, 2013, p. 83). Roderick Main, quoting Jung, states: "That Jung did not denigrate the limited 'here' in favor of the boundlessness of the 'hereafter' is powerfully shown by the myth of the afterlife that he developed, in which he speculated that 'the souls of the dead' are 'dependent on the living for receiving answers to their questions, that is, on those who have survived them and exist in a world of change' (Jung, 1963, p. 339), for 'only here, in life on earth, where the opposites clash together, can the general level of consciousness be raised. That seems to be man's metaphysical task' (p. 343)" (Main, 2021, p. 164). Christine Maillard

Jung stated: "I feel quite certain ... that the process of becoming conscious continues after death" (Jung & Jaffé, 2023, p. 149).

From 1929 to 1934, Jung presented his more mature thoughts about the mystery of death in three separate essays.[5] In one of these essays, he stated that "anyone should draw the conclusion that the psyche, in its deepest reaches, participates in a form of existence beyond space and time, and thus partakes of what is inadequately and symbolically described as 'eternity'" (1934/1969c, para. 815). Because of this, he also stated that as "a doctor, I make every effort to strengthen the belief in immortality, especially with older patients ... For ... death is not an end but a goal, and life's inclination towards death begins as soon as the meridian is passed" (Jung, 1929/1968b, para. 68). Jung argued that the crisis of the second half of life is a sign that "nature prepares itself for death" (1934/1969c, para. 808), hence, "it is hygienic ... to discover in death a goal towards which one can strive" (1930–1931/1969d, para. 792), since "dying ... has its onset long before actual death" (Jung, 1934/1969c, para. 809). Jung concluded that "the unconscious is all the more interested in *how* one dies; that is, whether the attitude of consciousness is adjusted to dying or not" (para. 809). Death, then, became for Jung not only a goal but also a reality that could enrich life. Death begins before it happens, in midlife, so how one lives *with* death, how one approaches that goal became for Jung of paramount importance. In 1928, Jung received a copy of *The Secret of the Golden Flower*, a Chinese Taoist-alchemical text that, together with a dream he had

---

writes that "*The Red Book* endows the dead with a real, or at least 'effective' existence" (2022, p. 195). Stephani Stephens states that in *The Red Book* "the dead proved themselves to be souls without bodies ... [and that in] all exchanges with the dead is the notion that the human being is both soul and body and that the soul possesses immortal qualities" (2020, p. 6).
[5] "Commentary on 'The Secret of the Golden Flower'" (1929); "The Stages of Life" (1930); "The Soul and Death" (1934).

which was set in Liverpool (1963/1995, pp. 220–223), confirmed to him that the goal of the individuation process is the self, "the archetype of wholeness" (1951/1968a, para. 351).

In 1944, following a heart attack, Jung had a near-death experience which led him to have "deliriums and visions" (1963/1995, p. 320) that he described as "the most tremendous things [he had] ever experienced" (p. 326). His visions not only made him consider "that he had died and had returned to life" (Shamdasani, 2008, p. 23), but also provided him with the courage to work and publish new formulations. Two years after his heart attack Jung enlarged his concept of the archetype, introducing the "psychoid nature of the archetype" (1947/1954/1969a, para. 419). This new theoretical development allowed Jung later to present the concept of synchronicity (1952/1969e), which, according to Shamdasani, "was clearly an attempt to render parapsychological phenomena comprehensible in terms of physics, and as such, opened the door to postmortem transcendence" (2008, p. 21). In his late work, *Mysterium Coniunctionis* (1955–1956/1970), referring to the 16th-century alchemist Gerhard Dorn (ca. 1530-1584), Jung presents the individuation process as consisting of three stages of psychological development, or "three conjunctions."[6]

---

[6] Dorn's description of the alchemical opus is divided into three unions or conjunctions. The first conjunction, called *unio mentalis*, is described as the union between psyche and spirit, which is a "purely intrapsychic" (Jung, 1955–1956/1970, para. 664) union, creating "the interior oneness" (para. 670). This, however, leaves the body unintegrated. The second stage of Dorn's description of the opus consists of reuniting the body with the *unio mentalis*. Dorn describes this union through the elaboration of what he calls *substantia coelestis* or *caelum* (para. 749). This mysterious substance "assists the 'spiritualization' of the body and makes visible the essence of Mercurius, the supreme chthonic spirit" (para. 687). Jung interpreted the *caelum* as his concept of "the self, as its symbolism proves, [since it] embraces the bodily sphere as well as the psychic" (para. 717). The transformation of the body and its union with the *unio mentalis* was considered by Dorn only as a *rite d'entrée* for what is the last stage of development, which

The third and highest conjunction Jung describes is the union of "the whole man" (1955–1956, para. 760), that is, "the integrated mind and body" (Main, 2021a, p. 23), with the *unus mundus*. Jung defines the *unus mundus* as "the potential world of the first day of creation, when nothing was yet 'in actu,' i.e., divided into two and many, but was still one" (1955–1956/1970, para. 760). In the *unus mundus*, matter is not separated from spirit, inner is not separated from outer, and death is not separated from life. The notion of the *unus mundus* points to the idea that only in death, or through the experience of death, can the individual attain the highest degree of psychological development. "'Over there,'" Jung writes referring to death, "separation does not exist: everything is being-in-one" (Jung & Jaffé, 2023, p. 170). With the concept of the *unus mundus,* Jung created a psychological framework that not only allows us to speak of the dead and of life after death within his psychology, but also encourages us to view death as a goal, as an experience of the other side of existence, as a culmination of our psychological development.

In short, when James Hillman wrote that "To understand early Jung, we must read late Jung. To understand events of 1896, we must turn to his writings of 1946" (1976, p. 133), he was probably thinking of the following sentence from *Memories, Dreams, Reflections* that summarizes my point: "my works ... are fundamentally nothing but attempts, ever renewed, to give an answer to the question of the interplay between the 'here' and the 'hereafter'" (Jung, 1963/1995, p. 330).

---

is described as the union of the body, soul, and spirit with the *unus mundus*. Main argues that Jung's psychology can be understood as a form of holism, which at "its deepest levels ... [is] cosmic and mystical as well as psychological and social" (Main, 2021a, p. 24).

How one dies

More precisely for the subject of this book, *how to prepare for death* was a paramount question for Jung. As Shamdasani notes, Jung came to consider that "his personal transformation, his individuation, was a preparation for death" (2020, p. 104). The following paragraph, recorded by Aniela Jaffé in a conversation she had with Jung three years before his death, describes well what I am here presenting.

> My exploration of the inner images serves the same purpose for me as philosophy did for Plato: It is a preparation for death. In a way it helps me to avoid ending my life in retrospection. Some old people are completely caught up in reminiscence and retrospection. They are imprisoned in their memories, while for me it is rather a case of *reculer pour mieux sauter*: I am trying to see the thread that has led me into my life, into the world, and will lead me out again. (Jung & Jaffé, 2023, pp. 150–151)

Shamdasani has reframed analysis as an *ars moriendi.* "Not how is your life going," he writes, "but how is your death coming along, would be the critical question from this perspective" (2008, p. 24). He partly bases his argument on Jung's account of the visions during his near-death experience, as recounted in a letter (2 November 1945) to Cary Baynes. In it, Jung writes:

> The soul seems to detach from the body pretty early and there seems to be almost no realization of death. What follows is well-nigh incredible. It seems to be an adventure greater and more unexpected than

anything one could dream of. *Whatever we do and try in analysis is the first steps towards that goal.* That is the only thing, which has accompanied me across the threshold. (Jung, cited in Shamdasani, 2008, p. 24; emphasis added)

This might lead one to think that it was Jung's visions from 1944 that made him understand his psychotherapeutic method as a preparation for death. But this is not the case. As mentioned above, even before the near-death experience Jung already saw analysis as a preparation for death. Already in 1929, Jung argued that the goal of the second half of life is death and that "shrinking away from it is something unhealthy and abnormal which robs the second half of life of its purpose" (1929/1968b, para. 68). In 1934, in "The Soul and Death," Jung asked: "why should not the older man prepare himself twenty years and more for his death?" (1934/1969c, para. 803), since "enlightenment or no enlightenment, consciousness or no consciousness, nature prepares itself for death" (para. 808). For Jung, nature, the unconscious, prepares itself for death not as an end but as a transition. That is why *how* one dies became important for Jung. The relevant question is how individuated a person is. One year after "The Soul and Death," Jung was asked by Walter Evans-Wentz, an American anthropologist, to write a commentary on *The Tibetan Book of the Dead* or *Bardo Thödol*. Jung described the book as

at bottom, nothing less than an initiation of the dead into the *Bardo* life, just as the initiation of the living was a preparation for the Beyond ...

The only "initiation process" that is still alive and practiced today in the West is the analysis of the unconscious as used by doctors in the therapeutic purposes. (Jung, 1935/1969b, para. 842)

The latter statement is the seed of this book. Since the individuation process was understood by Jung also as a preparation for death, my questions to the authors of this book were: How are you preparing for death? How have you dealt with death? Have Jung and his writings helped you to prepare for death? If so, how?

Where I come from

Personally, I have experienced analysis, first as analysand and then as analyst, as an intimate space for personal growth and spiritual development. Experiencing analysis, on top of that, as a container that permits death to enter the room has been profoundly enriching. "Minding" death, which is what I do while working with clients, especially older ones, has been not only transformative for some of my clients, but has especially brought me to a sense of home. Through death, Jungian analysis makes more sense to me. This is probably so because death and its mystery are familiar to me. I come from a culture, the south of Chile, where stories of ghosts and bewitched houses are not unusual. Almost everyone has a story to tell about a ghost. My paternal great-grandmother, Cotito, is remembered in my family for her deep interest in and possession of allegedly paranormal powers. She was a short, skinny old lady, with beautiful white hair, as I can see in pictures. I'm told she was kind and warm but had a mysterious side; she spoke to the dead. She had a three-legged table she used during the séances that she organized to connect with the spirits of the dead. In a conversation I had with my father, who was an introverted sensing-thinking type, he told me that in some séances he saw the famous table moving on its own as the spirits of the dead were responding to Cotito's questions. I do not think he was the type of person to believe in these sorts of things easily. In fact, I think he was the opposite:

As an accountant, he dwelt among concrete, touchable facts. My older sister, Mita, like the rest of us, grew up hearing these stories and she too developed, so it seems, paranormal capacities. During my childhood we moved out from two different houses that were, according to Mita, haunted. In each of these houses, Mita claimed, there was a ghost. She would describe it in detail, for the ghost would bother her at night while in bed—which, of course, terrified my other sister and me. I grew up profoundly afraid of ghosts. We literally ran away from them during my childhood. The possibility of a life after death—one that could affect us—was not just a possibility for me as a child, it was reality. And reality, accordingly, was rich, complex, and, above all, mysterious. That is why I can relate so intimately to Jung's statement that, "In psychological terms, what we call events in the land of the dead may actually take place in the unconscious psyche" (Jung & Jaffe, 2023, p. 152). From a feeling and also from an intuitive perspective, relating the unconscious to the land of the dead simply resonates with me.

Having said that, I am not certain that there is a life after death. I am not certain that ghosts are real. Nothing has proved it to me. But nothing has disproved it to me either. These have been lifelong questions for me, questions that have enriched my life. But I have no certainty. This is precisely what Jungian psychology helps me to do: to articulate these questions better, to test them, and to continue asking them not only for me but also, when appropriate, for my clients. Dreams, of course, are very helpful for this. Numerous times, for himself and for others, Jung interpreted dreams with dead figures objectively (1963, pp. 327, 336, 341; Jung & Jaffé, 2023, pp. 153–155; von Franz, 1984, p. xv), and just that, the possibility of allowing oneself to think and to work with dreams from that perspective, can be profoundly meaningful and even transformative. Jung's psychotherapeutic framework, to me,

13

is a unique modern space that allows the postsecular individual to confront the mystery of death and prepare for it. Just as Jung did.

I would like to say a few words about the following essays. First, I must say how in awe and how humble all these essays have made me feel. I am impressed by the openness, generosity, and above all, courage of these authors. I asked them to write from a personal perspective, showing how they confront death, and without exception they have done that. The first essay of the book is from its consulting editor, Murray Stein. As he is entering his ninth decade, Murray Stein reflects upon his life as a Jungian analyst. His reflection on the Self underpins his essay, as he writes about Tolstoy, the Bible, and Faust, to bring light in the shadow of death. Stating that "It is difficult, if not impossible, to confront death without confronting grief," Susan Olson, in her profound essay, shares her feelings and thoughts on the passing of her beloved husband and the closing down of her own clinical practice. Olson reveals her difficulties in accepting the death of her husband and how poetry and Jungian thought helped her slowly to come to terms with that reality. Ann Casement presents the concept of *death cafés*, a modern, collective, and therapeutic way of bringing death to life, something she argues, is much needed. Reflecting on a few of the foremost thinkers in the West who have dealt with the topic of death in their writings, she concludes that death, as a part of life, needs to be consciously integrated into each individual's experience of being.

Claire Costello's moving essay takes us to the world of AIDS and of dying. Her many years of experience working with dying patients show us how Jungian thought has helped her navigate the humbling, difficult, yet enriching experience of accompanying someone who is about to die. Costello relates how mystical experiences have helped her to walk through the grief of death. Joseph Cambray's essay discusses how Jung's psychological framework can be understood as a psychology that helps to reenchant our disenchanted world. Cambray explores *The Red Book* and concepts like synchronicity to try to make sense of dreams of death. Writing about Greta Gerwig's film *Barbie,* Stephani Stephens states that "death is everywhere, it has already arrived, and it sits in the seams that make living possible." She recounts some of her many uncanny experiences with death and the land of the dead and explains how the writings of Jung have helped her to come to terms with them.

The essay from Ann Ulanov shows how intimate accompanying a dying person can be for an analyst. Suffering, anger, admiration are experiences that Ulanov, as analyst, shares with us in her moving essay. Paul Bishop's essay presents how both Goethe and Jung, in different ways, related to the dead and to death in their writings. This rich essay allows us to appreciate how profoundly these two thinkers wrestled with the mystery of death. As an Anglican priest, Josephine Evetts-Secker has presided over many funerals, including that of her own husband. In her essay she explains how being a priest, a Jungian analyst, and an English teacher has helped her to become friends with death.

Ursula Wirtz's profound essay reveals her personal, long-standing relationship with death. Her experiences with it have made her conclude that the encounter with death, whether in its literal or symbolic form, lies at the core of the trauma experience. Through the death of her father, who passed away because of the COVID virus, Haruko Kuwabara takes us into the Buddhist Japanese ritual world of death. She discloses the rich symbolism of this tradition and how Jung's writings have helped her to make sense of a dream of her father in the afterlife. Henry Abramovitch, writing about the soul from a Jewish perspective, describes his many encounters with death, which had a profound effect not only at an immediate personal level but also in his journey toward becoming a Jungian analyst. Abramovitch, a specialist in the anthropology of death, discusses texts and clinical experiences that help us to reflect on how death affects analysis.

Larson Hinton, who writes that death exceeds all efforts to escape it and defies our capacity to understand, offers a profound account of several experiences with death and his reflections about them. One of these experiences is the dream of the *infernal machine*. In his beautiful essay, John Beebe, who confesses that it is not his mature old age that can teach him how to die but rather the soul in him that he must now listen to, takes us into the world of cinema with a discussion of Jean Vigo's *L'Atalante*. Beebe beautifully writes that "the dying body wants to be with the anima that has loved it in life, and that the anima wants to be with the dying body."

I want to express my gratitude to several individuals who made this book possible. First, Murray Stein, who, once again, has been a rock-solid supporter of a project of mine. When I first approached him, with doubts about whether or not this book was a good idea, he was not only very enthusiastic but immediately offered his help and collaboration. I would also like to thank each author of this volume. They all were brave to undertake my request. To sit down, reflect, and write about the suffering of death in one's own life is not an easy task. Neither is it easy to publish what one comes up with. To them, my deepest gratitude. Also, I would like to thank Gary Hayes, Emma Iovoli, Murray Stein and most particularly Roderick Main for offering constructive comments about my introduction. Diane Stanley not only gave me permission to use the powerful painting, called *Unus Mundus*, for the cover of this book, but together with her husband, John, actually created the cover. To both, thank you. I would also like to offer my deep thanks to the team at Chiron Publications, who from the beginning have believed in this project and have fully supported it. A big thank-you to them. Last but certainly not least, I would like to thank Anina, my wife, who often when I had to work on this book took our little and energetic Teodora Roma for slow walks so I could have some quiet space to read and write about death. Without her support this book would simply not exist.

Luis Moris
Zürich, March 2024

References

Charet, F. X. (1993). *Spiritualism and the Foundations of C. G. Jung's Psychology*. State University of New York Press.

Ellenberger, H. (1970). *The Discovery of the Unconscious: The History and Evolution of Dynamic Psychiatry*. Basic Books.

Hillman, J. (1976). Some early background to Jung's ideas: Notes on *C. G. Jung's Medium* by Stephanie Zumstein-Preiswerk. *Spring: An Annual of Archetypal Psychology and Jungian Thought*, 123–136.

Hillman, J. & Shamdasani, S. (2013). *Lament of the Dead: Psychology after Jung's* Red Book. Norton.

Jaffé, A. (1989). *From the Life and Work of C. G. Jung*. Daimon Verlag.

Jung, C. G. (1968a). *The Collected Works of C. G. Jung: Vol. 9, Pt. 2. Aion: Researches into the Phenomenology of the Self* (2nd ed.). Princeton University Press. (Original work published 1951)

Jung, C. G. (1968b). Commentary on "The Secret of the Golden Flower." In H. Read et al. (Eds.), *The Collected Works of C. G. Jung: Vol. 13. Alchemical Studies* (pp. 1–56). Princeton University Press. (Original work published 1929)

Jung, C. G. (1969a). On the nature of the psyche. In H. Read et al. (Eds.), *The Collected Works of C. G. Jung: Vol. 8. The Structure and Dynamics of the Psyche* (2nd ed., pp. 159–234). Princeton University Press. (Original work published 1947, revised 1954)

Jung, C. G. (1969b). Psychological commentary on "The Tibetan Book of the Dead." In H. Read et al. (Eds.), *The Collected Works of C. G. Jung: Vol. 11. Psychology and Religion: West and East* (2nd ed., pp. 509–526). Princeton University Press. (Original work published 1935, revised 1953)

Jung, C. G. (1969c). The soul and death. In H. Read et al. (Eds.), *The Collected Works of C. G. Jung: Vol. 8. The Structure and Dynamics of the Psyche* (2nd ed., pp. 404–415). Princeton University Press. (Original work published 1934)

Jung, C. G. (1969d). The stages of life. In H. Read et al. (Eds.), *The Collected Works of C. G. Jung: Vol. 8. The Structure and Dynamics of the Psyche* (2nd ed., pp. 387–403). Princeton University Press. (Original work published 1930–1931)

Jung, C. G. (1969e). Synchronicity: An acausal connecting principle. In H. Read et al. (Eds.), *The Collected Works of C. G. Jung: Vol. 8. The Structure and Dynamics of the Psyche* (2nd ed., pp. 417–519). Princeton University Press. (Original work published 1952)

Jung, C. G. (1970). *The Collected Works of C. G. Jung: Vol. 14. Mysterium Coniunctionis: An Inquiry into the Separation and Synthesis of Psychic Opposites in Alchemy* (2nd ed.; H. Read et al., Eds.). Princeton University Press. (Original work published 1955–1956)

Jung, C. G. (1976). *C. G. Jung Letters: Vol. 2. 1951–1961* (G. Adler, Ed.). Princeton University Press.

Jung, C. G. (1977a). Address on the occasion of the founding of the C. G. Jung Institute, Zürich, 24 April 1948. In H. Read et al. (Eds.), *The Collected Works of C. G. Jung: Vol. 18. The Symbolic Life* (pp. 471–476). Princeton University Press. (Original work published 1948)

Jung, C. G. (1977b). Foreword to Moser: "Spuk: Irrglaube oder Wahglaube?" In H. Read et al. (Eds.), *The Collected Works of C. G. Jung: Vol. 18. The Symbolic Life* (pp. 317–326). Princeton University Press. (Original work published 1950)

Jung, C. G. (1977c). On spiritualistic phenomena. In H. Read et al. (Eds.), *The Collected Works of C. G. Jung: Vol. 18. The Symbolic Life* (pp. 293–308). Princeton University Press. (Original work published 1905)

Jung, C. G. (1983) Some thoughts on psychology. In *The Collected Works of C. G. Jung: Supplementary Vol. A: The Zofingia Lectures* (pp. 21–47). Princeton University Press. (Original work written 1897)

Jung, C. G. (1995). *Memories, Dreams, Reflections* (A. Jaffé, Ed.). London: Fontana. (Original work published 1963)

Jung, C. G. (2012a) *Introduction to Jungian Psychology. Notes on the Seminar on Analytical Psychology Given in 1925* (W. McGuire, Ed.; S. Shamdasani, Rev. Ed.). Princeton University Press. (Original work published 1989)

Jung, C. G. (2012b). *The Red Book: Liber Novus. A Reader's Edition.* (S. Shamdasani, Ed.). New York: Norton. (Original work published 2009)

Jung, C. G. & Jaffé. A. (2023). *Reflections on the Life and Dreams of C. G. Jung. By Aniela Jaffé from Conversations with Jung.* Daimon Verlag.

Maillard, C. (1993). *Les Sept Sermons aux Morts de Carl Gustav Jung.* Presses Universitaires de Nancy.

Maillard, C. (2014). Jung's "Seven Sermons to the Dead" (1916): A gnosis for modernity—a multicultural vision of spirituality. In T. Kirsch & G. Hogenson (Eds.), *The Red Book; Reflections on C. G. Jung's* Liber Novus (pp. 81–93). Routledge.

Maillard, C. (2022). Death and the dead: Reflections on a figure of Thought in Jung's Red Book. In M. Stein (Ed), *Jung's Red*

Book for Our Time : Searching for Soul in the 21st Century. An Eranos Symposium. (pp. 191–201). Chiron Publications.

Main, R. (2004). *The Rupture of Time: Synchronicity and Jung's Critique of Modern Western Culture*. Brunner-Routledge.

Main, R. (2021a). The ethical ambivalence of holism: An exploration through the thought of Carl Jung and Gilles Deleuze. In R. Main, C. McMillan, & D. Henderson (Eds.), *Jung, Deleuze, and the Problematic Whole* (pp. 20–50). Routledge.

Main, R. (2021b). Mystical experience and the scope of C. G. Jung's holism. In E. Kelly & P. Marshall (Eds.), *Consciousness Unbound: Liberating Mind from the Tyranny of Materialism* (pp. 139–174). Rowman & Littlefield.

Main, R. (2022). *Breaking the Spell of Disenchantment: Mystery, Meaning, and Metaphysics in the Work of C. G. Jung*. Chiron Publications.

Oeri, A. (1970). Some youthful memories of C. G. Jung. *Spring: An Annual of Archetypal Psychology and Jungian Thought*, 182–189. Spring Publications.

Shamdasani, S. (2003). *Jung and the Making of Modern Psychology: The Dream of a Science*. Cambridge University Press.

Shamdasani, S. (2008). "The boundless expanse": Jung's reflections on death and life. *Quadrant: Journal of the C. G. Jung Foundation for Analytical Psychology 38*, 9–30.

Shamdasani, S. (2020). Toward a visionary science: Jung's notebooks of transformation. In C. G. Jung, *The Black Books 1913–1932: Notebooks of Transformation* (Vols. 1–7; S. Shamdasani, Ed.; Vol. 1. pp. 11–112). Norton.

Stephens, S. (2020). *C. G. Jung and the Dead. Visions: Active Imagination and the Unconscious Terrain*. Routledge.

Light in the Shadow of Death
Murray Stein

Introduction

Nothing brings individuals to the realization of their singularity like the prospect of immanent death. We're born alone and we die alone, as the saying goes. The difference between our birth and our death is the degree of consciousness we bring to the moment. We're born without consciousness of being singular, but we approach death with this acute awareness. The prospect of death separates us from all others even if they are present in the room. Socrates at birth and Socrates at death is the same man, but the two states of consciousness in this same person are vastly different. In a sense, the individuation process is the development of consciousness of one's singularity, and the prospect of death quickens this awareness to an acute degree.

An essential feature of individuation in its fullest expression is a lasting impression of the timeless moment, symbolized as light. This is a union of ego and Self, of temporality and timelessness. Time and eternity fuse together, and consciousness is permanently transformed. This can happen at any time in life, and of course more than once. And sometimes it takes place uniquely and most impressively at the point of death. This light is what I will speak about in this essay.

Coming to the realization of immanent death also has a strong effect on the moral function. As death approaches and the sense of singularity increases, people often feel a need to confess and to make apologies. A sense of shame or guilt accompanies their retrospective review of their life. They wish to speak of their shadow. A father confessor may enter the scene and bring relief by offering the opportunity for confession and last rites. However, the disclosure of shameful mistakes in the past and an attempt to make apologies to those affected are not necessarily of benefit to the recipients. I remember a widow telling me about a traumatic visit to the hospital when her husband was dying. On his deathbed, he told her in tears of an affair he had had with a mutual friend of theirs. This was for the purpose of clearing his conscience before it was too late. This revelation shocked her and spoiled her previously treasured narrative of a happy marriage. "If only he would not have told me," she said. "It was so selfish of him." One wonders why he felt compelled to tell her this secret. Was it out of fear, in anticipation of the Last Judgment? The moral function, or what we call conscience, can enter consciousness like a mighty daimon demanding action. Perhaps his confession also had a positive effect on his wife in the long run: The truth shall make you free! She could remarry with less conflict about betraying her earlier promise of eternal love.

"The Death of Ivan Ilyich" by Leo Tolstoy

In some great works of literature, we can find impressive examples of the experience of light in individuation as part of the psychology of dying. "The Death of Ivan Ilyich" by Leo Tolstoy is a classic. It is the story of a middle-aged man struggling with the surprising prospect of immanent death. As this shadow gradually settles upon Ivan, it has the effect of radically separating him psychologically from his previous life: from his history of obsessive preoccupation with personal comfort and professional success; from his self-absorbed children and narcissistic wife; from his hypocritical colleagues; in short, from everything that had meaning for him in his conformist bourgeois existence until now. For the first time in his life, he comes to himself as a singular individual. He realizes he is alone in his suffering.

The threat of death, coming as it does to him unannounced and by total surprise in the midst of his active life, changes all of his inherited collective attitudes about the basic purpose of life in this world, dominated as it has been for him by his social relations and position. It is a shock that forces him in a period of only a few months to revise his Weltanschauung. Until this time, he had felt quite secure in his perspective on the basic meaning of life, which was to rise to ever higher rungs on the social ladder in St. Petersburg. Now, confronted with the specter of death hovering so near to him on the horizon, he undergoes a transformation in his views. He sees shadows round about him ever more clearly: all the lies he has told himself and believed, and all the lies he sees the healthy people around him passing on among themselves without conscious reflection. His perception of the world is stripped of projections of a successful future for himself, and the erasure of such illusions is startling to him and to his family. His persona melts away as he spends sleepless nights in agony with legs propped up on the back of his willing and faithful servant while wife and children sleep soundly in their beds. He goes through all the typical sequences of denial and negotiating with God until he finally arrives to the dreaded conclusion that there is no escape and accepts his fate: He will die, and soon. His hypocritical colleagues show sympathy while quietly behind his back celebrating his removal from his high-level position and their expected promotions.

Then, surprisingly, in his last hours of life he is presented with an uncanny, irrational revelation of a brilliant and blinding light far beyond the ego's knowing. Until now, this had not been possible because of his absorption in his own sufferings and problems. Now that he has given up all hope of recovery, the way is cleared for the Self to appear.

> It was at this moment that Ivan Ilyich fell through, saw the light shining, and it became clear to him that his life had not been the one he should have led, but that it could still be put right.

Whereupon he proceeds to release his wife and son from his previous anger and hatred:

> He wanted to say "forgive me," but what came out was "Give me." And, lacking the strength to correct himself, he waved the words aside, knowing that He who needed to would understand him.

He leaves the matter in the hands of God. And now in the midst of dying, he has his moment of final individuation, the completion of his life's journey:

> He searched for the fear of death that he always used to suffer; but he could not find it. Where was it? What death? There was no fear, because there was no death.
> Instead of death, there was light.
> "So that's what it is!" he suddenly said aloud. "What joy!"
> All of this happened to him in one instant, and after that the meaning of that instant did not change[1]

Ivan's death process is the way to enlightenment.

---

[1] Leo Tolstoy, *The Death of Ivan Ilyich*, pp.208-9.

The Book of Revelation

A similar visionary breakthrough takes place for the biblical figure John, as described in the closing scene in Revelation, the last book in the Christian Bible. Revelation is the conclusion of the biblical story as Genesis is the beginning, two mythic accounts that serve as bookends to the historical narrative of the Lord God's relationship to humanity and specifically to the Chosen People, Israel, and the adopted heirs, the early Christians. The opening myth as told in Genesis 1 and 2 tells of the creation of heaven and the earth and features the Creator God brooding over the primordial waters, *Tehom* ("the deep"), out of which He fashions the world and all its creatures and plants. The concluding myth in Revelation 21 tells of a new heaven and a new earth and of "the holy city Jerusalem, coming down out of heaven from God, having the glory of God, its radiance like a most rare jewel, like a jasper, clear as crystal" (Rev. 21:10-11). The new heaven and earth replace "the first earth [which has] passed away, and the sea was no more" (Rev. 21:1), as the text declares. The radiance of the holy city expresses the glory of God.

This moment of radical transformation in history comes after intense suffering and tribulation earlier in the book and after the Last Judgment and the separation of saints from sinners. Those previous chapters represent the dramatic death process of the first creation: confessions of sins among the churches, judgments, the apocalyptic opening of the seven seals that announce the immanent death of the world, and the terrible suffering of the world in its death throes (hail, fire, and blood, the darkening of the sun, the opening of the bottomless pit). The shadow of death covers the earth. The new heaven and new earth and the holy city that appear to John after this are in a sense a postdeath image, but the vision occurs in this life to John who "in the Spirit" is "carried away to a great high mountain" and shown the new Jerusalem descending. Therefore, it is a predeath vision of the entry of eternity into temporality. For John personally, this would be an individuation moment, but it is also more broadly significant as an archetypal moment that life's ending brings—the union of time and eternity in a numinous symbol of light.

The Death of Faust

Coming to oneself as a solitary individual, confessional impulses for past injuries to others, radical separation from previous desires and ambitions, union with the Self—these are typical, perhaps archetypal, phenomena that accompany the dying process. What about a slower process of dying as age takes its toll, less dramatic and sudden than an unexpected diagnosis of an incurable disease such as Ivan Ilych received in the middle of his life? Perhaps it's the same but takes place at a slower pace and stretched out over a longer period of time.

An example is Goethe's famous protagonist, Faust, who lives to the age of 100 and has a long time to prepare for death, but he is so dedicated to the active life that he takes no time to contemplate the cessation of life. Death anxiety haunts him in the night, but come daylight, he turns heroically away and his ego-striving revives. Addiction to frenetic activity in the temporal, material world is his chief characteristic, and for most modern and postmodern people Faust is an exemplar of how life is lived.

Knowing that his days are numbered even while he denies this inevitability and now in extreme advanced old age, Faust undertakes a massive project of reclaiming huge territories of land from the sea and building a utopian paradise there for people to live in peacefully. It is a dream of heaven on earth, a secular new heaven and new earth, but it is not supported by the Lord who gave Mephistopheles permission to play his tricks with Faust. It is backed, however, by the cynical Mephistopheles, who is biding his time while waiting for Faust's soul upon his immanent death. And Mephistopheles hastens the willful Faust's death by killing the innocent couple Philemon and Baucis in order to clear the way for Faust's mad dream. Whereupon Faust is now decisively haunted by a ghostly figure named Care (*Sorge*) whom he attempts resolutely to dismiss like a Nietzschean Superman. But Care is not pushed aside without consequence:

> Experience it deep in your mind,
> As with a curse I now descend!
> The human being is, his lifelong, blind;
> Thus, Faustus, you shall meet your end.[2]

With this curse, Faust is struck blind and thus cannot see that Mephistopheles's helpers are digging his grave and not carrying out his reclamation plan. He hears the shovels and spades digging the earth, but he does not realize this will be his grave. He goes to death blind and unaware of what is happening to him.

This is not the end of Faust's story, however. There is a comic scene of battle between Mephistopheles and pretty young angels sent by the Lord to rescue Faust's soul. The angels distract the devils who are helping Mephistopheles and make him as well dizzy with desire for their pretty naked bodies. As the angels fly about, they sing:

> Blazes that give
> Those they're caressing
> Infinite blessing,

---

[2] *Faust*, Part II, 11,495-11,498.

While they yet live!
Gather up there,
Rise and adore!
Pure is the air,
Breathe, spirit, soar![3]

And thus they rise ever higher into the Empyrean, bearing off with them Faust's immortal soul into the light. The scene in heaven as Faust's soul is taken up celebrates his transformation and rebirth. His soul has been united with the spirit, and he regains "the radiance of his youthful strength."[4]

The meaning of this ending has been debated by scholars since the work was published after Goethe's death. Should Mephistopheles have been cheated out of possession of Faust's soul since Faust signed a contract with him in blood and he had fulfilled his part of the bargain? I believe the archetype of Light took over Goethe's imagination as he contemplated the ending of his epic. Faust experiences what Dante saw and experienced at the end of the *Divine Comedy*: light and divine love. Goethe wrote in a letter to his friend Karl Friedrich Zelter: "I was not born to be a tragic poet, since my nature is conciliatory; therefore the purely tragic case cannot interest me, which should actually be inherently irreconcilable, and in this extremely flat world, by the way, the irreconcilable seems completely absurd to me."[5] His imagination was guided by his psyche and the biblical tradition despite his preference for Greek and Roman culture, which did not shy away from tragedy by any means. I take the conclusion of Faust's life to be a statement of Goethe's fully achieved individuation process.

---

[3] Ibid., 11817-11824.
[4] Ibid., 12091.
[5] Letter to Karl Friedrich Zelter, October 31, 1831.
  http://www.zeno.org/Literatur/M/Goethe,+Johann+Wolfgang/Briefe/1831

Some Personal Reflections in Autumn's Light

Personally, I am not facing immanent death, but coming to the end of my 80th year of life the prospect is not as far off as it seemed in my younger days. The light of autumn is not as bright as summer light; it does not blind the eyes or make them squint. October offers a milder sun that does not burn the skin, and shadows display themselves at greater length and over longer distances. I was born in September, and I love the light of autumn.

As the inevitability of death becomes more present to consciousness, energies continue to flow but directed differently now. The creative impulse takes a different turn, toward reflection more than action. I look back to evaluate the motivations, passions, and activities that have driven and sustained me consistently throughout my life and ask myself: Are they the same today as they were before? When I try to test their present strength, because things do change significantly as the body ages, it seems to me that some motivations that made urgent demands earlier in life have weakened in intensity while others have grown stronger and more insistent. What made life interesting and meaningful earlier is not necessarily what matters now. "Love and work ... work and love, that's all there is," Freud famously summarized, and from these two prime sources flow the rivers of meaning, but the definitions of these terms change with time.

Questions I ask now are: Is there a myth I have consistently lived by throughout my life? Is it one myth that has given my life coherence, direction, and a sense of meaning in my youth and in the middle of life provide the same today? Or have I lived by different myths in earlier stages of life and today? We do need a myth to live by, as Jung correctly perceived in the middle of his life, but I find that we don't always know what it is or when it shifts imperceptibly, or even sometimes radically, to something new. We might not be aware of how things change as we age and grow old: "When I was a child, I spake as a child, I understood as a child, I thought as a child: but when I became a man, I put away childish things," St. Paul writes in his First Epistle to the Corinthians.[6] This has been my experience.

The celebration of Christmas, for instance, does not move me at all today, whereas when I was a child, it was a time of intense anticipation and excitement. Most things commercial and for sale in the shops leave me cold today. A new car? Not interested. A trip to some exotic destination? I can take a pass. Travel, once so attractive and enticing, has become tedious, and the prospect of passing through airports and staying in hotels, no matter how luxurious or special they might be, holds little attraction. What set my juices roiling in earlier years no longer has the same effect. I have seen a lot and done a lot. Life is simply different now. Adding new objects (toys, people, offspring) to my collection and pursuing new experiences no longer seem quite so attractive.

So, what makes life interesting and worthwhile now? Some interests do remain constant and form a basis of continuity with the past. I realize that one of my greatest pleasures has been the joy of learning, and this remains as compelling and sustaining as ever, perhaps even more so. I am as curious about ideas and works of the literary imagination as I was in my youth and middle age. For many years after graduating from Yale University in 1965 with a major in English literature and from Yale Divinity School in 1969, I had many dreams of returning to these beloved places—the streets, the hallowed halls, the glorious libraries—and having the leisure to study there again as I did as a young man. These were dreams that I awoke from with a feeling of nostalgia and longing. Would

---

[6] I Corinthians 13:11-12.

that they were true, I thought. I have also realized in retrospect that my teachers in high school, universities, and the Jung Institute in Zürich have been marvelous guides into the life of the mind and soul. This activity of learning continues to satisfy me deeply as I read on through my eighth decade. Reading and learning have given me great pleasure and joy in the past as they still do in the present, and I hope and pray they will continue to do so in the future. And writing is almost an addiction (I hope it is a positive one!).

Learning makes life worth living, and more! Living with the great minds of the past—and here I include importantly, of course, C.G. Jung—and with stimulating thinkers of the present time, is a central feature of my everyday life today, and this gives me a strong and continuing incentive to go on living from day to day. I am so grateful for my inspirational teachers, and I remember them one by one almost every day. I wish the same for the next generations and that my grandchildren too will be blessed with similarly inspiring guides into the life of the spirit.

I sometimes wonder: What are "hungry ghosts," such as those who haunted Jung and begged for answers to their questions? What are they hungry for? It seems to me that they might be hungry for sensual pleasures—tastes, smells, sounds, touch. Then I wonder: What will I miss after my days of life on earth come to an end? I have no answer. But this does lead me to realize how much I look forward to good meals, to walking in the hills around Goldiwil, where we live, to the pleasure of listening to classical music, to sharing a glass of wine in the evening with my wife in front of a cozy fire in the fireplace. Pleasures of the flesh do not vanish with age, although they change. In some ways, they even deepen. The key to sensual enjoyment is mindfulness, taking the time to savor the moment of sensate experience. I find this to be closely linked to the pleasures of the mind: Careful sensual uptake is akin to deep reading.

What about aesthetics? I wouldn't say that I absolutely live for beauty the way an aesthete like Oscar Wilde did, but it is important to me nevertheless even if at a more moderate level. I don't think I would want to live in an ugly world. I am not a true stoic, although it is in my blood from my mother's side of the family, who were German Baptist pioneers in the wilderness of 19th-century Saskatchewan, Canada. At my age and in sight of the terminal station on life's journey, I continue to look for beauty and find it in many places: in nature, in the beautiful city of Zürich at certain times of day in the calendar year (especially the fall and winter), in the lovely Asian-style home my wife has created for us in the Bernese Oberland, in music and art, in cinema, in noble animals. I am fascinated with the human face, and when a smile opens a somber Swiss face wide and makes the eyes sparkle, I feel joy in my whole being. I observe faces on the train, in the streets, in shops, in my office, in the classroom. Everywhere and in all places, I've ever visited, there have been beautiful faces, women's and men's.

Nowadays the prospect of becoming "enlightened" attracts my attention and interest more than it did in the past. I ask my aging friends and occasionally myself: Can one justifiably anticipate finding wisdom in old age? I don't think it is automatic or a given of human nature because many people, as I've seen, have died in advanced age without the grace of discernable enlightenment. This development seems to depend on cultivating mindfulness and imagination in a specific way. Personally, I do not meditate in the traditional sense, as for instance Zen Buddhists practice by sitting on a cushion for hours and thinking of "nothing" (i.e., the Void). Instead, I use the practice active imagination as I've learned about it in Jung's writings and studied how this process develops in *The Red Book*. The practice of active imagination has paid rich dividends and given me a sense of an inner community. And of course, dreams, my own and those of others who share theirs with me, often bring me to a flash of enlightenment, as from the following dream told me recently by my wife:

> A friend of mine is carrying a statue of the crucified Christ mounted high on a pole. As he moves forward toward a barn, I see the Virgin Mary floating in the air beside the Crucified figure. Another person, who is identified as the biblical Job, accompanies them. When they reach the barn, the three of them enter, and my friend and I remain outside. The three figures—Christ, Mary, and Job—become enormous living persons, each at least five meters in height. Suddenly, a Voice sounds and speaks the words: "All that is broken is made whole!" A clap of thunder and a bright flash of light that brilliantly illuminates the scene in the barn follow this. We can hear the Voice clearly and see the light through the cracks in the wall of the barn. Had we been inside, we would have been blinded.

Such astonishing messages from the unconscious come from time to time, unbidden, unsolicited, totally by surprise. They give me much food for thought, and beyond that, they deliver a numinous feeling (*Mysterium tremendum et fascinans*) of the sacred in our midst. They suggest enlightenment, if in a realm beyond ego consciousness.

Sometimes such revelations come also from the dreams that analysands bring into my practice. I look forward to my work each week with analysands. The continuous and long-term contact with people in psychological depth is, I find, immensely nourishing. Their dreams fascinate me and give me much to contemplate. And what deep satisfaction we experience together when we witness complexes untangled, compulsions dissolved, relationships stabilized, hostilities inner and outer neutralized—in short, when we experience together the psyche moving toward its goal of becoming whole and fully realized.

This brings me to the importance of "service" in my life. This is an abiding motivation that keeps me going even when the waves are high and the troughs between them are deep. From my father and mother, I inherited an indefatigable sense of service. My father was a pastor, and the last words I heard him speak as he lay dying and some fellow pastors were visiting him in hospital was: "I would still like to be of service!" He said this with tears in his eyes. I have had the same sense of willing obligation to serve a community, and in my life, it has been the community of Jungians worldwide. In the past, this was carried out partly through working in the various institutions such as training institutes and the International Association for Analytical Psychology, and now I do this primarily by writing and teaching. This motivation shows no sign of abating. It is one of the continuities in my life.

A most important item, which I've saved for last and which is the foundation of a satisfying life for me, is relationship— family, wife, children, friends, colleagues, students, analysands, and neighbors. If any one of these is disturbed, especially the close ones, I quickly lose a zest for life. As I grow old, my emotional stability depends absolutely on close and harmonious relationships. On this everything else depends—creativity, sensual enjoyment, the joy of learning, a sense of service, and all else that give my life interest and meaning. Without it, there is no ground under my feet, only an abyss of emptiness and futility. It's strange, because I am not a feeling type. Or maybe it is because of this that I depend so profoundly on solid and loving relationships. In this, I have been blessed for my entire life from childhood onward. I have had dear friends all along the way, and my family has been, if not without troubles and conflicts at times, the source of whatever resilience I can claim. In my opinion, the real test of individuation, in the sense of maturity, comes from relationship. This means to love, to sustain, to contain, to endure, and to learn from deep and powerful and often conflictive interactions with other individual human beings. This is the masterpiece of the individuation process, in my opinion, and its acid test (*Prüfung*).

I have used the phrase *Amor fati* over the years to express a particular feeling I often have about my life. With all its twists and turns, beginnings and endings, openings and closings of doors and windows of opportunity, my life has shown a distinct pattern of meaningful coincidences. I call this grace. In retrospect, I would say that most, if not all, of the most important decisions in my life have had the element of synchronicity at their center.

As a consequence, I have the strong feeling that a hidden hand has guided my destiny. Casual meetings have turned into life-changing events and have brought me into territories I would have never discovered by means of will or intention. This is how my life has unfolded, much less by deliberate conscious planning and design on my part than by sudden openings, by the intervention of messengers of meaning, by angels appearing in the guise of strangers on the path of life. It is these who have created opportunities for love and work, service and creativity, and ultimately for meaning. The ego has cooperated, but invisible forces at work have laid down the pattern in the dim background. I owe it to Jung that I have any understanding whatsoever of such a mysterious process. This has convinced me that meaning is not something made by the ego's hands but rather something discovered by taking "the next and most necessary step" as this reveals itself in the course of living one's daily life.

This brings me to reflect on the "myth of return," a journey akin to Homer's Odyssey, that has governed the pattern of my later years. In 2003, at the age of 60, I returned to Switzerland after an interlude of 30 years in the United States since graduating from the Jung Institute in Zürich in 1973. But the "return" was more than geographical. It was a "return" to the spiritual source and center of my life as a Jungian. It is where I had been born into the profession and nurtured in the way of living in daily contact with the unconscious through attending to dreams and engaging in active imagination. When people would ask me, "why in the world did you move to Switzerland at your age," I would jokingly say, "because of a love affair." As odd as it may seem, this is my home. I love it.

But there is more to the theme of "return." Shortly after my wife and I moved into our apartment in Zürich, I happened to walk into an exhibition in the Grossmunster Church recognizing the 500th anniversary of the birth of Heinrich Bullinger, the successor to Huldrych Zwingli, the great Protestant Reformer. The exhibition featured Bullinger's long career as pastor of the Grossmunster Church and his illustrious contributions as a leading theologian of his time. One of the topics displayed in this extensive review of the Protestant Reformation in Zürich was the Reformers' vicious persecution of the small sect known as *"Taüfer"* (Anabaptists) who lived in the nearby village of Zollikon. In January 1527, Felix Manz and several other leaders of the Anabaptist movement were taken on a boat into the Limmat River and forcibly drowned at the instigation of the Zürich Reformers. As a result of the persecutions, the Anabaptists fled Switzerland and moved northward into German lands, and eventually many migrated to North America. As I studied these materials on display, it suddenly dawned on me that these were my ancestors. On my mother's side, the family name was Reiman, and to my astonishment I discovered that this was also the name of some of the Swiss Anabaptists. (To this day the name is familiar in the Zürich region.) I realized that in moving back to Zürich I had returned home in a deeper sense than I knew! Now it seems to me that a circle has been closed, a family circle that has taken 500 years to complete.

There is yet a further dimension to the myth of return that I have been living since the age of 60. In a personal sense, the return to the homeland of Jungian psychology has also meant a return to the original sources of this field, namely the writings of C. G. Jung. The 30 years between leaving and returning, which I spent in the United States living primarily in Chicago, were filled with studies of many fields related to analytical psychology and with discovering and integrating other schools of depth psychology into the theory and practice of Jungian psychoanalysis. During this time, I was also very much occupied with founding new Jungian societies in the United States (the Inter-Regional Society and the Chicago Society of Jungian Analysts) and with traveling and serving the worldwide Jungian community as a member of the IAAP Executive Committee (1989-2004) and finally as President (2001-2004). These years were characterized by expansion of horizons, personal and professional, and explorations that resulted in a genuine appreciation of many different features of contemporary Jungian work and its place in the professional world of depth psychology. The return to Zürich in 2003 inaugurated a return to the source and core of Jungian psychology. Since then, I have been focused on a return to basics. When *The Red Book* was published in 2009, I was drawn to it, as were so many others, and during the past 10 years I have frequently circled around this primary text, its relation to Jung's later writings, and its interpretation for our times. This has brought a new dimension of depth, I believe, to my long-standing interest in the theme of individuation, about which I have written extensively throughout my career,

Age intensifies one's focus on the center and brings the essential matters and values more clearly to the fore, renders them less clouded over with extraneous matters and ancillary interests. It is a return to the Self. For me, these later years have been a time of gathering in and subjecting the contents accumulated previously from so many sources to a process of distillation. One hopes a Grand Cru will come of it. This *opus* calls for patience and concentration, selection and discrimination, rejection of the extraneous and steady attention to the essentials. It is a work in progress as I enter my ninth decade.

References

Goethe, J.W. von (1963). *Goethe's Faust*. Translated by Walter Kaufmann. New York: Anchor Books.

Tolstoy, L. (2015). *The Death of Ivan Ilyich and Other Stories*. Translated by Nicolas Pasternak Slater. Oxford: Oxford World's Classics.

The Ever-Moving Caravan:
Reflections on Aging, Dying, and Death

Susan Olson

Calm at last, eyes closed, hands resting at his sides, my husband, Don, lay almost motionless in his hospital bed. With each shallow breath the light blanket covering his chest rose and fell slightly. The wires and tubes tethering him to life were finally gone, except for an oxygen cannula and an IV port through which the Hospice nurse administered his medication. I sat in a chair beside him holding his hand, hoping that through the fog of sedation he could feel my presence. Although it was 4 o'clock in the morning, I did not want to fall asleep and miss a second of this liminal time. But I must have dropped off for a moment, for when I opened my eyes, I sensed that something had changed. The blanket was no longer rising and falling. The soft "puff" of his exhaled breath had ceased. I held his hand and watched for a few more minutes, just to be sure. Then I opened the door and called the nurse. "I think he's gone," I said.

I had lost loved ones before, but this was the first time I had been present at the moment when a living body becomes a corpse and the soul flies … where? After the nurse left for a few minutes, I stayed at Don's bedside, still holding his hand, wondering if he knew that he had died. Was his soul flying around the room, seeing me sitting there? Was he watching as the nurse returned and placed her stethoscope on his chest? Did he know that his heart continued to "flutter" (her word) for almost an hour after he stopped breathing? Was he having a "near-death experience," choosing to leave his tired body behind and walk into the light? From what he had told me, I knew that both he and his mother had almost died when he was born. So it seemed like justice, a balancing of the scales, that his departure should be easy and gentle.

Nevertheless, as Jung writes:

> [D]eath is indeed a fearful piece of brutality; there is no sense pretending otherwise. It is brutal not only as a physical event, but far more so psychically: a human being is torn away from us, and what remains is the icy stillness of death. There no longer exists any hope of a relationship, for all the bridges have been smashed at one blow. ... This is a cruel reality which we have no right to sidestep.[1]

In my 81 years of life, I have not been a stranger to the "icy stillness of death." One grandfather died before I was born, and the other was killed in an auto accident when I was 11. My father died at home of a heart attack when I was 14. Both grandmothers died of "old age" when I was newly married in my early 20s. My mother died of breast cancer when I was a young mother of 27, soon after the birth of my daughter. The cruelest blow of all was the death of that daughter in an auto accident when she was 18. As fate would have it, I was not present when these beloved souls left their bodies and crossed the threshold into death. The closest I had come was lying awake in my bedroom while my father lay moaning in great distress in his room across the hall. I did not want, and probably

---

[1] *MDR,* p. 346.

would not have been allowed, to enter that room as the EMTs tried to revive him. But after he died, while our mother and the doctor waited downstairs for the hearse to arrive, my brother and I cracked open the door and peeked into our father's room. In the dim light we saw a covered mound lying on the bed. We had thought we wanted to see our dad's dead body, but when it came right down to it, we were too frightened to come closer. Quietly we shut the door and tiptoed down the hall, never telling our mother (or anyone else) what we had done. Somehow our adolescent selves knew without being told that crossing the threshold into that room would have violated a great taboo, an age-old proscription intended to protect the living against the contamination of death.

Several days went by before we saw our father's body again. By then the taboo had been neutralized by the ministrations of the funeral home. Lying in his casket, Dad was all cleaned up with his hair combed, eyes closed, and lips glued shut in a tight artificial line. He was immaculately dressed in the white shirt, suit and tie we had chosen, wearing the golf-club-shaped tie clasp we had given him for Christmas. As I approached his casket and gazed down at his body, I knew immediately that it was not my father lying there. Where he was I did not know, but his lively, fun-loving, perfectionistic, hardworking essence had flown, leaving an empty husk behind.

In my family the denial of death, as Ernest Becker calls it,[2] was so strong that after Dad's funeral, we rarely spoke of him. In a few days my brother and I returned to school, hoping that no one would mention our loss. Our mother tried to "keep calm and carry on," maintaining a semblance of what passes for "normality." But the denial had its price: She began drinking late at night, when her loneliness became more than she could bear. My brother and I

---

[2] Ernest Becker, *The Denial of Death.* New York: Free Press, 1973.

maintained our "good kid" personas in public, while doing more than our share of teenaged acting out behind the scenes. Now, after years of therapy and analysis, I know more about the cost of denial: the emotional energy required to maintain it and its corrosive effect on the psyche. But after Don's death I felt my old defenses creeping in, infiltrating my thinking, my emotions, my behavior, and even my language. For example, when breaking the news of his death I found myself avoiding the "D" word and using instead the phrase *passed away*, a euphemism I have always disliked. "Why am I doing this?" I asked myself. It did not take me long to realize that I was sidestepping the cruel reality of Don's passing, clothing it in language that felt less abrasive than the harsh "D" word. These days I am making an effort to say (to myself as well as to others) the blunt words: "Don died. My husband is dead." There is no sense pretending otherwise.

Don had his own euphemism for death, borrowed from William Cullen Bryant's poem "Thanatopsis," which he must have been made to memorize in high school. Paraphrasing slightly, he referred to death as "the ever-moving caravan," often facetiously abbreviated as "the ever-moving." Bryant's poem ends with these lines:

> So live, that when thy summons comes to join
> The innumerable caravan, which moves
> To that mysterious realm, where each shall take
> His chamber in the silent halls of death,
> Thou go not, like the quarry-slave at night,
> Scourged to his dungeon, but sustained and soothed
> By an unfaltering trust, approach thy grave
> Like one who wraps the drapery of his couch
> About him, and lies down to pleasant dreams.[3]

---

[3] William Cullen Bryant, "Thanatopsis," 1817. Wikipedia.

Don has joined the "ever-moving" now, and I wonder what that "mysterious realm" is like for him. Did he walk into the light to be enfolded in loving arms? Or did his soul wink out and disappear like a dying star? He claimed to believe that death is "It," the end of all things, but his defense against misfortune was often to anticipate the worst, so as not to be blindsided when the axe fell. How surprised he would have been if at the moment of death, he found himself entering another realm, like a butterfly emerging from its cocoon! Sitting with his body before the funeral director came to take it away, I remembered what I felt when viewing my father's corpse: He is not there. His tired old body, whose hand I am still holding, is an empty container now. His tender, bruised, feisty, wise, loving spirit has departed, and only God knows where it has gone.

My own euphemism for death is derived from lines in Hamlet's "To be or not to be" soliloquy in Shakespeare's play:

.... To die; to sleep; —
Perchance to dream! Ay, there's the rub;
For in that sleep of death what dreams may come,
When we have shuffled off this mortal coil,
Must give us pause.[4]

Back in 1964, just before I married her son, my soon-to-be mother-in-law gifted me with tickets to see Richard Burton playing Hamlet in New York. I'll never forget that evening or that performance, especially Burton's serpentine movement while speaking the lines "when we have shuffled off this mortal coil." His head dropped forward, and his whole body gyrated as though he was casting off not only the black turtleneck he wore, but his entire skin. As graceful

---

[4] Hamlet, III, I, 64-68.

as a dancer, his body conveyed in one fluid motion the implicit meaning of Hamlet's words, which liken death to the shedding of an old, outworn garment. A few years ago Don and I found along our garden fence a long, slender snakeskin, perfectly whole, with even its eye openings intact. That snake had shuffled off its mortal coil and slithered away, leaving its dead, fragile casement behind. Carefully we coiled it up and placed it in a pottery bowl high on the shelf of a bookcase, where our curious cat could not get at it. It is there to this day, reminding me that death may be no more than shedding the outgrown clothing of the body, which we must discard before we move on to whatever comes next.

It is significant to me that both Don's euphemism for death and mine include references to dreams. In "Thanatopsis" death is compared to lying down to pleasant dreams, a fate Don would have welcomed since many of his dreams near the end of his life were dark and terrifying. The quote from *Hamlet* suggests that what comes after death "must give us pause." Perhaps Hamlet is remembering what the ghost of his dead father had told him in the first act of the play:

>   …. But that I am forbid
> To tell the secrets of my prison-house,
> I could a tale unfold whose lightest word
> Would harrow up thy soul, freeze thy young blood,
> Make thy two eyes, like stars, start from their spheres,
> Thy knotty and combined locks to part
> And each particular hair to stand on end
> Like quills upon the fretful porpentine.[5]

---

[5] *Hamlet*, I, v, 13- 20.

Although they lived centuries apart, both Bryant and Shakespeare take it for granted that dreams have meaning, for better or for worse. The two poets also suggest that the dead are conscious and continue to dream after they have shuffled off their mortal coil. Of course we cannot know, on this side of the veil, what dreams may come after we die. But we know for certain that the living often dream about the dead. In the two years immediately following my daughter's death I had a series of dreams about her, dreams which shaped my experience of grief and which eventually became the subject of my books *By Grief Transformed* (Spring, 2010) and *Images of the Dead in Grief Dreams* (Routledge, 2021). Both books also include examples of dreams reported by others, which held meaning for them and even helped to alleviate their grief. So after Don died, I hoped that he would come to me in a dream, although I knew that I could not command that to happen. Then two months after his death I dreamed:

> Don is sitting in his usual chair, alert and awake and very present. I notice that he is no longer tethered to the oxygen machine which had been his constant but unwelcome companion in his final months of life. He is wearing one of his favorite shirts, a soft flannel which I now often wear for comfort. His right hand is resting on the arm of his chair, so close that I can reach out and touch it. As I do so, I am glad to feel that his flesh is alive and warm again, not still and cool as it was in death. We don't speak or even look at each other, but it feels as though he has incarnated again in imaginal form. After two months, just as I am growing accustomed to his physical absence, he is present again in the form of a vivid dream image.

Like many couples, Don and I had two customary chairs that we sat in to read, talk, watch TV, share a cup of coffee or a glass of wine. We often ate our meals on tray tables pulled up next to our chairs. With a table and lamp between them, the chairs were just close enough for us to reach out and touch hands, but not so close that we could jostle or crowd one another. The circle created by the chairs, the table and lamp, the tray tables, even the TV set, became a familiar comfort zone, representing our connection but also the respectful distance between us. These days when I sit in my chair, I am painfully aware of the emptiness of his. Our cat seems to sense his absence too, for she often curls up in his chair, as though wishing (if cats can wish) to fill that empty space. To me, my dream suggests that Don's essence continues to occupy his chair, even though his physical life has ended and his body has been reduced to ashes. In the imaginal realm of the dream world, he is alive and warm and quietly present.

It is difficult, if not impossible, to confront death without confronting grief. But since I have written about grief before, I will say only a few words about it here. After my daughter died, I learned that grief affects the body as well as the psyche. As the psyche faces the "icy stillness of death," the body goes into survival mode, as if to hoard what energy it has for the basic functions of eating, sleeping, bathing, dressing, and minimal daily activity. I found the same to be true after Don's death, only more so. It was as though my whole being contracted and withdrew into itself, waiting for a bit of life energy to return. At 81, the healing process is slow and occurs in tiny, almost imperceptible increments. Some days I have bursts of energy, while other days demand hours of "down time" doing absolutely nothing. Consequently, this go-round of grief, like Hamlet's encounter with the skull of Yorick,[6] is a *memento mori*, a

---

[6] *Hamlet*, V, I, 200-215.

reminder of my own limitations and my own inevitable mortality. One day it will be my turn to shuffle off my mortal coil and join the ever-moving caravan. This is a cruel reality which I have no right to sidestep.

The shock of Don's death reverberated through my practice as well. These days my clientele consists mostly of a core group of people with whom I have worked for many years. Many of them are in their 60s, 70s, and 80s and are dealing with the realities of aging and death themselves. I know them well and have accompanied them through life transitions such as graduations, marriages, affairs, divorces, the arrival of grandchildren, retirement, the onset of age-related illnesses, and the deaths of parents and spouses. I have listened to their fantasies and dreams, supported their creative endeavors, confronted their complexes and defenses, and validated their hard-won insights. I try to minimize self-disclosure in my work, but as Don's health worsened, I told them that I was reluctant to leave him alone and would not be able to come in to the office as often as I would like. And so we reverted to the virtual format we had adopted during the pandemic, occasionally meeting face-to-face if possible. For the most part this transition went smoothly, with some clients even saying that they preferred to work online. The change also alerted them to the fact that my husband was in declining health with little chance of recovery. When he died, the idea of hiding behind a screen of analytic inscrutability felt like another form of the denial of death to me. Without going into detail, I wanted to acknowledge that I was grieving and needed time to regain my equilibrium. So I wrote my clients a brief email (BCC'ing them to preserve confidentiality), telling them that Don had died and saying that I would be taking several weeks off from work. Although I could not give them a precise timeline for my return, I said that I would stay in touch and hoped to resume within a month or two. To a person they expressed their condolences and assured me that they would be waiting when I was ready to begin again. If they had feelings of anger, fear, or abandonment, they put them on hold to be dealt with later. When we finally resumed our work, they wanted to know how I was doing before plunging back into their own concerns. On a human level I appreciated their sympathy, but I also interpreted it as a transference reaction, a need for reassurance that their analyst had not fallen apart, disappeared, or died herself. Several clients confided that during the break they had thought about stopping analysis but had decided to continue. Two whose work was already drawing to a close decided to terminate—one to seek a spiritual director and one, a therapist herself, to take a break from therapy for a while. But most had plenty of stored-up material to present and were ready to pick up where we had left off. So after a two-month hiatus, our analytic connections held, affirming the durability of the relationships we had formed over many years. It occurred to me that the break might have been preparing them psychologically for the permanent separation that would occur when I eventually died. But since my health is stable, I decided to hold that interpretation in my mind for now, to be introduced later if the time felt right.

Shortly before Don's death, another form of death was looming, this one involving my office. After 25 years, my office space had become a home away from home for me and a *temenos* for my analytic practice. A dear friend and colleague occupied the room next door, and I cherished my relationship with her even when we saw each other only briefly in passing. Don's energy was present in the office too, since he had shared it for several years before his retirement as a clinical psychologist. Some of his furniture, pictures, books, and mementoes were still there, lending their ambience to the space. But the 45-minute commute on a busy interstate highway was becoming troublesome for me, especially during rush hour, at night, or in bad weather. Since I was using the office infrequently, the rent had become an unnecessary and unwanted expense. So when my lease came up for its annual renewal, I could see the writing on the wall. As I weighed the pros and cons, I often confided in Don, who in spite of his compromised health listened patiently and (good therapist that he still was) did not try to make the decision for me. Gradually it became clear that this was a head vs. heart decision: My head knew that it was time to close the office, but my heart did not want to let go. In the end the decision was made easier by my two officemates, who planned to move to a smaller space nearby. When I finally told them that I had decided not to renew my portion of the lease, the three of us could breathe deep sighs of relief and begin the process of choosing a moving date, notifying our clients, arranging for movers, and packing our belongings. But right in the midst of this process, Don entered the hospital and then the inpatient hospice unit where he died. So the move went onto the back burner for several weeks while I made funeral plans, spent time with family, and began to tend to the legal and financial details that follow a death. I finally moved out of the office about a month after Don's death, but my memory of that time is fragmented and blurry. Somehow I went on automatic pilot and arranged the move, but I don't remember much about it now. When the office furniture was delivered to our (now my) home and the boxes were stacked in the dining room, waiting to be unpacked, I was too exhausted to feel anything but immense relief. The grief hit me later as I assured myself that although I had left my office, I was still an analyst. A chapter of my professional life had closed, but I had not retired and did not intend to do so. My clients wanted to continue our work and were adjusting to the virtual format. And yet I wondered if it would be possible to re-create the *temenos* of analysis in the two-dimensional form of computer-generated reality. As I write this six months after the move, the transition seems to be proceeding smoothly. But the verdict is still out on how it will unfold in the future.

Reflecting on those weeks now, I think that the coincidence of Don's death and the closing of my office hit me like a double whammy of loss. Not just one but two bridges were smashed at one blow, one by circumstances beyond my control and one by my own reluctant choice. As an introverted feeling type, my thinking function is the first to go when I am stressed. So for weeks it was all I could do to think straight about all the tasks that required my attention. Journaling helped, but when I read those pages now I encounter a mishmash of to-do lists, outbursts of emotion, a few fragments of dreams, and loose stream-of-consciousness ruminations. The fog is lifting now, but I know that the process of healing will be slow. At my age (how I dislike that phrase!), everything takes longer than it used to. No, scratch that, *I* take longer than I used to. Once again, the losses I am facing serve as *memento mori*, unmistakable evidence of my own aging and mortality. I try to honor that reality by paying attention to my need for simple food, moderate exercise, quiet time, and rest. I need contact with close friends and family, but I cherish the luxury of quiet days when I can sleep in, read, sit on the porch with the cat, watch the birds, notice the leaves turning, and begin to reflect upon the meaning of this season of life. More lines from Shakespeare, this time from one of his sonnets, drift into my mind:

> That time of year thou mayst in me behold
> When yellow leaves, or none, or few, do hang
> Upon those boughs which shake against the cold,
> Bare ruin'd choirs, where late the sweet birds sang.

In me thou see'st the twilight of such day
As after sunset fadeth in the west,
Which by and by black night doth take away,
Death's second self, which seals up all in rest.[7]

It may seem strange, but I find these lines comforting rather than depressing. Even though their tone is melancholy, they portray aging and death as ordinary events, as natural as the changing of the seasons. The luminous images of the yellow leaves, the bare boughs, and the fading light suggest that the transient beauty of autumn is also found near the end of human life. I know that I found Don's weak, tired, painfully thin body beautiful as his death approached. (He did not believe me when I told him so, but it is true.) Now my aging body reminds me daily that I am in the autumn of my own life and that winter will inevitably follow.

It is a cliche that in our twilight years we begin to suffer life-changing limitations, frequent falls, and debilitating illnesses, all pointing toward the day when we will join the ever-moving caravan. In recent years several of my close friends have died, and three have lost spouses. Many others are dealing with chronic health issues. None of my clients has died, but several are coping with their own infirmities and the illnesses and deaths of friends and family. Under these circumstances it is not surprising that the subjects of aging and mortality arise often in my conversations with friends and clients. These feel like important subjects to be faced head-on rather than avoided as we approach the end of our lives.

As I enter this season, I find myself thinking often of Jung's attitude toward aging and death. From an early age he was fascinated with death and did not shy away from addressing its impact on his

---

[7] William Shakespeare, Sonnet 73, ll. 1-8.

life. In his memoir he recounts many of his dreams of the dead, including several of his parents and his late wife. As he grew older and suffered his own health crises, he reflected on his own aging with characteristic honesty and depth. His reflections are now shaping my own attitude toward aging and death and are prompting me to approach my own mortality with as much acceptance as I can muster, even with curiosity about what comes next.

Early in his memoir Jung describes his first encounter with death as a young child. He recalls that one day a corpse floated down the Rhine Falls near his home. He was eager to go with his father to see the dead body, but his mother forbade him and held him back. Later he sneaked into the garden and saw blood and water trickling out of a drain in the washhouse where the body was being kept. "I found this extraordinarily interesting," he writes. "I was not yet four years old."[8] Later, after a great flood, he found the body of a dead man half-buried in the sand, its arm over its eyes. He was also fascinated to watch a pig being slaughtered, much to his mother's horror. Despite her reaction, "the slaughtering and the dead man were simply matters of interest to me," he writes.[9] These childhood anecdotes indicate that from an early age Jung did not shy away from the reality of death. On the contrary he was interested in, even curious about, the gory details he witnessed while watching the butchering of the pig. He does not offer an interpretation of his own youthful behavior, but I wonder whether his inordinate interest in death was unhealthy for a young child, or whether it reflected his unfazed response to something he regarded as a natural process. At any rate, he refused to abide by his mother's apparent belief that young children should not be allowed to witness such horrors. She

---

[8] C.G. Jung, *MDR*, p. 22.
[9] *Ibid.*, pp. 30-31.

may have been bound by the taboo against contamination by death, but evidently her inquisitive young son was not.

In 1896, when Jung was a university student, his father suffered a lingering illness from which he eventually died. Standing by his father's bedside, Jung watched with fascination as the sick man drew his last labored breath. "I had never seen anyone die before," he writes, implying that he was curious to observe the process. Once again, his mother was involved in this incident, as she was knitting in the next room while her husband lay dying. This time it was the son who appeared to be protecting his mother from "the icy stillness of death," or at least softening the blow. Rather than revealing that his father had already died, he went to her and said, "He is dying," allowing her to observe the truth for herself. I wonder if by not summoning her sooner, he was shielding her from witnessing the horror of death. Or was he wanting to separate himself emotionally from her and to satisfy his own curiosity unimpeded by her presence? Perhaps he was glad that his father's long suffering was over but did not want to reveal his relief to her. Of course, these interpretations are pure conjecture and are most likely projections of my own feelings. Nevertheless, the fact remains that Jung was fascinated, not repelled, by his father's death, and thought the incident important enough to include it in his memoir.

As I reviewed this event in Jung's life, I found myself remembering my own experience of sitting with Don as he died. Like Jung, I was curious about what happens at the moment of death. But my memory of my father's suffering, as well as the shock of my daughter's untimely death, had impressed on my psyche a deep fear of the end of life. In contrast to those two deaths, Don's last moments were so quiet that I hardly noticed when his breathing stopped. Witnessing his death did not erase my traumatic memories, but it did cushion their impact by allowing me to experience a death that was not painful and violent, but gentle and peaceful.

After his father died, Jung felt "a bit of manliness and freedom" awakening in him as he assumed his father's place as head of the family.[10] But six weeks later his feelings were shaken when his father appeared to him in a dream and told him he had made a full recovery and would soon be coming home:

> I thought he would be annoyed with me for having moved into his room. But not a bit of it! Nevertheless, I felt ashamed because I had imagined he was dead. Two days later the dream was repeated. My father had recovered and was coming home, and again I reproached myself because I had thought he was dead. Later I kept asking myself: 'What does it mean that my father returns in dreams and that he seems so real?' It was an unforgettable experience, and it forced me for the first time to think about life after death.[11]

Years later Jung recounted this dream to Freud, who apparently regarded it as an expression of Jung's death wish toward his father.[12] Jung, on the other hand, viewed the dream as an expression of his ongoing relationship with his father, or at least with his father's dream image. In the ensuing years he dreamed of his father several more times, each dream tracing the accomplishments in his own life and even the stages of his father's postmortal development.[13]

---

[10] *Ibid.*, p. 116.

[11] *Ibid.*, p. 117.

[12] Cf. Greg Mogenson, *Greeting the Angels,* pp. 27-29.

[13] I consider these dreams in detail in my book *By Grief Transformed* (2010), pp.

As I reviewed Jung's memoir in preparation for writing this essay, I was struck by his confidence that dreams of the dead have meaning, even when he cannot state with certainty what that meaning might be. He never states unequivocally that dream images represent the actual souls or spirits of the dead, although he comes very close to that position. But through decades of analyzing his own dreams and those of others, he became convinced of the reality of the objective psyche, which he also termed the collective unconscious. His visions of the sacred marriage during his recovery from a heart attack in 1944 confirmed his experience of the "absolute objectivity" of the eternal realm. A dream after the death of his wife had the same objective quality:

> I saw her in a dream which was like a vision. She stood at some distance from me, looking at me squarely. ... Her expression was neither joyful nor sad, but, rather, objectively wise and understanding, without the slightest emotional reaction, as though she were beyond the mist of affects. ... Face to face with such wholeness one remains speechless, for it can scarcely be comprehended.[14]

This compelling vision of his wife, along with many other dreams and visions, led Jung to imagine "life in the hereafter" as "a continuance in the world of images. Thus the psyche might be that existence in which the hereafter or the land of the dead is located," he wrote.[15] In other words, Jung's dream images of his father, his wife, and others, and my dream images of Don and my

---

67-82.

[14] C. G. Jung, *MDR*, p. 327.

[15] *Ibid.*, p. 351.

daughter dwell in the imaginal realm of the psyche. Many dreams of my daughter had the same quality of vivid immediacy that Jung describes in his vision of his wife. This leads me to wonder if after my death, my image will find its place in the objective psyche and visit my loved ones in *their* dreams.

"After my wife's death in 1955," wrote Jung, "I felt an inner obligation to become what I myself am."[16] Toni Wolff had died in 1953, so at the age of 80 Jung was left without the companionship of the two most important women in his life. I find it remarkable that at his age, and in his bereaved state, he wrote about becoming his authentic self, as though he knew that his individuation journey was not over and that he still had important work to do. His Tower at Bollingen, begun in 1923, had always been to him a "representation in stone of my innermost thoughts and of the knowledge I had acquired."[17] And so in 1955, he added an upper story to the central section of the house, which "signified an extension of consciousness achieved in old age."[18] In his last six years of life Jung was in frail condition and suffered several health crises. Nevertheless, he continued seeing a few patients, carving his stone tablets at Bollingen, going for long drives with his friend and caretaker Ruth Bailey, spending time with friends and colleagues (even when it tired him to do so), working on his memoir, and writing his article "Approaching the Unconscious" for *Man and His Symbols*, completed just a few weeks before his death.[19] His own account of his final years, supplemented by Barbara Hannah's biographical memoir, is a testament to the resilience and creativity

---

[16] *Ibid.*, p. 251.

[17] *Ibid.*, p. 250.

[18] *Ibid.*, p. 252.

[19] cf. Barbara Hannah's account of Jung's final years in *Jung: His Life and Work,* 1976.

of a fruitful old age. It reminds me of Don, who, having retired at the ripe old age of 81, planned our trips, built bookshelves for our library, carefully constructed a stone wall at the back of our garden, planted flowers and vegetables, and wrote down memories and stories of his early life. He no longer saw patients, but he heard from many of them and always responded. Even near the end of his life, when he had energy for very little else, sitting on our screened porch watching the birds and butterflies brought him great pleasure. As I live into the autumn of my own life, I now think of it as a time to "become what I myself am." I hope to be as intentional as Jung and Don were about taking on creative projects that are important to me and living fully into old age until my time comes to die.

Near the end of his memoir, Jung devotes an entire chapter to his ideas about life after death. "Perhaps one has to be close to death to acquire the necessary freedom to talk about it," he writes.[20] For most people, he continues, "it means a great deal to assume that their lives will have an indefinite continuity beyond their present existence. They live more sensibly, feel better, and are more at peace."[21] With this in mind, he encourages his readers "to form a conception of life after death, or to create some image of it—even if [they] must confess [their] failure. Not to have done so is a vital loss."[22] He goes on to describe his own "myth" of the afterlife, based on his dreams of the dead and certain synchronistic experiences. He also explores the belief in reincarnation, concluding that his skepticism about it was modulated somewhat by "a series of dreams which would seem to describe the reincarnation of a dead person

---

[20] C. G. Jung, *MDR*, p. 330.
[21] *Ibid.*, p. 332. In the next paragraph he goes on to say that others "far prefer absolute cessation to continuance."
[22] *Ibid.* p. 333.

of my acquaintance."[23] He sums up his myth in the statement, "[t] he meaning of my existence is that life has addressed a question to me."[24] He goes on to speculate that perhaps his ancestors had not been able to answer certain questions that had preoccupied them during their lifetimes, leaving him with the task of addressing those unsolved issues in *his* life. In any case, he concludes with the often-quoted statement, "The decisive question for [humanity] is: [Are we] related to something infinite or not?"[25] I think this is the main question that life addressed to Jung, which he attempted to answer in his long life's work and then bequeathed to us.

This essay has been a reflection on my own experience of aging, dying, and death. I have written it in a season of grief for the death of my husband and the closing of my office. Jung's comments on death and the afterlife, familiar to me from working on my books, have surfaced again to guide me in this study. But now I read them with new eyes, or perhaps I should say *old* eyes—the old eyes of a woman who knows that death will come for her one day. I am preparing for that day by doing the tasks that will make life easier for my loved ones when I am gone: making a new will, planning my funeral and burial, clearing my house of unneeded furniture and possessions. It may be that before long I will leave this house, which Don and I planned and built together, and move to an independent living community with help for assisted living, should I need it. These practical matters are important, but they are not my chief concern. The inner questions are far more important — questions about the meaning of my life, my legacy, my care for those I love. Above all, I want to face death with a settled mind, an open heart, and a curious spirit. Achieving that attitude is a work in

---

[23] *Ibid.*, p. 351.

[24] *Ibid.*, p. 350.

[25] *Ibid.*, p. 356.

progress which will occupy me for the rest of my days. Accepting that I will die one day is not easy: I know it intellectually, but my stubborn ego does not want to believe it. It is difficult to imagine not being, ceasing to exist, taking my place in the silent halls of death. I do not want to go kicking and screaming and full of fear, that is for sure. So I want to follow Jung's lead and form my own conception of life after death, to create my own myth about it. That seems like a worthy occupation for a woman in the autumn of her life. As I sit on the screened porch where Don and I used to sit together, watching the leaves turn purple and bronze before they fall, I am ready to begin.

References

Becker, E. (1973). *The Denial of Death*. Free Press.

Bryant, W. C. (1817). "Thanatopsis." https.//en.m.wikipedia.org wiki.Thanatopsis

Hannah, B. (1976). *Jung: His Life and Work: A Bibliographical Memoir*. G. P. Putnam's Sons.

Jung, C. G. *(1964) "*Approaching the Unconscious*." Man and His Symbols. C. G. Jung & M.-L. von Franz (Eds.).* Doubleday & Company, Inc.

Jung, C.G. (1983). *Memories, Dreams, Reflections*. Aniela Jaffe (*Ed.),* Richard and Clara Winston, (Translators). Fontana Paperbacks, Flamingo edition, Random House.

Mogenson, G. (1992). *Greeting the Angels: An Imaginal view of the Mourning Process*. Baywood Publishing Co.

William A. Neilson and Charles J. Hill, Eds. (1941). *The Complete Plays and Poems of William Shakespeare*. Houghton Mifflin Company, The Riverside Press.

Olson, Susan (2010). *By Grief Transformed: Dreams and the Mourning Process*. Spring Journal Books.

Olson, Susan (2021). *Images of the Dead in Grief Dreams: A Jungian View of Mourning*. Routledge.

Death Cafés

Ann Casement

Death is Dasein's own most possibility
(Heidegger: Sein und Zeit)

Preamble

The first half of this chapter, preceded by a brief Introduction, is a piece of reportage culled from various online articles by a U.K. national newspaper titled The Guardian. This is not my usual fare as I do not indulge in a daily dose of the kind of tedium that passes for reporting in newspapers these days, but that particular paper serves the purpose for the first half of my chapter as it gives quite a lot of coverage to the topic I shall be exploring initially, i.e., death cafés.

Introduction

As India is my Mataram (motherland), I was accustomed, in childhood and early adolescence, to seeing death on an almost daily basis on the streets of Mumbai. This took the form of Indian funerals, which were public affairs with the corpse being carried on a stretcher, its face exposed to view with the rest of the body covered in flowers. This was generally followed by a large cortège, some members of which—presumably close family—would weep and wail as the body was carried through the streets of the city. Despite the abandoned displays of grief, there was nothing remotely gloomy about Indian funerals, which were colorful affairs, and I would sometimes join the followers and interact with members of the cortège who were not too grief-stricken to talk with them in Hindi in order to find out what I could about the dead person.

I have also had the truly extraordinary experience of being with two close family members as they died suddenly of heart attacks—the first when I was age 11; the second was in my maturity. On each occasion, there came the death rattle at the end as the ka, or life force, literally left the body. These are among the two most profound experiences of my long life.

In my late teens, I moved between London and Paris, where I was studying at the Sorbonne—though, more often than not, I was to be found at the Café de Flore talking hot air about existentialism as Sartre was all the rage at the time. I was torn between remaining in Paris when I'd finished my studies or returning to London. A part of what finally drew me back to London was the proliferation of what were known as coffee bars where an insipid fluid called cappuccino was served at Italian-inspired cafés—sadly without real Italian coffee—with accompanying live music played by rock groups, some of whom went on to fame and fortune.

One such café in London's Soho was called the Macabre, where edibles were served on tables shaped as coffins. Being young, we all thought the idea of dining off coffins was great fun—as a teenager, the reality of one's own death being a distant mirage which only happened to old people. I have included these reminiscences in my presentation as they are in marked contrast to the way death is generally experienced in contemporary times in the U.K. and other Western countries where the dying "are now requested to exit on the tips of their toes" (Zoja 1995: p.186). Death itself is often preceded by force-feeding of the terminally ill or similar indignities. In addition, death has become an embarrassment never to be discussed in public and, in some countries, it appears to have been banished altogether. Juxtaposed with this denial of death, there is a voyeuristic devouring of television footage—shown as part of the evening's entertainment—of people being killed whenever a war is raging in any part of the world or there is one of nature's devastating eruptions such as an earthquake or tsunami. As these events generally take place in far-off parts of the globe, the viewer is kept at a safe distance from scenes of death on television, which do not pose a threat to one sitting comfortably at home.

As the phenomenon of death has been around since the beginning of life on earth, this split reaction to it in the West can only be viewed as pathological.

The Guardian

I first heard mention of the existence of Death Cafés in the course of a talk given by Baroness Rabbi Julia Neuberger at The Royal Society of Medicine at the beginning of the pandemic that was ravaging— and continues to ravage—our world. The Four Horsemen of the Apocalypse—War, Pestilence, Famine, Death—have been and continue to be around us, which makes it an eminently suitable time to research Death Cafés, which is the reason why I am presenting this topic today. When I first started to research the subject, I discovered, much to my surprise, that there were 2,765 Death Cafés in existence in the U.K. and 13,893 in other countries around the globe, including Afghanistan, Algeria, Argentina, Australia. Cambodia, China, Czech Republic, France, Germany, Hong Kong, India, Lebanon, Nigeria, Peru, Turkey, and Uruguay.

What follows in this part of the chapter has been taken from various online issues of The Guardian, a national newspaper in the U.K. One article stated that the first Death Café to be founded in the U.K. was at London's district of Hackney by a man named Jon Underwood in 2011 before he died in 2017. The following extensive extracts are from the aforementioned articles, written by a variety of journalists for different issues of The Guardian, all of whom visited Death Cafés in the U.K. At one event, the journalist was told by the organizers of that particular meeting that people were interested, as there were not many places where talking about death was acceptable. One of the organizers went on to say: "Talking about it can only be a good thing: not only does coming to terms with your own mortality mean you're more likely to live life to the full, being open about it means we can support each other, our families and ourselves when death arrives in any of our lives. It makes for a healthier, happier community."

This statement resonated with the journalist, as his sister was a doctor working in palliative care and who had told him about the reaction of families of frail, elderly patients with multiple comorbidities. When the time came to tell family members their loved one was going to die, they could not believe what they were hearing, as they were not equipped to deal with it or even to support the person who was dying. "How have we got to the stage in our sanitized society where we can't bring ourselves to believe anyone is going to die?"

The journalist goes on to say that 100 years ago death would have been a constant presence—as a result, people had big families because it was expected that some would die in infancy. Men went to war and did not return, women frequently died in childbirth, and not many people made it past middle age. If one compares those facts with the contemporary world, people live much longer, as medical care and sophisticated technology have made it possible to prolong life expectancy. The result is that an individual can live to 35 or even 40 without ever having a relative die. Through this lack of exposure to any direct experience of death due to the "outsourcing of death" as Jon Underwood expressed it, people have become ill-equipped to deal with it when it occurs. As a result, we live in a state of denial of death—the one thing that comes to us all and that, as Heidegger expresses it, no one can do for us.

Death Cafés

The following is a description—written in the anthropological present—of what takes place at an actual death café, which begins with the moderator hushing the conversation by announcing the start of the meeting. Customers who don't realize they are in a death café leave hastily, staring at the remaining people in concern and fascination. Menus are passed around that list questions for discussion and are divided into "starters," "mains," and "tea and coffee." The moderator reassures the assembled company the questions are just conversation starters which do not have to be stuck to rigidly. Between each course the assembled company moves around to ensure everyone present has a chance to interact with different people.

The journalist writing this particular piece sat down next to a woman in her late 50s, and together they scanned the items on the starters menu: "Cremation or burial?"; "Nature taking its course or assisted dying"; "Where would you like to be when you die?" The journalist expresses it amusingly, saying these are certainly ice-breakers and that it is easier to talk about death and dying with a stranger than trying to start a discussion with a spouse or partner after work. The journalist's companion started to discuss why speaking about death is a taboo subject; she thought that the real problem was having to face becoming dependent, i.e., returning to childhood. This is an ever-increasing phenomenon as more and more people are choosing to live alone because they have no wish to be dependent on another. My own thinking is that one may be better off thinking in terms of codependency, which is something death cafés can provide.

For the next course, the journalist sat with two young women who had about them all the hallmarks of bereavement. They had sought out a death café as their recent loss had made them more open to talking about death in general, but they tellingly added that talking about themselves dying with others would be morbid. As the assembled company were now on the "mains," the discussion had become more in-depth with topics such as: "What do you think makes for a good death?" and "What words do you want on your tombstone?" All this was done in the tone of animated discussion and was not accompanied by tears or hushed voices. When the company swapped around again at the tea and coffee stage, the two topics were: "What song would you like at your funeral?" and "How would you like to be remembered?" This time the journalist was seated next to a death doula, a nonmedical person who accompanies people as they are dying. These are the counterparts to birth doulas, who stay with women who are giving birth. This gave rise to the question of why there is so much planning and forethought given to birth and rarely to the event of dying.

The death doula had this to say about her role: "I have a background in nursing, which gives me essential experience, but a death doula is not a nurse. It is a completely different approach in that it is not allied to medicine or the medical 'narrative.' It's led by the individual—the person who is dying. It's somewhat similar to the role of a birth doula." One can learn to function in either of these roles for which the training contact details are online.

She had attended the death café to experience other people's feelings about the possibility of dying. She also wanted to find out how people felt about having someone being with them at the time of dying who was not a family member. She was impressed by the discussions she had taken part in at the death café, particularly the fact that people were keen to personalize their death—and their lives.

When the café wound down to its natural end, many people lingered deep in conversation. When he left, the journalist hailed a taxi, and the driver asked him what he had been doing. This prompted a discussion between the journalist and the taxi driver on death on the way to the former's home, where they sat chatting for 20 minutes after they arrived there. As a side note, some of my best conversations have been with taxis drivers—especially in London, as they know so much and have had a great many fascinating experiences. If you ever want to dish the dirt, there's no one better to do that with than a London taxi driver.

In concluding this part of the presentation, I want to mention that due to the pandemic, I have been unable to implement any sort of death café in London. This is much needed as, in a recent communication with Baroness Neuberger, she informed me that though they were very much around in England when she spoke about them to the Royal Society of Medicine, she can find nothing about them at the present time. They seem to have ceased to exist, very likely due to restrictions on meeting others during the pandemic lockdowns—ironically at the time when they were most needed. The Baroness and I shall continue to try and find out more, and I am also in contact with the President of the Psychiatry Section of the Royal Society of Medicine in the hope of taking this idea forward at some point in the future as life becomes increasingly normalized.

Philosophy as Death

The oldest burial site I have been able to locate online is situated at the Theopetra Cave at Thessaly in Northern Greece. It is approximately 135,000 years old and displays signs of some sort of ritualized burial. Mourning the loss of the dead has passed down through the ages—the best-known burial sites being, of course, the pyramids erected for the pharaohs at Giza on the outskirts of Cairo. Those are from Egypt's earlies Dynasties though the pharaonic burial sites moved to Upper Egypt in later times when Thebes— now Luxor—became the center of Egyptian society. The Valley of the Kings and the Valley of the Queens are incredible to visit as one can go into many of the tombs there, including the tomb of Tutankhamun, probably the most famous pharaoh of all because of the discovery of his tomb in 1922 by the Egyptologist Howard Carter. The impact of the wondrous treasures in his tomb has had a huge impact on Western society, including fashion and architecture, since that time. They are on display in the new museum at Giza and make one gasp with delight—which makes one wonder what enormous treasures must have accompanied the more important Pharaohs but of which much less evidence remains than the more-or-less intact tomb of a minor Pharaoh such as Tutankhamun.

I have spent several Christmases in Egypt, at which time I visited Giza and various tombs and temples in that incredible country, including Abu Simbel in Upper Egypt. Many of the monuments are well preserved due to the dry climate and desert landscape, and most are dedicated to the dead. One could almost think of the Ancient Egyptians as having a death fetish, though what they were actually aiming at was a continuation of their lives on earth after death, hence the burial of their possessions with their embalmed bodies, including slaves, if they were royals or members of the hierarchy. One may speculate from this that the Ancient Egyptians were as much in denial of death as people who are alive today appear to be.

Part II of this chapter will be reflecting on a few of the foremost thinkers in the West who have dealt with the topic of death in their writings. Many of them, including Freud and Jung, have borrowed extensively from the Hindu Upanishads and from Mahayana Buddhism for help when confronting the one ineluctable experience of all living organisms, viz., death, which, by its very nature, has been ever-present in the thinking of introspective writers throughout the ages. Most philosophers, including Socrates, view death and philosophy as synonymous and indeed think of the latter as a lifelong preparation for death. The pages of the Phaedo, that contain a moving depiction by Plato of the death of Socrates, are made up of a symposium lasting several days. For myself, this work has a poignant symmetry with the approaching death in 2005 of the Jungian psychoanalyst Phillip Zabriskie. Over that summer, a few of us, family and close friends, gathered around him in New York, the Hudson Valley, and on the coast of Maine. Each was inspired by the stoicism with which Phillip faced his final days on earth. He was even present at a rendering of his memorial where there were poetry readings and presentations, and, following his death on Christmas Day 2005, every one of us dedicated the creative work we were engaged in at that time to Phillip. Throughout the summer that led up to his death, his beatific smile and gentle manner were ever present in the way Plato describes Socrates calmly receiving the love and companionship of his close circle on the day before his death. Following his death, he was exalted by them as "the best, the wisest too, and the most just" (Plato 1993: p.79).

For Christians, the Phaedo has a familiar ring as the martyrdom of Socrates prefigures that of Jesus; the resemblance being furthered by Socrates—or, possibly, Plato's—thinking of the soul as separate from the body with an afterlife following the death of the body. In addition, Plato's notion of the ideal forms are the original precursors of the perfection to be found only in heaven— bearing again an obvious resonance with Christian doctrine. As a result, it has often been suggested that quite a lot of what is attributed to Socrates by Plato in the various books the latter dedicated to his mentor, is more Plato's thinking than Socrates' own. Two millennia later, Nietzsche critiqued Plato as the true founder of Christianity, "the slave morality," as Nietzsche scathingly refers to it.

Schopenhauer and Death

Schopenhauer, the last great Kantian Idealist—whose writing is a model of clarity that stands out as the clearest expression of ideas of any philosopher apart from Plato—is paradoxical about the inevitability of death as the final denouement of the horrors of this life, the latter seen by him as a giant penitentiary. In addition, life itself is dismissed as illusion (maya). According to Schopenhauer, every good, like every ill, presupposes existence, hence its absence contains no ill at all; here, he is referencing Epicurus's quotation: "When we are, death is not, and when death is, we are not" (Schopenhauer 2011: p.523). Epicurus arrived at this conclusion as he was trying to reassure his followers in their fear of death—one that Schopenhauer takes as a touchstone of truth in the following quotation: "…the true symbol of nature is the circle, because it is the schematic representation of recurrence … which is implemented in everything, from the course of the stars to the death and origination of organic beings" (Ibid: p.533). This will have a familiar ring for Jungians as does his quotation from Hermes Trismegistus, the latter often referenced by Jung: "You are not nothing" (Ibid: p.547).

Schopenhauer's borrowings from Epicurus, as well as the latter himself, are critiqued by the Heideggerian scholar Johannes Niederhauser, for whom Heidegger's dasein (being) is inseparable from death - in other words humans are being-towards-death – some Heideggerian thinkers prefer to state it as being-unto-death, the eminent Hubert Dreyfus for one, from the first moment of the existence of dasein. According to Heidegger, one is ready to die from the time of one's birth or thrownness into the world.

Schopenhauer often reverts to his well-known "pessimistic" estimation of human existence in the following: "…the individuality of most people is so miserable and worthless that they truly lose nothing with it, and that what in them may still have some value is the general fact of their being human; but to this we can promise imperishability" (ibid: p.548). Somewhat reminiscent of Freud's often quoted saying from *Studies on Hysteria*, while not offering imperishability, does state that the goal of psychoanalysis is to transform neurotic misery into ordinary human unhappiness.

Though he was not a conventionally religious thinker and, in fact, declared himself an atheist, he wrote compellingly about religions. For example, one vital source of Schopenhauer's creative work was his discovery of the wisdom embedded in the Upanishads, the religious-philosophical Sanskrit texts of Hinduism, as well as in Mahayana Buddhism. Many of the terms he borrowed from those texts will be familiar to Jungians, viz, Ultimate Reality, the World Soul, the Atman, and the self. But, "reflecting reason" is always the ultimate goal for Schopenhauer as evidenced in the following: "… just as everywhere in nature a remedy, or at least a compensation, accompanies every ill, so the same reflection that introduced cognizance of death also facilitates metaphysical views" (Ibid. p.518).

As with much else in his thinking, Schopenhauer turned to Kant for inspiration on the topic of death, which I shall set out at some length as it has a great deal to tell us:

> The most thorough answer to the question of continuation of the individual after death is to be found in Kant's great doctrine of the ideality of time... Beginning, ending and continuing are concepts that derive their meaning simply and solely from time, and consequently are valid only under its presupposition. But time has no absolute existence, is not the mode and manner of the being in itself of things, but rather merely the form belonging to our cognizance of the existence and essence of ourselves and all things which just for that reason is highly incomplete and limited to mere phenomena. Thus, with respect to the latter alone do the concepts of cessation and continuation find application, not with respect to that which is displaying itself in them, the essence in itself of things, in application to which such concepts therefore no longer have any true meaning. (Ibid: p.550)

In other words, to seek for an answer to what happens after death from temporal concepts becomes impossible as the problem transports us onto a stage that nullifies time while, at the same time, posing the question in temporal terms. According to Schopenhauer's reading of Kant, the problem is transcendent, and death remains a mystery. That is not the end of the dilemma that confronts us as we can assert that an individual is a phenomenon and transitory, but that his/her essence in itself is not affected—the temporal concepts having been eliminated, one cannot talk of its survival but, at the same time, it is indestructible. The argument is complex, and Schopenhauer tries to work around it by agreeing with Kant that we cannot know the thing in itself but rather recognize that it can be sought in what Schopenhauer calls Will. For knowing is only a secondary property of one's essence, whereas the Will is the ultimate core of reality, the opposite of outer reality or illusion (maya). Schopenhauer is not a religious thinker, so he is certainly not talking about the soul here but, rather, what Freud and Jung later came to call the unconscious. There, in the unknowable realm that we share with all other humans, lies our common humanity and it is this that is imperishable.

Nirvana

It is important to bear in mind that brevity barely describes the manner in which I have summed up what Schopenhauer elegantly and at length spells out on death and the Will, but it is not possible in a short presentation to do anything like justice to this great thinker's work, let alone his all-important influence on the development of psychoanalytic theory. Before leaving Schopenhauer to look at two other contributors' thinking about death, it remains to be acknowledged that he was among the first Europeans to take Eastern philosophy seriously, in particular the Vedantas. To mention just one overwhelmingly important outcome of that venture on Schopenhauer's part is Freud's later thinking on the death drive and the Nirvana Principle—the latter still vitally important in neuroscience as the homeostasis of the living organism. In the course of a two-day-long seminar given by Mark Solms, the founder of the International Neuropsychoanalysis Society, I was responding in this vein to a question by one of the participants when Mark smiled ironically and said: "Yes, Ann, there is a case to be made that Freud's thinking is entirely prefigured by Schopenhauer." For Freud, the ideal state of being was that of Nirvana—a calm acceptance of oneself not being pulled in contradictory directions by the Id, the drives or the demands of society.

Authenticity: Dasein v. Duende

In this section, two contemporary publications—*Martin Heidegger* by Rüdiger Safranski and *Heidegger on Death and Being* by Johannes Niederhauser—are employed to provide commentaries on Heidegger's ideas on death. These are juxtaposed with my own view that Heidegger's thinking on death is another example of the fact that he was never really able to expunge Catholicism from his psyche or from his "thinking path"—the term applied to the genius of Heidegger's output from the decades from the 1920s to the 1970s utilized by both Niederhauser and Safranski. Although Heidegger overtly rejected Catholicism in his 20s, one can distinguish traces of it showing through in much of what he goes on to write—as already indicated above all in his emphasis on death. Catholics are brought face-to-face with death from early childhood by the image of Jesus' death on the Cross, the central symbol of Catholicism, and encircles them in so much Catholic ritual as a preparation for death. In several other ways, too, Catholicism is deeply embedded in his thinking, for example, when he was thought of as the head of a university in Berlin that would turn out professors imbued with Nazi ideology. Heidegger wanted to found a "monastery of philosophers" living a communal life but with monastic cells for contemplation and learning (Safranski 1998: p.279).

In this section, I am seeking to discover family resemblances (Schopenhauer and Wittgenstein) between death and its link to authenticity in the work of Heidegger, as well as in the notion of duende from the Spanish poet Federico Garcia Lorca. The origin of that Hispanic term is from the words duen de casa which translates as "master in the house"—the very way in which it manifests in Heidegger and Lorca—both of them cradle Catholics. For them, authenticity is closely related to a heightened awareness of death—Lorca calls it "emotional darkness" and "the spirit of the earth" in his paper "Play and Theory of Duende," delivered in Buenos Aires in 1933. One encounters this dark power in certain places and certain individuals, for instance, the Daimon in Jung and James Hillman's writings; Freud and Lorca's Eros and Thanatos; the Mana of Oceania; the Dionysian in Nietzsche about whom Lorca writes: "...that same duende that scorched the heart of Nietzsche, who searched in vain for its external forms on the Rialto Bridge and in the music of Bizet" (Lorca 1933). Duende is always about closeness to death—never more so than in the corrida (bullfight)—where the crowd's cry of Olé! Olé! as the matador plays the bull with the cape, that evocative sound which closely resembles the Islamic cry of Allah! Allah! at ecstatic moments in Islam whose culture permeates the Spanish psyche.

Momento Mori

One is ready to die the moment one is born—that is the gospel according to Heidegger and Lorca, i.e., death as the fulcrum of duende and dasein. I contend that Heidegger had duende above all when he was, for a while, an ardent admirer of that personification of duende, Hitler, in its manifestation as an evil spirit or goblin. Hitler and the Third Reich represented for Heidegger a longed-for return to his ghostly yearning for Ancient Greece, in particular the

Pre-Socratics, though above all, Parmenides. Heidegger's yearning is preceded by Nietzsche's in the same vein:

> One longs back for that place in which alone one can be at home: the Greek world! But it is in precisely that direction that all bridges are broken – except the rainbow bridges of concepts…But what happiness there is already in this will to spirituality, to ghostliness almost…the digging up of ancient philosophy, above all of the pre-Socratics—the most deeply buried of all Greek temples. (Nietzsche in Safranski 1998: p.277)

Socrates himself could triumph over death as he was seized by thinking so that his body could be killed, but his soul would live. He had no need for momento mori as he had passed beyond the shadow of death to a place where he was untouchable. This "triumph over death" is the final act of authenticity and duende—only available to one who has faced momento mori in other words, has faced the fact that: "I must die." This is what the matador with duende possesses that raises him above the merely brave matador—death being the greatest universal archetype which can only be experienced as such by each individual being and not by the generality of "We" or "They" —the inauthentic in Heidegger's philosophy.

The Seventh Seal

The seventh seal is to be found in a passage in the Book of Revelation which reads: "And when the Lamb had opened the seventh seal, there was silence in heaven about the space of half an hour" (Revelation: 8:1). The "silence" refers to "the silence of God."

The renowned Swedish director Ingmar Bergman's masterpiece *The Seventh Seal* takes its inspiration from The Book of Revelation. The theme of Death runs throughout the film with the plot centering on a disillusioned knight and his squire who have returned to their country after the Crusades to find it ravaged by the plague. He encounters the personification of Death clad in black, whom he challenges to a chess match which is played on a beach—the liminal place psychologically. The knight believes he can survive for as long as the match lasts, but at the end the knight and Death go off together in a final dance of death. As Death states: "No one escapes me," which is the motif that runs through the paper that is presented in this chapter.

Jung

This piece draws to its conclusion in paying homage to Jung's thinking on death as the following quotation illustrates: "…the man who despairs marches towards nothingness, the one who has placed his faith in the archetype follows the tracks of life and lives right into his death. Both, to be sure, remain in uncertainty, but the one lives against his instincts, the other with them" (Jung, 1963, p. 284). The above insightful quotation from Jung summarizes the gist of this presentation which is that death as a part of life needs to be consciously integrated into each individual's experience of being. The genius of Jung, Heidegger, and Lorca lay in the fact that they confronted that ineluctable fact of life, i.e., that death is with one every moment and is, as Heidegger puts it, dasein's ownmost possibility. Thus, the ultimate transformation in psychoanalysis is to become properly mortal—the outcome of the union of dasein and duende.

Bhagavad Gita

The final word rests with the Lord Krishna who states: "I am death that carries off all things" (Bhagavad Gita 1962: p.50). (As an interesting aside, Robert Oppenheimer, the leader of the Manhattan Project, at the moment the first atom bomb was exploded at Los Alamos on 16 July 1945, quoted or rather paraphrased this as: "Now I am become Death").

References

Anonymous. (1962). *The Bhagavad Gita*. Penguin Books.

Anonymous. *The Book of Revelation.* Spuyten Duyvil.

Heidegger, M. (1967). *Sein und Zeit*. Max Niemeyer Verlag, Tübingen.

Jung, C. G. (1963). *Memories, Dreams, Reflections*. London: Collins and Routledge & Kegan Paul.

Lorca, F.G. (1933). *Play and the Theory of the Duende*. Buenos Aires Lecture online.

Niederhauser, J. (2021). *Heidegger on Death and Being: An Answer to the Seinsfrage*. Switzerland: Springer Nature.

Plato (1993). *Phaedo*. Oxford: Oxford University Press.

Safranski, R. (1998). *Martin Heidegger*. Harvard University Press.

Schopenhauer, A. (2011). *The World as Will and Representation*. Vol. Two. Upper Saddle River, New Jersey: Pearson Education.

Zoja, L. (1995). *Growth & Guilt*. London: Routlege.

Accompanied Through the Resonant Field
of Grief and Healing

Claire L. Costello, Ph.D.

The Soul would have no Rainbow if the eyes had no tears.
Guy Zona (1994, p. 66)

In moments of grief, the sanctity of actually being alive reveals itself in shards of rainbow light. It was Joseph Henderson who led me through the valley of loss as we explored how the psyche prepared me in my dreams during the year before my Jungian analyst, Don Sandner, suddenly and unexpectedly died. He also taught and encouraged me to allow my experience of grief in as fully as I could when my mother died. And in so doing, I was opened to a transformative healing experience with the Rainbow Serpent.

Inspired by the writings of Jung, other Jungian mentors, my analytic relationships, my devotion to mind-body healing, my spiritual teachers and practices, and my mother-line, I came into awareness of the understanding and acceptance of moments where I felt validated, companioned, held, nurtured, and responded to by the Infinite. And this guidance has anchored my trust in the communication process between psyche, spirit, and body that leads to healing, something I have come to know since childhood.

I am grateful for this opportunity to put into words what has helped me in times of being with death and dying, grief and mourning, healing and living. I am grateful for the grace that has guided my awareness. I hope that these stories affirm your own experiences that have led your way as you approach death or the dying of a loved one or patient. May they light your way or affirm what it is you already know and intuit. There is glorious freedom in the way we each grieve.

Childhood Experiences

From a young age, I have been captivated with trying to understand the unique processes of healing within each of us. As a third-grader in Catholic school, I had conscious conversations with God, the Holy Spirit, my Guardian Angel, and Mother Mary. Dreams wakened me to being alive and believing that we were all born in this time to be agents of a change that would possibly happen sometime around the year 2020. Concurrently, there was a sinister undercurrent that I was keenly aware of as my country reeled from three major assassinations—John F. Kennedy, Martin Luther King, and Robert Kennedy—while teenagers protested the Vietnam War and *Cherish* persisted on the radio. As Jung (1961) describes experiences of his own childhood in *Memories, Dreams, Reflections*, we sense collective culture in our young life and are deeply affected by it. And it was reading C.G. Jung's *Memories, Dreams, and Reflections* (1961) in my early 20s—while studying at University of California, San Francisco, to become a child and adolescent therapist and working at Langley Porter Neuropsychiatric Institute—that affirmed those events that, as a child, set my life course and vocation in motion: an experience of healing through an exchange with God that required a vow, which I have kept.

In the fourth grade, I encountered symptoms that subjected me to many invasive procedures in a variety of Chicago medical institutions, including a brief hospitalization. How medical professionals related to me influenced whether I had the courage to not be scared when they took me behind closed doors for some procedure. I learned to tolerate the sensations through imagery of the sounds, scents, and warmth of the South Carolina shore or focused concentration on the experience itself. It was determined that I had a mild bleeding disorder. I remember asking the doctor if I was going to die. He told me no, but we would need to be careful if I ever needed surgery or had an accident.

In the following year, when symptoms began to resurface, I had a frank conversation with God. Irritated, I implored, "God, take this thing off my face, and I promise to teach what I learned." (At the time, this was about teaching health care professionals that their kindness could embolden patients to have courage in this foreign medical land and they could help their patients to bear procedures with imagery or focused attention.) Within a week, the symptoms I had experienced for over a year were gone. Shocked, I realized that I had been heard and responded to from an invisible source. God was relating to me! And then I uttered with a gasp, "I have taken a vow. I have made a covenant with God!"

As a freshman in high school, on my first trip to San Francisco with my parents, the minute my foot hit the tarmac, a jolt of energy shot through my body and a voice said, "You are going to live here one day." I hadn't even seen the place yet. I have come to respect these moments that seem to leave my consciousness until it is time for them to be remembered.

My College Years

Before my move to San Francisco, while still in college, I had some profound encounters with dying. I learned to pay attention, if only in retrospect at times, to a subtle voice that tried to guide me, offering a warning, which I often did not heed, that made it clear I needed to turn toward that slight voice without dismissal, if only I could catch myself before batting it away. I began to listen more closely.

At Duke, I trained in the system's theory of nursing health care and gravitated toward the new field of interdisciplinary comprehensive health care, helping Duke to originate curriculum for its medical health care students in this emerging field. This ultimately evolved into the new primary-care wellness field and finally, decades later, into integrative medicine. I lived this growth from the ground level. As a nursing student at Duke, this work led me to a Robert Wood Johnson interdisciplinary team preceptorship in Bangor, Maine, the summer between my junior and senior year of college. I was 20.

One of the hospital's beloved cantankerous nurses was dying of cancer. Her room was next to the nurses' station and had a large glass window. Not being able to handle their feelings or hers, the nurses assigned me to her care. One day she witnessed my first blatant encounter with power differential when a male physician came into the station where I was sitting and writing a note and demanded that I get up and give him my seat. I looked at him incredulously and said, "What?" He repeated himself. And then I said, "I will get up when I'm finished writing my note, then you are welcome to have it." Well, my patient witnessed that, and this endeared me to her. Laughing, she told me she had seen that interaction and assured this budding new nursing student that I had done the right thing!

Over the next few weeks, this patient taught me much as she grew quieter and more internal. One night, I noticed a change in her breathing. Caught between I don't know what to do, how to be, I also felt I was receiving instruction. It was time to call the family; when I did, it became clear that they might not make it to her bedside in time. Back in her room, I felt her say that I needed to leave the room. I wasn't sure whether this was my own fear of being with her as she was dying or her request. Then I heard it again. I felt that she clearly wanted me to leave the room; she wanted peace; she wanted to die without me present. I left wondering, "Am I leaving because I really feel that this is what I am understanding from you?" I believe I heard a "yes." Shortly thereafter, she died.

During this late night and early morning, a compassionate nurses aide taught me how to respectfully and lovingly bathe and prepare her body for the journey to the morgue. I was in awe as we did this together, and then I became queasy as we placed her body in a bag and zipped it shut. This was difficult and incomprehensible. Yet, this learning helped me the following week, when a complicated birth became a death. A compassion awakened in me that I had never known, as I grieved and offered a tender ritual of bathing, honoring the bruised and deceased baby all by myself, feeling my recently passed nurse-patient beside me.

These experiences opened a doorway, and I wanted to understand more about how to listen and understand tacit communication in the field between people within the healing arts. I wanted to know more about how healing happened. What were the conditions and properties of eliciting a healing response within the patient, within myself? My maternal grandmother and I seemed to share an uncanny capacity to call right when things were needed. Did it have something to do with this subtle communication?

These experiences alerted me to listen more deeply to this subtle, calm voice or feeling. And it has grown in my work over the years, particularly in the realm of conscious dying.

Early Professional Years

After college I moved back home and began working in acute psychiatry on a locked unit in a Chicago medical center. Late that summer, I visited San Francisco with a friend and remembered the tarmac moment back in high school and decided to move there in November 1978. The week I did move to San Francisco, there were high-profile murders: political, spiritual, some on the trails through the beautiful hills of California. I felt evil in the world and I understood I was not free; my newfound freedom felt curtailed.

I entered therapy for the first time, afraid that I would not live past 25. This fear confounded me, especially in consideration of my third-grade dream of feeling born for the coming times and my fourth-grade conversation with God, although at the time I did not think about it like this. My therapist accepted my fear of dying young and encouraged me to begin reading Stephen Levine's *Who Dies* (1982) along with his other books. I attended his workshops, and he taught me how leaning into dying and pain allowed for a more conscious attitude toward healing, which awakened me more to living. This made sense to me.

I discovered Angeles Arrien, a cross-cultural anthropologist, Basque medicine woman, and professor at California Institute of Integral Studies (CIIS) who wrote and taught the *Four-Fold Way* (1993), a path that encouraged coming into authenticity through practices that she distilled from the universal teachings of cross-cultural, indigenous, earth-based religions. My study with her remarkably spanned more than 30 years. I also began following the writings and teachings of Rachel Naomi Remen, who explored the mysteries of life on the edge with her oncology patients. Reading and training in meditation with Jack Kornfield began to ground me. These learnings helped open, soften, and lessen my fear of a young death and dying in general. They helped connect me to nature and to the joy of life with the spirit. Consciously and with intention, I opened to the mysterious liminal space between life and death. Reading Jean Bolen's *The Tao of Psychology* (1979) and June Singer's *Boundaries of the Soul* (1972) and *Androgyny* (1976) also validated my trust and perspective in such things.

Dora Kalff, a Swiss therapist who created a Jungian version of sandplay therapy, came to San Francisco while I was in graduate school in my early 20s. Her sandplay slide presentation of a 10-year-old girl with a medical condition made me feel my own 10-year-old-self healing within them. This experience catapulted me into a new professional trajectory, and I went to study with Frau Kalff in Zürich in my late 20s. Frau Kalff encouraged me to continue my sandplay experience and to study with Jungian analyst Kay Bradway, who became my first consultant as I established my private practice back in San Francisco.

Dora Kalff activated my deepening interest in Jung, and our group continued to work with her for many years both in the U.S. and again in Switzerland. The movies *Matter of Heart* (Whitney, 1986) and *The Way of the Dream* (Boa, 1988) awakened me to the possibility of contributing to the balance of this world by becoming aware of my shadow. I took Don Sandner's courses on Jung and the Vision Seminars at the C.G. Jung Institute in San Francisco. This nurtured a desire to become an analyst, to create more ground from which to understand healing, and to offer something to this world.

Frau Kalff also affirmed my study with Angeles Arrien and my evolving interest in sweat-lodge ceremonies with a Káruk medicine man and a Hawaiian Kahuna. She also directed me to study with Stan Grof, a psychospiritual psychiatrist who created Holotropic Breathwork. These teachers guided me in growing my psychospiritual interest in healing, first activated by my encounter with spiritual forces and my physical health at age 10. These experiences and trainings nourished my relationship with the invisible world, made me more conscious of intuition as a resource, and synchronized my spiritual guidance with a deep affinity with the healing arts. Kay Bradway nudged me to begin doctoral study, and I began Jungian analysis with Don Sandner. We had a shared interest in healing and in the quality of the ecstatic in that process.

AIDS Work with Dying, Grief, and Compassion

In 1986, I began my doctoral studies and quit my job in adolescent psychiatry. A good friend from nursing school offered me a part-time time job as the director of psychotherapeutic services at her new company, Lifesource, an innovative interdisciplinary pharmacy and nursing agency. My role was to offer in-home counseling and consultation to patients who had cancer and Crohn's disease and were receiving intravenous chemotherapy and nutritional treatment.

Six months into this new work, the early AIDS epidemic exploded in San Francisco, and most of my patients became young men trying to survive AIDS. A part of me identified with the vulnerability of this disease, not only because it was affecting young men in my community, people I cared about, and was devastating the sense of freedom to be oneself in San Francisco, but also because my own bleeding disorder made me feel at risk lest I need a blood transfusion. This created an indelible bond with my patients. I could not believe the lack of compassion from society, which was then so palpable in our culture.

In my attempt to understand my own fear of dying young, I had already begun a deep exploration of death, dying, and healing. Maybe this was how the Self began to prepare me for the call that summoned me. What I learned from and with my patients is embedded in my being, some of which I hope to share as I explore this territory of grief, death, healing, and awakening compassion.

I continued to work during the initial AIDS crisis, for seven years, when almost all patients were dying, before there was hope. During this time frame, I completed my doctoral dissertation on *The Impact of Religion and Spirituality on AIDS-Related Bereavement* of my patients' partners and family members in collaboration with Stanford University and the National Institutes of Health. My research in bereavement revealed that protection from depression is available when one's spiritual beliefs and practices are aligned and linked and as one experiences personal growth from caring for a dying beloved (Costello, 1992).

As I wrote in "My Brother's Keeper" (2020), "I didn't choose to work in the AIDS field. I found myself in the middle of it. It cracked me open like a bishop pinecone in wildfire. And some new spring poured forth that I never knew existed" (p. 69). I drove through the Bay Area knocking on patient doors, one home after the other, three days a week for the next seven years. I entered the privacy of my patients' universes weekly or bimonthly—often for about two years, sometimes shorter, until death came. We created a temenos, a sacred space, in living rooms, around kitchen tables, or in bedrooms—a chair at their bedside, and later still I followed my patients into hospitals, skilled nursing facilities or hospices. I learned that sometimes being as present as possible was the only thing to do.

None of us knew what we were doing. We were firsthand witnesses to a horrific disease that had no hope, and our hearts ached as we tried to find ways to alleviate the suffering. We had to carve an inner, deeper, wider temenos to be of service. Each person we worked with taught us something to help our next patient. There was a web of support from our patients as they knew we were helping others and together we were trying to create more healing for all.

Two years into the work, my patients began to die. The first two died in the same week. I was bereft. It felt as if I needed to help each patient navigate the liminal state after death, but this was new territory for me, and understanding the bardo, that intermediate state between life and death, was beyond me.

That difficult week, I took a dream into my Jungian analysis. *I was bleeding from my eyes, my ears, my nose, my mouth, lying on the ground losing consciousness.* I heard Don Sandner command, while pounding his hands on the arms of his chair, "You cannot go with them! You must tell them your time on earth is not yet done." I awoke from a trance I did not know I was in. And I knew I was listening to the guidance and wisdom of a shaman.

Over the next five years, I witnessed my patients slowly deteriorate, become debilitated, succumb to horrible infections, get worse, get better, become disfigured, blind, demented, ultimately slip into semi comatose states, and eventually let go. I mourned the death of 200 beloved men. To this day, I cannot write or read this without a well of grief rising in me.

Experiencing the slow deterioration and death of my patients as we sorted through dreams, memories, hurts, traumas, and fears forced me to delve deeply into my soul to be of any help or comfort. As the disease progressed, my presence was the most I could offer, for the person was in an altered state of consciousness, or comatose from the disease, medication, or dying process. I had to process and grieve many times. I could feel the numinous quality of the dying process as a person began to step out into the beyond, then come back for brief periods to seek comfort and courage for the final journey. I could feel these happenings and recognize how it could pull for me too. I likened it to the myth of Icarus, with wings that could get too close to the numinous and that transitional liminal state in between life and death. This was no place to be in long and still be on your feet connected to the earth. Marie-Louise von Franz, in *On Dreams and Death* (1986), acknowledges this potential.

There was a moment when the rapport between me and my patients began to shift. As they entered a liminal realm where we both would drift, they began to teach me how to be with them as they were dying, if I could listen well enough. This taught me very clearly how to go and return, go again and return. A presence seemed to come into form that directed the learning that would then evolve my awareness so that it would recognize this moment and help me help others, for every situation and personal passing was unique.

I had to fall into the pain of the loss, the razor's edge, back through to life. What do we do with all that energy of care when the person we have worked with is no longer living? This transition during bereavement was hard to bear, as there was no path to follow. It was a new trail. How do we manage such experiences? How can we continue to help those in need, so that our life may be enriched and not torn apart by the experience? It was a dilemma not only for the health care professional but for all those suffering with AIDS, as they were losing their friends, partners, mentors, brothers, and health care providers. It was truly a relentless disease in an unrelenting time.

It took everything in me to find the necessary resilience, the inner capacity, and religious spiritual attitude from which to hold this healing temenos, for the grief and the horror were immense.

I learned to create a blessing ritual for each person as he or she transitioned. At times just prior to or after death, I told each of my patients, as Don instructed, "I cannot go with you. My time on earth is not yet done. Please help me do this work when you are able." I told them the Native American teaching I had learned at an American Psychological Association conference from Ed Duran about the eagle and the sweetgrass, a tale that helped to guide the spirit of the dying. Then wherever they were—whether in their home, hospice, skilled nursing facility, or in my own home, if I could not be with them—I burned sweet grass and called upon the eagle, the Great Spirit, Kwan Yin, and Mother Mary, asking for support for their journey from their ancestors and the beyond. Not once did anyone, including nurses or doctors, object. This ritual became my prayer and sanctuary, a solace to myself and my departing soul friend, who taught me how to offer my presence and to open to the sacred as together we encountered the flow of life and death on the edge.

Cultivating a New Religious Attitude

Spiritual practices of renewal and self-care called to me. Dora Kalff had introduced me to Kwan Yin, the one who perceives the sorrows of the world, and I found myself immersing in her compassion for strength. I reclaimed my Catholic devotion to Mary and the rosary while in Switzerland visiting the Madonna del Sasso in Locarno and then later while walking upon Monte Verità, located on Lake Maggiore. I returned to Native American purification rituals, doing sweat-lodge ceremonies and traditional vision quests with Angeles Arrien, Káruk, and Lakota medicine men to hold my heart and body to this earth. Time in nature, the hot springs of Tassajara in Big Sur, backpacking the Grand Canyon in Arizona, Zion National Park in Utah, and the Marble Mountains in California anchored me as I bore witness to immense places and dunked myself in cool streams or hot springs.

My first vision quest was in the sacred Marble Mountains. The intention of my quest was to seek understanding and inspiration to be with the dying. I had no food or water for three nights and three days, and I was five miles from anyone. No one knew where I was. I began to feel what my patients might feel as they lay in their weakened state prior to death. My mind was clear; my body was hardly able to move. Dreams and extraordinary realizations came as I looked all night into the stars and encountered a brown snake as I swam in a stream. When I found my way from where the black-and-white marble of the mountain joined, back to the camp at the end of those intense days and nights, I was guided by a force that protected me on those trails alone in that altered state. I was taken directly into the sweat lodge and given a sip of water. I felt the return of life with that drop of wetness. Later I learned that one of my patients left his body nearly at the same time. This synchronicity of returning to life and leaving life helped me realize that there was wisdom in what had been experienced that may reveal itself over time.

Surrendering to the vision quest process opened my senses to the subtle awareness of the "not-yet-known," and these experiences opened me further to the capacity to attune my awareness to the subtle source. Sacred practices offered by earth-based religions, when practiced for the intention of understanding healing and broadening my capacity to observe and communicate with the invisible realms, guided by wisdom teachers, helped prepare me for death: my own and others.

Moments of synchronicity, analysis, and consultation were my salve. There were moments of sanctity, glimpses of grace that held me to this earth and allowed me to reach for Spirit. They helped me bear what was unbearable and taught me to trust that I was being companioned by the invisible world through tears of grief.

Over time, a new religious attitude began to materialize that expanded my awareness, promoted a new attitude toward mystery and healing, and carved a well of compassion within my heart. Some things learned that helped me do this work:

- If we meet the moment and offer our listening, caring selves, that will be enough.
- If we let ourselves be moved and mourn and share our grief with others grieving, there will be healing.
- If we pay attention to the graces that nature offers, we will be nourished enough to keep trying another day.
- If we act from our heart, the Self comes in to meet us.

Many who died during the AIDS epidemic purposefully tried to help us learn how to help others as we endured with them their suffering through our presence. Though deeply painful, it was a time many of us continue to treasure. Being a part of something I did not choose engaged me to become someone I had not known. I learned to build a trust with an inner feeling or guidance or intuition, whatever one wants to call it, that I listen to or sense with today. I hope this guidance from within or beyond may serve you as well.

May They Serve

It was following my heart's aspiration to become trained in Jungian analysis that led me to the extraordinary encounters with those who taught me about the natural processes of healing, death, and dying. It seems fitting that the work to cultivate analytic presence (Costello, 2018) would entrain me to trust the liminal experiences of soul that traveling the land of in-between required as I cared for my patients dying of AIDS. These experiences deepened my capacity to be in the transformative field as holy ground, not just as a Jungian theory but as a living reality. I say this to you now in hopes of engendering some ease, for this territory is not unfamiliar to you. And it is sacred.

It was through reading Jung that I was taught to trust the relationships I had with the spiritual, to know my vocation was in line with my soul. Don Sandner, my analyst and mentor, taught me to trust the rituals of purification of the sweat-lodge ceremony and to use the vision quest to help grow my awareness of the healing process and to foster the development of my analytic presence. He also taught me how to return when I went too far to comfort my patients as they slowly and painfully died of AIDS.

And after Don died, it was Joseph Henderson who taught me to grieve and thus heal as I spoke of my dreams and experiences on the edge of death and dying in my personal relations. Mary Jo Spencer taught me to know that, indeed, the Self was a willing responsive witness to me. Dora Kalff deepened my affinity to Jung and affirmed that the earth-based spiritual practices of our native lands help to fine-tune our relationship to the Self and anchor us onto this earth. Later, June Singer (1990) asserted that we are accompanied by the invisible; Murray Stein (2006), Lucy Huskinson, Ann Casement (2006), and Ann Ulanov (1996) affirmed within me the awareness that the scintilla field is real enough to grow an actionable ethical stance.

I have come to realize that the capacity to be in what we, as Jungian analysts, term the analytic attitude, is the same resource that helps us be with dying, grief, healing, and transforming. This process is more familiar than what we might imagine. It took many years of training and insight to understand that Dora Kalff's "free and protected" space within the sandplay process was resonant with her Tibetan spiritual practice. This realization allowed me to recognize a field of analytic presence that can be nurtured and cultivated through mindfulness meditation as well as by compassionately being with one's grief and with a being who is dying.

What I have come to understand is that the elements that broaden our analytic attitude are what is needed to be with the dying while we are in our own grief: to be open to what arises without judgment; to tether ourselves to our own inner experience while opening to attune to another's, to the space between us, to the facile, fluctuating moments of going with and then returning from the reverie of images, dreams, reflections, memories, and myths while anchored right here in real time. Here we receive the glimpses of healing through communications from the subtle divine.

So, we need not be afraid to familiarize ourselves with the land of grief. Like the shaman, we are letting ourselves travel out or in and to return, again, to home. Each journey opens the channel wider for the healing in the universe to refill our vessel so that our well-being can serve others for whom we are caring. We must release and rinse our body, as vessel, after our care for another, lest residue remain, and then we must solidly ground back into our place here now, feet on the earth in our own life. I learned this important and necessary action long ago from Marion Woodman and often need to remind myself of it after a day's work.

Finite and Infinite

Here is an invitation to explore this territory of grief, healing, and compassionate resonance that can serve life, our own and others.

I love how Jung (1961) writes, not just in *Memories, Dreams, Reflections* but often in his papers, about his encounters with his conscious and unconscious play and also what he experienced in the consulting room with his patients, or something of his patient's experience that activated him. Then he speaks to how it took him years, sometimes decades, to integrate and understand that experience. This feels true for me.

My hope is that these experiences can thus guide choices and ultimately link us even more strongly to the web of life as continued connection with loved ones—passed and present—arrive. The scintilla and gossamer threads sometimes recede as we live our life so linearly. I remember Theodore Abt telling me once that if I could string each of my dreams or synchronistic moments like pearls on a necklace and wear them, this bridge to mystery and reality would imbue great meaning into my life.

Jung (1961) offers us specific reassurance that our own experiences are meaningful and that there are things that can be comprehended by consciousness only when the time is ripe. "Images of the unconscious are not produced by consciousness but have a reality and spontaneity of their own" (p. 324). I understand this to mean that as we experience something, while we may be awake to it, there may be yet more to receive when the time is right, and it may be years later. When it does arrive, it will bring new nourishment. The timelessness of this brings it all home, there is no regret it did not come sooner, that the moment of awe has arrived now. Henderson (1976) also shares a parallel reflection about the expansion of the cultural consciousness when he says that evolutionary change (in cultural consciousness) takes place only against a strong conservative resistance and in its own time.

> The psyche at times functions outside of the spatio-temporal law of causality. … A complete picture of the world would require the addition of still another dimension; only then could the totality of phenomena be given a unified explanation. … I have been convinced that at least part of our psychic existence

is characterized by a relativity of space and time …
this relativity seems to increase … to an absolute
condition of timelessness and spacelessness. (Jung,
1961, pp. 304–305)

Marie-Louise von Franz (1986) and Barbara Hannah (1992) both reiterate that for Jung (1961) the decisive question for humans is: Are we related to something infinite or not, as that is the telling question of our life. "In knowing ourselves to be unique in our personal combination, that is ultimately limited, we possess the capacity for becoming conscious of the infinite" (p. 325). This recognition of our limitedness keeps us from succumbing to the reverberations of the numinous experience as something created with our particular relationship with the divine or consciousness. We have not called it forth; it has landed autonomously from the unconscious. It is because of our humble awareness of our limitation, our finiteness, that we can even enter dialogue with the infinite. This creates the right relational balance within the ego-Self rapport and is both protective to the ego and respectful to the mystery of life. This reminds me of two of my favorite lines from *The Prophet* (1923) by Kahlil Gibran: "Think not that you direct the course of love, for if love finds you worthy it directs your course" (p. 14). And "For this I bless you most, you give much and know not that you give at all" (p. 63).

As we face and endure loss, we question how to call upon the resources of the psyche and our practices to tend to our feelings and care for ourselves, a loved one, or patient. The experiences shared here may offer examples that resonate with what the reader knows and understands. The hope is to encourage, validate, allow, attune, and savor these experiences that reveal themselves on the subtle edges of reality in life, death, or healing, thus allowing them to inform, transform, and contribute to living fully now. These sacred experiences beckon us to receive the blessing of being and feeling known. And Jung (1961) encourages us to turn toward them to find the ethical stance that engages us in life in deeper heartfelt ways from having had the experience. Turning in that direction, toward letting our life be informed by our sacred experiences further, connects us to something greater than ourselves (p. 193).

Gifts

Don Sandner's Vision: The Spaceship

A year or so before his death, Don shared a vision he had during an Ayahuasca medicine ceremonial journey in the Amazon. This is the essence of what I remember.

Don was allowed and able to bring everything most important to him, throughout the course of his lifetime, his work and development into a spaceship. Nothing of his accumulated essential experience would be lost, all was relevant and secure. He saw himself get into this round ship and take off. This was reassuring to him and gave him great peace. Was this vision an illustrative example of the subtle body Don built over his lifetime?

It echoes the subtle body that Barbara Hannah describes as a central wisdom in the *Secret of the Golden Flower* (Hannah, 1992, p. 42). She speaks to the possibility of one's soul becoming spiritual already in life. A spirit with consciousness that can survive death by building a subtle body, which becomes refuge in the Beyond just as our body provides on earth. The subtle body is a being like an ectoplasm, autonomous, "sort of a mandala like refuge of an enduring kind" (Hannah, p. 43). I imagine this spaceship as Don's soul's subtle body, something he seemed capable of creating as his psyche and soul prepared him for his physical death.

There is resonance in the writings of Holger Kalweit (1984), an author Don directed me to as the author of one of his favorite books, *Dreamtime & Inner Space*. Kalweit states that the shaman trusts in *philosophia perennis—Perennial Philosophy*—the universal mystical teaching of the unity of all beings (p. xii). To the shaman, the universe is pervaded by a creative essence that not only transcends normal existence but also lends to it an inner cohesion.

> The notion of soul ... is the notion of a life principle beyond the body is central to all tribal cultures ... these ideas have been preserved throughout history and nourished again and again by Man's spontaneous experiences. ... The existence of a soul and its postmortal connection with our lives is the ground of all traditional spiritual philosophy. (Kalweit, 1984, pp. 10–11)

Shamans develop skills to journey to the realm of death, to the beyond, to be reborn as they return in order to understand the natural transformative process of death, rebirth, and impermanence in everyday life. The vitality of life is watered by awareness of death and the beyond.

Altered and heightened states of consciousness exist, and the natural transformation of the psyche, a process infused with an understanding of impermanence, death, and rebirth, approaches us in liminal times and in birth-to-life and life-to-death transitions. Thich Nhat Hahn (2003) instructs us there is no birth and no death as everything continues to exist in new form; the cloud becomes rain becomes river, sea, and mist. Kalweit reminds us that Plato's last words were to practice dying. Thich Nhat Hahn also encourages a practice to see death and birth in everything. Cultural anthropologist Angeles Arrien guides us to practice dying by doing something not ever done before on one's birthday. And Wilhelm and Jung acknowledge that we need strong roots in the here and now to become conscious of eternity, and that this is only possible with respectfully realizing one is finite. Our natural losses and renewals may help prepare us for death. Perhaps Don could let go in peace, knowing what was essential to his nature would accompany him on his spaceship.

In our last year of work, I felt like a child asking him to repeat this vision to me and to tell me again what he thought it meant. I overcame the childish feeling several times. He was always gracious and delighted to repeat it to me. There was something comforting that resonated with me, which I later came to understand.

Soon after my husband and I married we were hoping to become pregnant. I was 39. Before a final attempt with fertility treatments a year or so later, I considered pausing analysis based on Dora Kalff's teaching suggesting that when pregnancy was difficult, it may be best not to be in analysis. But as I considered proposing this option, I heard in my mind a question: "What if it's the last time you see him?" I pushed this question aside, attributing it to anxiety from a younger part's fear of separation. Several times I heard that question. I tried to dismiss it, but the voice insisted firmly: "No, I'm asking you to answer, what if it's the last time you see him?" Shocked, I considered it thoughtfully. That inner voice seemed satisfied only when a conscious decision was submitted: I would be OK with myself, even if it was the last time I saw Don. So we talked about pausing and scheduled an appointment a few months out. I asked him whether he thought there was enough time to do all we wanted to do and whether he thought we knew when our death was near. And as we stood by the glass doors as I was leaving, I asked him, "Are you OK?" With a quizzical look, he said,

"Yes, I'm fine." I hadn't told him the question I kept hearing when considering pausing. I wish I had.

And it was the last time I saw him.

The week before we were to meet again after our several-month hiatus, with no success with pregnancy, I had a pressing feeling to call to confirm our appointment. I tried to push that aside too, saying of course he has it in his book, no need to check. The inner voice said call him now, so I did. It was Good Friday. He picked up. "Oh! It's been so long!" he said joyfully. My heart melted with the sweetness of it!

A couple of days later, on Easter Sunday morning, I woke with this dream.

Dream: The Hogan

Don is sitting on the earth inside an empty Navaho Hogan. He motions for me to come and sit cross-legged beside him on his right, and he takes my left hand with his right, conveying everything is OK. I see a friend who also works with Don, leaving on the left; again, Don indicates all is well with his presence, no words, my concerns understood and resolved. The feeling is of presence, connection, and groundedness, as we both sit on the earth next to each other, hand in hand.

When I woke from this dream, there was a shift in feeling, for I had been angry in grief that such a longing for motherhood would come too late, after consciously choosing in my 20s not to bring children into this world, anticipating future ecological hardships. The urge to give life after being immersed in death, at mercy to an internal procreative biology, why all that, to have it come to naught? Mad at God, mad at the analytic process for swinging me to opposite poles for nothing. Later in time, a deep gratitude flowed for the feeling that the maternal call came at all, initiating a mammalian belonging. But, for now, this anger subsided into heavy grief.

Late that Easter morning, my friend from the dream called to tell me Don had died. Beset with grief and disbelief, I understood the dream to be a visitation from Don as he was passing. And I am exquisitely grateful for it.

My profound sadness grew those few days following the news of Don's death. We had told one another that we would meet at our regular time come Thursday. I felt I needed to be in the room at the time we said we would meet. I did not want to *not* show up; maybe his spirit would be there, waiting. I called Don's wife and asked her if I could come to the office at the time of our appointment. She said yes and made arrangements.

So I went to his Marin office on the San Francisco Bay where his son's family lived. I was comforted to be in the presence of the healing sounds of water and wind, of being in a place so familiar with Don, with us.

Hearing it, sensing it, seeing it, I lit and burned some cedar, buckbrush, and sweetgrass, and traced the pictures and objects that were companions on our journey all those years. I bowed to things in the room gratefully, for their healing. I petted the polar bear and wolf.

I sat in the places where I sat and lay. I sat in the places he would sit. I sat on his meditation cushion, felt peaceful there; although it seemed sacrilegious in a way, it also felt like sitting in my dream when he held my hand. While there, the phone in the office rang three times; the cat in the house meowed three times.

As I turned to leave, touching the handle of the sliding glass door, the thought I had when that door first opened and closed for me over a decade ago flashed through my mind. "I wonder what it will be like when this door opens and closes for the last time." Feeling startled, compassion followed, "Ah, so this is how it is. I am opening and closing this door, with my own hands, without Don, by myself, this last time." Later, solace seeped in, that psyche seeded that question in my consciousness long before, and it came to mind then. Filled with both awe and sadness, my legs heavy, I trudged up those wooden stairs to the road one final time.

At Don's burial, as we greeted the seated family after each poured earth over his casket. I introduced myself to the daughter-in-law who lived in the home where the office was and thanked her for letting me come that day. Her eyes opened wide, and she said with excitement, "Oh, I have something to tell you." I was taken aback, given the moment. We agreed to talk at the reception. She told me that she and her 3-year-old son had left that day to give me privacy. When they came home, her son began to run down the stairs, crying out, "Papa! Papa!" which was Don's grandfatherly name, and threw open the door—which he knows not to do—and threw his arms around the air in an embrace, "Papa is here! Papa is here!" he shouted. She knows her son was seeing him. I was deeply comforted.

The reality of losing Don before our work was done was tempered by realizing that psyche had prepared us for his death, and thus, our work together, our shared life in analysis, his death itself, was our work. Don helped me midwife the deaths of so many young men and others, and the real and mystical experiences held within that work helped me walk through the grief of Don's death too. Burning sweetgrass and sage, I invoked their spirits to assist Don in crossing over as he had blessed their journeys. That first week I wrote a poem for him. And the Hale-Bopp comet so bright in the vast night sky reached its perihelion, the point in its orbit when it was closest to the sun, the day after he died. It sparkled in front of me on the long stretch of road home every evening for months. This held me, thinking of him shepherding others there. I see Don as a rainbow bridge.

The Rainbow Serpent

Joseph Henderson tended to my personal grief, as he supported me through the deaths of my first analyst, my mother, my marriage, and as I lose those I love. He taught me about the healing field within grief and that our surrender to it brings a newfound relationship with the beloved.

He shared that as he felt his grief from the loss of his wife alight upon him, he also felt his wife's presence close to him. This pairing helped him appreciate these visits from her, and compassion grew for these moments of grief and connection.

He encouraged me to create time to attend my grief following the death of my 72-year-old mother, to follow the stream wherever it led without pushing it away. Building a sanctuary within me, I leaned into the precious time of grief as a healing process. Henderson shared that it often took one or two cycles of all the seasons to fully comprehend the loss. He assured me that a rapport would come with an invisible presence that would integrate and reveal, not remain stuck in some sphere of body or mood, but one that might inspire, comfort, and be available through the course of days. I came to appreciate the space of grief as loving, sad, yet merciful. The initial grieving time was temporary; the veil thin between the worlds as subtle moments of communication emerged. Grief was the journey that returned me to life and knitted together the heart with invisible presence and meaning. Not fearing it, I began to notice it leaving.

Several months after my mother passed, I was backpacking in Zion National Park with my husband and friends. On our last day, I walked along the river to find a spot to watercolor and write my Dad a letter. The pen streamed across the page as I reviewed those weeks with Mom in the hospital. I wrote tearfully, hoping she was aware of our presence and love as we sang to her. I knew this was probably true, but I was deep in my grief, whispering it all out loud. Coming to the end of page three, I paused and looked up, gazing without thought, in anguish, then I saw it. In that blue sky was a square rainbow, all colors—blue, green, red, yellow, purple—floating. No rain in sight, no cloud nearby. I jumped up excited, called out to my husband to see, but no one could hear. Was this just a vision? I wanted him to validate it somehow. But I sat alone and watched it float out of sight and dematerialize.

Seeing this rainbow in the desert, through my tears, as I wrote to my Dad about Mom's dying, is a treasured moment. Glimpses of the sacred stay with us and nurture us forever. Later I realized this moment brought her close to me, that she was in harmony as Nature, as Don had written about in his book *Navaho Symbols of Healing* (1979).

When I shared this with Henderson, without a pause he claimed, "You saw the Rainbow Serpent." And he told me about this ancestral communication. The rainbow serpent continually rotates around this earth. There can be openings where communications from the ancestors are offered, especially near rivers. "You invoked the universe and your mother and in your lament looking up—the Rainbow Serpent came to you as the answer, communication from the land of the ancestors." Henderson's wisdom opened my heart in awe. From the moment I experienced that square rainbow floating in a cloudless, brilliant blue sky in Zion National Park, my grief lifted. My returning to those grief-filled images of my mother dying in the ICU hooked up to all kinds of machinery ceased. And instead, I feel the visitation of my mother.

Support from the Invisible World

I have come to trust in the support from the invisible world, and this helps me attune to or to notice, or be willing to register in my neuroception, a possibility that may be approaching. Why not? We understand atoms and quarks, black holes, mitochondria, tiny bacteria, and viruses, all unseen, all a blanket of life. Sometimes moments come in just glimpses, like the sun as it hits the dew on a blade of grass and sends a rainbow-arc of light. These moments allow me to still and be with my sadness, my joy and awe, the feelings of others, the scintilla, in this resonating field of sparks. This keeps me awake to aliveness dancing about in nature. Dreams seem to come sometimes from another realm—the myth living itself out in the images of the night. There are times to purely be with these moments, and there are times from which one needs to act because of these experiences. Act as in to take heed and say or do the thing that came to mind. Listen as if spoken to because you have been. Trusting that as real. Did it come from the heavens? Did it come from the body? Maybe one day we will know for sure. In the meantime, this growing awareness of being communicated with from the unseen is trying to be known.

The realm of healing and the realm of dying share something similar that is tacit. And the cultivation of our analytic presence helps us be awake to it. The realm of unconscious communication via dreams or synchronicities may also share a similar space. Or is it all in the same field?

The sandplay process also works in this field. It is a process of potential, uncertain—a process that needs respect and protection to keep open, as we wait or are awestruck, trusting. The sandplay field is an alchemical field of healing experienced in the relationship between the sandplayer and sandplay therapist (Costello, 2008, p. 16). A vibratory exchange between two objects within a third creates an experience in the interactional play between the objects and the analytic dyad, and between the contained/limited space of sandbox, the sand, the objects, the analytic dyad, and the objective psyche that potentially activates healing.

Maybe this is why the experience of healing and the experience of dying and grieving can, in certain conditions, create a sense of meaning and belonging to the web of life, a weaving of life, that brings solace—that we are not alone with the misery of it all, somehow. The field of healing and the field of dying into death and rebirth are well known to the shaman and the analyst.

There are ways we have learned as Jungians to trust in the possibility of transformation that can be utilized when caring for or communicating with a patient or loved one, a person or a pet that opens a doorway to a magnetic invisible field of potential presence and communication, encouraging us to recognize timelessness and spacelessness, or like Jung, to believe in life after death. Yet, it may also just be holding the presence of continuity—as Thich Nhat Hahn (2003) says, no birth, no death—to the reality of the nature of existence we do not yet understand. Certain conditions create manifestation or no manifestation in a continuing cycle of death and rebirth. As Jungians, we understand the transformative power of symbolic death and rebirth that can guide us as we travel, open to outcomes in the worlds of individuation, body death, and the natural cycle of the seasons. Here, also, is consolation from Khalil Gibran (1923): "And could you keep your heart in wonder at the daily miracles of your life, your pain would not seem less wondrous than your joy" (p. 39).

The anguish of loss, the land of the dead in dreams or at the bedside of a dying loved one or patient, or in the consulting space with another, takes a pulling and a toll. That is because it is real, and the real requires energy. We can't be there too long, or it feels like it begins to take us, too. This is our limitedness in the face of the infinite. There is no shame in understanding this respectful balance. Knowing this, we can practice with the traverse of leaving and coming, going and returning, like the shaman, using the body as vessel, releasing ego but inviting the vessel to be used or filled, as one is allowed to return across the threshold, rinsing and inhabiting the body as vessel once again, with our ego. We come to trust our capacity to return. And as we grow familiar with perceiving the quality of the synergistic feeling of awe and sadness that is grief, we are opened to the heart of compassion. As we cross thresholds, we come to understand that our grief is what keeps us in right relation between the finite and the infinite. Our awakened awareness of the preciousness and interconnection of life is our gift for having placed ourselves in service of midwifing transmutation. Its price, deep grief; its outcome, the potential for evolving a compassionate heart—perhaps a contribution to the evolution of World Soul.

The compensatory function to be active in life, taking a dream image and turning it into something within life is life-enhancing, healing, rejuvenating. These actions keep us tethered to this earth.

In Parting

When I review my life by piecing together brief resonant communications within spaces lived, between breaths, dreams, healing, dying, and death, it makes sense. Everything in our lifetime prepares us for the moments we must meet. A gift of the psyche. Yet, allowing those lived moments (for often it is in retrospect) to help us attune to an emerging, current experience requires our conscious awareness to notice and make use of them. Doing this serves our capacity to act in accordance with our guidance and our heart. Our trust in this grows. Our experience of compassion deepens. This opens us to relating with the interconnectedness within all of life and to a feeling of belonging to this life we have that we are living now.

Being with our grief follows a similar river course as the analytic process. Being with death and dying flows in this way as well. Our growing resonant analytic presence helps us traverse these transformative compassionate fields. It's the tears of our grief that bring us alive.

My patient Fred's last words uttered to me when I asked him what it was like to be consciously dying, were, "Being Nature." Don Sandner (1979) wrote that the Navaho religion revolves around a great secret, quoting Gladys Reichard, who states that at one's final dissolution they not only become one with the ultimate harmony, they are that harmony (p. 273). I feel that Fred was sensing himself becoming harmony in the universe. These two teachings from Fred and from Don would weave together and evolve a profound understanding that is instrumental in the way I live my life, feel my grief, and communicate with my loved ones in the Beyond. This revelation feels like a profound blessing and its wisdom helps me today when I lose someone I love and when I grieve those I serve, for it helps me see and hear my loved ones all around me.

References

Arrien, A. (1993). *The Four-Fold way: Walking the Paths of the Warrior, Teacher, Healer, and Visionary.* San Francisco: Harper Collins.

Boa, F. (Director). (1988). *The Way of the Dream: Conversations on Dream Interpretation with Marie-Louise von Franz.* Windrose Films.

Bolen, J. (1979). *The Tao of Psychology: Synchronicity and the Self.* San Francisco: Harper Collins.

Casement, A. & Tacey, D. (Eds.), (2006). *The Idea of the Numinous: Contemporary Jungian and Psychoanalytic Perspectives.* East Sussex: Routledge.

Costello, C. (1992). *AIDS Related Bereavement: A Study of Partners and Family Members.* Unpublished Doctoral Dissertation. Pacific Graduate School of Psychology: Palo Alto.

Costello, C. (2008). Sandplay Within the Context of Relationship. *Journal of Sandplay Therapy, 17* (2), 12–19.

Costello, C. (2018). Cultivating Analytic Presence Through Mindfulness: A Day of Practice and Exploration. Presentation: C G Jung Institute, San Francisco, CA, United States.

Costello, C. (2020). My Brother's Keeper: Born Through Grief and Awe During the Early AIDS Crisis in San Francisco. *Jung Journal: Culture & Psyche, 14*(3), 68–77.

Gibran, K. (1923). *The Prophet.* New York: Alfred A. Knopf.

Hannah, B. (1992) & Frantz, D. (Ed). *The Cat, Dog, and Horse Lectures and "The Beyond."* Wilmette: Chiron.

Henderson, Joseph. L. (1976). *Psychological Attitudes and Cultural Change.* San Francisco: C. G. Jung Institute.

Jung, C. G. (1961). *Memories, Dreams, Reflections.* New York: Pantheon Books.

Kalweit, H. (1984). *Dreamtime and Inner Space: The World of the Shaman.* Boston: Shambala.

Levine, S. (1982). *Who Dies? An Investigation of Conscious Living and Conscious Dying.* New York: Anchor Press/Doubleday.

O'Donohue, John. (2008). *To Bless the Space Between Us: A Book of Blessings.* New York: Doubleday.

Sandner, D. (1979). *Navaho Symbols of Healing: A Jungian Exploration of Ritual, Image, & Medicine.* Rochester, NY: Healing Arts Press.

Singer, J. (1972). *Boundaries of the Soul: The Practice of Jung's Psychology.* New York: Doubleday.

Singer, J. (1976). *Androgyny: Toward a New Theory of Sexuality.* New York: Doubleday.

Singer, J. (1990). *Seeing Through the Visible World: Jung, Gnosis, and Chaos.* San Francisco: Harper & Row.

Stein, M. (2006). On the Importance of Numinous Experience in the Alchemy of Individuation. In *The Idea of the Numinous: Contemporary Jungian and Psychoanalytic Perspectives* (A. Casement & D. Tacey, Eds.) (pp. 34–52). East Sussex: Routledge.

Nhat Hanh, Thich. (2003). *No Death No Fear: Comforting Wisdom for Life.* Riverside: Parallax.

Ulanov, A. (1996). *The Functioning Transcendent: A Study in Analytical Psychology.* Wilmette, IL: Chiron.

von Franz, M. (1986). *On Dreams and Death: A Jungian Interpretation.* Boston & London: Shambhala.

Whitney, M. (Director). 1986. *Matter of Heart.* Kino International.

Zona, G. (1994). *The Soul Would have No Rainbow if the Eyes had No Tears.* New York: Simon & Schuster.

Re-enchanting the Realm of Death

Joseph Cambray, PhD, IAAP

Introduction

From the late 16th century through the early 21st century, first Western and then more broadly many cultures have gone through "disenchantment." The cosmological shift from an animated universe to a dead, soulless, mechanistic view has been seen as the outcome of the scientific revolution in the West. The form of science promulgated here became increasing algorithmic, starting with Newton's laws, equations of motion, which seemingly reduced the world in subsequent generations to a rational machine without a soul and leading to the death of God[1]. This collective loss of divinity associated with the world has cast a rather dark shadow on the experience of death and intensified the fears associated with dying for modern people. The atheistic conception of death is a terminus in oblivion. This is engrained in cosmological imaginings of the gradual but inevitable extinction of the entire universe, evaporating into nothingness, a nonfertile void. In the face of such bleak predictions, what might depth psychology, especially a (post) Jungian approach have to offer?

---

[1] For Newton and many of the new breed of natural philosopher/scientists of the pivotal 17th century, the new epistemology was not yet divorced from the past religious worldview. This rupture took place with increasing strength in the 18th century with the "Enlightenment." For example, Newton wrote far more on alchemy as Warden and then Master of the Royal Mint than he did on physics, see Dobbs 1975.

To address this question, an appreciation of Jung's project to invigorate a despiritualized psychology provides an initial pathway forward which can be further developed in terms of new understandings of the notion of "the unconscious" that have been emerging over the past three decades or more. The basis for this approach can be found in Jung's experiment in self-exploration captured in his elaborated transcription of his journals (*The Black Books, BBs)* into an illuminated manuscript, *The Red Book* (*RB*). His project for individuation, as will be shown, required him to go beyond personal realization of the Self. This led him to the notion of synchronicity, which even today has not been fully understood in terms of its consequences for our cosmology.

In this paper, I hope to show that Jung was seeking reenchantment, not only for himself but for his society, and by extension to the world. He left us valuable tools, but much remains to be accomplished to this day. I believe that only by seeking to further this project will our relationship to death be impacted at a collective level; it will require a revisioning of our lives in this world in order to recontextualize our deaths into an experience in touch with "objective" as well as "subjective" meanings and going beyond these categorizations. In this regard, we do not prepare for death, but if fortunate, nature prepares us for it.

From the Death of God to *The Red Book*

Friedrich Nietzsche was perhaps the most powerful modern voice to openly proclaim the death of (the Christian) God. Initially in *The Gay Science* (first edition in 1882), with various proclamations, such as:

> God is dead. God remains dead. And we have killed him. How shall we comfort ourselves, the murderers of all murderers? What was holiest and mightiest of all that the world has yet owned has bled to death under our knives: who will wipe this blood off us? What water is there for

us to clean ourselves? What festivals of atonement, what sacred games shall we have to invent? Is not the greatness of this deed too great for us? Must we ourselves not become gods simply to appear worthy of it? (p. 181, 1974)

We are left with an enormous lacuna, which ironically, he suggests we would have to fill with ourselves in an act of extreme grandiosity equivalent to a schizophrenic delusion.

A few years later in *Thus Spoke Zarathustra* (first published in four parts in German from 1883-1885), Nietzsche repeats his concern but now in a parable that finds echoes in some of Jung's encounters with various inner figures in the *BBs* and then *RB*. Most notably, Zarathustra speaks with an aged ascetic who recognizes him and sees that he has changed. At the end of their exchange Zarathustra remarks:

"What should I have to give you! But let me go quickly that I take nothing from you!" And thus they parted from one another, the old man and Zarathustra, laughing as two boys laugh.

But when Zarathustra was alone, he spoke thus to his heart: "Could it be possible! This old saint has not heard in his forest that *God is dead*!"

(p. 41, 1969)

Nietzsche goes on in the next parable to speak of the *Uebermensch/* Superman, his replacement for the god. In his *Zarathustra Seminars* (2009), Jung does discuss the "death of god" on numerous occasions but curiously never refers explicitly to Nietzsche's parable of the aged ascetic. At a feeling level he seems to stay distant from parallel experiences of his own, as in Chapter VII of *Liber Secundus* in the *RB*, "The Remains of

121

Earlier Temples." There Jung encounters two figures with whom he has had previous exchanges, Ammonius (A) the desert monk, and the Red One (R), a devil figure. In their initial exchanges Jung had been wary but respectful of the figures. Now, he has become more certain of himself and bold in his treatment of them to the point of being dismissive:

> I [Jung]: "Dear friends, it does my heart good to see you enjoying yourselves together."
>
> Both: "We are not pleased, mocker and adversary, clear off, you robber, pagan!"
>
> I: "But why are you traveling together, if you're not enjoying each other's company and friendship?"
>
> A: "What can be done? Even the devil is necessary, since otherwise one has nothing that commands a sense of respect with people."
>
> R: "Well, I need to come to an arrangement with the clergy, or else I will lose my clientele."
>
> I: "Therefore the necessities of life have brought you together! So let's make peace and be friends."
>
> Both: "But we can never be friends."
>
> I: "Oh, I see, the system is at fault. You probably want to die out first? Now let me pass, you old ghosts!" (p. 276, 2009)

While Jung is in quest of transcendence, the previous, historical ways are not sufficient for him. He soon goes on to meet Izdubar, in whom the perspective of the science of the day wounds his mythological spirit. The healing of Izudbar requires his transformation into fantasy, an insight which more broadly leads to the emergence of the psychic reality of the imagination. These steps hold the key to a renewed relationship with the divine.

By the time Jung was engaged in the active imaginations of the *BBs*, he was unhappily ensconced in the disenchanted world of rationalistic science. Nietzsche's prophetic comments were in place, and Jung was seeking a way out of a despiritualized world, one that lacks "objective" meaning, including for death. To contextualize his explorations further, we will look to the sociologist Max Weber and his 1917 lecture "Science as Vocation."

Disenchantment

In his 1917 lecture, subsequently published as "Science as Vocation," Weber, drawing upon the German Romantic philosopher-poet Friedrich Schiller, spoke of the embrace of science by modern cultures as leading to an *Entzauberung der Welt* a "de-magicization" of the world, which has been embraced in English as a disenchantment of the world. This state is marked by loss of meaning, lacking access to divine, spiritual, or metaphysical realities (Weber 1946/1919). For Weber this created significant personal distress along with desires for mystical experiences. Weber went to Monte Verità in Ascona to be with a group of occultists who met there (Josephson-Storm, 2017, pp. 269ff.); this preceded Olga Fröbe-Kapteyn and the Eranos of Jung.

Weber saw the disenchantment occurring in several steps, beginning with a differentiation of priests from magicians, then on to the shift from "pagan" belief systems to monotheistic religions, which brought totalizing systems of meaning and values, culminating in the Puritan ethic of vocation. From there it became possible for science to delegitimize monotheistic religion as irrational, displacing them and creating a unified worldview for a completely secular world (Weber, *ibid*).

Weber's hypothesis has gained widespread interest over the past century and has become a topic of considerable interest in academia—over 200,000 articles are noted in Google Scholar as of July 2023. Weber (1864-

1920) was a contemporary of C. G. Jung, and although they have no known correspondence, there are distinct parallels in their thinking. Roderick Main has recently published a valuable comparative study of their work, which emphasizes the importance of the trajectory: enchantment, disenchantment, reenchantment. Jung's individuation model along with synchronicity are seen by Main as key to Jung's efforts at countering the despiritualization (Main 2022), which is roughly equivalent to disenchantment. Main notes that this also offers a viable path to building some solid bridges between sociology and analytical psychology.

Reenchanting Jung

In following Jung's path through the *RB*, one of the questions arising for me had to do with his motivation for continuing the project, especially after his 1927 "Liverpool dream" (*RB* p. 217).

Jung makes clear that this dream brought with it a realization of the Self, imaged in the magnolia tree with its shining, golden blossoms on an island in the center of the city that those around him could not see. He subsequently captured the image in his painting of the "Window on Eternity" (*RB*, p. 159; 318 n. 296). On the surface, this realization seems the paramount achievement of the individuation process, yet it was not the end of the *RB* exploration.

The following year (1928), while continuing his work on the *RB* Jung painted a well-armed, or heavily defended castle (*RB* p. 163). During the painting, he received a manuscript from his sinologist friend, Richard Wilhelm, of a translation of a Taoist alchemical text, now known as *The Secret of the Golden Flower*. Wilhelm was seeking a foreword or commentary from Jung (both of which he supplied). Jung was deeply impressed at the coincidence of the image of the Vajra mandala, which was included in the manuscript as it bore a striking resemblance to his castle painting. He claims this coincidence is what refocused his attention onto alchemy, a subject he explored for the remainder of his life.

In November of 1928 Jung began his private dream seminar course and rapidly came upon a series of remarkable coincidences stemming from a dream under discussion. Asked to comment on how he understood these phenomena, Jung remarked:

> ...we would make a mistake to consider them [the coincidences] as causal; events don't come about *because* of dreams, that would be absurd. ... But it is wise to consider the fact that they do happen. We would not notice them if they were not of a peculiar regularity ... a sort of irrational regularity. The East bases much of its science on this irregularity and considers coincidences as the reliable basis of the world rather than causality. Synchronism is the prejudice of the East; causality is the modern prejudice of the West. (pp. 44-45, 1984)

William McGuire's footnote to the term synchronism identifies this as "Jung's first use of this term in the sense of 'synchronicity'" (*ibid.*).

As I have shown elsewhere (2014), the notion of synchronicity finally released Jung to "return to the human side and to the world" (2009, p. 219). Thus, it seems Jung was not ready to end his confrontation with the unconscious even with a personal revelation of the transpersonal Self, as meaningful as that was to him. Rather, it took the revelation of a new cosmogonic principle, a fourth term to be added to the physics of the day with its energy/space-time/causality model to provide the desired exit from the madman/prophet dilemma constellated at the onset of his inner work which led to *RB* (Cambray 2014).

In accord with Main, I would place individuation and synchronicity as the essential requirements for a (post) Jungian reenchantment psychology. Following the implicit trajectory of Jung's thought, I would further extend the model of individuation to include a broader, environmental dimension, not only including a transpersonal but also include an ecological vision of the psyche and the Self. Further, in the recognition of the cosmogonic significance of synchronicity, a complex, postcausal holistic science is required for our fuller understanding of the world we live in. The reanimating aspect of this will be discussed shortly, but first a story about a dream synchronicity associated with death.

A case of the dead in dreams

There is, of course, an extensive literature on oneiric experiences in which figures in our lives who have died return in our dreams. There is not space here to review this material, but the link of psyche with death goes back to the very notions of what psyche may be, e.g., that aspects of ourselves survive the death of the body. Classicist Erwin Rohde wrote extensively on the origins of the concept in *Psyche* in cults of the dead (1925). In addition to Jung himself[2], important texts were published by Jungians Edgar Herzog, *Psyche and Death*, (2001); James Hillman, *The Dream and the Underworld* (1979); and Marie-Louise von Franz, *On Dreams & Death* (1987), among others. Occasionally dreams involving deceased friends or relatives have synchronicities associated with them, which tend to give a profound feeling of existence of the soul. Recently I had such a dream.

> Having completed administrative duties at an academic institution, I was in the process of retiring and was about to attend a party to commemorate this life transition event. The night before the party, I had a dream of a friend and colleague from my place of employment, who had sadly died rather suddenly about a year after he, himself, retired. This had been a difficult loss for

---

[2] For a compilation of Jung's reflections on death, see the volume edited by Jenny Yates, *Jung on Death and Immortality* (1999).

me as he and I had grown quite close, especially during the period of COVID-enforced isolation when we were often together alone among a skeleton crew on campus. We had made plans for a variety of activities we would do together in retirement, so his death was a bitter blow. In my dream, the first I had had of this friend: *We were amiably catching up when I mentioned aloud that I thought he was dead and asked him about it... at this point he disappeared.*

The next day at the party I was presented with some parting gifts. As I unpacked one, it was a lovely carved crystal bowl with an inscription on it. *I was asked to read the dedication aloud and as I began to do this, I saw that it was dedicated to my deceased friend, not to me.* While some of the staff were highly distressed at the engraver's mistake, I decided to relate my dream, with a strong sense of the presence of my friend at the gathering. Indeed, he would have been one of most important guests there for me had he still been alive.

The synchronicity provided comfort and felt a preparation by the world for death, revealing the deep bonds that transcend our mortality. Like Jung, I cannot comment on any metaphysical reality to such experiences, but I do feel my heart is gladdened by them. In reflecting on the dream, it seemed my insertion of the notion of death into the dream of our catching up was part of the loss/disappearance of my friend. Perhaps our egoic framing of loss associated with death is what is mirrored back from the unconscious, *rather than death being a cold, hard "truth," the psyche recedes into invisibility at the insistence of disenchantment?* Alternatively, the ability to tolerate the suspension of choice may keep engagement alive, analogously to "Schrodinger's Cat" before an observation is made.

Jung as visual thinker

To appreciate the implicit reenchantment motif in Jung's work more fully together with its relationship to death, I would like to direct attention to some recently published drawings and paintings by Jung. In particular, consider some works not included in *RB* but recently published in *The Art of C. G. Jung* (Jung 2018), where we learn that Jung had a serious case of "Spanish Flu" (now called the 1918-1920 Great Influenza epidemic) in which he reported, "I was losing my hold on life" (p. 137). In his near-death state, he had several dreams and visions which he subsequently painted in a series of "Spheric Visions" (*ibid*, pp. 131-137). These are marked by a floating sphere with a cross quadrating it; this image eventually made its way into the *RB* on page 125. As I have shown elsewhere, this image itself bears a remarkable resemblance to the image of a juvenile sea squirt found in the paintings of the marine biologist Ernest Haeckel (2014). The suggestion is that there is a deliberate interplay between biology and analytical psychology captured in this figure. The biological argument at the time was considering the creature to be a manifestation of a transitional form between invertebrate and vertebrate organisms. In Jung's image, from my perspective, the radiant quadrated sphere seems a transitional form between the mundane and heavenly worlds. In effect, science and spirituality are placed in a new dialogue with Jung showing himself to be an impressive visual thinker, working out complex problems in visual representations of a path toward reenchantment.

Now with the newly published images of Jung's art, we can return to the quadrated sphere and reassess its *bio-mythic relevance*. As Jung was beginning his recovery process from the flu, he recalled another dream occurring at a repeated location: "a wonderful evening sky vaulted over the island. Between the two trees a sphere floated or had settled there [cat. 58]" (2018 citing a conversation with Aniela Jaffe on February 6, 1959). This image is a clear precursor to the one on page 131 of the *RB*; here, the sphere is more complexly formed with an eightfold structure and is the source of illumination for the entire figure. From an alchemical perspective we are looking at the philosophical tree radiant with light of the *lumen naturae*, giving further evidence to the evolution of Jung's capacity for synthetic, visual thinking.

An important way to understand Jung's visual intuition in this image is to leap forward to our own pandemic, that of COVID-19. Scientific images of the novel coronavirus produced in early 2020 revealed its circular crownlike form in electron microscopy, and subsequently the spheroidal form in X-ray crystallographic studies. Of course, nothing similar was available in 1919 during the pandemic Jung experienced— the first virus to be crystallized was the Tobacco Mosaic Virus in 1935, also the first to be imaged by electron microscopy in 1939, 20 years after Jung's illness. Nevertheless, I suggest Jung's visual intuition captured an image related to his illness during recovery. A comparison of the "Spanish Flu" virus (based on samples preserved from that time) with the novel coronavirus show morphological similarities in their spheroidal form (**Figure 1**); perhaps even more curious are the triadic and quadrated

COVID-19   Spanish Flu

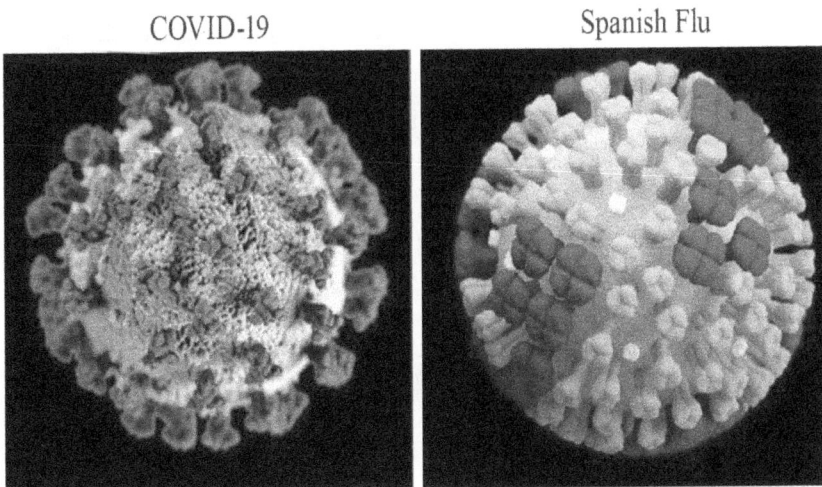

Figure 1 https://newsgranularity.com/2020/05/11/
covid-19-vs-spanish-flu-a-societal-comparison/

forms of the surface proteins on the crystallographic study of the Spanish Flu virus, perhaps a harbinger of his later reflections on the psychological significance of shifts from trinitarian to quadratic forms.

Although this information was clearly not available to Jung's conscious mind, it does seem his visual intuition was acute enough to give this image prominent representation in *RB* as noted. I will explore this with what I term the psychoid imagination in the next section, but here, I would like to suggest Jung's visual work with the spheroidal form can be appreciated in terms of reenchantment. Sadly, the author of "the disenchantment of the world," Max Weber, died in 1920 of the "Spanish Flu" before he was able to work out next steps to counter this disenchantment. Jung seems to have carried this cultural task forward on his own in the depth psychological realm, without reference to parallel attempts by others. Perhaps his most aphoristic statement on the state of our disenchantment is his remark, "The Gods have become diseases" found in Collected Works 13, par. 54, in his commentary on *The Secret of the Golden Flower* first published in German in 1929 where this aphorism is stated as *Die Götter sind Krankheiten geworden* (Wilhelm 1929), at the very time he is privately articulating the synchronicity hypothesis.

In elevating his illness-dream-vision of the sphere to the source of illumination in the tree of life, he offers us a way to reclaim the mythic imagination, as he often said, by going through the problem, not around it. If we have lost our connection to the divine, and with it the meaning of death, reducing them to pathologies of mind and body, then by embracing the illness, following the images which emerge from it, we may indeed lead to a new consciousness.

I would argue that COVID-19 has been driven by global warming[3] and if we are not to suffer further outbreaks, perhaps of even more dreadful

---

[3] In support of this, see Harvard's T. H. Chan School of Public Health website, e.g., https://www.hsph.harvard.edu/c-change/subtopics/coronavirus-and-climate-change/

illness, we must regain a respect for the ecological wholeness of nature—could we treat our illnesses as pathways back to relationship with the cosmos, can our diseases show us the way to reenchant our world? Can the realm of Hades, which has been evacuated by our Herculean sciences, be reenvisioned in the psychoid aspect of the *unus mundus*?

The psychoid imagination

The previously unidentified talent Jung displayed in accessing and visually representing aspects of nature unknown to science of the time, through what I have termed "the psychoid imagination," is not unique to him. In previous publications I have pointed to a number of artisans and artists who have displayed such abilities, for example Jackson Pollock's perception of fractal realities well before Benoit Mandelbrot formulated his classic sets, or Vincent van Gogh's capturing of turbulence in certain of his paintings, including a twinkling of light that is one of the unsolved mysteries of classical physics (2016). One way to formulate these feats is through considering potential noetic qualities of certain altered states of consciousness, especially ones which might transcend our usual subject/object splitting.

Noetic altered states have historically been the purview of select mystics and shamans. William James, a figure of important influence on Jung, famously defined the noetic quality of mystical experiences as:

> states of insight into depths of truth unplumbed by the discursive intellect. They are illuminations, revelations, full of significance and importance, all inarticulate though they remain; and as a rule they carry with them a curious sense of authority.
>
> (1902/2011 p. 312)

James, although a skeptic, also saw noetic potential in telepathy, clairvoyance, and communication with the dead. Like Jung, he knew mediums and attended seances, seeking bridges between the living and the dead through psychical research. His view of consciousness was critical of the materialist view that consciousness was merely a product of the brain and thus in close accord with Jungian thought in its rejection of the finality of disenchantment.

The psychedelic revolution has opened the doors for many more people to access altered states with potential noetic significance. Nevertheless, sorting out the veracity of the knowledge gained in such experiences can be quite a challenge. Historically, the *vera imaginatio* of alchemists offered such a noetically rich and informative experience which revealed a profound and difficult achievement. In discussing this phenomenon Jung implicitly directs us to its enchanted nature:

> We have to conceive of these processes not as the immaterial phantoms we readily take fantasy-pictures to be, but as something corporeal, a 'subtle body'... Imagination is therefore a concentrated extract of the life forces, both physical and psychic.
>
> (CW 12, par. 394)

He notes the alchemists worked "[i]n an age when there was as yet no empirical psychology ... because everything unconscious, once it was activated, was projected into matter" (*ibid.*). The projections of unconscious contents were an integral part of the enchanted world, and Jung's observation provides a significant reason why it is not fruitful to simply try to return to such ways of processing experience. This leaves Jung, and ourselves in turn, to find new pathways to this true imagination not contingent on either projection or rational dismissal. The synchronicity hypothesis was Jung's best effort at how to approach this as it manifests at the edge of the subjective and objective, partaking of both in an inseparable manner and perhaps transcending their supposed opposition; it inherently involves a psychoid dimension.

Synchronicities and death

Since the moment of death has a psychoid archetypal aspect, if we do not accept a purely materialistic cosmology (death of the body with no soul to transition), we may take reports of near-death experiences, visions, and dreams at or around time of death, as well as supposed communications with the deceased as providing additional anecdotal glimpses of the psychoid realm being accessed through the deep imagination. Obviously not all synchronicities are associated with imminent death; still they do put us in touch with a realm that is outside our mundane perceptions, what might be interpreted as a realm outside time, either before, after, or transcendent to it.

As Jung mentioned in his essay on synchronicity, the absence of causality in synchronistic events is related for him to conditions in which space and time are essentially reduced to zero and the laws of physics have not yet come into being (CW 8, par. 855), effectively approaching the conditions of the singularity in our scientific cosmogony—an archetypal moment of birth and perhaps death of the cosmos. A bit later in the same essay he refers to synchronicities as "acts of creation in time" (CW 8, par. 965), again arguing for an expansion of the scientific view of the origins of the universe. So, looking through the lens of synchronicities, might we be peering into a portal or window on eternity from which time emerges? Perhaps a clinical report will provide a microcosm hint.

About 18 months prior to a move across country to take on a new position, I was going through my analytic case load deciding how and when to discuss the upcoming change with clients and potential options for their ongoing analytic work, either with other analysts or through telecommunication with me. In the midst of my deliberations, I received a phone call from a client about whom I was in the deepest quandary on this issue. She was calling to cancel our session that day, because of physical difficulties which would not let her drive—cancellation was a very rare occurrence for this person, so I knew it was something serious. She instead went with assistance to a medical exam and was diagnosed with an aggressive cancer that left her a very short time to live. Attending to her dire condition superseded any discussion of my future move, as her prognosis suggested her death would come long before I moved.

As we both were reeling from the shock of her news trying to decide how to meet with the least disruption, the medical staff decided to place her in a nursing care facility. While I wanted to try and see her as often as possible during this most stressful time, I was unsure how this might be accomplished. Within a few days, we discovered to our surprise that she would be placed in a facility less than a five-minute walk from my office! This decision had been made for medical reasons without any consultation or consideration of how the location might impact on our work; the choice was, under these very difficult conditions, a real boon. I was able to maintain our regular schedule of several times a week analysis (though at times in silence depending on her strength) right up to the end of her life. While the client's dying process was tragic in many ways, and we had to process our grief in an accelerated manner, we were fortunate to have the time and space in which to engage in a review of our years together and meaningfully say our goodbyes—in some ways time felt elastic as her psychic life unfurled in what was a matter of weeks. It was a privilege to accompany her on this final chapter of her life; we were both deeply moved by how there seemed to be an unconscious facilitation of the work as if helping her prepare for a premature death.

Death has often been envisioned as a movement of the soul back into nature and the cosmos: the material substances of the body gradually returning to elemental forms, while some dimensions of consciousness rejoin a cosmic consciousness, variously framed in different religions. There is an implicit ecological aspect to this type of vision of death, disintegration, and reintegration into the larger whole. As I've discussed previously (e.g., 2017), Jung used the image of the rhizome to capture this:

> Life has always seemed to me like a plant that lives on its rhizome. Its true life is invisible, hidden in the rhizome. The part that appears above ground lasts only a single summer. Then it withers away – an ephemeral apparition. When we think of the unending growth and decay of life and civilizations, we cannot escape the impression of absolute nullity. Yet I have never lost a sense of something that lives and endures underneath the eternal flux. What we see is the blossom, which passes. The rhizome remains.
>
> (Jung 1961, p. 4)

The rhizome image holds the truth of our profound interconnectedness as an underground secret. By analogy, synchronicities point to the rhizomatic forms undergirding our world, transcending mortality, and giving meaning to the archetypal events in our lives and deaths. As I noted, this leads to an expanded vision of the psyche in its distributed, nonlocal dimensions, making it an ecological system that we are just beginning to appreciate from the perspective of complex adaptive system (the model I have used in the past to formulate clinical synchronicities, 2002).

If complex adaptive systems are one of our best tools for understanding ecological systems and if synchronicities can be framed in terms of such systems, then we might consider relevant synchronicities as communications from/with the ecosystems we live within and are a part of. This would offer one form of access for dialoguing with the environment. Might we begin with deep listening to meaning of synchronicities associated with experiences in nature. Let me give an example from my own experience associated with the death of my parents:

> As my parents aged, they told my sister and me of their wish to be cremated, and once both had died to have their ashes commingled and scattered at sea. To honor this wish, after they were deceased and cremated, my sister and I chartered a boat in a city at the seaside where my parents had begun their marriage. We traveled together with our spouses out of the harbor and into deeper waters with the captain playing "swing music" from the era of our parents' romance. Upon reaching a desirable location for the scattering of ashes, we had a ritual and said our goodbyes. As we watched the ashes swirl into the depth, we were amazed to see a mother whale and her calf surface close to our boat. The whales, which the captain claimed were unusual to see at this time of year, then proceeded

to swim in elegant circles around the boat. They leapt into the air, displayed their tails, and generally performed what felt like a water ballet. We all watched the pair for almost 45 minutes, until the captain informed us that we needed to return to the harbor. We left the whales still swimming on the surface as we said our farewells; all were profoundly moved by this seeming tribute from these intelligent creatures from the depths. It felt as if we had all been blessed by this extraordinary moment celebrating life and death. This brought us another type of gratitude to our parents for having had us enact this ritual which held so much unexpected richness. The sense of interconnectedness with the environment was palpable. That day our parents transitioned into being ancestors as they entered mythic depths, saluted by these figures of rebirth and new life.

Multiple "Lives"

The psyche in my experience has not only been productive of dreams and synchronicities about death but also about the possibilities of multiple existences. These have not been experiences that insist on literal past lives but offer possibilities of alternatives in metaphoric language that open up mysteries of types of existence. I will offer one dream in this regard.

At an inflection point in life, a time of various potential directions for careers, the following dream offered another way to consider the issue:

The dream begins with a scene with a certain feeling of urgency in a closed room. Stepping outside the room, I not only exited the space but had a shift in perspective, finding myself first outside the building, then as if stepping further back, a large vision emerged. Now, a large tapestry was before me, extending beyond my vision in all directions, perhaps to infinity. As I moved back closer to the weaving, I realized I could enter through any point of intersection, the knots, which would open into another room, and with that into another life. I awoke to the room I was sleeping in.

In exploring what had been envisioned in this image, my associations went to the little I knew of the Akashic records at the time, a somewhat fanciful notion of 19th-century occultists drawing on Sanskrit term *Akasha* meaning "space, atmosphere, or sky" (Nash 2020). Later I would come to recognize other similar images with related meanings, such as Indra's Net derived from the Buddha's *Avatamsaka* or "Flower Garland" Sutra and further developed by the Hua-yen school in Chinese Buddhism. The metaphor of Indra's Net is told as follows:

> In the realm of the god Indra is a vast net that stretches infinitely in all directions. In each "eye" of the net is a single brilliant, perfect jewel. Each jewel also reflects every other jewel, infinite in number, and each of the reflected images of the jewels bears the image of all the other jewels—infinity to infinity. Whatever affects one jewel effects them all.
>
> (O'Brien 2020)

This is read as an image of the interconnectedness and interdependency of all things in the universe. The Hua-yen vision of the universe is compatible with a synchronistic cosmos in which there is a fundamental interconnectedness based on meaning rather than causality. While these visions do not explicitly take positions on death and afterlife or rebirth, they would necessarily argue that death should not be seen in isolation but rather as a part of the continual flow of existence. As interdependent aspects of a cosmic web or tapestry, life and death should not be separated. The mystery of how they are interrelated remains a question that many religions wrestle with. For this essay, I suggest they are archetypal images upon which beliefs about afterlives and/or rebirths are imagined. At a practical level, this dream helped me transition from a career in science to becoming a Jungian analyst and then seeking links between these approaches to life and reality, still at play in this essay.

Conclusion:

In this brief essay, a group of synchronistic experiences have been linked to different experiences associated with death. The intent has been to acknowledge our lack of understanding beyond medical rationale and to see how depth psychology may offer another approach to facing death. This will not have the precision of a technical-medical explanation but can bring us closer to the fullness of the experience, even if remaining at least somewhat inarticulable in the end.

In exploring the topic, we should be clear that there are many synchronicities that do not involve death in a concrete manner and reciprocally many deaths do not involve known synchronicities. Nevertheless, if death is taken as a realm of ultimate mystery beyond ordinary human understanding, then synchronicities may indeed offer a portal to the afterlife, in the sense that they compel us to consider the impact of an acausal coincidental meaning of certain events, which only comes through reflection after the events have been "lived" in an immediate manner. Perhaps as noted, synchronicities bring us into contact with realms of experience that conform neither to subjective nor objective definitions. Rather, in their emergent qualities they engender an awareness of a larger psychic ecology.

Here, we close the loop in bringing our discussion back around to reenchantment. The two concepts, synchronicity and reenchantment, have a secret, untold history that has been pointed toward here and in Main's new book. This started with the grim awareness, in various forms, of the soulless condition of modern humans being articulated by the end of the 19th century. Various pioneers have sought to challenge this trend, which has continued to intensify through the 20th century. The glimmer of hope to move beyond this wretched state of affairs has come from experiments, like Jung's described in the *RB*. In that case, the effort culminated in a vision of individuation that required a synchronistic universe to reach fulfillment.

How then do we move this forward in our lives? Cultivation of awe and wonder, which should also include the sublime and its sense of terror[4], would offer an emotional path that does not require the sacrifice of all we have gained through science and technology but would help us reassess the cost and value of how we employ our gains (for an up-to-date view of these emotions including current neuroscientific understandings see Keltner, 2023). Does death take on a new appearance when these emotions are present? I believe this is a cultural, or even global, narrative we would do well to explore together.

References

Cambray, Joseph. "Synchronicity and emergence," *American Imago* 59 (4), pp. 409-434, 2002.

_____. "The Red Book: Entrances and Exits," in *The Red Book: Reflections on C. G. Jung's Liber Novus*, ed. T. Kirsch and G. Hogenson. (New York & London: Routledge, 2014).

_____. "Intuizione artistica e immaginazione psicoide: un ponte tra realta simboliche e ecologiche," (Artistic intuition and the psychoid imagination: bridging symbolic and ecological realities) in *Enkelados*, 4, 117-133 (2016).

_____. "The emergence of the ecological mind in Hua-Yen/Kegon Buddhism and Jungian psychology," in *J.Anal.Psy.*, 62 (1), 20-31, (2017).

Casement, Ann. "The complex pleasure of the sublime," in *Thresholds and Pathways Between Jung and Lacan: On the Blazing Sublime*, ed. Ann Casement, Phil Goss and Dany Nobis. (New York & London: Routledge, 2021).

Dobbs, Betty Jo Teeter. *The Foundations of Newton's Alchemy or "The Hunting of the Greene Lyon"* (Cambridge: Cambridge University Press, 1975).

Herzog, Edgar. *Psyche and Death: Death-Demons in Folklore, Myths, and Modern Dreams*, 2nd ed. (New Orleans: Spring Publications, 2001).

Hillman, James. *The Dream and the Underworld.* (New York, San Francisco: Harper & Row, 1979).

James, William. *The varieties of religious experience.* Digreads.com. Available at: www.digireads.com. (1902/2011).

Josephson-Storm, Jason A. *The Myth of Disenchantment*. Chicago and London: The University of Chicago Press, 2017).

Jung, C.G. *Memories, Dreams, Reflections*. (New York: Vintage Books, 1961).

_____. Commentary on "The Secret of the Golden Flower," in *CW*, vol. 13 (Princeton, NJ: Princeton University Press, 1967).

_____. *Psychology and Alchemy*, *CW* 12, 2nd ed. (Princeton, NJ: Princeton University Press, 1968).

_____. *The Structure and Dynamics of the Psyche*, *CW* 8, 2nd ed. (Princeton, NJ: Princeton University Press, 1969).

_____. *Jung on Death and Immortality*, revised edition, ed. Jenny Yates. (Princeton, NJ: Princeton University Press, 1999).

_____. *The Red Book: Liber Novus*, ed. Sonu Shamdasani, trans. John Peck, Mark Kyburz, and Sonu Shamdasani (New York, NY: W.W. Norton, 2009).

_____. *The Art of C. G. Jung*, ed. The Foundation of the Works of C. G. Jung, Ulrich Hoerni, Thomas Fischer, Bettina Kaufmann, trans. Paul David Young and Christopher John Murray. (New York, London: W.W. Norton & Company, 2018).

Keltner, Dacher. *Awe: The New Science of Everyday Wonder and How It Can Transform Your Life*. (New York: Penguin Press, 2023).

Main, Roderick. *Breaking the Spell of Disenchantment: Mystery, Meaning, and Metaphysics in the Work of C. G. Jung. Volume 8 of The Zürich Lecture Series*. (Ashville, NC: Chiron Publications, 2022).

Nash, Alex. "The Akashic Records: Origins and Relation to Western Concepts" in *Central European Journal of Contemporary Religion* 2, 109-124, 2019, online 3 October 2020. DOI: 10.14712/25704893.2020.3

Nietzsche, Friedrich. *Thus Spoke Zarathustra*, trans. R.J. Hollingdale. (New York, NY: Penguin Classics Edition, 1969).

Nietzsche, Friedrich. *The Gay Science: With a Prelude in Rhymes and an Appendix of Songs*, trans. W. Kaufmann. (New York, NY: Vintage, 1974).

O'Brien, Barbara. (2020, August 26). Indra's Jewel Net. Retrieved from https://www.learnreligions.com/indras-jewel-net-449827

Rohde, Erwin. *Psyche: The Cult of Souls and the Belief in Immortality among the Greeks*, trans. from the 8th edn. by W. B. Hillis (London: Routledge & Kegan Paul, 1925).

von Franz, Marie-Louise. *On Dreams & Death*. (Boston & London: Shambhala, 1987).

Weber, M., Science as a vocation. In H. H. Gerth & C. Wright Mills (Eds.), *From Max Weber: essays in sociology* (pp. 129–156). (New York: Oxford University Press, 1946/1919).

Wilhelm, Richard. *Das Geheimnis der Goldenen Blute*, mit Kommentar von C. G. Jung. (München: Dornverlage, Gret Ullmann, 1929).

Barbie's Question

Stephani Stephens

The opening scene of Greta Gerwig's film *Barbie* is almost seven full minutes of sway and swing and joyousness as it effortlessly revels in the perfection confection that is Barbie Land. The fun is high pitched veering between very fun to really, really very fun. There's a pace and pink and unwavering enthusiasm for living the Barbie way, and we all know that Barbie Land has always been like this. In celebration of all that they are, Barbie captures the spirit of the place by proclaiming this is "… the best day ever and so is yesterday and so is tomorrow and so is every day from now until forever …"

So, it comes as a surprise with hands clapping and arms waving while line-dancing with the Kens, that Barbie wonders that quiet part out loud: "Do you guys ever think about dying?" The question is such a shock and in such contrast to the prevailing mood that it is laughable. And in melodramatic fashion, Barbie Land freezes; the dancing stops, the music stops, and the Barbies stand agape. They are not so shocked by the content of the question as they are by its occurrence, which has interrupted the unconscious living they all enjoy. This is only matched by Barbie's realization that her heels have fallen and now rest oddly yet solidly on the ground signaling a condition that no one in Barbie Land has ever quite considered. And as the film moves on to Weird Barbie who has been "played with hard" (embodied hilariously by Kate Mackinnon, Gerwig's real and former college roommate), we are left reflecting if all decisions in the Barbie universe come down to that choice: either those silk pink heart-buckled Manolo Blahniks vs. those brown Birkenstocks.

The question is Barbie's, she asked it out loud, and now she is tasked with answering it because things in Barbie Land aren't quite right. There are odd happenings and tears in the perfection that are interrupting the bliss that is their unconscious dance. In fact, some of the Barbies aren't too bothered about the question and are more concerned why Barbie is so unlike her Barbie self.

As she journeys to the Real World, the otherworld, to be tossed about by all that duality has to offer, it is the question of mortality if not the messy side of a striving conscious life that gets Barbie's pink convertible rolling. It's the question that hangs around everything and what introduces an anxiety that is foreign to Barbie (whose name literally means "foreign woman"). We learn through Barbie's journey that the dark thoughts are attributed to a Real woman in the Real world (played by the impassioned America Ferrara), and it is her misgivings and deep loneliness about being a woman, mother, and office worker that has propelled Barbie into her question. And the question itself is never really directly answered by the journey's end. Yet, Barbie's anthem is to embrace her humanness, and this could only have been done with that seminal question. Barbie's travails also beg consideration: "Can we really live, either in Barbie Land or in the Real World, in either place, without grappling with *that* question?"

I grew up during the '60s and '70s, at the moment of cultural expansion, which stretched beyond the black and white television, beyond the nuclear family structure, beyond the A-line skirts and during the rise of the political protest. In a one-television household, I still had plenty of access to the TV shows that nurtured my childhood dovetailing into unreal realms that furthered the scope of possibilities. On a diet of *I dream of Jeannie, Bewitched, The Ghost and Mrs. Muir,* and *The Flying Nun,* here were women fancifully and magically playing with standard operating conditions while stretching and using the unseen to enhance a given life.

Fantastical, yes, but also posing a question: "What would happen if you didn't accept those suburban, nuclear family, black and white narratives of *Leave It to Beaver*, *Father Knows Best, Dick Van Dyke,* and *My Three Sons* (although shifted to color)?" Were these fantasy narratives the hint of not just liberation of women's lives (certainly) but perhaps more so of women's psyches? Or were they saying perhaps, just perhaps, there is something more going on. And just about the time Barbie came on the scene in 1959, there must have been DNA deep in the narrative that charted a course for girls and women not just farther into the world but farther into the dimensions of the psyche. I'm not saying that because Barbara Montgomery could twinkle her nose and produce effects that gave me permission to trust all of my nonordinary experiences. But the whimsy of magical if not flexible possibilities gave my psyche space and room to explore those "what ifs." In a sense, Barbie's question might be the one to address the nature of living itself.

"Ghostly matters are part of social life. ... Haunting is a part of our social world and understanding it is essential to grasping the nature of our society and for changing it."
                                                                Avery Gordon

Jung was very open if not transparent about his uncanny experiences with ghosts. As was he reflective, doubtful, and interrogating. Even over a century later we are not really any clearer on what precisely these experiences say about the deceased, about us, or about the moment. Jung too felt that it was far too simple to dismiss these encounters as projections, but of course after that line was drawn in the sand, he struggled to bring form to the formless. The topic sits in the back row of his psychological ideas, never really emerging as a discernible entity or an elucidating concept.

Adrienne Harris, Speilrein scholar, suggests the idea with respect to Sabina Speilrein's work, that is a distinction between an amorphous ghost who sits in that back row and a definable ancestor who occupies a lineage on center stage. That is one who steps into a proper sense of place. The movement from ghost to ancestor is a compelling one because it grants agency. It grants a direction to follow from what has previously and traditionally sat as a confused "hunh?" to the sorting out of "why this, why now, and so what?" These questions are for conscious's sake, a way of living with the unknowable. And yet, we live with plenty of unknowables: the mystery of love, why we are here on Earth, and could we be the only conscious beings in the universe? We live with these questions in the back row too, but these don't often unsettle us as does a presence in the kitchen at midnight.

When I was living overseas and far away from the Texas city where my grandfather was aging and moving toward the end of his life, I became a meditator. Not a religiously oriented meditator, but a close your eyes, calm the mind, and create some peace in life meditator. I found that it was a perfect antidote to the busy life I was living, teaching in an inner-city secondary school and enjoying the nightlife whenever I had the chance. When I was speaking to my grandfather on the phone, I could tell he was only half there, not deteriorating mentally, just his presence seemed not fully there. He would talk about his wife, who had died several years previously, yet never really said anything about the wife caring for him at the time. But he remained sharp, knowing who I was whenever I called, remembering stories and laughing and poking fun. So, feeling a sense of frustration that I wasn't there and feeling as if I could be doing more for him, I began a meditation practice that I read in Songyal Rinpoche's wildly popular book *Tibetan Book of Living and Dying*. The Phowa meditation, or the "transference of consciousness," at the time of death seemed so easy, and it gave me focus as I imagined moving light and energy to him. It was a type of prayer but seemed a bit more dynamic, as at the end of each meditation I felt I had sent him something of myself, and as I did, I became aware of how my own anxiety seemed to dissipate. I did this over a period of about two weeks, and as I was walking home one evening, I heard his voice pop in my head "I'm going now." It was clear yet a bit distracting, as I was on a busy city street. But I responded by assuring him it was indeed time, that he should be ready and confident of his next step, and that he had all of our support. I continued to do Powha as I walked, which was quite new for me, meditating on the fly as it were. And so, it was no surprise that when I arrived home to phone him, I learned that he had passed earlier that evening. I was grateful that the meditation had worked for us both. Every once in a while, I will be someplace and see a tall, gangly man with wispy grey hair sticking out of a cowboy hat and I think of him.

In the early '90s, I was teaching in southwest London at a private school. Recognizing the cost of living in this part of London, the school wisely had purchased several teacher flats within walking distance to the school, and I lived in them my entire time there appreciating both cost and convenience. One, very close to the Richmond train station, was a ground-floor flat in a Brutalist building, perfect for my single life as a teacher, but it was haunted. Maybe I should clarify "and it was haunted." At first, this was unsettling, the odd sound, not noise exactly, but sound that you think you hear but aren't quite sure; the hum of people speaking and realizing no one was in the breezeway, the running of water only to realize the faucet was not on. Then the more menacing intrusions: waking up to the sound of silverware shaking in the drawer only to walk into the kitchen to find the drawers open; and other times when clothes and books were scattered when I had specifically placed them on shelves. One night about 3 a.m., on the bed where I was sleeping, I felt something, that sense you get when the bed leans to one side. I quickly opened my eyes to just make out an impression on the mattress next to me *as if* someone were sitting there. That was the last straw. I stood up in the middle of the room and yelled: "Enough, knock it off, either pay rent or get out!" At that moment, I saw the outline of an elderly man, who had moved to the other side of the room. I just made out the smile on his face as he faded away. I never saw him again, and after that night the whole flat exhaled into a rather everyday place to live.

What gave way to a peaceful home for Jung prompted him to produce *Seven Sermons*. Places and people and history itself have loose ends flitting about, and if we are paying attention, or perhaps not paying attention, is when you see such things. Maybe we are called into these spaces to seam together in some sensical way that which has been untended or ignored. Jung's significant point in the Nox Secunda commentary is that the work in these spaces, on behalf of the dead is *our* work, necessary work, and to pretend the dead aren't there somewhat misses the point.

When I first discovered Jung, or as many say, "when Jung found me," I consumed his perspectives on how he was living with his "confrontation with the unconscious." And yet it was his growing into an understanding of his unconscious that seemed most remarkable. He held the experience, his doubt about it, his possible explanations of it and his gauging alongside the prevailing literature of the day in order to bring some sense to himself and the kind of person he was evolving into. This is what I found so reassuring about his own accounts. His honest acknowledgement that he was transfixed by something while still being onto something is what resonated with my own unfolding.

I studied in St. Andrews, Scotland, for one year, and it is the spookiest place I've ever lived. St. Andrews is a cathedral city, and the cathedral was built in 1100. The entire town sits dramatically windblown on the coast that abuts a lengthy, white sanded beach. The cathedral ruins are perched above the North Sea, and the sea stretches in a mix of blue water and cold gray sky. I lived in Deans Court, thought to be the oldest building in the city and was the manse for the Archdeacon of the cathedral. It sits directly across from the cathedral ruins, and from the living room, you could look right across the street, through the ruins and into that stretch of sea. It was beautiful and cold and, well, spooky except for the few days in the month when the sun splintered through the cloud cover. My dorm building was added sometime in 1400 or later. You could be standing next to the window and not only see your breath, but wisps of your hair move around from the draft that made its way inside no matter how insulated the buildings were. I went to lunch at a friend's who lived in town, and she invited me to eat under a stack of blankets on her bed with a space heater running on high in front of us, and I couldn't help but think this was the coldest moment eating or otherwise that I had ever experienced, while my nose was running and I became too distracted by the inside weather to have a conversation.

The temperature is why most of the time we congregated in the living room of the main building where it was convivial and warm and where you could always find someone to chat with.

Except very late at night, which for some reason over my entire time at St. Andrews, I found to be the most conducive for studying, translating, and jogging. I managed to find those midnight hours to flow like other students' day hours, and this time proved most productive. I always seemed to want to take lengthy runs all over town during these hours too. Down North Street and over to West Sands, alongside the golf course and where you could just imagine the *Chariots of Fire* cast running and cursing the blistering winds as well. One night, I had caught a second spurt of energy and increased my running pace. It must have been nearing 2 a.m. as I was coming along the curve of a sidewalk along the Scores and just approaching the corner of a building when I felt a smack. It wasn't as if someone had hit me, it was as if someone had stood solidly in front of me and I ran into them. I bounced back almost falling and gasped in shock, looking around for some explanation only to realize that had I continued on the path, I would have run right into a scaffolding steel pole positioned right level with my forehead. I was shaken and yet so grateful for whatever stopped me literally in my tracks, saving me from a potentially devastating injury. I've often remembered what that felt like to be stopped with just air and space between me and that scaffolding.

I had a graduate study office in a building right on the sea aptly named Castlecliffe. Graduate students had offices all over campus, but some of them, as I settled in, mentioned, shuddering, "it's kind of spooky over there." I didn't think much of it at the time other than "compared to the rest of this place?" So, of course I found myself walking to Castlecliffe late at night arriving around 10 p.m. and often studying until 2, 3, 4 a.m. The window, of course, looked out over the sea, and the wind blew constantly with a steady stream of sea spray. Often the wind would whistle, the way wind does making its way around and through the cracks of a building.

One evening as I settled into work, I heard clearly, as if it was just underneath the window, the music of bagpipes, not the *sound* of bagpipes, but music playing. It lasted for about five minutes and happened several different times. I raised it with some friends who said, "Oh, yes, it's haunted over there. Have you heard of that story about the bagpiper who went down to play music near the cave on West Sands and never returned? Now you can still hear him playing; they call him 'Jock the piper.'"

Another night as I wandered for a study break hoping to catch someone in the living room and found no one, I turned the lights on and walked over to the window, and out near the entrance of the cathedral were two figures, walking, well really floating, side by side and entering the cathedral grounds. I rubbed my eyes and blinked to find they were still there making their way across the ruins. After that night, I grew a real respect for the spirit of place and how history lives far apart from our trespasses and busy lives among it.

My family has had a run of good luck when it came to family dogs, and it is my sister who seemed to fall in love with a canine, nurture, nourish, and then suddenly be called to work assignments involving travel and decided my parents would be well off with another dog. Emma was a small, short brown-haired Swedish terrier, not so much a Swedish breed, but that she was adopted in Sweden. Emma spent her elder years with my parents in the U.S., and as is often the case with our beloved furry family, she soon lost her vision and became diabetic. Her days were numbered, and my parents each were inconsolable that she was coming to the end of her life. At the time, during their sharing of sadness, I do not remember thinking this, but in the middle of their account of her illness I said, "You will know when she has passed over completely, because you will hear bells." As soon as I said it, I thought, "Now why would I say such a thing that I could not possibly guarantee, know the outcome, or prove?" And I didn't think much more of it as I tried to console them for the next few weeks. Soon, it happened, and Emma passed peacefully, and the next day my father called and said, "This is so weird; in the middle of the day, I heard loud bells, like church bells clanging in the kitchen. The TV wasn't on, and the phone hadn't rung, it was just bells chiming." It was then he remembered what I said a few days prior and realized its significance. He asked, "How did you know that was going to happen?" And of course, I didn't. But it did give me pause: Did I plant the idea in his head that he would hear bells? I think that's giving me way too much credit. Did he remember in his grief and produce the sound himself? Perhaps. Yet, the way he reported hearing it seemed too explicit to be conjured. But truly, the real point: Does it matter? Did it matter that he/we could not explain how he came to hear the bells, given the deeply peaceful understanding that the sound gave him in relation to his beloved dog?

Many years ago, I was watching my 2-year-old nephew who was cranky and feverish and not interested in sleep. With fitful activity and occasional moments, he lay his head down on the bed with eyes wide open. I remember the bedroom had a large window that was covered to keep the light out in hopes he would sleep more easily, but he thought it much more fun to pull at it until shards of sunlight lit the wall and floor and made visible dust balls floating in the air. His fever seemed to be getting worse as did his reddening hot cheeks. I was worried and became very quiet in the hope of listening to how his body and temperature might reveal either a serious sickness or something he might shake. As I stilled, the atmosphere in the room changed and as soon as I wondered, "What is going on here?" the room felt full of sunlight, the air thick, and a group of people appeared. It was a strange gathering as it seemed to be made up of members of the family, but in different generations. My father was standing there to my left, yet as far as I knew he was thousands of miles away and quite alive. His mother, my grandmother who was deceased, was also standing there on the other side of my nephew and next to her, my grandfather who had been deceased for many years. In the center was my nephew, hair matted to his sweaty forehead, a bewildered look as if he too could tell the air hung with presence. And there was movement, like a constellation in space, a movement of patterns throughout the room with stillness and motion, if that's even possible. Again, I wondered what was happening with four generations assembled in this dappled room, surrounding a sick little boy. Then it came in flash of recognition: My father had lost a brother, my grandparents a son, almost 62 years before from scarlet fever, and I felt a rush of fear that this is what my nephew was suffering and did this mean the same for him? Or was there something more complex at work here? Was my nephew in fact my father's younger brother who had died as a child and now was a child again? My thoughts were jumbled, and sense-making wasn't revealing a clear conclusion. Yet, I knew I needed to assimilate something given the data in front of me. The group went still, and the constellation continued to move slowly as my nephew paused, looked up and smiled. I looked at all three of them who were gazing down at my nephew, just watching with no expression to indicate an outcome. I had the thought again: Could my nephew actually be this deceased child, and could he once again be taking a place in the family lineage? Or was there a need to call into memory the uncle I would never meet, who had died so many years ago? Or was the extended family asking for his memory to be honored? As I paused and looked to ask each of my relatives, they faded away. The constellation stopped, the thickness in the air lightened, and my nephew looked at me, still smiling, and stretched his hand into the air. I too felt relieved, I don't know why, and yet less than an hour later, my nephew's fever disappeared, he settled and finally fell asleep.

Some 10 years later, when I eventually read Jung's garden party dream in *Memories Dreams Reflections*, I felt I understood how he experienced multiple awarenesses simultaneously or rather one awareness giving way to multiple perceptions, as you can see even the language here obfuscates the experience. And of course, the important question: Why would I be able to see this and so what? What did it all mean? Simply a sneak peek behind the veil? Was I meant to do something about this, or had I already? Had I looked into an intersectional space that held the possibilities of each person so as to calibrate an existing imbalance and as such everyone had deeply seen what I had? When we consider the work of the dead, perhaps this means we tend to what is in front of us even if we don't understand. Maybe because I witnessed this, a healing of sorts initiated in me that rippled in three different dimensions? And perhaps the questions around the encounter are more important than any discernible answers. By holding the question of my nephew's origin and illness, is that more importantly placed than the answer that he could have been my father's brother? Or was the point that we all happened to share the same DNA and there was a pattern about to emerge, had I not, had *we* not, borne witness to the grief and damage that a little boy's death in the 1940s had on four generations?

I have shared this story with the Jungian community before, but it deserves a place here as I couldn't really grasp or explain it at the time. Almost 25 years ago, again in London, I remember the day clearly, as I was on my way to pick up a part for my computer, and later I remember thinking how ironic that this technical need was that steered me across this space in Southwest London. I had gotten off a bus and was walking across a square, when suddenly, as I was walking, I emerged into a different setting, the square was still decidedly there, but the people were different, dressed in bright colors almost in costume with hats and blousy trousers and leather shoes. There was a huge party with dancing, song, instrumental music and merriment. It took about 20 paces for me to walk through this celebration and out of it, at which time I found I had crossed the square to the other side and was about to enter the computer shop.

A bit dazed, I asked the shop attendant if he knew anything about the square, and he said, pointing back to where I had walked, that the stone sitting in the center was where the ancient kings of Britain were crowned; that is why this area of London is called Kingston, referring to the King's stone. I was stunned, wondering had I walked "into" something, had I walked "through" it, had I shifted awareness, or what exactly happened? What I did understand from that day is that places have their own present(ce), and London from that time became a very different city for me. Again, perhaps history isn't really a past idea but rather a tab appearing on our laptop screens, there but not open.

I had a client once many years ago who was grieving. His story was confronting and to this day the most violent story from a client I've worked with. His female friend had been murdered not long ago, and the loss was still fresh as was his anger, bitterness, and need for revenge. In fact, he was certain he knew who had murdered his friend, and the focus of our sessions was on managing these feelings of vengeance. As his thoughts began to mull over the possibilities, I had the strangest and most distracting experience, an overpowering aroma of strong, black coffee. I dismissed it as I was tracking my client's emotional space and exploring with him how he would feel after reconciling his loss with violence. Again, the black coffee aroma was so strong I looked around to see if perhaps

I had left an open container and that was what I was picking up. But no, there was no coffee in the room. After a few minutes, for the third time, the aroma arose, and this time it appeared with a flash, an image of a coffee cup, like a fast-food paper cup. I focused back on the client and how he was expressing his plan, but the aroma was so distracting I simply could not ignore it. I thought hesitantly, "Should I mention this to him?" If it doesn't mean anything, then I have interrupted an important piece of therapeutic work: his clarity on revenge. But if I do share and it is meaningful, I'm not sure where it will all go. So, I took a leap and said, "As you are talking, I have the impression of strong dark coffee in a paper cup." He looked shocked and paused and then began to weep, and through his tears he explained that the two of them often met to have coffee; she liked it strong and black with no sugar, and they always met at a local fast-food spot.

Who knows where the coffee scent came from: his psyche, his memory, which was strong in grief? Or did it come from her to him, and I intercepted it, or from her to me? And yet, how could it have been just me?

Over the years I have landed on the fact that the resolution to these questions doesn't matter and really is not the point. For this man, his focus shifted immediately as he considered that a gesture of vengeance and violence really had no part in his loving memory of her and had he decided on that direction it would have dishonored the bond they shared.

As a Latin teacher, I spent several summers in Rome studying and wandering around the ruins with other graduate students, priests, nuns, and scholars who needed a functional level of Latin to research at the Vatican Library. We were a motley crew of all ages and all with a bent of enjoying this ancient language in a place that had been its home. One year, I managed to secure a summer job with a prominent American architectural scholar who was hosting a seminar for architects to study ancient buildings. He needed an assistant, and I had just enough Italian to support him and his efforts with the seminar as well as to assist the participants settling into the city with their various needs. He was a wonderful academic to work for and included me at seminar meals and at family gatherings. When I think about my time during that particular summer, it was the convivial gatherings at the American Academy as well as the on-site visits around the city that remain memorable. Four years after that summer, I returned to Rome, unplanned, last minute, with a friend who had never been. I was excited to show her the many places I found amazing for such a city that seems to live in contemporary and ancient ways simultaneously. We hopped on the #70 bus near Trastevere, and she asked me when I was in Rome last, and I began sharing stories about that memorable summer with the architect, how lovely he and his family were, and how intriguing the seminar topic turned out to be, and how we secured special access to Nero's palace, which was just then beginning a substantial excavation. There was a lot to tell as the bus weaved its way across the Tiber and into Largo Argentina, where we were deciding to hop off. As I finished reminiscing, enjoying how strong story and memory can be, I looked up to see the architect and his family climb into the front of the bus; he glanced at me and smiled, he greeted me, and we chatted briefly. My friend and I got off the bus there and she asked, "Who was that?" She couldn't believe this was the same architect we had been chatting about for the previous 15 minutes, the one I had not seen since the last time I was in Rome four years previously. I have friends who say that this is the universe's way of fact checking. I have grown to understand this is really about living close if not alongside the unconscious.

Jung stepped into the lineage of psychology with his own fascination of human behavior; his cousin Helly, his doctoral work, his own experiences with the uncanny, his No. 1 and No. 2, his own ghost sightings, his obsession with the Nekyia. These are so much a part of Jung's psychological model that to try to conceptualize his theories without being conscious to this is like only working with half of the unconscious. And as he emerged out of those early years of his confrontation, he knew undoubtedly that he was becoming more himself and embracing a sort of psychological interoception that would serve him well while being of service to others.

When considering the challenges that life offers, the struggles, disappointments, humiliations, frustrations, and agonies, to think Death could be any harder than this, I don't think is possible. Death could not be any sadder than the feeling of heartbreak and the stubborn stain it leaves, which makes it harder to love. Or the cold knowing of a missed opportunity or the surprising emptiness that moves in when your children leave home. Would we choose to grow old in the way that it comes, probably not. That Achilles had the choice is more than any of us get; live a long life but unknown or die young in glory, but never knowing it as such? The cruelty is not in Death but rather in the daily and often minor battles that we all wage over a lifetime, the *prima materia*, that we struggle to cast into a life that we can live and do so in peace with ourselves.

If I had to imagine an afterlife, it would be something like Burning Man with air conditioning and less sand, or perhaps a Full Moon rave in Goa with easy access to a comfy hotel. In any case, I suspect the afterlife isn't so much a break or a vacation as it is a different type of work. We get down to business, observational business, just skewed toward the unconscious with an optional upgrade to consciousness.

We can't unhear Barbie's question. It was already sitting just underneath all that pink paint, "planned choreography and ... bespoke song." I could no less ignore these episodes in my life than Barbie could ignore her flat feet and angst-inducing journey into consciousness. Death is everywhere, it has already arrived, and it sits in the seams that make living possible.

References

Gerwig, Greta (Director). (2023). *Barbie* [Film]. Heyday Films/ LuckyChap Entertainment/NB/GG Pictures/Mattel Films

Gordon A. (1997). *Ghostly Matters: Haunting and the Sociological Imagination*. University of Minnesota Press.

Harris, Adrienne. "'Language Is There to Bewilder Itself and Others': Theoretical and Clinical Contributions of Sabina Spielrein." *Journal of the American Psychoanalytic Association* 63.4 (2015): 727–767. Web.

Jung, C. G. (1995). *Memories, Dreams, Reflections* (R. Winston & C. Winston, Trans.). Fontana Press.

Sogyal, Rinpoche. (1992). *The Tibetan Book of Living and Dying*. San Francisco: Harper.

Living and Dying

Ann Ulanov

When Luis Moris invited me to be one of the authors in his book on Jungian views on the afterlife, I found when I pondered the subject, it was as if it pondered me. It drew me back to work with analysands who unexpectedly included me accompanying them in dying and into death. And the material was still hot! As if yesterday, I felt tears at their loss, anger at their suffering, admiration at their completing resolution of the specific complex that dogged them. I accompanied them in the work as they struggled to meet their approaching death and the loss of their living which they loved. And they accompanied me in the changes wrought in me in relation to theory and practice required when working in such an archetypal field. The paradox of a person's aliveness when confronting the insult of death cutting off life struck me, and that one way we survive into afterlife is through such double companioning. Me for them and them for me—the person lives in me. I was surprised how near still was their living and dying—what they reached as meaning in their life, and indeed that kind of love that dwells between two people working in deep analysis; it endures.

Jung had several views about the afterlife. He thought it impossible to have sure knowledge of what may await us after death as it is not within the range of our understanding, not perceptible to us or subject to our rational, logical comprehension. As a result, however, it is imperative not to impose preconceived doctrines, opinions: "There is no way to marshal valid proof of continuance of the soul after death" (Jung, 1963, p. 312). Yet, the unconscious gives hints, speculations, and images. Jung insists, pay attention to these signs of what death might mean to us, to have our myth about death and life after it. For reason shows one "nothing but the dark pit into which he is descending" and then we march "toward nothingness." But for the one "who has placed his faith in the archetype follows the tracks of life and lives right into his death" (ibid., p. 306). Jung's words reminded me of Winnicott's opening line beginning a notebook when "the reality of his own death had to be negotiated." He wrote: "Oh God! May I be alive when I die!" (Winnicott, 1989, p. 4).

Jung talks about living and dying in terms of conscious and unconscious and stresses the "Myth is the natural and indispensable intermediate stage between unconscious and conscious cognition" (Jung, 1963, p. 311). Jung felt Christianity was the worldview he was born into, and like many "modern" people he fell out of it and found in early writings one of his purposes vis-à-vis religion was to provide the missing bridge to sacred traditions. He saw the link to archetypal images of Christianity, for example, to images arising in individual psyches (Ulanov, 1971, p. 111ff). In his later pivotal experience recorded in his *Red Book* and *Black Books*, he locates life-changing personal transformation as happening in the "innermost psyche" of each of us in relation to the ultimate value, called God.

Personally, Jung needed and hoped to find his own myth; he looked for it. He found it, finally, when beholding the vast Athi Plains of Africa with "gigantic herds" of wild animals moving "forward like slow rivers ... this was the eternal beginning, the world as it had always been, in the state of non-being; for until then no one had been present to know that it was this world" (Jung,

1963, p. 255). There Jung found his myth that expressed "the cosmic meaning of consciousness." By our human consciousness of the world and its multiotherness, we reach the objective existence of all these phenomena. They exist outside our subjectivity but need the validation of our seeing and responding to them to establish their external realness. "Human consciousness created objective existence and meaning, and man [*sic*] found his indispensable place in the great process of being" (ibid.).

All these thoughts of Jung's life came to us in his *Memories, Dreams, Reflections,* recorded and edited by Aniela Jaffé (1963). Now, in the July 2023 publication of Jaffé's "protocols"—all the things Jaffé was forced by the publisher to leave out—are made available to the reader. Here we read Jung's view of what is included in the afterlife: "I feel quite certain, though, that the process of becoming conscious continues life after death" (Jaffé, 2023, p. 149).

Jung was surprised, however, to learn from the dead, specifically the figures of Elijah and Salome, that at death, the sum of their knowledge is capped. The dead learn nothing new once dead, hence they show great interest in the experiences of anyone just crossing over from life to death. What have you to tell us of life now? Jung cites dreaming of his father consulting him for new insights in marriage counseling to help him resolve the difficulties of his marriage to Jung's mother. The mass of dead (from wars, plagues, natural disasters, but mainly souls who have not tended to their individuation) crowded into Jung's presence to demand answers to the haunting questions they did not struggle with when alive and hence could not now die to rest in peace. What is Nothingness, God, Sexuality, Community, Spirituality? How to live? What is the meaning of life? (Jung, 2009, pp. 338f, 346f,

352f). This fantasy in *The Red Book* in effect, said yes, there is an afterlife, and yes, there is an individual identity carried over in it.

A later theory of Jung's imagined life after death as issuing from an ego-related-to-Self kind of consciousness might endure after death (Von Franz, 1986, pp. 20, 92, 108-111). That meant ego, as initially the center of consciousness, moves out of center stage to consent to greater power of Self, as the center of the totality of personality including unconscious as well as consciousness. Further, I see a connection between Jung's idea of an ego-related-to-Self kind of consciousness that lives on after death and his idea of reaching the "objective ego" in life, often reached through illness, aging, or development of keener insight into inner growth of psyche toward wholeness. The objective ego is painfully stripped of all illusions, called maya, to reach a solid consciousness and perspective of an ego formed only from experiences that have been integrated into one's individual identity. All usual ego preoccupations of problems to be solved, responsibilities to be performed, accomplishments to be achieved, plots, greeds, fears, power-grabs are shed. What is left or revealed is what is genuine, real, authentically oneself—who one is, what one is, to what one belongs, to cite Dorn's view of the alchemists' aim. What is truly one's own—whether from suffering or talent— is integrated into consciousness of what one really is, for better and for worse, with a unique history and relationships.

Such specificity answers another ubiquitous question about the afterlife: If there is one, will I be me in life after death, or will I be an anonymous drop in the vast ocean of being, no longer individual in any sense? Jung suggests some kind of personal something enduring after death, but different from what we mean by personal identity before death. Hence this question of afterlife touches another question too. Is it only people who have when alive achieved recognition for a huge contribution, whose consciousness, whatever personal form it assumes, that endures after death? I mean their consciousness, not their fame and name for the huge gift given to the rest of us by their invention or crafting of the new. The answer seems to be "No" in Jung's mind. It isn't fame or even recognition for a great contribution (like the Salk vaccine against polio) that decides individual consciousness after death. The speculation seems to be that individual consciousness after death depends on the quality of consciousness achieved in life. An ego-related-to-Self objective ego kind of consciousness may endure after death.

If it is the version of consciousness of ego-in-the-Self of the objective ego, then the deciding factor is what one has really integrated into one's personal identity, not fame, or even honor. Here we have people never known in their living who may have suffered well, reaching some insight that helps everyone's suffering. They knew it and shared it by living it. The thought is that this knowing, or degree of insight into truth, or reaching of a greater degree of loving, is deposited into a collective reservoir of knowing, of insight or resilience, of truth or love from which everyone else may draw. Such a person deposits something valuable that others do not yet see. They fill the well for others to get the *aqua permanens*, the living water. Examples might be sages of wisdom traditions or an ordinary person who does something extraordinary.

Their individual integrated ego is like an external objective object that leaves its mark of accumulated insight or even wisdom; they refresh and expand the living water in the collective unconscious. The source of water is increased, flowing like a river from which others can drink. We bless the person who found the polio vaccine or who invented the can opener or heard a new kind of music, for example, Mozart who sometimes said he just copied melodies singing in his head. We are blessed by the unknown fourth-grade teacher whose effect on one's child was as if to make geraniums grow from his head—the creative power of imagination. If this collective reservoir is true, then people can reach the verity. They experience, "I found what mattered; I gave to it; I contributed my experience of it; I am worthwhile." This is a registering of value, rather than of progress of more growth to make more profit.

The example I will come to below, of the man I named Fred, in the national press of his obituary was thought to have a "blessed death." People who came to see him before he died or to honor his passing at his memorial service said they found something from him that opened them to a saving insight of their own. Members of our therapy group said something got firm in themselves—to end a relationship, to risk a marriage, to grab hold of something essential in themselves, and to close off fake paths. Jung said of the Self that it multiplies in others when we live from it. The second example, also below, is a woman I named Jan, who impressed others coming to see her in her very long day's dying, amazed by her spirit and livingness which forced them to face their own capacities to live what came to them, find their ownmost way in it.

People who make such contributions to the collective reservoir of strength, truth, goodness, justice, kindness, usually experience some insistence growing up that there is something they must be doing in this life, but they do not know what it is. An example of this is a philosophical point: the power of beauty to prevent war. The potency of sheer beauty in its many forms, if noticed and felt infiltrating one's pores to flow into one's blood circulating in every aspect of one's emotional, social, spiritual, physical body, would go a long way to defeat war. It would. To be opened by this life force of the feminine would make it impossible to wield weapons to cut off a woman's foot, or thigh, or forearm, make impossible to hold malicious envy to diminish an other to a commodity. This recognition of beauty is not sentimentality; it is living the brute strength of a vigor, a force.

Avivah Gottlieb Zornberg, the Hebrew scholar of the Midrash and Torah, cites a wonderful illustration that the potency of "becoming holy is a function of being moved by a beauty that comes from elsewhere." In the film "The Shawshank Redemption," one of the prisoners plays a Mozart aria over this maximum-security prison's speakers (for which he is punished by two weeks in solitary). Its "pure sound" disrupts the prison's routine and everyone—guards, prisoners, warden "stops in his tracks." Zornberg writes, "the experience is one of freedom, from another place and another time" (Zornberg, 2022, p. 166). Beauty makes a space free from the oppression of brutal murders and the brutal system punishing the murderers.

I. The Questions Asked

Living and dying are linked, I find, by the same questions that come up. They are not identical but analogous. Is life a random chance or guided by a meaningful path? In dying, we feel up against a limit, a punct, a period that ends the sentence of my life, facing I will be no more. If I continue to be, it will be so different from the way my being alive is now, on this side of the life/death line. Questions mount up. What does my life amount to? What lasts in value for me? Where did I wander away, let go of the good and make bad mistakes, or just not see the options because of ignorance? What has been the point of my life? Is everything just hit-or-miss, or is there a purpose? Have I served anything, given to others and to life's fulfillment for all of us? What goal or hope has guided me? What am I doing here? What is anybody doing here? What is the meaning of existing?

These questions also come up when facing the depth of the problem that has brought us to analysis for help in discerning what is going on, what purpose this problem serves. People might wonder if there is another dimension to living beyond this ego rush of daily doing. How do we reach it and what is it like? Sometimes people get relief resolving the problem that brought them to analysis but, in effect, stay on the surface and get on with living there. Analysis is done. Sometimes the problem opens to another one, deeper than its first expression. That means a deep dive for the analysand. With Fred, the split of himself between competing opposites drove him to consider suicide. The immediate problem drove him deep into, what am I to be doing with the life given me? With Jan, she knew her dread of aloneness was a deep problem and she would land in it if her beloved partner died first. She persisted in getting me as analyst across the continent despite many good analysts in her neighborhood. Why? She wanted from outside her familiar territory some kind of assurance and insurance for the quality of her living and for her ways of living her dying.

One privilege of being an analyst is getting to see the archetypal background moving the problem or symptom into the person's new awareness of the principal archetype and of its arc through one's whole life. My patient discovers, as Jung says, her or his own mystery play. Jung urges in *The Red Book*, do not imitate mine; you have your own.

The common element in the questions stirred up by coming death and by depth analysis is to be able to differentiate the ego function—duty to life—from the nonego dimensions of psyche that move personality toward some kind of unity, perhaps best described as a unity of diversity, diverse parts. This shows in the two directions of analysis: to break down and analyze the parts of the symbolic fantasy-material of a complex that interferes with ego functioning into its material components, and to support the synthetic process of gathering these parts into a general and intelligible statement about our shared human life (Jung, 1966, para. 121).

Facing death and facing depths sooner or later confront us with a fact we share in common: basic helplessness. I am impressed how this shared fact is avoided and then gets faced. Life confronts us: We are not in charge. I heard a wonderful example from a student years ago. She was hired to make a city hospital Emergency Room speed up in efficiency and empathy in dealing with people who arrived there frightened and feeling helpless. She was to train new young male residents, just graduating from previous classes and chock-full of knowledge and confidence, how to greet and put at ease people arriving in stress, so their medical problems could be more swiftly and accurately diagnosed for treatment. However, the new residents could not believe my student, a middle-aged, plump Southern woman, was in charge of them. They looked down on her and dismissed whatever she had to teach in her Southern accent. What could she, who is not medically trained, have to tell us, new residents! They had no problem asserting their superior knowledge. She cut to the chase by putting them into the experience of the patients—feeling helpless, embarrassed to be there, not knowing how to handle themselves, hence delaying any processing of their needs. She saw their thick defense against human helplessness and the fact most people arriving in the ER were consumed with helpless fear for themselves, their loved one, especially their children. The young men had no connection to their own human helplessness except through their superior knowledge. They were not emotionally available yet to the task confronting them.

She told them to strip to their underpants, put on a hospital gown open at the front, and some to sit on the plastic chairs in the waiting room, others to lie on the table in an examination room, and all of them to wait until called. The point was immediately taken.

They felt like a patient in crisis and then told to wear an awful gown exposing them. They felt vulnerable, helpless, dependent on the new teacher as the new patients will depend on new residents, probably younger than the patient's own children and now in charge of them. They learned fast and came to value this smart woman who found the link of common humanity, fear of helplessness. They also began to differentiate between ego concerns with persona, upwelling panic, prejudice, and nonego illness in the body as a vital part of the whole personality bigger than the ego, to be addressed in dignified and considerate ways to gain full information and cooperation with the healing procedures to follow.

In my experience, when dying comes up to an analysand because of medical causes, the questions about living and dying alternate with greater emphasis falling on the living side of the line between living and dying. Also, one's context changes, and the change becomes part of the analytical sessions such as what is going on medically—hospital visits, tests, doctors, internet research into the disease threatening, let alone the symptoms causing suffering. The analyst must be prepared to hear and manage how to hear, I suggest, the medical facts bombarding one's patient. For that is the new context of the person's life. I found it useful to listen to a brief sum in each session of the medical processes going on and the emotional living of it. Then we could listen in, inquire, explore, comment on the person's emotions, dreams, insights, thoughts, despair, angers, tracing symbolic meanings of this raw material, just as much as we would do with a business context, a parenting context, or a relationship context, or experience of the sacred. The template of sessions is analogous; the details are unique in each case, and so is the archetypal particularity unique in its interactions with the actual facts of the person's daily process. The emphasis lands on the questions stirred up of meaning, value, purpose, blessing. The word soul often appears.

II. The Gradient

In sum, afterlife cannot be known or proven, yet we can give attention to hints indicating something persists and that it may include some individual awareness of one's own personal authentic being. In the West, we seek to make meaning and assume the universe has meaning, and we want connection with it both within our inner life and outside ourselves. We resonate with our own psyche's seeking a wholeness, not perfect but completely, including all the parts of us, good and bad, then facing death gains a curiosity. What will this process of growing old or facing terminal announcement be like? Jung senses life addresses a question to him and he must answer it. Otherwise, I remain dependent on the world's answer. If I attain a degree of being an objective ego based on the sum of what I have integrated from my life experiences and shed all else, then what is living and dying like?

From the ego point of view, death is often pictured as catastrophe, loss, a sad ending whether with a whimper or a yell. From the Self's point of view that Jung ponders from dreams, arriving on the other side, one is greeted with celebration, dancing, a festive occasion. We bring news to the dead. The truth we learn again is that the biggest mistake is unlived life, missing our chance because we wandered off, lay about in inertia, denial, ran away all the time. Think the thought you can still think, yells Jung in *The Red Book*. Who will if you don't? Trust the primordial kernel of light in you, do your work whatever that is, contribute to the reservoir of life force in its many varieties of kindness, sagacity, exploration, and courage and always respond to the seriously funny in life.

What does this mean psychically? Jung compares it to water always seeking its own gradient. Unconscious psyche is like water finding its entrance at our lowest point through the gradient that goes down. We cannot make change happen by wishing it, nor by willpower, nor sets of "shoulds," nor even by sound common sense, nor by remaining unconscious, nor by swallowing wholesale a traditional view of what is to come after death without having our own experience factored in—does it click or not? Jung says life can flow forward only along the path of the gradient. Energy to do so comes about only by tension of opposites; libido will find its gradient just as water finds the lowest possible entrance. Energy must be released from unserviceable forms; we must trust in nature (Jung, 1966, paras. 94-96). Further, Jung recognizes in his time changes going on in the culture, and new different ways of being arising, causing upset and unguessed liberation—the opposites again appearing right together. We live in such a time now. Flexibility has increased so that we are conscious of new forms of gender that before we could not even think about in public. Jung in 1913 gave his approach which is pertinent to us in 2024. Gender is fluid, in all of us; we have to see where the water of psyche follows a gradient new to us. Jan did this in living with her soulmate of 42 years and having a male companion friend for some of those years. Follow that water, the life of the unconscious and live it but, Jung stresses, don't make a new rule about where you land or how you got there that now everyone must follow, or condemn. That leads to a new rigidity. The crucial thing, Jung writes, is the individual situation and the actual context in culture, to see what complex in you and in the culture is being worked out or unfairly forced. It depends on the individual and the situation (Jung, 2009, pp. 263-264). This is struggle for life, for aliveness.

The best way to pursue all these matters, I suggest, is through actual examples. I will give two and do so incompletely because giving full cases would take space we do not have. I will also mention in each case an idiosyncratic flair of each person to give you their unique personality.

III. Clinical Example: Fred

Fred was 43 when he came to do his first and only analysis in 1968. He came from a distance of several states twice a week for sessions in person. This lasted three years. Then, he joined my therapy group and also had irregular sessions with me for another three years. He died in 1975.

He was a genial man, friendly in nature, and enjoyed the game of life. In university, he was not good enough at football to make the varsity team. But he was good enough to make the junior varsity team. He loved the game and played football all four years on the junior varsity team. He was married 20 years; they divorced, retaining most of their friendship during his analysis; they had three sons whom he dearly loved.

He sought analysis out of desperation. He felt caught in excruciating conflict and saw no way out but suicide. Suicide was present in the air, hanging there as a possibility, as an immediate part of the presenting problem. He felt strung out in conflict. On one side was his vocation, which he felt called to despite an earlier, different plan for him and his wife to work in the wilderness. He felt guilt toward his wife for not pursuing the wilderness plan for which she was more suited.

A helping profession drew him, which he loved and was deeply committed to and highly successful in. He was not a power-grabbing man but one who served a greater good, humble, ordinary, and warmly related to others. With it went a fine public reputation in his community and devotion to his sons to set an ideal of finding their own rewarding paths in life.

On the other side of the conflict was his secret sexual life, without which he felt he could not live. It included brief meetings, a long relationship that ended when he divorced, another significant unusual relationship, and a final one before he died, as an outcast from life with others. He felt guilt toward his wife for his extramarital sexual life. He was mad at her sexual rejection and having to say she found him "unattractive" and for her general disapproving tendency "to tell the truth when it did not need to be told." Though friends to some degree, they were locked in a sexual struggle. She wanted him to be celibate, to which he said no, though he dreamt early on of dousing himself with gasoline and setting it afire. She called him a hypocrite and coward with his guilty secrets, while she was at least honest about her out-of-marriage liaisons.

He felt his mother's positive love for him but had the odd sensation it lacked some sexual something. She made him her confidante. His father was demonstratively affectionate but ruthless in business and spoiled and worshipped by his mother. He began to see in analysis how he was enthralled to the Mother in her archetypal manifestations, depending on women's approval, remembering no fights between his parents, or any need to gain his independence from them. In his extramarital relationship, he discovered he felt it intolerable when she was mad at him and likewise doomed when his wife told him she felt "blah" about him. He felt cheered, rejuvenated when he was accepted and loved by a woman and began to see he was at the beck and call of the woman's responses. He dreamt of volunteering to go into a house where he could be castrated. Gradually, he was able to distinguish between his feelings and his needs and seeing he used women to fill the deficits he felt in himself.

After much analytic work, Fred dreamt his dilemma in a new way that summed up the split in himself: Two women, whom he associated to wife and other woman, but who were not so identified in the dream, armed with revolvers, hold him and each other captive. All three can see each other. Each woman might shoot him or the other woman, but each is halted because her opponent can see her take aim and might shoot first. Fred feels trapped as well as pulled apart.

But he also felt in the dream a change in himself. First, working on the dream, he saw these women in the dream as parts of himself, not stuck onto the two women in his life at that time. Second, he saw his being trapped: He did not have a gun. Third, he was not asking in the dream how can I get out of this standoff, that is, his suicide solution. He was asking, what does it mean that we three see each other? The possibility of some communication drifted in. He wanted the meaning of his suffering.

A technical name for Fred's dilemma is to say he was afflicted with a split-anima. In his transference, he used me as the anima bridge (Ulanov, 1996, p. 163). I emphasize Jung's notion of these archetypal figures of anima and animus as "unwelcome intruders," who compel our attention through irresistible attraction as dream or fantasy personages, or in projected form, through their lure to other people. By making the personifications of these complexes conscious, "we convert them into bridges to the unconscious. It is because we are not using them purposefully as functions that they remain personified complexes" (Jung, 1966, para. 399). To the degree we actively try to understand them, "the personified figure of anima and animus will disappear. It becomes a function of relationship between conscious and unconscious" (ibid., para. 370).

In Jung's vocabulary, the contrasexual bridge functions to connect ego and Self; it is a two-way traffic that depends on ego telling the personified anima/us what matters to the ego and the anima/us showing the ego what the unconscious Self is aiming toward. The conflict then is taken off the outer people in projected form and placed squarely within one's own personality to get a sustained functioning relationship so conscious and unconscious—specifically ego contents and aims and Self contents and aims—

converse back and forth (Ulanov, 1996, pp. 160ff.; Ulanov and Ulanov, 1994, pp. 10-12).

In my opinion, the contents of our contrasexual factor are peculiar to each personality, not a set, fixed content, the same in everybody that then is misapplied to actual women and men. The sexual tonality of anima or animus refers to an urgent way psyche makes spiritual factors conscious—the sense of joy in living, pleasure in body contact, laughter and lightness as well as stirring up soul issues of meaning and emotional purpose one serves. Additionally, Self includes the collective unconscious, so social mores come into play in personal ways and also in standing up to them in the process of differentiating one's individuating path. Our personal struggle includes living in relation to groups and society and even nations and ancestors (Ulanov, 1996, p. 161). As the philosopher/theologian Vladimir Solovyev put it, only sexuality is strong enough to counter our egotism (Solovyev, 1945, pp. 2, 35, 77).

Not relating to these archetypal forces so intimately touching our sexual and spiritual lives leaves us in a position of suspended animation in living. We do not live on the ground materializing real potentialities. We float above them with fantasies of what might be possible but is never tackled. The analysis brought Fred down to earth. His aggression, cut off from conscious use in relation to the conflict that entangled every aspect of his life, left him with aggression turned against himself in merciless self-condemnation, hopeless to find his way out. That gave the suicide possibility a lot of energy to which we devoted a lot of time to deflate it.

Several dreams midway in our work and then later showed Fred to use his aggression, not suffer its criticism and possibility of killing him. He dreamt of one of his sons (whom he thought of as "too good" and who joined the Marines); they were stirring up the fire to cook their steaks, and "rats came out from everywhere." In a later dream, "there is a bad guy in the trunk of my car. Should I turn him in or keep driving? He tried to get me. Now I have got him." He tried hard to deal with all the rats. He stopped blaming his wife for his sexual problem and took responsibility for his own actions, realizing it was not just her rejection that set him off into affairs, but his dissatisfaction with their relationship. He faced the other woman's wrath and pain when he decided not to marry her and told her so. He managed to see it through with both women, so that although he made them angry and hurt them, they also saw and respected his firmness in deciding he could not go on with two lives. He bought a motorcycle and did not worry about his community's approval, though they did approve. He decided with his wife to divorce and made it public and carried the consequences to his work and to help his sons through the turmoil the divorce caused them.

After some years of work, this anima split softened in him; it was not gone, but he felt he could live with it because he accepted these two parts as parts of himself. He decided to live alone. He felt in our work he had reached the limits of as far as he could go now. The threat of suicide had moved into the far background. Against my counsel, which he sought, he terminated treatment. He kept in touch over the ensuing months until I was again brought into sustained contact with him. That contact was initiated by his phoning to announce he had lost his balance and fallen from his motorcycle. He then learned from the doctor he was gravely ill with an incurable and fast-moving brain disease. Indeed, he was dead in three months.

The disease was rare, and every one of the few recorded cases followed a predictable, set pattern: to go psychotic before dying. Suicide moved swiftly into the foreground, again presenting

181

the solution. He was back at the beginning, fearing for reputation, hurting his sons, keeping secrets, afraid of disapproval, tempted to defend by destroying. Analyzing this same old complex down to its component parts made Fred realize he was not the same man anymore. The synthetic questions analysis poses moved into the foreground. What purpose could psyche be following that his old defense popped up again with such force? He used his aggression now and took hold of his death. A teaching hospital from which he sought help had never seen his very rare disease, and doctors clamored to examine him, run tests, interviews, procedures, etc. He allowed it for some weeks and then put an end to it. He did not like the way they treated him—as a commodity to be inspected without acknowledging he was a person facing the end of life. He phoned his sons, who came to take him home where he wanted to be to die.

Our contact was sporadic due to his physical tending and his increasing disability. But we had enough time to locate his fears, link them up with the old ones which put them in their past place, no longer relevant to the present. He dreamt of his death: "I dreamt my watch stopped" and of his distress: "I dreamt of one of the worst battles in North Africa (where he served as an army Sergeant in World War II); I was wounded, hot, face down in the sand with no water." He was gripped again with the fear his secret sexual life which continued, but because of the work in analysis, he took responsibility for his actions and related in an upfront way to his partner, not using a woman to fill in deficiencies in himself (Ulanov, 1996, pp. 129-143, 159-190). During that previous work, anima figures in dreams pushed under his nose his evasions of taking his own stand, and the therapy group members did the same, indicating how the women in his life bore the strain of his split anima relationships. He needed to carry the burden, the group members would say; do not hide under the image of affability. That was when he started to dream of guns, shooting, and killing in military life. It was then that he decided to live alone as a single man in his own right for better or worse, holding those empty spaces in himself.

With this announcement of his coming death, spiritual questions loomed. Was it morally right to use suicide to escape what he did not accept in himself, his secret of sexual complex, his fear that details of his sexual history would spill out into the public domain when he became psychotic? Suicide could again be the solution. We did the usual work naming the suicide lure as the defense against his fears. That analytic approach seemed to put suicide in its place but left him with no resolution of his terrors. In its own proportion, he was an esteemed public figure; hence, there was a social consequence of condemnation if he was exposed. We tackled basic synthetic questions: What meaning might be assembling in the face of this illness? Was there a purpose, still unclear, toward which the threat of psychosis this disease was moving him? What was the renewed threat of exposing this long-held secret aiming at? The burden of his exposure fell on the living side of the living/dying border—that he would be rejected as a reprobate; it did not concentrate on punishment in the afterlife or visions of what would happen there.

In the midst of these open-ended questions, Fred announced his huge surprise. He spontaneously made a lavish gesture, which paradoxically both astonished him and confirmed his struggle. Gathering his fear of psychosis and exposure and his temptation to make a getaway through suicide, he renounced control and sacrificed his escape route. He handed over this bundle of dreadful emotions to a presence beyond himself. He just gave everything he had and was to the Source of his life, to God, withholding nothing, not even his sanity and his solution of killing himself. At the uttermost boundary of death, he came to accept his life fully.

With gripping directness, he confided himself to the power that had created him.

We talked over this extravagant gesture and marveled at its arrival. Fred seemed to be at greater peace during these talks. I was stunned and moved. I saw Fred for the last time the day before he died. Although he could no longer speak by then, I knew he knew me as I spoke to him. He made whalelike noises (whales had interested him recently), hailing me from a far distance, from the midst of the "blue fog" he lived in now that he had described in previous meetings. What amazed us those last days was that he did not become psychotic. His was the only one of the recorded cases of his disease to have missed that fate. Thus, he was spared what he most deeply feared because, I believe, he faced his fears and willingly submitted to them and offered them up. Fred was going back to his Creator, the gift of his life in hand in response to the Creator's gift of life to him.

For myself, I registered a permanent shift in my commitment to analytic methods, theories, and practice that seek to enlarge consciousness. They remain valuable, now with a space between me and them, more as methods that frame the mysterious meeting of our psyche and its source.

IV. Clinical Example: Jan

Jan was 60 when she started analysis with me, her third analyst. She died when she was 74. We worked the 13 1/2 years on the phone, at first one session a week and increasing to three, a double session one day she requested saying she needed that extra time to get beneath daily tasks to what really mattered, and a single session the other day. Annually (until it was impossible medically, e.g., COVID and then her disability), she would come from her far distant home to meet in person for several sessions. Halfway through, Jan said she needed to see me, my face, so we used half of each session on FaceTime. She described her first analysis as brief and dealing with ego problems in daily life. Her second analysis was long, with a Jungian who specialized in children, and reached, I believe, the left-out child in Jan and brought her through to greater trust that she could be loved for herself and that her love was valued. The latter half of that analysis got complicated with the analyst's changing appointments, not seeing Jan, and left her feeling betrayed. But, Jan said, when I love, I go on loving, and she did so, persisting in her relationship, which dwindled to nothing. It was then discovered the analyst was succumbing to Alzheimer's disease. The presenting problem with me was this bundle of hurt and confusion, but I also had to deal with her fear of being alone, which she projected onto her beloved partner's death yet to come but was probable, as her partner was much older. Her partner did die within some years of our work. Jan forecast she would be in trouble being alone, and I was her insurance to work on it.

She and her partner were soulmates, and their love endured their conflicts. Jan said her partner was an immovable object, and she was an irresistible force. They pledged to grow in consciousness, both being analysts, and so faced and worked on opposites between them, and their love deepened. It was full of conversation, arguments, conflicts, laughter, humor, international travels, shared writing projects, and the recovery through Jan's efforts of bringing her partner's children and grandchildren into a closer family bond and enjoyment. Jan was unable to achieve pregnancy which she wanted strongly but learned in retrospect that had she succeeded, it would have killed her because of strain on her complicated serious medical conditions. She learned this through emergency surgery for a threatening brain aneurysm.

Jan was intellectually brilliant, publishing books of significance, and multitalented in the creative arts—as painter, poet, professor (emerita now), and a practicing analyst, earning a psychology degree and teaching, which emphasized nourishing creativity as a source of spiritual life. She was heavily influenced by Jung's work and devoted herself to the study of his methods and contemplative process in painting *The Red Book* pictures. She was unusual in suffering a creative complex, namely being driven to respond to creative intuitions in writing, creative visions in painting, and poetry. When a creative idea or image appeared, she responded and worked hard to find its form outside her in the external product of painting, poem, book, teaching, reorganizing curriculum to emphasize creativity. At times she felt driven. It was not neurotic, though she needed to develop the capacity to pause, rest, not get whipped into shape all the time. She was simply multigifted, and space was made to accommodate all this life-giving energy in external forms.

The opposite, though, of Jan's talents and accomplishments was serious medical problems from birth to death. Some were so rare that for her to seek help in a nursing home or even extended stay in hospital was life-threatening and out of the question. Treatment for these rare maladies required specialists whom Jan hunted, and they took her on as a patient. I saw she acted almost like a consultant, reporting in weekly consultations her precise observations of change in the distressing symptoms, what medicines needed change or decrease of dosage, etc. The doctor said she helped him treat his other patients with this disease, most of whom just turned their faces to the wall and gave up on life.

Jan never did that. She faced the threat of death time and again from the many syndromes she suffered, and along the way had surgery for breast cancer, which eventually became necessary because that doctor did not listen to Jan and ignored her report, and thus she got cancer and a later cancer from the first one, which eventually contributed to her death. She also suffered gastroparesis of the gut, eye problems that necessitated a regular hypodermic shot in her eyeball, threat of necrosis of the jaw, tumors along her spine and those in her abdominal wall that necessitated regular painful procedures to drain the hugely increasing fluid in the abdomen. She said the worst of all was recurring nausea due to dysautonomia. Here again she was unusual. She was amazed by people who came to see her and wondered why she didn't feel resentment for this troublesome medical life that was going to kill her, complaining, "Why me?" Jan replied, "My question is why not me? Why not me? I am one of many, and through gene pool I get to carry this. My question is how to live when I am dying? I want to be seen as a person who has illnesses, not the illness who happens to be a person." She had multiple conditions, more than I am listing.

She made two plans: first, conditions for quality of life— the necessity of beauty; wanting to be of use; to be able to love; to be in touch with creativity. If she could not meet them or lost that aliveness experience, then time for the second: an exit plan. She researched ways to do this, which changed over the years in relation to what she learned about laws regulating selected death and about frustrating regulations that surrounded hospice. At first, she planned a wolfpack—a group composed of the neuropsychiatrist she consulted regularly and her cancer doctor, her lifelong friend, like a sister, another professional woman in psychology, and she asked me. This request opened a running theme between us: my place in her life. I had to get clear what it meant to be her analyst in these dire life/death situations. I got some clarity and felt a handwritten letter was the most appropriate response, not email, not inserted into a session, though we talked it over in later sessions. I felt it needed a very personal response to a woman under steady threat of death and trying to make a plan how to face it. Jan wanted me to be a constant companion on the phone and to hear about my life as a friend to fill her with stimulating things I might say about living and dying. I felt the circumstances demanded a personal response from me. I gave it, and it stood me in good stead to do the work, which was demanding over ensuing years—crises often of health, persistent searching for ground under her aloneness, despair at first about living at all without her soulmate, the one she loved and still loved.

I wrote Jan a letter; I wrote no, I would not join the wolfpack. In essence, I was her analyst, plain and simple, neither friend nor consultant, nor mentor, nor combatant. Though any of those realities could and did flow through both of us in our work, at core I was her analyst, and we had work to do. Jan accepted it without rancor or sorrow, and that durable connection survived all the years we worked with living and dying. We did a lot of shadow work; she faced spiritual questions and came to something that settled her. She developed her feeling function, which I found remarkable— that it could happen when beset by illness and that it did emerge. It made me remember Jung insisting transformation comes from the inferior function. Our durable connection allowed us both to see together without naming it, in what was to be our last session, that her dying was very near. She died two days later.

But one last physical medical experience needs mentioning. Jan could not see clearly until she was 6 years old, and it was remedied by the time she was 7, with glasses and contact lenses. She was extremely nearsighted, and neither parent noticed. It was a teacher seeing Jan squint all the time trying to look at the blackboard. Jan remembers everything was a blur.

That fact of not seeing contributed to Jan acquiring, and then mastering to an extreme degree, the capacity to attune to the other person. All her other senses sharpened to take in who the other person was because all she saw was a blur. Hence, attuning to the other person's scent, tone, timbre of voice, body movement or stillness, gestures, pace of sentences, all developed to a big degree in Jan. Her father was a strong and firmly fixed man in his opinions and ideas, often good, yet narrow and surged by affect. He was right, and one must obey. For example, Jan started school, tried it for a few days, then said she did not like it and was not going anymore. But her father made it clear: No, she would go to school. Argument followed, setting off a pattern of explosive conflicts between them, each determined in their own view. Jan gradually developed another way around his having to be right. He was a large and also loving man, but one not to be brooked; she was small with short legs as she put it; he was loud and towering. He held out. She, as an adult, wrote in her book of short stories the encounter of a father and daughter over this school impasse. Jan vividly remembered her father bringing to the conversation a pair of large scissors, left lying there on the table next to his hands. Jan did not think she was beautiful, but she thought her hair was—long, thick, light brown with golden lights, with soft waves. Somehow it was conveyed that no school-going meant her hair was to be cut. This equation filled her up with terror. Her father had found the lever to unseat a determination as strong in his daughter as it was in himself. She was 5, and he was a big adult. She submitted.

She went to school, where an excellent wide-viewed teaching was going on; she loved it. It was the best, with its all-girls excellent high level of academics, languages, art, student government, friends. In the last years of dying, she created for that school two full scholarships for girls outside the social class and economic benefits of the usual students. Two such grants were needed, though Jan was not superrich, so the girl(s) would not be alone as the only different one(s) for this full education.

As an only child of two creative parents and sundry relatives, Jan learned to attune to others at an early age when she could not see them, partly as a way of listening and hearing tones of the other person, and partly because her parents adored her and could be said to abuse her with the demands of their loving. Her mother was a composer and known for it. Her father became a public person recognized for military service, leadership in academies and in Protestant church. Father had to be right and could not allow his own doubts or the proof of the other's argument to surface. Force followed—emotional never physical—when persuasion failed. He could not yield. Jan developed sophisticated, automatic ways to protect her father, whom she loved, from his own unconscious fears. She put things so tactfully and indirectly when they differed to forestall his boiling over. Even when dying and still faithful in FaceTime calls, she would dress and use skillful makeup to conceal failing health because she felt her father could not stand her suffering. She never told him her terminal diagnoses. Through analysis, she came to see the high cost of being the defender of her father against his own unconscious opposite emotions. That whole mechanism softened and relieved her of the degree to which she carried for him what he could not carry. That happened with her mother too, but in a different way.

Her mother was a famous composer of her country's music and dependent on her daughter to substitute for her mother's frail ego in daily tasks and demands of her husband. In panic at his unhappiness or anger, she would sometimes bang her head against the wall. Both parents resented Jan emigrating to America, saying, "Why don't you live here because we love you and because it is right." This was also a loving family; all the frailties and demands were also imbued with loving. Her father loved his wife inordinately and married again to survive his mourning her death, though without making room for Jan's mourning for her mother, whom she loved dearly and nursed into death. Instead, her father sent Jan— so talented at organizing everything—the dozens of boxes of her mother's music and interviews to order for archiving for museums and historical societies. Jan did it when confined to bed in between bouts of throwing up.

The culture in which the family lived was divided up into groups of class and ancestors and social level. Anyone outside its rules was dealt with by shunning rather than murderous attack. I felt Jan had to emigrate to another country completely opposite in order to get hold of a life of her own, to find her individuating path. Her parents resented Jan emigrating but finally agreed to visit Jan in her new country and home, not just to accept her annual long visit home. They were disappointed not to have grandchildren, though that was modified when they learned pregnancy could threaten her life.

But back to attunement. It was so skilled and so inwardly enforced that it kept her alone, not feeling accepted or acceptable as her own self. Not only was she to surmise what was going on in the other person and adapt to it automatically, but she had to want what the other wanted. Getting conscious of this automatic habit and getting liberated from endorsing it was an important area of Jan's development that involved skirmishes between us now and then. In retrospect, our exploring attunement showed us it sustained her dread of aloneness because she did not yet attune to herself! Challenging that automatic defense made space for her later development of her introverted feeling function in sharp contrast to her superior and more extroverted thinking and intuition. She did not know what she wanted after her soulmate died; she just wanted to be with her again, in this or the next life. Jan's creative output was remarkable, producing more when ill than most of us produce when healthy. Getting attunement conscious and related to as a choice to do or not to do freed up space for looking into her own desires. At first the space was empty, nothing there. Eventually her own feelings and certainties developed.

In the process of arriving there, I felt crowded by her attuning skills, but we could get that through mutual consciousness and not allow it to take over our conversations. And my keeping in mind to inquire and be curious about what did Jan sense, want, or feel, not substituting Jan wanting to know what I felt, built up a protospace from which developed in Jan's hard last years her feeling function, which astounded her and made us laugh often. It did seem amazing that in the midst of all this sickness and its endless medical procedures, which were painful, awful, ever increasing, that we could do any analytic work. But we did. It confirmed in me the power of Jung's methods—analytic and synthetic analysis, looking back to regressive factors and looking forward to prospective functions just emerging and not yet here. In addition, allowing the full turmoil of affects, instincts, emotions, unbridled energies, and spying the archetypal images that gathered them and then finding words or concepts to talk about what was actually emerging into symbolic meanings really worked. Awareness of collective factors differentiated from the delicate unfolding of this individual personality and its precious integrity was a necessary sustained task. I was amazed and full of admiration for her psyche, for the human psyche, and Jung's approach to analysis.

But I found myself resisting the full pointing of Jan's attuning skill that had dictated her not just to attune to the other person but to want what they wanted, a full attunement amounting to identification. Here was the left-out girl alone and getting conscious of finding what she wanted and did not want and needing full dependence at first. Here was the little girl who could not see clearly for the first six years of her life needing to see my face in sessions. Here was my task of differentiating from my shyness to say yes to being looked at fully, taken in through FaceTime. Once we saw Jan's aim to know her desires nestled into, hiding, in that attuning identification skill, it became easier. We slowly sorted out Jan wanting my life to gain her responses to her life. As we sorted my desire for Jan to have her life and me to have mine, space was made for each of us and for the big back and forth between us.

The joke also was on me. When Jan let me be me, I was sometimes apt to offer something from my life pertinent to what Jan brought up and to let her benefit or dismiss whether this shed light or got us off course, or signaled a life connection between us. The work got easier. It flowed. Periods where Jan was too enervated to speak might spontaneously prompt me to play a bit of music, which was important to her all her life. Or one day I hummed, and she rested, and once, she, much talented (learning from her musician mother) and me not, we sang a melody together. It was restoring, peaceful. In retrospect, I see the burden of so much sickness, pain, and awful procedures weekly was a lot for both of us to carry. Her suffering and the weight of compassion affected the sessions always. We learned to play by ear what was the best response to the day's situation, two different and related persons, not a merger or one eclipsing the other.

Jan's attunement was also a strength. She got along with people and was broad in her interests, easily crossing over to see what reality looked like from the point of view of the other person or other discipline and could envision bringing them together into fruitful conversation. She did this in her teaching and creating a wide-ranging curriculum for the educational institutions that employed her. Her professorship in the last was long and rich. This capacity was part of her performative nature, including the inner pressure to perform—to find external forms for inner creative intuition, for receiving the other even when opposed, like the grown-up children of her partner. The results were beneficial and included some people who did not like her, maybe envied her, or felt intimidated by her accomplishments.

We got a clue about this performative skill through its very exact opposite. She suddenly suffered a violent physical collapse, literally strung out on the bathroom floor with every orifice protesting by evacuating whatever was inside. The nausea and disequilibrium were quelling. Even to move her eyes or have a thought or say a word started another paroxysm of evacuation. She was rendered completely, utterly helpless. Looking back, she saw she had the same collapse but to a much less degree of violence starting in her twenties, and, looking forward, the collapse was to repeat itself. It was not named medically then, attributed to being overtired, etc. This now was terrifying and overwhelming.

Jan's detailed description of helplessness struck me hard. She grew alert to when collapse might strike her and assembled different means to moderate its impact. I mulled over what these attacks of helplessness could mean in psychological terms. Insight arrived: Only an opposite as strong as her gifts could make some kind of difference. She had to be silenced, made utterly still, struck down, unable to use her strong will to aid herself, to manage, recover, get the ego in charge again. To gain her full life, this helplessness countered her multiple talents to do and to produce, to effect. She was seriously unbalanced, one-sided, with the left-out side in dread of being alone. Her body forced her to change through encountering helplessness.

Nonetheless, after its passing, she grew curious, open to learn, find the medical name for this disorder to see what it might mean psychologically. She found the medical name for this different mode of being that defeated her: dysautonomia—no cooperation between parasympathetic and sympathetic nervous systems. In essence, parasympathetic helps us relax, let go, and sympathetic alerts us to fight or flight. Translated in body terms, the attacks let everything go—bowels, vomit, air, heartbeat, breathing. Any intense emotion, whether traumatic or ecstatic, could trigger an attack. Jan learned to manage it by strict attention, conscious relation to details of the condition, and readiness to try medication, change of behavior, diet, etc. She also created preventive measures, such as making herself throw up a bit of a meal to prevent an oncoming emptying of everything in her body onto the floor, or bed, or herself. Her various illnesses made constant trips to hospital for transfusions, paracentesis (painful draining of fluid from the abdomen cancer tumors), infusions of calcium/magnesium (to prevent heart attack) and on and on. From this crowded context of physical ailments, I can see what made me say one day, "The way to your soul is through your body." That hit home for Jan, and I was surprised I said it. Jan gathered many sufferings into watching herself dying and wanted to do it with grace and pleasure in living. I only saw in retrospect, for someone strongly asserting an exit plan, I have never known anyone who fought so hard to adapt to the next medical crisis in order to stay alive. She reached toward, and we were reached by symbolic meanings that made Spirit real to her.

She had been speaking all along about religion, her experience of it, her loss of it, and her need for some connection to Spirit now. In early teenage years, she had mystical experiences of God that she valued highly and kept secret, knowing that her father, an ardent Protestant Christian would pounce. In her university years, she fell in love with a Catholic fellow, who fell in love with her and again kept its intensity secret to avoid her father's prejudice against Catholicism. The presence of God felt central to her and undergirded her active life in studies, family, friends, fun.

A corollary of religious experience was what she called now a powerful projection of Spirit on a sequence of women she found numinous. They were independent, dedicated to mind, truth, service, and faith. Examples were a teacher, the headmistress, a top assistant of a guru, the second analyst. Jan was drawn to dedication to something beyond the personal—teaching English after graduating university to children in New Guinea, joining a Hindu ashram and rising to become one of the leaders, joining with her soulmate in social activism through a Congregational church. These religious experiences did not sustain, usually because the leader betrayed the trust or simply moved to another group. But Jan was socially active all her life, even when ill, contributing to causes and setting up donations. She took all her paintings before her death, the ones not sold, and put them online at prices to be negotiated and donated the funds to Ukrainian refugees and/or women's groups. The numinous woman projection figured in the disarray of the ending of the second analysis. She did not project a numinous woman role onto her soulmate; that connection was unique. Nor did it fall on me, and I was glad to endorse that absence. She did eventually dream what she thought was the core truth of our relationship. Dreams were few and far between because of the heavy doses of meds that interfered with recalling them. The dream: She and I were seated before a fire, together, silent, focused, with much feeling, looking at and into the fire, beholding it. The fire was the numinous.

By the time of our analytical work, Jan had no viable religious connection and wanted one. What slowly emerged was under the banner of Spirit. She felt it did exist in many forms, and in that fire dream we beheld it. That enabled us or was part of us both, being together and feeling the numinous—something beyond the present passing of days and illness and whatever was going on. Spirit, she felt, is beyond, not defined by daily events but very much living in and through them. Later she gathered up her feeling about being so ill, not asking why me, but why not me. Why not me, I am one of the many. The picture of being one of many grew into a sense we are all one large organism, all connected, so that what happens at one side of this huge breathing ball affects the rest on another side. Our job, so to speak, is to live the best we can, carry what falls on us, live the pleasure of living in all its forms, do our part and sustain and regard this great one organism.

In her plan A, Jan aimed to live with quality of life, even though, as she put it, she was like a head of lettuce in the supermarket, past her due date. She wanted to live being a person who happens to be ill and to deal with it as best she could. She wanted to give something to others, in person and from afar; for example, she set up on the internet for people (from all parts of her life as teacher, analyst, traveler, writer) to send in photos of beauty for all to enjoy. She wanted to connect with meaning and felt here she was striving but not yet completing. She wanted to enjoy each day, which meant not having overwhelming pain all the time. In her international travels, she built close relations with relatives from Russia, Lebanon, and with friends she made in Greece, Japan.

Her plan B, to exit by choice if quality of life was no longer possible, underwent various changes, dealing with complications to secure how it could be done because, for example, she could not depend on taking a pill; she might throw it up. She could not rely on a shot because her weight and skin were so stressed, it was uncertain her vein could receive a shot. That left suppositories, which law required to be administered by a hospice official which put Jan

right off. Her wolfpack doctor came up with a helpful picture—
think of that person as a technician; the others of us will be there.
Jan's condition of being of service to others included seeing former
patients if they wished a session and if she was up to it, leaving
herself freedom to cancel at the last minute if it was a bad day. That
worked and kept various appointments to a minimum. Jan's concern
for the women who helped her, as she had, in fact, arranged a nursing
home of her own, training them, outfitting them especially during
COVID, taking care of them if they got the virus by continuing to
pay their wages as many of them were undocumented and needed
the job. Jan was both chief administrator and chief patient, which
made me tired just hearing about all the troublesome details of
running this outfit. It worked, and she arranged a method of reliable
payment that kept the fees affordable. The spirit Jan sought made
her think of these women's needs after her death. She set up a
severance pay to sustain their transition to another job.

The later analysis centered on Jan landing in the bottomless
pit when her partner died and how to live and arrange connection—
was it even possible—with the loved one now gone. She paid close
attention to any wisp of connection while looking into the dark.
She suffered feeling abandoned, not knowing how to connect to
meaning, being unwilling to live with a belly full of anger and
angst. "I'm diving in search of pearls of my spirit and the Spirit,"
she said. "I want to keep to the center and just breathe in and out,
and maybe God is breathing in and out. I want to live my feelings,
not talk about them. I want to digest them even if I cannot digest
food (though that medical condition let up, and there were periods
of enjoying eating again). To love is spirituality to me and to know
my love is valued." She pursued, "What do I want?" and tethered
her desire bit by bit to answers and laughed at how slow she was
to see the obvious. For example, she took to heart the fact that she

and her soulmate, despite arguing and big mistakes, also lived 42 years of loving that lasted, deepened, grateful for battles that ended in laughter. Both are so intelligent, and one interrupts the argument by correcting the other's grammar. That dissolved fighting into laughing.

The last session we had, on a Monday, a double session, Jan recounted an awful experience of the previous week when she had been taken to the hospital because of an upset in her breathing. She came out of it ready to go home, but the hospital people could not understand what she was saying and thought she had had a stroke. She knew she hadn't, but because of her chronic lack of saliva and rushing to the hospital without her saliva tablets, she could not form words clearly. She went home. But her cancer doctor came to visit and spent two hours tactfully raising that the end might be near and whether she would want to set a date for the exit plan at which this doctor would be present.

Jan's answer impressed me. She said, "If I set a date at which I must then act with a plan, it will trigger my old complex about performing. I will rise to the occasion and perform with all the gusto I did in graduate school. My partner only read what she liked and skipped everything else, and I had to fast tutor her to pass her exams. But I came out with all A's and never wanted to read again. And she came out passing and never stopping reading only what interested her and moved her and enriched all her living. I do not want to exit performing."

The doctor then said with gracious concern, "I do not want you to get to a place where you are unable to make a choice and then are stuck with the disease in charge as that can get very nasty." The doctor was encouraging Jan to make a choice now. They parted on very good terms.

Jan brought it up in our next Monday session. She explored all she had said about performing and what the doctor said, and what was she to do? So, we did what we usually do—I asked, are there any feelings here? Any clue? What comes up? She said no, in the dark. Jan was in a dilemma. It was quite possible she would become unable, helpless to effect any choice, be left with nasty pain. Yet performing—setting the date to exit and doing it, performing—well did not feel right to her. It did not. I wondered later, did I remember my old saying to Jan, your body is the way to your soul? Because after a while of silence and near the end of our session I said, "Ask your body: What does it tell you?" That clicked for Jan. The session ended, and we seemed to communicate without words that the body would tell her. We knew the body knew death was near. We looked at one another. Jan said, "Something big has happened, and we know it and don't have to say it." I nodded.

The body did decide. She died two days later. I was told she felt distress breathing very early Wednesday morning, two days after our Monday session. She told her helper, "Take me to the hospital." That moved me deeply because Jan hated the hospital and would never go there if avoidable. It meant the body told her it was time. I felt she chose the hospital to spare her helpers the very hard messes of the body dying at home. The hospital knows how to deal with all that effectively and efficiently. Jan loved her helpers, and they loved her; she chose to spare her ladies. I laughed and wept.

My deep gratitude to the two individuals for permission to draw from their material described in the section Clinical Examples.

References

Edinger, E. F. (1998). *The Anatomy of the Psyche, Alchemical Symbolism in Psychotherapy*. LaSalle, Ill. Open Court. Jaffé, A. 2023. *Reflections on the Life and Dreams of C. G. Jung from Conversations with C. G. Jung*. Trans. Caitlin Stephens. Einsiedeln, Switzerland: Daimon Verlag.

Jung, C. G. *Encounters with C. G. Jung: The Journal of Sabi Tauber (1951-1961)*. Eds. Irene and Andrus Gerber. Trans. Marianne Tauber. Einsiedeln, Switzerland: Daimon Verlag. Jung, C. G. 1953. *Psychology and Alchemy. CW 12*. Trans. R. F. C. Hull. New York: Pantheon. ____. 1966. *Two Essays in Analytical Psychology CW 7*. Trans. R. F. C. Hull. New York: Pantheon.

____. (1963a). *Memories, Dreams, Reflections*. Recorded and edited by Aniela Jaffe. Trans. from the German Richard and Clara Winston. New York: Pantheon.

____. (1963b). *Mysterium Coniunctionis. CW 14*. Trans. R. F. C. Hull. New York: Pantheon.

____. (2009). *The Red Book Liber Novus Ed*. Sonu Shamdasani. Trans. Mark Kyburz, John Peck, and Sonu Shamdasani. New York: W. W. Norton.

____. (2020). *The Black Books. Vol. 7 of seven vols*. Ed. Sonu Shamdasani. Trans. Mark Kyburz, John Peck, Sonu Shamdasani. New York: W.W. Norton. Mutu, W. 2023. *Wangechi Mutu: Intertwined*. New Museum, New York: Phaidon. Solovyev, V. 1945. *The Meaning of Love*. Trans. Jane Marshall. London: Geoffrey Bless. Ulanov, A. B. 1971. *The Fem-*

inine in Jungian Psychology and Christian Theology. Evanston, Ill.: Northwestern University Press.

_____. (1996). "Transference/Countertransference, a Jungian perspective," pp. 123-143, and "Disguises of the Anima," pp. 150-190 in *The Functioning Transcendent*. Ed. Murray Stein. Asheville, NC: Chiron. Ulanov, A. and Ulanov, B. 1994. *Transforming Sexuality: The Archetypal World of Anima and Animus*. Boston and London: Shambhala.

_____. (2019). "Scapegoating, Projection, and New Forms Emerging" (Oregon Jung Society, unpublished manuscript).

_____. 2022. "The Shadow's Shadows." IAAP Congress, Buenos Aires, Argentina.

_____. (2023). "Uncertainty: Is It a Gift?" in *Our Uncertain World, Challenges and Opportunities in an Uncertain Time*. Ed: Leslie Sawin. Asheville N.C.: Chiron.

von Franz, M-L. (1986). *On Dreams and Death*. Trans. Emmanuel Xipolitas Kennedy and Vernon Brooks. Boston and London: Shambhala.

Winnicott, C. (1989). "D.W.W. A Reflection" in *Psychoanalytic Explorations*. Eds. Clare Winnicott, Ray Shepherd, Madeleine Davis. London: Karnac.

"I Don't Permit the Winter":
Death and Life in Goethe — and Jung

Paul Bishop

In January 2020, the roof fell in on my world. Literally—the ceiling in my study collapsed, as a result of what turned out to be a long-standing problem with the chimney and an ingress of water, slowly weakening the structure of the ceiling. So, I set about finding a roofing company and an interior decorator to do the repairs, and by the end of February had agreed start dates for the work to begin. Then in March 2020, the roof fell in across the entire world, as the coronavirus pandemic went global and spread across Europe, until the U.K. went into lockdown at the end of the month—and there was no chance of getting repairs or anything else carried out.

Trains and buses became eerily quiet; at the university, lectures and meetings were quickly canceled, and soon the campus became completely abandoned. Everything went online: hastily organized Microsoft Teams groups were set up, and suddenly everyone discovered Zoom. In England, the news turned into a body count; government ministers and the Prime Minister himself were hospitalized with COVID-19; across the U.K., Nightingale hospitals were rapidly built. In the face of—potentially—a brush with death itself, everyone was tense, nervous, anxious, waiting to see what was going to happen, not least about the imminent examinations. Surprisingly (or perhaps not so surprisingly), the decision was taken for exams to go ahead—in virtual form.

Two-hour Honors exams were replaced with "takeaway" essay questions, oral exams were conducted (despite the evident distress of some of the students, or so it seemed to me) via Skype or Zoom, and the machinery of examination boards was cranked into operation online. In its emails, Internal Communications offered congratulations on "the design and roll out of the online examination diet" as an "incredible achievement," while recognizing the times were "challenging." Yet it was all becoming too much for some: In an email sent to the entire faculty, an administrator could not contain her anguish at "both the tone and content within the deluge of emails we are currently receiving from senior management and the VC," and at a failure to acknowledge "the trauma, suffering and grief" that both students and staff were likely to be experiencing during the pandemic. It seemed that, when it came to the crunch and in the face of death itself, the academic community had revealed what was most important to it: exams, grading, marking, assessment.[1] Meanwhile, in America and in other countries (including the U.K.), Black Lives Matter protests in the wake of the death of George Floyd as a result of police action saw statues of colonial slave traders being pulled down. For some, this was an example of the kind of "psychic epidemic" predicted by Jung.[2]

As the year unfolded, so the chaos grew: Students were invited to return to the campus for the new university year, despite

---

[1] By contrast, in March, April, and May, the German National Academy of Sciences Leopoldina issued a series of ad hoc statements on the coronavirus pandemic, to which scholars from a variety of disciplines (including the humanities) had contributed; in the U.K., academics were busy working on their institutions' submissions for the bureaucratic exercise of the REF.
[2] For the notion of "psychic epidemics," see Jung's lecture to the *Kulturbund* in Vienna in November 1932; see CW 17 §302 and CW 10 §471.

the risk of infection (and despite the protests of the lecturers' union); a BBC investigation into the spread of COVID-19 on Scotland's college and university campuses concluded that, when students were allowed back to halls of residence during the pandemic, profit had been placed before safety (BBC One Scotland 2020), while subsequent research by Sarah Armstrong used an analysis of financial and student data to show that through the pandemic (2020-2022) Scottish universities, far from losing money or students, actually gained both and accelerated income growth during COVID (Armstrong 2023). In remarkable scenes at the University of Manchester, protesting students pulled down metal fencing that had been erected around their halls of residence at a cost of £11,000 as part of lockdown measures to control the spread of coronavirus (Hall, Gayle, and Quinn 2020). And despite the heightened consciousness in the wake of the BLM protests, a Black student at Manchester complained of racial profiling by one of the security guards (Halliday 2020). Across the country, students incarcerated in university accommodation struggled to cope with the impact on their mental health of an imprisonment for which, through their rent, they were actually paying. It was as if the whole university system had turned into a giant Milgram experiment; and, in a way, it had. Or to put it another way, as the Italian philosopher Gorgio Agamben did (in an amazingly frank intervention of 23 May 2020), what we were witnessing was the final death of a form of life that had evolved over the centuries from the *clerici vagantes* of the Middle Ages to the student movements of the 20th century; and all that remained was to sing a "requiem for the students" (Agamben 2020).

On a more personal level, the period since the outbreak of the pandemic has involved the deaths of family and professional colleagues: the death of my mother, shortly followed by the death of her sister, my aunt; the death of several neighbors in the street; the deaths of various colleagues at my university, including the suicide of one of our graduate students; the deaths of several recently retired colleagues; and, in a way that has brought home to me my own mortality with peculiar acuity, the deaths of my French teacher at school and my German tutor and doctoral supervisor at university. In 1920, following the death of his daughter Sophie from the so-called "Spanish Flu," Freud asked in a letter to Ernest Jones, "Can you remember a time so full of death as the present one?" (Paskauskas [ed.], 1993, p. 370). While struggling to come to terms with these personal and professional losses, the remarkable lines of Paul Claudel's poem on the occasion of the Commemoration of the All the Faithful Departed in his "Corona Benignitatis Anni Dei"—and its reference to the Office for the Dead as *Le psaume à longs cris vers par vers et l'obsécration entrecoupée / Par les neuf Lectures terribles* (that is, the nine readings for Matins taken from the Book of Job) which the poet recites at night on the 2nd November while outside the thick fog of a Hamburg night reminds him of Purgatory (Claudel, 1967, p. 458)—have since begun to acquire a new significance for me. And then, in the midst of all this chaos and death, in the summer of 2020 the *Black Books* arrived on the publishing scene.

These seven hefty volumes of Jung's *Black Books*, containing facsimiles and translations of the notebooks he wrote between 1913 and 1932, come in a black cardboard box that makes the set more than vaguely reminiscent of the black monolith that appears at the beginning of Stanley Kubrick's 1968 film version of Arthur C. Clarke's *2001: A Space Odyssey*. If the discovery of the ominous monolith by a primordial horde of starving prehistoric hominids triggers a shift in the evolution of consciousness by somehow inspiring them to develop and use tools, might the *Black*

Books, I wondered, bring about a similar shift in my understanding of *The Red Book* (to which the *Black Books* are the forerunner)— and at the same time speak to my sense of loss? For both works, *Red* and *Black*, involve the figures of the dead.

In an entry in the *Black Books* for 17 January 1914, Jung records a fantasy in which he encounters the figures of the dead— whose appearance is marked by "a roaring sound fill[ing] the room like a horde of large birds with a frenzied flapping of wings," which turns into "many shadowlike human forms rush[ing] past"—on their way to Jerusalem to pray at its holy sepulcher (BB 4, p. 207). (Their return from Jerusalem, and their plaintive cry that they have "come back from Jerusalem, where [they] did not find what [they] sought," will turn out to be the occasion for Jung—and later, in *The Red Book*, for ΦΙΛΗΜΩΝ—to deliver the first of what becomes a series of seven sermons to the dead (BB 5, p. 283; and RB, pp. 507-508). And in the entry for 26 December 1915, Jung's soul tells him that "community with the dead is what both [he] and the dead need," and at his request she teaches him the prayer to the dead (BB 5, p. 255). In the revision of the material in the *Black Books*, the theme of the need to encounter the dead advances in *Liber secundus* to the fore of its argument.

In "Nox secunda," Jung comes to understand that the chaos behind everyday life is "not formless […], but it is filled with figures"—the figures, that is of the dead: "Not just your dead, that is, all the images of the shapes you took in the past, but also the thronging dead of human history, the ghostly procession of the past" (RB, p. 340). The task of encountering the dead is an imperative in itself, but it brings with it further requirements: "When the time has come and you open the door to the dead," Jung tells us, "[…] withdraw and enter solitude, since no one can give you counsel if you wrestle with the dead" (RB, p. 342). Far from becoming their "blind spokesman" (*verblendeter Sprecher*), it is enjoined on us to become (in the words of the *Draft*) their "legal executor" (*Anwalt*), to "turn to the dead, listen to their lament and accept them with love" (RB, p. 344). The task enjoined on Jung—and on us—is to work for the acceptance of the dead and indeed for their salvation (RB, p. 343)—whatever exactly that might mean.[3] By the time of "The Magician," however, and a section dated to 2 February 1914, Jung claimed—after the Cabiri finish constructing his Tower and in the wake of his conversation with a hanged man—that he was "no longer threatened by the dead," that he had "taken over something of the dead into [his] day," and that whereas previously he had wanted to "satisfy only [his] own demands" and was therefore "living in the sense of the world": "When I recognized the demands of the dead in me and satisfied them," he declares, "I gave up my earlier personal striving and the world had to take me for a dead man" (RB, p. 433).

This encounter with the dead illustrates a key aspect of what Jung was seeking to do in the *Black Books* and in *The Red Book*: namely, to engage with "the matrix of a mythopœic imagination which has vanished from our rational age"—an imagination that, while "present everywhere," is "both tabooed and dreaded" (MDR, p. 213). As a result, it appears to be "a risky experiment or a questionable adventure [*als zweifelhaftes Abenteuer*]," which involves entrusting oneself to the "uncertain path that leads into the depths of the unconscious"—the path of "error, of equivocation, and of misuderstanding" (*des Irrtums, der Zweideutigkeit und des Mißverständnisses*) (MDR, p. 213). In this respect, he insists, the

---

[3] For further discussion of how there is "a sense of the 'debt' to the dead that one can find in some ancient works—above all in Homer and Sophocles—and that in this notion of some debt to the dead we find something of great import for our ethical lives that is effaced in philosophy," see Schmidt, 2006, p. 123.

Black Books and *The Red Book* are "more than a literary exercise," just as the second part of Goethe's *Faust* is; as a way of establishing "a link in the *aurea catena* which has existed from the beginnings of philosophical alchemy and Gnosticism down to Nietzsche's *Zarathustra*," this path is said to be "unpopular, ambiguous, and dangerous," because it is "a voyage of discovery to the other pole of the world" (MDR, pp. 213-214). Moreover, this Faustian dimension is all the more significant, given Jung's quotation of two lines, not from the second part of *Faust*, but from the first: "Yes, let me dare those gates to fling asunder / Which every man would fain go slinking by!" (*Vermesse dich, die Pforten aufzureißen, / Vor denen jeder gern vorüberschleicht*) (ll. 710-711).

On the one hand, this quotation serves as a companion to another quotation, *Quaero quod impossibile* (that is, "I seek what is impossible"), inscribed above Jung's stone fireplace in his Tower at Bollingen (Kingsley, 2018, vol. 1, p. 104). As Peter Kingsley has argued, this Latin saying was most likely inspired by a passage in the second part of Goethe's *Faust*, where Manto the seer—in some sources, the daughter of Asclepius, the god of healing, while in others the daughter of the blind prophet Tiresias)—invites Faust to descend into the underworld to meet Persephone, saying, "Him I love, who seeks the impossible" (*Den lieb' ich, der Unmögliches begehrt*) (l. 7488). (Confirmation of this thesis can be found in Jung's own copy of *Faust*, where he has underlined this passage and the lines that follow [Kingsley, 2018, vol. 2, p. 529].) As not just a seer but a Sibyl (l. 7455), Mano's titular status recalls the figure in Book 6 of Virgil's *Aeneid* who accompanies him on his journey to the underworld (Hamlin, 2001, p. 428); but here Manto remains motionless and asleep, if nevertheless dreaming, within the temple of Apollo where she serves (p. 428); thus the descent into the underworld is—like the more famous journey to the realm of the Mothers as described by Mephistopheles to Faust in Act I—essentially a journey inward, a journey into the unconscious (p. 428). Here we are in the realm of mythology or the realm of psychology. And the passage from Homer's *Odyssey* about how Hermes serves as a guide into the underworld "toward the gates of the sun and the land of dreams" (book 14, line 12), quoted by Jung in an inscription on a stone on the outside of the Tower at Bollingen (Kingsley, 2018, vol. 2, pp. 101 and 529), can be seen to find its Faustian equivalent in these lines from Part One.

On the other hand, however, these lines from Part One speak to a very different aspect of death, and a very real one: for the immediate context of these lines is the opening "Night" scene, where Faust is in despair and contemplating suicide. There is a saying that "too many of us die at 30 but get buried at 80," and in this "Night" scene, we are shown what this looks like: The academically successful but intellectually (and probably not just intellectually …) frustrated Faust regrets his study of "philosophy, / Jurisprudence, and medicine, / And help me God, theology" (ll. 354-356), and after having turned from contemplating the sign of the macroocosm to the sign of the earth spirit, he conjures up the *Erdgeist*, only to be rejected and mocked as "a fearful writing worm" who mistakenly thinks of himself as a "superman" (ll. 498 and 490). Seizing a vial of poison, Faust pours it into a chalice, and he is just about to drink it when the sound of the Easter bells and a chorus of angels distracts him. In this sense, what the "Night" scene presents is a kind of near-death experience; Faust is about to commit suicide but is distracted, yet we have been shown the state of mind he is in which will lead to his signing the pact with Mephistopheles. Significantly, the terms of that pact—first, its rejection of rest or *Ruhe*:

If on the bed of sloth I loll contented ever,
Then with that moment end my race!
Canst thou delude me with thy glozing
Self-pleased, to put my grief away,
Canst thou my soul with pleasures cozen,
Then be that day my life's last day!
That is the wager.

> (ll. 1692-1697, Goethe, 1908, part 1, pp. 77-78)

and second, its promise of permanent, perpetual activism:

When to the moment fleeting past me,
Tarry! I cry, so fair thou art !
[*Werd ich zum Augenblicke sagen:*
Verweile doch! du bist so schön!]
Then into fetters mayst thou cast me,
Then let come doom, with all my heart!
Then toll the death-bell, do not linger,
Then be thy bondage o'er and done,
Let the clock stop, let fall the finger,
Let Time for me be past and gone!

> (ll. 1699-1705; Goethe, 1908, part 1, p. 78)

—involve not the abolition of mortality, but merely the postponement of death; as if Faust (or Goethe) realizes at some level that a life without death would itself be not worth living.[4]

The immediate effect of the pact, once agreed (and signed in blood), is to effect a kind of reverse of the midlife crisis from Faust has been suffering: by going for a drink (or several) and lots of entertainment down at the pub—or going to Auerbach's Keller; by being rejuvenated through artificial means—or going to the Witch's

Kitchen; and by getting in touch with his emotions (and especially his erotic drive)—or befriending (and seducing) Gretchen, with catastrophic consequences. The catastrophe lies in the fact that, at the end of Part One, it is Gretchen who is about to die; imprisoned and awaiting execution for the murder of her mother and her own child. Thus, Part One could be read as showcasing three different kinds of rejuvenation—social, physiological, and psychosexual—but none of these can compete with the rejuvenation undergone by Faust between Parts One and Two, the second of which opens with the remarkable scene *Anmutige Gegend* (or "Charming Landscape").

Jung captured the difference between Part One and Part Two of *Faust* with admirable concision when he said that "in the first part of *Faust* Goethe has shown us what it means to accept instinct and in this second part what it means to accept the ego and its weird unconscious world" (CW 7 §43). Whereas Part One closes with Faust and Mephistopheles hastening away from the dungeon where Gretchen is languishing, awaiting execution, Part Two opens in what is literally another world—but still part of this one. In a "Charming Landscape," we see Faust lying on flower-covered grass, weary and restless, while above him a ring of spirits as graceful little shapes floats and weaves. Accompanied by Aeolian harps, the spirit Ariel, a figure from Shakespeare's *Tempest* who had concluded the intermezzo of the "Walpurgis Night's Dream" in Part One, sings of how the elves and fairies will wipe Faust's conscience clear, for "good or evil be his nature / Pity they the luckless man" (ll. 4619-4620). (The figure of Ariel, whose name in Hebrew means "lion of God," derives from the biblical Book of Isaiah, where Ariel serves as another name for Jerusalem.)

In one of his lectures published as part of his *Geisteswissenschaftliche Erläuterungen zu Goethes «Faust»*, the anthroposophist Rudolf Steiner (1861-1925) described this scene as Faust's "initiation with the spirits of the earth." In this lecture given at Dornach on 22 May 1915, Steiner tried—despite the disastrous global situation—to draw a link between the liturgical season (that is, Pentecost) and this opening scene of Part Two: "This Pentecostal mood is having an effect on Faust. And afterwards he continues on his life's journey" (Steiner, 1982, vol. 1, p. 105). Thanks to the magical intervention of the elves, Faust finds himself once again rejuvenated and renewed: "Life's pulses newly-quickened now awaken," he says (l. 4679). The source of this rejuvenative power, however, is not this time, as it had been in Part One, the witch's magic spell as cast at the instigation of the Devil, but rather the Earth: "Thou girdest me about with gladness," Faust says, "priming / My soul to stern resolve and strenuous keeping, / Onward to strive, to highest life still climbing" (*Zum höchsten Dasein immerfort zu streben*) (ll. 4684-4685), thus restating the great Faustian themes of striving (*Streben*) and intensification (*Steigerung*).

In this refreshed and renewed state, the natural world around now seems paradisiacal to Faust: "A very Paradise about me lightens!" (l. 4694), and the radiance of the sun, whose approach had earlier in the scene made a stupendous clangour—an acoustic recapitulation of the "far-thundering progression" attributed to its "appointed round" in the words of the archangel Raphael that open the "Prologue in Heaven"—causes Faust to be "blinded" (l. 4702). What Empedocles saw as a pair of opposites, love (*philotes* = φιλότης) and strife (*neikos* = νεῖκος)—[5]and the theme of the opposites is one of the great Jungian themes—are here understood by Faust as reciprocally related, as a *Wechselwirkung*: "Is't Love? Is't Hate? that

---

[5] See Empedocles (DK 31 B 26 and D|K 31 B 35). For further discussion of the relation between Presocratic thought and psychoanalysis, see Arkin, 1949; and Tourney, 1956.

yonder glowing spindle / In bliss and bale alternating [*wechselnd*] tremendous / About us twines, till we the dazed beholders / To veil our gaze in Earth's fresh mantle wend us" (ll. 4711-4714), and the shining of the sun through the waterfall produces a phenomenon that is as symbolic as it is meteorological—a rainbow:

> Nay then, the sun shall bide behind my shoulders!
> The cataract, that through the gorge doth thunder
> I'll watch with growing rapture, 'mid the boulders
> From plunge to plunge down-rolling, rent asunder
> In thousand thousand streams, aloft that shower
> Foam upon hissing foam, the depths from under.
> Yet blossoms from this storm a radiant flower;
> The painted rainbow bends its changeful being,
> Now lost in air, now limned with clearest power,
> Shedding this fragrant coolness round us fleeing.
> Its rays an image of man's efforts render;
> Think, and more clearly wilt thou grasp it, seeing
> Life in the many-hued, reflected splendour.
> [*Am farbigen Abglanz haben wir das Leben*].
>   (ll. 4715-4727; Goethe, 1908, part 2, p. 15)

Now Jung, in his seminar on *Dream Interpretation Ancient & Modern* (given in Zürich between 1936 and 1941), quoted this final line, suggesting that in it Goethe expresses "approximately the same opinion as that of the Romantics," namely: that "reflection is a reality, illusion is reality" (Jung, 2014, p. 80). (According to Jung, this notion "corresponds exactly to the Eastern conception of *maya*," and he takes issues with the translation of *maya* simply as "illusion": rather, we should say "real illusion, which emanates from something unknowable.") Perhaps (for once) more tellingly, Steiner comments that "after this night Faust has reached the point where he no longer wants, like the Faust of the first part, to hurl himself into life, just as it has thrown him into guilt and into evil, but he turns to its *many-hued, reflected splendour*," adding: "It is the same *many-hued, reflected splendour* which we call *Geisteswissenschaft*, which appears to him as a *many-hued, reflected splendour*, and by means of which we gradually raise ourselves to experience reality" (Steiner, 1982, vol. 1, p. 116).

After agreeing to the pact, Mephistopheles agreed to show Faust "the small world, and then the great": correspondingly, in Part Two we see, not the evening to Auerbach's Keller, the visit to the Witch's Kitchen, and the Gretchen episode of Part One, but instead the Carnival at the Imperial Court, the Mothers scene, and the conjuring up of Paris and Helena (Act 1); the Classical Walpurgisnacht (Act 2): the Helena episode (Act 3); the war between the Emperor and his rival (Act 4); and the concluding act and its concluding acene (Act 5). Over this period, Faust does grow older; so, it is an aged Faust whom we encounter, wandering around in the spacious ornamental gardens of his palace in Act 5. (In his conversation with Eckermann of 6 June 1831, Goethe suggested that Faust lives to be a hundred years old [Eckermann, 1998, p. 413].) We shall, however, see not just the aged Faust: We shall also see his death and witness his progress in the postmortem state.

In a lecture given in Dornach on 14 August 1915, Rudolf Steiner begins with a methodological, if somewhat unexpected, move of discussing Goethe's obscure work, *Weissagungen des Bakis* (or *Soothsayings of Bakis*), in order to demonstrate the difference between exoteric and esoteric interpretations (Steiner, vol. 1, pp. 143-145). His own task, he declares, is to show that "while Faust is supposed to be led under the influence of Ahriman-Mephistopheles through the confusion of the world, the deepest of what is embodied in the human heart is not supposed to be able to be consumed by what comes from Mephisto-Ahriman" (pp. 145-146). (In Steiner's extraordinarily intricate—or perhaps simply extraordinary—system of anthroposophy, Ahriman—whose name derives from Ancient Persia, where he is the opponent of Ahura Mazsa, the Persian sun god—is a divine being whose influence causes all those processes that harden and materialize those spiritual realities originally underlying all creation [van Oort, 2011, p. 4].)[6]

On Steiner's account, the goal which Goethe himself had set himself in his *Faust* drama was to show us how Faust was finally able to be taken up into the spiritual worlds (Steiner, 1982, vol. 1, p. 146). In his lecture given the next day, however, Steiner made a shrewd observation by pointing to the complicated publication history of *Faust*: In Goethe's own lifetime, Part One of *Faust* was first published as *Faust, A Fragment* in 1790 and then, as Part One, in 1808; Act 3 of Part Two was published as *Helena, an Intermezzo for "Faust"* in 1827; and the opening scene of Part Two, i.e., *Anmutige Gegend*, and the first three of the six scenes in the section *Kaiserliche Pfalz* (as far as verse 6036) were published in 1828.[7] According to Steiner, in Goethe's lifetime many people must have wondered how *Faust* was going to conclude;[8] and many rightly suspected that, as indeed happens, Faust's soul was going to be redeemed and taken up into the spirit world. (That said, this aspect

---

[6] The role of Christ in maintaining a balance between, on the one hand, Ahriman and, on the other, Lucifer is depicted by Steiner in his sculpture "The Representative of Humanity," displayed in the Goetheanum in Dornach.

[7] See Steiner, 1982, vol. 1, pp. 161-162; cf. "Chronology of the Composition of *Faust*" (Atkins [Ed.], 1984, pp. 306-307; and "The Composition of *Faust*" (Hamlin, 2001, pp. 505-513).

[8] In fact, in conversation with Eckermann on 20 April 1825, Goethe reported having received a letter from a young student, who wanted to be sent the plan for Part Two with a view to completing the work himself (Eckermann, 1998, p. 102)!

arguably remains the most controversial aspect of Goethe's *Faust*; in 2018, Peter Kreeft was still able to argue that "in *Faust*, Goethe told the traditional moral story of Faust, the man who sold his soul to the Devil, from an antitraditional, antimoral point of view" (Kreeft, 2018, p. 103). Changing the original tale by 180 degrees, "in *Faust* God and the Devil turn out to be allies, because they both move Faust up the ladder of enlightenment and maturity and away from his earlier moralistic innocence," so that "the whole point and end of the old Faust story is turned into its opposite": "Faust is not damned at all but enlightened," and "he is not punished but rewarded for disobeying the moral law" [p. 103].) So, the question for Goethe was: How was this going to be represented?

As Steiner reminds us, in his conversation with Eckermann of 6 June 1831, Goethe pointed out that "the conclusion, where the redeemed soul is carried up, was difficult to manage," adding: "Amid such supersensual matters, about which we scarcely have even an intimation, I might easily have lost myself in the vague [*mich sehr leicht im Vagen hätte verlieren können*]" (Eckermann, 1998, p. 414). The solution, Goethe told Eckermann, had been to give his "poetical design" (*poetischen Intentionen*) a "desirable form and substance" (*eine wohltätig beschränkende Form und Festigkeit*) by using "sharply-drawn figures, and images from the Christian Church" (p. 414). And, as we shall see, this is indeed the case.[9]

---

[9] In his *Erläuterungen*, Steiner is insistent on "this miracle" (*dieses Wunderbare*) of Goethe's old age: having completed something "entirely pagan, entirely pre-Christian" in the form of the *Helena* Act (or Act 3), as well as something "certainly not anti-Christian" in the form of Act 4 (although one might disagree about that), it is only in his old age that Goethe must "emerge out of all the pagan cult and implant Christianity into *Faust*." "Goethe had to become eighty years old," Steiner concludes, "for him to be able to say to himself that he is in a position to use Christian representations in such a way that they are a change of clothes [*Umkleidung*] for the way which the soul of Faust has to go" (Steiner, 1982, vol. 1, p. 162). On this reading, the Christian iconography of the *Schlußszene* has to

Act 5 of *Faust*, Part Two, is full of darkness and death. It opens with the episode of Philemon and Baucis, whose cottage with its tiny chapel Faust orders to be destroyed as incompatible with his great land-reclamation scheme, and who end up being murdered; the moves in "Midnight" to Faust's encounter with the Four Gray Crones, representing Want, Debt, Need, and Care (*Sorge*). Blinded by Care, Faust nevertheless continues with his great project, unaware in "Great Outer Precinct of the Palace" that the Lemures—in classical mythology, the spirits of the evil dead—are not implementing his plans, but digging his (i.e., Faust's) own grave. After a final speech in which Faust appears to trigger the conditions of the pact when he almost entreats the "fleeing minute"—"Oh tarry yet, thou are so fair" (ll. 11581-11582— he sinks backward; the Lemures break his fall and lay him on the ground; Faust is dead. In the ensuing "Entombment" scene, Mephistopheles goes to claim Faust's soul; as the ghastly jaws of Hell open on the left, however, an aureole and a heavenly host appear above right, and Mephistopheles is distracted from seizing his prey by a chorus of young, naked, Cupidlike angels, strewing roses and drifting all about. (In crucial respects, this scene reenacts the dynamic of the opening "Night" scene when Faust is distracted from committing suicide by a Chorus of Angels.) Soaring up, the Angels carry off Faust's "immortal essence" (in German, *Faustens Unsterbliches*), and the Act—and the entire work—concludes with the "forests, cliffs, wilderness" of the "Mountain Gorges" scene.

Unlike Steiner, this development profoundly worried Jung. In his "Epilogue" to *Psychology and Alchemy* (1944), Jung described *Faust* as "steeped in alchemical thought from beginning

---

be taken at face value, rather than a kind of intellectual-historical, crosscultural quotation.

to end" (CW 12 §558). In the scene where Faust conjures up Paris and Helena, Jung argued, a medieval alchemist would have seen "the mysterious *coniunctio* of Sol and Luna in the retort" (as depicted visually in the woodcut illustrating the stage of *fermentatio* or the symbolic representation of the *coniunctio spiritum* in the *Rosarium philosophorum* [1550]). "Disguised in the figure of Faust," however, the modern individual "recognizes the projection and, putting himself in the place of Paris, takes possession of Helena or Luna, his own inner, feminine counterpart" (CW 12 §558). On Jung's account, this is a big mistake, because "instead of watching the drama, he has become one of the actors" (§558); as a result, "the real goal of the entire process—the production of the incorruptible substance—is missed," and all attempts at rejuvenation or "rebirth" end disastrously—exemplified by the Boy Charioteer (in Act 1), the Homunculus (in Act 2), and in particular Euphorion (in Act 3) (§558). (Unmentioned by Jung, however, is the exception: the successful rejuvenation of Faust by the elves in the *Anmutige Gegend* scene.) As Faust cannot resist "supplanting Paris in Helena's affections," so these minor figures are "destroyed by the same greed," and here, Jung concludes, is "probably the deeper reason why Faust's final rejuvenation takes place only in the postmortal state, i.e., is *projected into the future*" (§558; my emphasis).

On this reading, Faust's identification in Act 1 (and in Act 3?) with Paris "brings the *coniunctio* back from its projected state into the sphere of personal psychological experience and thus into consciousness"—a fatal development because if, on the one hand, it is a "crucial step," which means "nothing less than the solution of the alchemical riddle" (inasmuch as it involves "the redemption of a previously unconscious part of the personality"), then nevertheless, on the other, it triggers an inflation, suggested by Faust's Übermensch-like powers (CW 12 §559). For Jung,

Faust's death is "hardly a satisfactory answer"; and, by locating "the rebirth and transformation that follow the *coniunctio* [...] in the hereafter, i.e., in the unconscious," the problem is left "hanging in the air" (where it is taken up again, Jung adds, by Nietzsche in his *Zarathustra*—a claim which is an entirely separate matter for discussion) (§559). Yet is the matter quite as simple as that? Let us look at the *Schlußszene* more closely.

It opens with a stage direction about four Holy Anchorites (that is, early Christian desert hermits), who are shown as scattered up the mountainsides and dwelling among rock clefts. (It is likely that frescoes showing stories about the Desert Fathers or the Thebaid in the Campo Santo in Pisa or Titian's painting of St. Jerome in the wilderness were among the visual sources for this scene.) A Chorus and an Echo speak the following lines:

> Billows the forest on,
> Lean them the cliffs thereon,
> Grapple the roots thereon,
> Trunk crowding trunk upon;
> Wave gushes after wave,
> Shelters the deepest cave;
> Softly the lions, dumb-
> Friendly about us come,
> Honour the holy seat,
> Sanctified love-retreat.

(ll. 11844-11853, Goethe, 1908, part 2, p. 333)

In his *Erläuterungen*, Steiner comments repeatedly—almost obsessively—on these lines, but some of his remarks contain useful insights about them. After all, there is a genuine problem: How does one depict the afterlife? Goethe could not simply represent Faust ascending into heaven and depict everything in "abstract-allegorical images" (*abstrakt-allegorische Gebilde*) because that would have been "symbolism" or mere "straw," and because he was "in the most intimate and in the highest sense an artistic nature," he did not want that—"he wanted art" (Steiner, 1982, vol. 1, p. 146). However sophisticated the stage machinery at his disposal might have been, Goethe had "first of all to find the worldly medium [*das Weltenmittel*] by means of which Faust can ascend as a soul into the spiritual world," and the only means to do this is not through the air, not through external physical elements, but through the only thing that can represent the spiritual, namely: the spiritual (*das Geistige*). Or in other words, Goethe needed to create "a reality of consciousness that can embrace the spiritual," and he does this by placing in the scenery human beings in whose consciousness the spiritual is alive: namely, monks or anchorites, so that one can say that "the ascent of a soul into spiritual worlds is a real process [*ein realer Vorgang*]" (p. 146).

And not just the Holy Anchorites: In these opening lines, the Chorus (which Steiner imagines as a chorus of monks [cf. p. 157]) and its Echo demonstrate that they can "perceive in the sensuous-physical realm the elementary world of the spirit"—the spiritual world, into which the soul of Faust has to ascend. These lines—especially the first line, *Waldung, die schwankt heran*—are, Steiner insists, not "depictions of physical processes," but an expression of how one can "feel the elementary world as proceeding from natural things" (p. 147). (The presence of Echo, Steiner adds, is "not without significance"; its function is to illustrate "how everything which comes from elementary nature is really omnipresent [*allseitig*]" (p. 147). In the remaining lines, Steiner explains, "the world of the spirits of form slowly begins to turn into the world of the spirits of movement"; or, as he puts it, "what we encounter as elemental" now "becomes spiritual [*es vergeistigt sich*], it begins to become moved," so that "everything goes into motion" (pp. 157-158). On this account, the language and imagery of Goethe's text actually shows us how "a soul can ascend from this earthly being, the physical plane, into the spiritual world" (p. 158). According to Steiner, "we cannot imagine that we could have the presentation of the ascent of Faust's soul into the spiritual worlds magically presented to our soul, if we cannot place in front of the soul's eye [*vor unsrer Seelenauge*] the lively way in which nature becomes alive and the release from the life of nature in the case of Faust's soul" (p. 158).[10] In fact, Steiner even goes so far as to talk about Goethe's "occultism" while insisting that it is an occultism that is "entirely healthy" and "rooted in the firm ground of the reality of worlds" (p. 158).

As it happens, Jung too was struck by these opening lines, citing them in his letter to Bernhard Baur-Celio (1895-1981) of 30 January 1934. Now Baur-Celio, a teacher of French and Italian in Küsnacht, had asked Jung whether he possessed any "secret knowledge" not contained in his writings, in response to which he received the intriguing answer that Jung had had "experiences which are, so to speak, 'ineffable,' 'secret' because they can never be told properly and because nobody can understand them"; indeed, Jung was not even sure if he had understood them himself (Jung, 1973-1975, vol. 1, pp. 140-141)! He went to describe these experiences as "dangerous," "catastrophic," and "taboo-ed": dangerous, because 99% of people would declare Jung to be mad if they heard such things; catastrophic, because the prejudices caused by telling them might block the way to "a living and wondrous secret" (*zu einem lebendig-wunderbaren Geheimnis*) for other people; and "taboo-ed," because they are an ἄδυτον (*adyton*, that is, something "not to be entered," an "innermost sanctuary or shrine," often an area

---

[10] For discussion of the notion of a *geistiges Auge*, see Hanegraaff 2018.

where the cult image of the deity was kept), protectively surrounded by δεισιδαιμονία (*deisidaimonía*, i.e., "fearing or reverencing the divine")—the latter being correctly described by Goethe in the conclusion to *Faust II* in the words of the Chorus and Echo:

Shelters the deepest cave;	*Höhle, die tiefste, schützt.*
Softly the lions, dumb-	*Löwen, sie schleichen stumm-*
Friendly about us come,	*Freundlich um uns herum,*
Honour the holy seat,	*Ehren geweihten Ort,*
Sanctified love-retreat.	*Heiligen Liebeshort.*

(ll. 11847-11853)

"And already," Jung added, "too much has been said" (1973-1975, vol. 1, p. 141).

Too much—or not enough? Coming from vastly different (although arguably compatible) theoretical starting-positions, Steiner and Jung agree in their intuitive sense that these lines are highly significant. This intuitive sense is borne out by Cyrus Hamlin in his interpretative notes in the Norton edition of *Faust*. Here Hamlin suggests that the 10 lines of two-stress dactyls introducing the "Mountain Gorges" scene call for "particularly close attention" (Hamlin, 2001, p. 485). The assignment of these lines to Chorus and Echo is especially "cryptic," he notes, comparing them to the hymn of the Archangels in the "Prologue in Heaven," the self-presentation of the Earth Spirit, and the spirit chorus that holds Faust in hypnotic fascination in the first study scene in Part One; and to the chorus of nature spirits that accompanies Ariel in the opening "Charming Landscape" scene and the songs of the Sirens in the "Classical Walpurgis Night" in Part Two (p. 485). In them, Hamlin suggests, Goethe "give[s] voice to nature itself"— "powers of the spirit express the activity that gives them identity in a language that perfectly fuses sign and signified" (p. 485). The

223

concluding couplet, he adds, constitutes a "remarkable formulation of blessing, consecration, and love"; in Hamlin's estimation, this Chorus and Echo is "just as remarkable—indeed, astonishing—a poetic achievement as the concluding Chorus Mysticus," yet it "as not received much attention from critics" (p. 486). Nevertheless, it did not, it seems, escape the attention of Jung or Steiner.[11]

Moreover, in the "Mountain Gorges" scene, we too—as readers (or spectators)—embark on a kind of ascension, through the hierarchy of four Anchorite fathers: the Pater Ecstaticus (who floats hither and thither, reminiscent of St. Philipp Neri about whom Goethe writes in his *Italian Journey*),[12] via Pater Profundus and then Pater Seraphicus, and finally Doctor Marianus. (These titles evoke such historical figures as St. Anthony, Johann Ruybroek, and Dionysius the Carthusian (*ecstaticus*); St. Bernhard of Clairvaux (*profoundus*), who acts in the *Paradiso* as a guide to Dante's ascent to the mystical vision of God); and St. Francis of Assisi (*seraphicus*), while name Marianus reminds Jung of one of the early alchemists, usually spelled Morienus [CW 12 §558; cf. §386, n. 88]). At the same time, the prayer addressed by Doctor Marianus to the Mater Gloriosa (in ll. 11997-12012 and 12020-12031) echoes the prayer to the Virgin spoken by St. Bernhard in Dante's *Paradiso* (canto

---

[11] In his commentary to his translation, Albert G. Latham suggests another possible visual intertext for the lines, "Softly the lions, dumb- / Friendly about us come," again from a fresco in the *Campa Santo* of Pisa: namely, the *Anchorites in the Thebaïa*, with its depiction of huge cliffs on the banks of the Nile, to which trees cling with their roots, while hermits sit in huts and caves, some lions dig a grave for a dead anchorite, and other lions guard the abodes of the hermits (in Goethe, 1908, pp. 406-407). And Goethe's collection of engravings included one representing St. Jerome in the Wilderness, with his signature lion. As a biblical source informing these two works, Latham suggests the famous prophecy of Isaiah about the coming judgment, in which "the wolf and the lamb shall feed together, the lion and the ox shall eat straw" [Isaiah 65:24].)

[12] See Goethe's entry in his *Italian Journey* for 26 May 1787 (cf. Steiner, 1982, vol. 1, p. 160).

33, ll. 1-39). Indeed, Dante is clearly one of the models or cultural reference-points for Goethe's *Schlußszene*.

As we ascend through the patristic hierarchy, so we become aware of something else. After the floating figure of the Pater Ecstaticus, we move from the Pater Profundus (in a deep region) up to the Pater Seraphicus (in a middle region); and, before moving further up to Doctor Marianus (in what is described as "the highest, purest cell"), the Pater Seraphicus describes how a wispy morning cloud floats up, containing a chorus of Blessed Boys—children, that is, who had died unbaptized and immediately after being born, and who, in traditional Catholic theology (until recently revised), were believed to be in the Limbo of Infants.[13] Pater Seraphicus urges them to continue on their *Steigerung*, that is, their ascent, reassuring them: "For in ether free, supernal, / This as spirit-food still holdeth, / Revelation of Eternal / Love that unto bliss unfoldeth" (ll. 11922-11925); until, finally, the chorus of Blessed Boys is circling around the highest peaks. Here, among these higher peaks, we see angels, floating in the higher atmosphere and bearing Faust's "immortal essence" (*Faustens Unsterbliches*). Originally, Goethe had used the word *Entelechie* ("entelechy"): a notion found in Aristotle as *entelecheia* (ἐντελέχεια), where it is related to *energeia* (ενέργεια), and employed by Goethe in the sense of Leibniz's notion of the indestructible monad.[14] Thus an entelechy is a kind of secularized

---

[13] See the report of the International Theological Commission, commissioned by Pope John Paul II and authorized for publication in April 2007 by Benedict XVI, titled "The Hope of Salvation for Infants Who Die without Being Baptized."
[14] See Goethe's conversation about the entelechy with Eckermann on 3 March 1830, where he remarks that "the obstinacy of the individual, and the fact that man shakes off what does not suit him […] is a proof to me that something of the kind exists," adding: "Leibnitz had similar thoughts about independent beings, and indeed what we term an entelechy he called a monad" (Eckermann, 1998, p. 353). For further discussion, see Gaier, 1999, pp. 720-722; Kohlschmidt, 1974; and Seppänen, 1983.

notion of the soul, understood as a dynamic principle that turns what is *potential* into something *actual*.[15] (John Peck has argued persuasively for the importance of Aristotle's "action template" in his *Poetics* and his notion of *entelechy* in his biology and natural history for Jung's theory of individuation.[16] In an interview with Jung in 1952, Ximena de Angulo suspected that Jung may have had a prejudice against Aristotle because of the "intellectual aridity and doctrinaire rigidity" of so-called "Aristotelian" thinking in the Church; but, when she pushed him on whether individuation was "what made a tree grow into a tree" and "if it was not the same thing as the Aristotelian entelechy," Jung—after hesitating—conceded it *was* the same thing.)[17]

Amid the highest peaks and in this higher atmosphere, these angels bearing Faust's immortal essence now declaim lines which, according to Goethe in his conversation with Eckermann of 6 June 1831, contain "the key to Faust's salvation":

---

[15] See Schöne, 2005, p. 800; cf. Aristotle's *Metaphysics*, where the notions of potentiality and actuality are introduced in book 8 (Z) and analyzed in book 9 (Θ) (Aristotle, 1984, vol. 2, pp. 1623-1644 and 1651-1661). On 19 March 1827, Goethe wrote to Zelter: "The entelechical monad must preserve itself in unceasing activity alone"; and on 1 September 1829 he said to Eckermann: "I doubt not of our immortality, for Nature cannot dispense with the entelechy," and adding: "But we are not all in like manner immortal; and he who would manifest himself in future as a great entelechy must be one now" (Eckermann, 1998, p. 331).

[16] "The sections of Aristotle's *Poetics* devoted to the structure of action rendered symbolically [...] supplied Jung with his terms. [...] The nugget for Jung in this action template is the pressure or drift in psychic energy, the apparent purposiveness in life processes, which is akin to the finalistic perspective invoked by him for certain dreams, but which typically remains a bane in modern science, and certainly is baneful to theorists of unconscious processes when those processes are tied to the least shred of traditional teleology" (John Peck, "Introduction," in Jung, 2014, p. xxxiv).

[17] "Comments on a Doctoral Thesis" [1952], in McGuire and Hull, 1977, pp. 205-218 (p. 211); cited in Peck, "Introduction," in Jung, 2014, p. xxxv.

Freed is the noble scion of
The Spirit-world from evil.
»Him can we save that tireless strove
Ever to higher level.«
And if Supernal Love did stoop
To him with predilection,
Then him shall hail the angelic troop
With brotherly affection.

(ll. 11934-11941; Goethe, 1908, part 2, p. 336)

So, in what sense do these lines contain the key to Faust's salvation? As Goethe himself explained, "In Faust himself there is an activity which becomes constantly higher and purer to the end, and from above there is eternal love coming to his aid. This harmonizes perfectly with our religious views, according to which we cannot obtain heavenly bliss through our own strength alone, but with the assistance of divine grace" (Eckermann, 1998, p. 413). Except it's perhaps not *quite* as simple as that.

For the two lines telling us that whoever strives (*strebend*) and makes an effort (*sich bemüht*) is someone whom they (as angels, and presumably hence as agents of God) can redeem (*Den können wir erlösen*), not only raise questions about the model of redemption (*Erlösung*) with which Goethe is operating (is it a Christian notion of redemption from the consequence of original sin through the redemptive power of the death of Christ, God become Man, on the Cross? Or a more Neoplatonic notion of redemption as a kind of cleansing, stripping-away or removal (= *Abstreifung, Ablösung?*),[18] but they are also placed within quotation marks; marks, not present in Goethe's handwritten manuscript (H[33]), but added in pencil to

---

[18] See Schöne, 2005, p. 801; Gaier, 1999, p. 1143.

the final manuscript (H), and hence to be regarded as passively authorized by Goethe (see Schöne, 2005, pp. 800-802). What these quotation marks mean remains unclear, but they can only serve as some kind of distancing device. Sensing this, perhaps, Steiner (the published version of whose lecture omits the quotation marks!) comments on the immediately following lines spoken by the Younger Angels that this is "an occult sentence," implying that "to Mephisto-Ahriman love is a consuming fire and a terrible gift of darkness" (Steiner, 1982, vol. 1, p. 151).

The following lines, spoken by the More Perfected Angels, invoke the notion of "eternal love" as alone being able to separate "*Geeinte Zwienatur*," prompting Steiner to observe that "angels hide their face before becoming human," indicative of "a secret which can only be seen by those beings who can descend deeper than angels who have not become human" (vol. 1, p. 152). Even Steiner then shows himself to be surprisingly materialist when he interprets the line, "*Löset die Flocken los*," spoken by the Blessed Boys, as a reference to the tradition practiced by Benedictine monks of dressing those about to die in a brown gown, or *flocca*, in which they are then buried; another example, he suggested, of how Goethe "connects with physical processes in order to characterize spiritual processes" (vol. 1, p. 152). Yet Steiner soon gets back onto his anthroposophical track, identifying the Anachorite called Doctor Marianus with Faust; acclaiming how in the Chorus of Penitent Women (including the figure of the Penitent, formerly called Gretchen) Goethe has taken love in its sensuous form and religiously transformed it; and finally emphasizing, with reference to the celebrated words of the concluding Chorus Mysticus, how Goethe has depicted the final scene "really properly [*wirklich sachgemäß*], from spiritual knowledge" and that he knew how to "create the real basic structures [...]: the basic structures of consciousness [*Bewußtseinsgrundlagen*]" (vol. 1, p. 155).

Of course, one does not have to follow the (anthroposophical) reading offered by Steiner or the (archetypal) reading offered by Jung to find in *Faust* as a whole and its concluding scene in particular a remarkable resource, intellectually as well as emotionally speaking. For my part, I would read the concluding scene not so much as a representation of the afterlife-as-the-unconscious (Jung) or of spiritual worlds (Steiner) as a representation of representations of the afterlife as a theological construct or an iconographical tradition. The text also sits in a productive tension with remarks made by Goethe elsewhere in letters and conversations. For it seems that, aside from *Faust* and from his impromptu criticism of Karl Friedrich Lessing's "Monastery Courtyard in Snow" (see below), Goethe's own personal response to death reveals a more vulnerable side to the great poet and thinker.[19] At the beginning of 1805, or so Heinrich Voß told (August Hermann) Niemeyer on 12 August 1806, Goethe had awoken with a premonition that either he or Schiller were going to die that year (see Steiger [ed.], vol. 4, p. 546). Very soon both men were unwell, in the case of Goethe with fever and pneumonia, then a kidney infection (vol. 4, pp. 556 and 567). In a letter to F.I. Niethammer of 4 March 1805, Hegel remarked on how cold the winter in Jena was being and on how concerned he was about Goethe and Schiller. While ill himself, Goethe's reaction to Schiller's ill health was to remain silent about it, as Christiane Vulpius told J.H. Meyer on 20 May 1806 (vol. 4, p. 573). For his part, Schiller went from one fever to another, telling Goethe in a letter of 27 March 1805 that although he had "finally clung with all seriousness onto [his] work" and was "now

---

[19] See the accounts in Wulf, 2022, pp. 308-310 and 340. For drawing this refreshingly lively portrait of the "Jena Set" to my attention, I am grateful to Murray Stein.

back underway," it had been "difficult to reassume his post after such long pauses and unfortunate incidents" and that he had had to "force [him]self" (Schiller/Goethe, 1990, vol. 1, p. 998). Only a few weeks later, however, Schiller was dead.

It says something not just about Goethe's attitude to death but about that of early 19th-century German culture as a whole that no one wanted to tell Goethe about the death of his dearest friend and closest collaborator at the age of 45. According to Voß's account, it was only when Goethe asked Christiana about how ill Schiller had been the previous day that, breaking down in tears, she finally told him that Schiller was dead (Biedermann [ed.], 1909-1911, vol. 1, p. 387). Goethe's response was, understandably, one of great emotional intensity, but it was not extravagant. He locked himself away in his study, and although the burial took place in the graveyard of the St. Jakobskirche, a short walk away from Goethe's house in Weimar, he did not attend the funeral. In a letter to K.F. Zelter of 1 June 1805, Goethe wrote: "I thought I was going to be lost myself, and now lose a friend and in him half my own life," adding: "In fact I was supposed to begin a new way of life [*eine neue Lebensweise*]; but in my years there is no longer a path to this. So I now see only each day in front of me, and do what is immediately required, without thinking of further consequences" (Goethe, 1962-1967, vol. 3, p. 7). With the death of Schiller, Goethe had (so he told Zelter) lost "a friend and, with him, half of my own life" (*einen Freund und in demselben die Hälfte meines Daseyns*) (vol. 3, p. 7), someone who was both "excellent" (*vortrefflich*) and "irreplaceable" (*unersätzlich*) (Steiger, vol. 4, p. 580).

The strength of Goethe's response was a source of concern to others. Writing to his brother A.W. Schlegel on 24 May 1805, Friedrich Schlegel expressed the fear that "the old man will now turn entirely to stone, or will not survive it for very long" (*ich fürchte der alte Herr wird nun ganz versteinen, oder* überlebt *es nicht lange*);[20] no one dared mention Schiller's death to Goethe; and although Goethe undertook to finish work on Schiller's drama *Demetrius*, later telling Förster on 4 August 1831 that he and Schiller had discussed the play in such detail that Goethe "could write the rest of his Demetrius" (Biedermann [ed.], 1909-1911. vol. 4, p. 383) and was determined to do this in order to "spite Death" (*dem Tode zum Trutz*) (Steiger [ed.], 1982-1996, vol. 4, p. 581), it proved to be impossible for him to do this because of Goethe's "hollowed out condition" (*den hohlen Zustand*) following the loss of his friend (Steiger [ed.], 1982-1996, vol. 4, p. 582).

We find a similar response on Goethe's part to the death of Christiana Vulpius, for many years his lover (and eventually his wife). When, after a long illness at the age of 51, she died, Goethe's response was, as it had been with Schiller, one of a refusal not so much to accept the fact as rather even to engage with it.[21] This strategy is reflected in his decision neither to talk about her death nor to attend her funeral, even though they had been together for 28 years—just as after the death of Schiller. Goethe's diary entry for 6 June 1815, however, reveals what he was feeling: "Emptiness and deathly silence, within me and without" (*Leere und Todtenstille in und außer mir*).[22]

---

[20] Friedrich Schlegel to August Wilhelm Schlegel, 24 May 1805; see Körner (ed.), 1936, vol. 1, p. 198.

[21] For further discussion, see Dusini 1998; Wulf, 2022, p. 340; and Damm, 1998, pp. 501-502.

[22] See Goethe's diary entry for 6 June 1816: "Slept well and much better. Nearing the end with my wife. Final terrible struggle of her nature. She departed from us around midday. Emptiness and deathly silence, within me and without. Arrival and festive procession of Princess Ida and Bernhard. Councillor Meyer. Riemer. In the evening brilliant illumination of the city. My wife to the mortuary at 12 o'clock at night. I am in bed the whole day" (*Gut geschlafen und viel besser. Nahes Ende meiner Frau. Letzter fürchterlicher Kampf ihrer Natur. Sie verschied*

Yet the notion of entelechy—adopted by Goethe from Aristotle and used as a motif in the concluding scene of *Faust*, Part Two—seems to offer a clue as to a Goethean response to the inevitability of death. In conversation with Friedrich Christoph Förster (1791-1868) in 1826, for example, Goethe recounted how a young painter from Berlin—he means Karl Friedrich Lessing (1808-1880)—had sent him a painting, subsequently identified as "Monastery Courtyard in Snow" (although it is uncertain which version),[23] which Goethe described as "betraying a definite talent for poetic invention as well as composition and execution," yet he added that he found himself in disagreement with the artist and his painting alike (Korrodi [ed.], 1944, p. 247). Whereas Dutch painters show us winter landscapes in which men and women go merrily ice-skating on frozen ice, he explained, Lessing (and his Romantic ilk) takes the spectator "into a winter landscape in which ice and snow appear not to be enough for him; he exceeds, or, we might say, he out-winters winter through the most repulsive additions," chiefly the staffage (or human figures): namely, "a procession of monks, in fact barefoot, in the snow, escorts a departed brother, who is being carried lying in a coffin on a black-draped bier to the crypt in a delapidated monastery" (pp. 247-248). Goethe's reaction was highly negative—"These are sheer negations of life and the friendly habit of existence, if can quote myself," and he continued:

> To begin with, the dead nature, the winter landscape;
> I don't permit the winter; then monks, refugees

---

gegen Mittag. Leere und Todtenstille in und außer mir. Ankunft und festlicher Einzug der Prinzessin Ida und Bernhards. Hofr. Meyer. Riemer. Abends brillante Illumination der Stadt. Meine Frau um 12 Nachts ins Leichenhaus. Ich den ganzen Tag im Bett) (Goethe, 1893, p. 239).

[23] For further discussion and reproductions of the works in question, see von Lorck, 1936.

from life, people buried alive; I don't permit monks; then a monastery, and a delapidated one, but I do not permit monasteries; and finally, just to make it complete, a dead man, a corpse; but I do not permit death. (Korrodi [ed.], 1944, p. 248)

This robust attitude toward death captures in a negative way the positive attitude toward life exemplified by Goethe in his last letter, written shortly before his death, sent to Wilhelm von Humboldt on 17 March 1832.[24]

In part of this letter, Goethe responds to Humboldt on the question of the composition of *Faust*—the work he regarded as his *Hauptwerk*, which was the sense in which Jung also understood it (MDR, p. 232)—and the six-million-dollar question as to whether there was an underlying intention:

The idea of *Faust* was present in mind more than sixty years ago in a youthful way — the opening part clear, the whole sequence less detailed. I have always kept the general intention at the back of my head and merely worked out the particular scenes that happened to interest me most. This left some gaps in Part II which had to be filled in without letting the interest decline. It was at this point that the great difficulty arose of achieving by means of determination and moral character [*durch Vorsatz und Charakter*] what really ought to be left to nature to do unforced. But it would be a pity if this did not prove possible after a life as long and as actively

---

[24] For further discussion of this letter, see Fairley, 1957.

reflective as mine. (Goethe, 1962-1967, vol. 4, p. 481)

This comment serves to confirm the interpretative approach taken by Jung (as well as by Steiner) that seeks to uncover an overarching intention in the work as a whole. Moreover, in the context of this letter *Faust* serves to exemplify other tenets expressed by Goethe about life. First, "the sooner a man realizes that there is an art or a technique that will enable him to improve and intensify his natural gifts in a controlled way, the happier he will be. Nothing that comes to him from without can hurt the individuality he was born with. The best-endowed mind [*Das beste Genie*] is the mind that can absorb anything, appropriate anything, without in the slightest degree impairing its primal bent or what we call its personality [*Charakter*], but rather enhancing it and bringing it to the highest capacity" (Goethe, 1962-1967, vol. 4, p. 480).

Second, what are the implications of this stance in psychological terms? Already we find in Goethe a recognition (and, indeed, an appreciation) of the unconscious: "It is here" — in other words, in personality (or *Charakter*) — "that the interrelation of conscious and unconscious occurs in its many forms. Think of a musician preparing an important score. Conscious and unconscious will interact like warp and woof, a favourite image of mine" (Goethe, 1962-1967, vol. 4, p. 480). (In fact, we find the image in *Faust*, when Mephistopheles tells the student in the second "Study" scene: "What though the thought-assembly shop / Is like a master-weaver's job, / Where one tread stirs a thousand points, / The shuttles back and forward fly, / Threads flow too swiftly for the eye, / One downbeat strikes a thousand joints [...]" [ll. 1922-1926]; cf. his essay of 1818, "Indecision and Surrender," where the same image—here deployed ironically—is used in an almost cosmic sense [Naydler, ed., 1996, pp. 98-100].) Finally, we find in Goethe's letter to Humboldt a description of the self that could easily be described as proto-Jungian, given its emphasis on the harmonious synthesis of consciousness and the unconscious: "By dint of practice, theory, reflection, encouragement, and resistance, and further and ever further reflection [*und immer wieder Nachdenken*] the human organs will unconsciously and in spontaneous action combine the acquired with the innate to produce a unity that is a wonder to mankind [*eine Einheit ... welche die Welt in Erstaunen setzt*]" (Goethe, 1962-1967, vol. 4, p. 480). This view of the self confirms the popular saying that "too many of us die at 30 but get buried at 80," which in turn restates the fundamental principle of Goethe's outlook, namely: that "the point of life is life."[25]

References

(a) Works by Jung (abbreviations)

BB = Jung, C.G. 2020. *The Black Books, 1913-1932: Notebooks of Transformation*. Edited by S. Shamdasani, trans. M. Liebscher, J. Peck, and S. Shamdasani. 7 vols. New York and London: Norton.

CW 7 = Jung, C.G. 1953. *Two Essays on Analytical Psychology* [*Collected Works*, vol. 7]. Trans. R.F.C. Hull. London and New York: Routledge.

CW 10 = Jung, C.G. 1970. *Civilization in Transition* [*Collected Works*, vol. 10]. Trans. R.F.C. Hull, 2nd edition. London and New York: Routledge.

CW 17 = Jung, C.G. 1954. *The Development of Personality* [*Collected Works*, vol. 17]. Trans. R.F.C. Hull. London and New York: Routledge.

CW 12 = Jung, C.G. 1968. *Psychology and Alchemy* [*Collected Works*, vol. 12]. Trans. R.F.C. Hull, 2nd edn. London: Routledge.

MDR = Jung, C.G. 1963. *Memories, Dreams, Reflections: Recorded and edited by Aniela Jaffé*. Translated by R. and C. Winston. London: Collins; Routledge & Kegan Paul.

RB = Jung, C.G. 2012. *The Red Book: Liber novus* [*A Reader's Edition*]. Edited by S. Shamdasani, trans. M. Kyburz, J. Peck, and S. Shamdasani. New York and London: Norton.

(b) Other works cited:

Agamben, G. (2020). Requiem for the Students. Available online <https://d-dean.medium.com/requiem-for-the-students-giorgio-agamben-866670c11642>.

Aristotle. (1984). *Complete Works*. Edited by J. Barnes, 2 vols. Princeton, NJ: Princeton University Press.

Arkin, A. M. (1949). A Short Note on Empedocles and Freud. *American Imago*, 6(3) (September), 197-203.

Armstrong, S. (2023). Profiting From Pandemic? Scottish Universities During COVID-19. Preprints 2023, 2023060832. https://doi.org/10.20944/preprints202306.0832.v1

Atkins, S. (Ed.). (1984). *J.W. Goethe: Faust I & II* [Goethes Collected Works, vol. 2]. Revised edn. Princeton, NJ: Princeton University Press.

BBC One Scotland (2020). *Disclosure*, "Covid on Campus"; broadcast on 19 October 2020.

Biedermann, W. (Ed.). (1909-1911). *Goethes Gespräche*. 5 vols. Leipzig: Biedermann.

Claudel, P. (1967). Œuvre *poétique*. Edited by Jacques Petit. Paris: Gallimard.

Damm, S. (1998). *Christiane und Goethe: Eine Recherche*. Frankfurt and Leipzig: Insel.

Dusini, Arno. 1998. "Leere und Todtenstille in und außer mir": Goethes Tagebuch zum 6. Juni 1816. *Germanisch-Romanische Monatsschrift*, 48(2), 165-178.

Eckermann, J.P. (1998). *Conversations of Goethe*. Trans. John Oxenford, ed. J.K. Moorhead. New York: Da Capo Press.

Ernest Jones, 1908-1939. Cambridge, MA; London: The Belknap Press of Harvard University Press.

Fairley, B. (1957). Goethe's Last Letter. *University of Toronto Quarterly*, 27(1) (October), 1-9.

Gaier, U. (1999). *Johann Wolfgang Goethe: Faust-Dichtungen*, vol. 2, *Kommentar I.* Stuttgart: Reclam.

Goethe, J.W. (1893). *Tagebücher*, vol. 5, *1813-1816 = Werke* [Sophien-Ausgabe], section III, vol. 5. Weimar: Böhlau.

Goethe, J.W. (1908). *Faust, Parts One and Two.* Trans. Albert G. Latham. London; New York: Dent; Dutton.

Goethe, J.W. (1962-1967). *Briefe.* Edited by K.R. Mandelkow. 4 vols. Hamburg: Wegner.

Hall, R., Gayle, D., and Quinn, B. (2020, 5 November). Manchester students pull down lockdown fences around halls of residence. *The Guardian.* Available online <https://www.theguardian.com/education/2020/nov/05/security-fence-manchester-university-student-flats >.

Halliday, J. (2020, 15 November). Manchester University suspends security guards after claims of racial profiling. *The Guardian.* Available online <https://www.theguardian.com/education/2020/nov/15/manchester-student-alleges-he-was-racially-profiled-by-security-guards >.

Hamlin, C. (Ed.) (2001). *Johann Wolfgang Goethe: Faust: A Tragedy* [*A Norton Critical Edition*]. 2nd edition. New York and London: Norton.

Hanegraaff, W.J. (2018). Rudolf Steiner und die hellsehende Einbildungskraft. In R. Steiner, *Schriften zur Anthopogenese und Kosmogonie* [*Schriften: Kritische Ausgabe*, ed. C. Clement, vol. 8] (pp. v-xviii). Stuttgart-Bad Cannstatt: frommann-holzboog.

Hennezel, M. de, and Vergely, B. (2010). *Une vie pour se mettre au monde.* Paris: Carnets Nord.

Jung, C.G. (2014). *Dream Interpretation Ancient & Modern: Notes from the Seminar Given in 1936–1941.* Ed. J. Peck, L. Jung, and M. Meyer-Grass, trans. E. Falzeder and T. Woolfson. Princeton, NJ, and Oxford: Princeton University Press.

Jung, C.G. (1973-1975). *Letters*. Edited by G. Adler and A. Jaffé, trans. R.F.C. Hull, 2 vols. Princeton, NJ: Princeton University Press.

Kingsley, P. (2018). *Catafalque: Carl Jung and the End of Humanity*. 2 vols. London: Catafalque Press.

Kohlschmidt, W. (1974). Faustens »Entelechie« — doch der Doctor Marianus? *Orbis Litterarum*, *29*(3) (September), 221-230.

Körner, J. (Ed.) (1936). *Krisenjahre der Frühromantik: Briefe aus dem Schlegelkreis*, 3 vols. Brünn: Rohrer.

Korrodi, E. (Ed.). (1944). *Goethe im Gespräch*. Zürich: Manesse.

Kreeft, P. (2018). *The Platonic Tradition*. South Bend, IN: St. Augustine's Press.

Lorck, C. von. (1936). Goethe und Lessings „ Klosterhof im Schnee". *Westdeutsches Jahrbuch* für *Kunstgeschichte: Wallraf-Richartz Jahrbuch*, *9*, 205-222.

McGuire, W., and Hull, R.F.C. (Eds). (1877). *C.G. Jung Speaking: Interviews and Encounters*. Princeton, NJ: Princeton University Press.

Oort, H. van (2011). *Anthroposophy A-Z: A Glossary of Terms Relating to Rudolf Steiner's Spiritual Philosophy*. Forest Row: Sophia Books.

Paskauskas, A. (Ed.) (1993). *The Complete Correspondence of Sigmund Freud and Ernest Jones 1908 - 1939*. Cambridge, MA: Belknap Press of Harvard University Press.

Schiller, F./Goethe, J.W. (1990). *Briefwechsel zwischen Schiller und Goethe in den Jahren 1794 bis 1805*. Edited by M. Beetz. 2 vols. Munich and Vienna: Hanser.

Schmidt, Dennis J. (2006). "What We Owe the Dead," in *Heidegger and the Greeks: Interpretive Essays*. Ed. Drew A. Hyland

and John Panteleimon Manoussakis. Bloomington and Indianapolis: Indiana University Press, pp. 111-126.

Schöne, A. (2005). *Johann Wolfgang Goethe: Faust: Kommentare.* Frankfurt am Main: Deutscher Klassiker Verlag.

Seppänen, L. (1983). Goethe und seine *Entelecheia. Neuphilologische Mitteilungen*, 84(1), 126-131.

Steiger, R. (Ed.) (1982-1996). *Goethes Leben von Tag zu Tag: Eine dokumentarische Chronik*, 8 vols. Zürich: Artemis Verlag.

Steiner, R. (1982). *Geisteswissenschaftliche Erläuterungen zu Goethes «Faust»*, 2 vols. Dornach: Rudolf Steiner Verlag.

Theophanidis, P. (2020). Giorgio Agamben and the coronavirus pandemic: interventions. Available online <https://aphelis. net/agamben-coronavirus-pandemic-interventions/> [Updated 13.04.2022].

Tourney, G. (1956). Empedocles and Freud, Heraclitus and Jung. *Bulletin of the History of Medicine*, *30*(2) (March-April), 109-123.

Wulf, A. (2022). *Magnificent Rebels: The First Romantics and the Invention of the Self.* London: John Murray.

Death's Cartography:
"Ours is a flame but borrow'd thence to light us thither"
(Herbert)

Josephine Evetts-Secker

Necessarily, this must be a very personal narrative, celebrating the fact that the only way I could come to where I am now is the way I have come. Let me say at the outset that in all my living, I have never been without the sense that "something else is going on." I could be no more specific. So where am I now?

A few months ago, standing between my son and my daughter, we lowered my husband of 53 years into the earth, in a burial site chosen by him just over the road from our home of 26 years in a small English village. A recording of a Haydn sonata was amplified in the churchyard, played on a fortepiano John had made for the player in his workshop nearby. Haydn saw him to his rest, music that had thrilled and consoled him especially since he became an instrument maker.

What follows holds in the background Jung's surprising description of death as "that unproblematical ending of individual existence" (Jung, 1934, Vol. 8 §796) and the ensuing remark that he was "astonished to see how little ado the unconscious psyche makes of death" (Ibid. §809). Though this paper and my life make much ado about death, I can also entertain Jung's understatement as true.

As an Anglican priest, I have presided at dozens of funerals and am very familiar with that arresting moment, when standing at the graveside, often with weeping families, saying the last blessing and feeling the resonance of those ancient words, so stark and yet consoling: "Dust into dust; ashes into ashes." These follow the words of committal: "Our days are like the grass; we flourish like a flower of the field; when the wind goes over it, it is gone and its place will know it no more." And then the final prayer: "Support us O Lord all the days of this troublous life, until the shadows lengthen and the evening comes, the busy world is hushed and the fever of life is over and our work is done. Then Lord in your mercy grant us a safe lodging, a holy rest and peace at the last" (Anglican Funeral Liturgy). In this last rite at the graveside, I have known, feelingly, that at some not-too-distant point in time I will be the one in the coffin.

Since my teenage years, Christian faith has always been in the background, sometimes in the foreground, of my living. It was relinquished during years of discovering Jung and training as an analyst, though I knew there would be a day reckoning, exploring my own relationship between analytical psychology and a more mature religious faith. One of the greatest gifts I derived from Jung is the core understanding of the both-and, with its release from "either-or" propositions. Release from "nothing-but" thinking. In more recent years, this has been richly supported by my layman encounter with quantum insights that reload those humble conjunctions, "and" and "but," extending into "but also" and "and yet." This move amplified psychologically is echoed for me in quantum thinking. Light is not either a wave or a particle, but it can be both wave and particle. In a lecture, the physicist Paul Dirac reputedly put a piece of chalk in one place and another at another place. In the everyday world, a piece of chalk is *here,* and a piece of chalk is *there*, he said. "But in the quantum world, the chalk is *partly* here and partly there. It's elsewhere too. Probably" (Nelson & Giberson, 2011, p.103).

In these troubling times, with the Israeli-Palestinian conflict raging, this capacity for duality both-and thinking and feeling, is a necessary political tension, more easily theorized than lived in the mixed emotional turmoil of our watching and witnessing world. But resistance to forced binary sympathies is vital to any possibility of a peaceful future.

Religious faith and analytical psychology offered me an "in between" space that I have inhabited with its inherent and fruitful tensions. It is my transitional space where I play most seriously. Under a different rubric these two fields entered my inner world through poetry. In a typical English grammar school education, I grew up with Shakespeare, and through subliminal paths, death entered my soul. Two soul-musings in particular held me: two young men in crisis. First, Hamlet, contemplating death by suicide:

To be, or not to be, that is the question:
Whether 'tis nobler in the mind to suffer
The slings and arrows of outrageous fortune,
Or to take arms against a sea of troubles
And by opposing end them. To die—to sleep,
No more; and by a sleep to say we end
The heart-ache and the thousand natural shocks
That flesh is heir to: 'tis a consummation
Devoutly to be wish'd. To die, to sleep;
To sleep, perchance to dream—ay, there's the rub:
For in that sleep of death what dreams may come,
When we have shuffled off this mortal coil ... (Act 3. Sc. 1)

The quandary debated in this soliloquy must surely be ours too at some point in life, literally or symbolically, the moment of crisis in which we must choose life. This existential dilemma is sometimes brought into therapy. Then, the therapist's dilemma ... to say or not to say ... what? At such times, Hillman's *Suicide and the Soul* offered support, (Hillman, 1964) a common experience of encouragement in the Jungian community, often felt through our shared literature. This is one of so many forms of suffering that come to us every day, reminding us of one principal aim of our therapy, "to help ... acquire steadfastness and philosophic patience in face of suffering" (Jung, 1943 §185). Much is expected of us, and we sometimes expect too much of ourselves in these inscrutable territories of heart and mind. In our helplessness, we can be helped by Jung's precious reminder that "we are always human and we should never forget that we carry the whole burden of being only human" (Jung, 1935, §169). I take heed of this limitation. It is at such times that we need to be in touch with our own deepest intimations about death. There is no faking fortitude or resolution. It can help to share realistic anticipation of actual death. For me there is no more compelling confrontation with death than the lusty Claudio, imprisoned and awaiting execution for getting his beloved "with child" in Shakespeare's *Measure for Measure*, a play about mercy and justice. Having been challenged by the Duke, disguised as a Friar, to "be absolute for death," Claudio responds with searing realism:

> Ay, but to die, and go we know not where;
> To lie in cold obstruction and to rot;
> This sensible warm motion to become
> A kneaded clod; and the delighted spirit
> To bathe in fiery floods, or to reside
> In thrilling region of thick-ribbed ice;
> To be imprisoned in the viewless winds,
> And blown with restless violence round about
> The pendent world.   (Act. 3. Sc.1)

Aye, but to die! How that resonates. Shakespeare never averted his eyes! Nor must I. It fascinated me that Hamlet was a young man attuned to the life of the mind, to philosophical reflection, to conscience and consciousness, while Claudio was drawn to the life of the flesh and instinct, more preoccupied with his body's fate. So differently might death be approached.

Shakespeare's drama, especially the tragedies, not only began my schooling in death and in depth, but also comforted me with its challenges. In one way or another, we are all offered such a challenge, to face or to turn away, to choose whether or how to respond. Freud suggested that the encounter with and acceptance of death was one goal of analysis. This has been my experience, however expressed and lived by typical analysands navigating the second half of life. Sometimes, and certainly for me, it is shaped in natural imagery of aging as with Wordsworth's

> The Clouds that gather round the setting sun
> Do take a sober colouring from an eye
> That hath kept watch o'er man's mortality; …
> Thanks to the human heart by which we live,
> Thanks to its tenderness, its joys, and fears,
> To me the meanest flower that blows can give
> Thoughts that do often lie too deep for tears. (Ode)

Such thoughts, in such words, entered my soul as a student in the first half of life and prepared me, without my awareness, for maturing life that ensued. It became more fully conscious as I traced Jung's own reflecting paths and shared in them.

For me, this felt emotion relates intimately with Jung's metaphor of the sun's passage in his musing on "The Stages of Life." Though this is a familiar topos, Jung gives it freshness, minted from his therapeutic praxis.

In the morning it rises from the nocturnal sea of unconsciousness and looks upon the wide, bright world which lies before it in an expanse that steadily widens the higher it comes in the firmament. In this extension of its field of action caused by its own rising, the sun will discover its significance; it will see the attainment of the greatest possible height, and the widest possible dissemination of its blessings, as its goal. ... at the stroke of noon the descent begins. And the descent means the reversal of all the ideals and values that were cherished in the morning. The sun falls into contradiction with itself. It is as though it should draw in its rays instead of emitting them. Light and warmth decline and are at last extinguished, (Jung, 1930/1, §778)

Body and mind change, they age and must find new energy centers and outlets. In such a context, how inappropriate the heroic "rage against the dying of the light," so positively engaged by those resistant to the required sacrifices and willingness to "decline" in significant ways. Always in touch with natural cycles in the world around me, I am attuned to Jung's concern with clinging to attitudes and living life "out of season." We watch the seasons of the soul used in complementary and contrapuntal ways in dream, as in a hot July, dreaming of going to teach a summer course along roads that were snowy and icy.

The medieval and early Renaissance topos of the candle also moved me on my first encounter with it, compelling the acceptance that I began to die at my birth. Death comes with life, part of what Jung sees as a larger self-regulating system. I was born into paradox and have lived in the tension between the two opposites. Our human predicament is visualized starkly in Francis Quarles' images, which I discovered when I was working on emblem literature as a young academic (1638). The emblems depict graphically the passage from when the light of life is first given, as soon as the candle is lit, it begins to burn and to burn down through old age to its extinguishing. Time comes with life, *Tempus erit* until the stage, *Invidiosa senectus.*

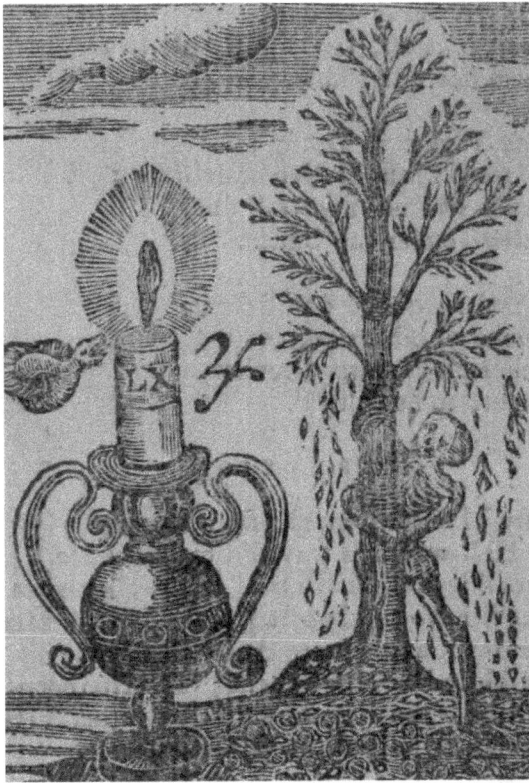

We live this natural cycle, falling from the tree of life like autumn leaves. This came to me in poetry and image with a peace that shocked me even as it consoled, assuring me of something Jung later impressed on me, that "natural life is the nourishing soil of the soul" (Jung, 1934, §800).

Death continued to school me through my increasing experience of poetic word and image, and my growing experience of the reality of psyche. I had to reconcile this with the excitement and richness that life was throwing my way! The interrogation of death's meaning and reality persisted and persists, with the acceptance that I will not be physically conscious when the final answer is met.

As an analyst, as I accompany men and women analysands as they become conscious of their inner life and make space for the engagement with mortality, all my experience gathers, impelling me to ask more formally, then, what is death, mysteriously not life's end but life's ending, a process not an event?

Death has always been inwardly alive in me, though my earliest contact was distant and public. I lost no one in the war (World War II) into which I was born. Death came in numbers I couldn't grasp, announced on the radio ... the wireless that seemed always to be on ... with solemn voices accounting the war dead. I recall that when someone on the street died, all neighbors' curtains were closed and all came out on the road as the hearse passed by, with bowed heads and in a large silence. I experienced no personal loss till adulthood, three grandparents dying (or disappearing) before I was born. I remember vividly the annual November 11 Service of Remembrance of the war dead at the civic cenotaph, the alarming and inchoately moving bugle's Last Post and the laying of wreaths, an impressive collective ritual. That was the impersonal background against which I began to shape my personal drama of life and death. How different that is now, today, as the horror of death rages in the Middle East and Ukraine and the appalling numbers register daily with global and personal impact, all graphically near in television images of bloody faces and torn bodies. War dead are no longer distant and public. The horror and

the pain are brought into analysis by distressed analysands who
may have fewer ways of dealing with the enormity of it all, for
them and for humanity. Fight or flight feels irrelevant. We are
helpless spectators, witnesses. There is nothing to be done; there is
no comforting. Sometimes it seems that all that is possible is simply
bringing the trauma into the safe analytical space and sharing our
grieving. All that can be done, all that can happen, is the conscious
willingness to be compassionately aware and to hold as much of
the tension between such appalling opposites as is possible. At such
times, it feels crucial to be honest about my own relationship to
the trauma and my own dealing with a kind of vicarious survivor's
guilt and my most personal relationship with those large verities.
Integrity in depth! Jung suffered the pangs of what he thought of
as "civilization in transition" among his exploratory reflections
on current contemporary events, acknowledging, that his "souls
shrinks," at realizing "all that man is capable of." Since that includes
us all, so with Jung we harbor "a terrible doubt about humanity …
[which]gnaws at our hearts" (Jung, 1946, p. 177).

These current wars in Ukraine and Gaza confronting us
with unbearable and graphic experiences of death follow two years
of pandemic deaths, close to us wherever we were. The major
trauma for most people affected was the fact that we could not be
with loved ones to accompany and comfort them in their dying,
neither could we perform those necessary rites of ending, funerals
and ceremonies of farewell, shared with the community of family
and friends. Burial rites are ancient and considered essential for
the deceased as well as for those who mourn. The denial of that
full experience wounded individuals and communities. Many
people were able to imagine and create their own unique rituals
of farewell, but more were left feeling that the dead had not been
honored and are left with grief, unhealed and unable properly to

mourn. Personally and collectively, these felt like dark Antigone times!

One troubling reality in all this is the dreadful truth that not all are fortunate or rich enough to die old; so many die young in poverty and needless sickness, not only in Third World countries and many die prematurely in natural disasters. Currently, in the Middle East, Ukraine, and elsewhere, thousands of lives are being cut short by violence of war and human evil. All of this confronts me with an urgency that sometimes makes my concern with individuation feel like an intolerable luxury. Then my own trust in psyche and soul is put to the test and the validity of convictions about the necessity, the potency, and viability of grain by grain of consciousness, willingly borne, as gift to humanity, can have its own efficacy. Then I feel challenged by Jung's insistence that if we dare embark on the path of individuation, we must atone for our betrayal, or at least our neglect, of convention and collective conformity. The ransom he claims that must be paid is the creation of "values which are an equivalent substitute for his absence in the collective sphere" (Jung, 1916, §1094ff). As one knows death draws nearer, one cannot and must not avoid this examination of one's own life, how it has been used and perhaps abused. As parent, as child and sibling, as friend, therapist and as priest, I hope that I have given back something of what was given to me and can perhaps rest in that hope. I pondered this challenge after a dream that has not lost its immediacy. I was simply aware of "two rocks, knowing them simply and starkly as a rock of doing and a rock of being." This was followed by an experience of people dying. The accounting that challenged me had nothing to do with conventional Christian judgment, about sin. It was a deeper, wider, and more subtle acknowledgement of my individual failures and darkness.

Yet I trust that enoughness is enough and find peace in a good enough life.

Traditional pictures of eternal life were always alien to me; they could not touch me, never becoming part of my Christian belief system. The traditional heaven did not inspire or beckon, which I had to interrogate as a priest conducting funerals where I must attend to the needs of traditional believers who wanted the comforting picture of Heaven awaiting the lost loved one and awaiting them. Yet I commit with deep feeling to the words of the liturgy that I have pronounced so many times on entering the church with the coffin, bringing the deceased to a final farewell. "O death, where is your victory. Where O death is your sting?" Followed by Christ's acclamation, "I am the resurrection and the life!" Resurrection is not resuscitation, and whatever resurrection might be, it will be wholly other, another, creation that cannot yet be known. I have lost, or am losing, my need for certainties, in sympathy with Polanyi's "unbridled lucidity" and Jung's advocacy of equivocation.

Awareness of ancestors is almost palpable in a village church where baptisms, marriages, and deaths have been celebrated for centuries, many forebears of current villagers. My husband chose his own gravesite in the older part of the churchyard, among "the old fellas." His nearest neighbors got there at least 200 years before him. Born in Holland and having lived long in Canada, he was no local. But he had a profound sense of belonging here, in this church, in this place, rich with Anglo-Saxon stones, near to the ruined abbey where Caedmon, first poet recorded in English, wrote his seventh-century hymn. We had shared the elegiac spirit of the wanderers and seafarers with their felt awareness that "lif is laene" (life is lean, i.e., transitory).

I have always been attracted to such places of the dead. Even as a young girl, I remember climbing over the not-very-high wall to get into a large urban cemetery and spending hours there. I loved the wildflowers that seeded around the edges and I was enchanted by the masses of flowers on graves. Climbing over the wall, rather than entering through the open gate, must reflect some vague sense of guilt, for I couldn't resist redistributing the flowers. It seemed so "unfair" to me that some graves had plenty and some were bare. I wasn't aware of actual wrongdoing, but I did behave furtively. I had some inchoate feeling of connection, communion with the dead strangers in the earth beneath me, whose names I read engraved in stone.

Once I was exposed to theological formulations, I was impressed by the doctrine of the mystical body and the communion of saints. This charge stayed with me and associated quite easily with emergent thinking about collective unconsciousness when I encountered it and began to explore its depths. The phrase "collective unconscious" always felt clinically cold to me, not eliciting the felt reality of universal community in depth, outside of time and space. I always felt comfortable burying the dead, especially where the ancestors were literally personal as well as symbolically collective. As I have conducted these rites, I have known myself part of humanity, if only as a grain of its consciousness. Since no one was prepared to provide a humanist to bury my atheist, absent father, I officiated at his cremation. As he was the notoriously black sheep of his family, I could only feel compassion that he had carried his family's huge shadow in a rather righteous socialist environment. I could not let him carry all of that into the flames, and needs must own my dark share of it. I smuggled God into the event with a recording of Handel's aria, "He shall feed his sheep like a shepherd," which led into God's calling all of mankind, "come unto me all ye who

labour and I will give you rest" (*Messiah*). It was the first of what
was to be a frequent experience as a priest, but it was the first time
I depressed the red button that took the coffin into the fires. There
is no escaping the reality of death at such a moment. The committal
of a father was nevertheless an existential jolt, with a faint miasma
of patricide!

I resonated richly with Hillman's remarks when articulating
"the lament of the dead" that he sustained some contact with dead
writers through footnotes, for me a vibrant recognition.

> … one of the reasons why I like to put scholarly
> footnotes, which seems almost irrelevant, is that I
> know if I don't bring it in here, no one will ever
> remember or pay attention to it. it's the only way
> to keep the dead. For me, the dead are very often
> what's gone before in the field, and these dead are
> remembered, because I've remembered to bring
> them back. … (Hillman, 2013, p. 187)

Contact with earth's ancestors (even the 2-million-year-old man in
us all) links us beyond the grave. We know its continuing activity
in our dreams, our myths, and our symptoms.

In contrast to my own impersonal and distant first
experience of death, my children's first loss was their beloved
elkhound. They dug the grave and scratched "Goodbye old Pal"
on a rock at the site of burial. Their love and their sorrow were
utterly pure. I was reminded of a poem for children, "Burying the
dog in the garden," (Patten) in which a miserable neighbor over the
fence told the children who were burying their dog that animals
didn't go to heaven. They were outraged at the very thought of
having "nothing to stroke for eternity" and decided that they didn't

want to go to heaven. They surely touched an archaic emotional truth. Our relationship to animals as sentient creatures has always been important, carrying our animal selves. Fairy tales, myths, and dreams metamorphose between animal and human selves, often revealing how animals carry our projections, which we must withdraw to carry our own animal nature, as psyche requires.

Clearly the question "What is death?" has never not been there for me. A physicist (who worked with a Nobel Prize-winning team researching the quantum world) left academia to become a priest. He was asked constantly why we must die. He replied that from a physics standpoint, death exists because of the second law of thermodynamics, which says everything heads inexorably downhill and ultimately to some kind of destruction. So, man must accept that death must make space for the continuing generation of life through the eons of evolutionary process. But his theological response affirmed that "God's final intention is the new creation drawn freely into such close connection with its Creator" that its "matter," "suffused with the direct presence of a God no longer veiled, will permit the everlasting process of eternal life" (Nelson & Giberson, 2011, p.153). At times the dialogue between priest and physicist within John Polkinghorne's thinking reminds me of that between Jung and Pauli. Psyche, soul, and science cohere.

Given the inexorable reality of death, which became for me an increasingly felt reality even before I started to experience the death of people who mattered to me, I of course had also to interrogate the alternative to mortality. Once again schooled by poetry, I was challenged by Tennyson's dramatic monologue "Tithonus." A mere mortal, Tithonus, fell in love with the goddess of the dawn, and immortality was bestowed on him by the gods so that they might unite. But as Tithonus aged, Aurora returned each morning, renewed in eternal youth. He agonizes at his condition,

"Immortal age beside immortal youth." His lament opens in melancholy mood:

> The woods decay, the woods decay and fall,
> The vapours weep their burthen to the ground,
> Man comes and tills the field and lies beneath,
> And after many a summer dies the swan.
> Me only cruel immortality
> Consumes;

What a gripping thought, to be consumed by "cruel" immortality! Knowing that "the Gods themselves cannot recall their gifts," Tithonus grows envious "Of happy men that have the power to die,/ And grassy barrows of the happier dead." What shocked and delighted me then were those words, "happy men that have the power to die." What a realization! This introduced into my soul a kind of existential itch that persists. It lives on in me at the graveside, in the contrapuntal beauty of "our days are as the grass" being followed by the knowledge that something unknown must follow on, come after. This experience always brings with it Wordsworthian "thoughts that do often lie too deep for tears" (Ode). Never dying becomes deadly. The value and beauty of transience is overwhelming, for me making horrific the very thought and sight of artificial flowers.

Reading Hillman's *The Souls Code* brought vividly to mind a girlhood experience that is oddly pertinent to these reflections (Hillman, 1996). The mature personality, Hillman suggests, is already present *in nuce* in early life, in some particular experience that is remembered with particular efficacy. This for me was the moment when I first really knew that "something else was going on," mysteriously and incomprehensibly beyond me. Sitting in the middle of a meadow around the age of 10, I was so overwhelmed with the beauty—or whatever it was—around me and with a profound inexplicable sense of being given something momentous, I wanted to express—whatever it might be—gratitude or wonder—whatever "It" was. I responded with the thought that I would count the blades of grass around me to register my "appreciation." I could not have described it at the time, of course. I had no language or categories with which to contain it, but I later realized that in Jung's sense of the religious experience, I was relating to something transcendent, awesome, and infinite, so beyond me that I could scarcely breathe with its enormity. I had a sense of another world, another dimension somehow interfused with the green grass in which I was sitting. That unformulable past experience came vividly to mind when in later years I encountered Polanyi's thinking about a "tacit dimension" (Polanyi, 1966). In my other language, it was an apprehension of sheer grace. The 17th century for me later became a spiritual home where such intuitions were illuminated; these yearnings and excitements were intellectual emotions that I shared. Henry Vaughan often catches me, as in his elegiac lyric "They have all gone into the world of light/ And I alone sit lingering here ..." The final lines retain the same charge for me today as when I first met them:

> And yet as angels in some brighter dreams
> Call to the soul, when man doth sleep:
> So some strange thoughts transcend our wonted themes
> And into glory peep (Vaughan).

A "peep" seems often to be our allotted portion! A glimpse is good enough; it is always enough. Jung's recognition and empathic insight into the phenomenon of the numinous, especially experienced in dreams, opened up for me so much inner territory of soul. It remained a useful and enriching model, our commerce with the "ganz andere." This in turn influenced my reading of biblical literature.

There are moments in life and in analysis, one's own and that of one's analysand, when one experiences what I can only name "sheer grace." Jung quite often mentions "divine grâce" without ever elaborating what it is. He calls upon it in a rather "it goes without saying" kind of way. But it is always in the context of enabling. It feels mysterious, can feel miraculous, always unsought, unwilled, unpredictable, unknowable, empowering, ennobling even. A *je ne sais quoi* energy that can feel pneumatic. Gracious, feels like a gift. One is left feeling awe and gratitude and surprise. Something moves, something happens, feeling accidental—even supernatural. Sometimes it happens in the field of synchronicity. It can appear like a meeting of Hermes with the Paraclete, acceding to both models. It heals contradiction and impossibility and like "the wind it bloweth where it listeth and is seen no more" (John 3.8). It fulfills a need of which one is usually unaware and often activates the dynamic of transformation. I experience it often in the field of the transcendent function, where it holds but transforms opposites. I am left with a feeling of something "other than"— sometimes fully *ganz andere*. I intuit this as a kind of visitation, a fresh "signal of transcendence," as Peter Berger so aptly heralds it. He speaks of phenomena experienced within our "natural" reality that point beyond that reality (Berger, p.59). For me it has a whiff of the sacred. All this I intuit in relation to death and its beyond.

It is obvious from what I have written so far that language has been a medium through which I have lived and live my life. It is not surprising therefore that I found such a fellow soul in George Steiner, who sees us as a "short-lived mammal made for extinction," but he argues that "we are a *language*-animal, and it is this one endowment more than any other, makes bearable and fruitful our ephemeral state" (Steiner, p.85). I once dreamed about discussing tenses with my analyst, complementing conscious experiences. I marveled, as I am sure Jung would have done, in considering the evolution of our speech, the amazing grammatical phenomena that serve us, "subjunctives, optatives, counter-factual conditionals and of the futurities of the verb" (ibid). These kinds of linguistic maneuvers allow us to tell our stories, even about a thousand-year future, or as I ponder death's time map, the fact that I can imagine the very morning after my death. I can begin even to imagine a world without me in it. This fictive human gift enables us to "deny, reconstruct, alter, past, present and future mapping otherwise the determinants of pragmatic reality." Such an endowment ensures that our lives are "worth experiencing." Death is part of such language and imagination mapping.

One massive gift that came with my discovery of Jung's map of the soul was the 'undoing,' as it were, of Weber's premise of the disenchantment of the world. For me the inner world was freshly re-enchanted through embrace of Psyche. Jung opened the door to the wonder of consciousness, entry into archetypal world of myth and dream. Weber diagnosed the "eclipse of magical and animistic views of nature, following the rationalization that disinherits modernity and uprooted us from a sacred context for thinking about the world" (Weber, 1919). One aspect of this renewed enchantment was openness to dreamlife, alarming and satisfying by turns. I remember keenly a dream that was simply a statement when my children left home for university. It was simply, "Now I can get on with the age-old business of dying." Almost banal but invigorating and big! Interestingly, the dream was a bald statement, I simply *heard it written*. I didn't see words, but the hearing was somehow the writing. My experience echoes Jung's in experiencing spoken words in dreams as having particular significance. There was no image, but inevitably, images came!

Dream:

> ... I am being executed. I am in a cell ... it's bright, light ... white walls. I can choose the method execution. Electric chair, hanging, guillotine or a poison capsule. I decide on the capsule. It is all horrific and terrifying but also quite calm. X is there, vaguely with me. There is no sense of an ending. It was painful and comforting. I knew then that one could only really discover one's ultimate reality (shorthand for 'it') if one was awaiting execution, only before death, only in dying can one know this is it, this, alone, is me. Everything else, adaptations, and needs and love and constraints interfere with one's being.

On waking, I was aware of a newsflash from the night before ... a fleet of whales were beached off the Tasmanian coast. (X's home) They could not get back to the sea and officials decided to shoot them. I heard a biologist say that shooting them was the easy way out. Then, I flash to the idiom, 'biting the bullet.' All of this was painfully complicated, but oddly enlivening. It left me wondering whether in some strange symbolic way, we choose the way we die, unconsciously choreographing our ending, while living.

Frank Kermode's exploration of our experience of endings affected me significantly. He stirred an arresting sense of inner and outer time. In the background to his work and to our lives is the sound of the clock ... maybe I should now say *used to be* ... the regular tick-tock of the clock, now digitalized and so depriving us of this ancient rhythm of measurement. He suggests that "tick is a humble genesis, tock a feeble apocalypse" that gives force to "humanly uninteresting successiveness" (Kermode, p.45). While this is happening, constantly, he sees us "remain in the middest. ... the future moves in on us." We are always *in medias res*. I know of no more compelling drama of the clock ticking life away than in a 17th century drama of *Doctor Faustus* (Marlowe, 1631). Faustus' bargain with Mephistopheles cannot be revoked. He waits for the final severance from life, a trauma magnified by the ticking of the clock and the striking of the hours, resounding agonizingly in theatrical performance.

> O Faustus
> Now hast thou but one bare hour to live,
> And then thou must be damned perpetually.
> Stand still, you ever-moving spheres of heaven,
> That time may cease and midnight never come.
> *The watch strikes.*

> O, half the hour is past! 'Twill all be past anon.

Like Tithonus he has to face eternal time but as a damned human, wishing for escape from his knowing of time. If metempsychosis were true, he groans, then

> This soul should fly from me, and I be changed
> Into some brutish beast.
> All beasts are happy, for when they die,
> Their souls are happy, dissolved in elements (Act 5. Sc.2).

Then the clock strikes midnight, signifying his hope-less end, the last tock in his last scene of his last earthly act.

Time can be torture for the bereaved who must look forward to a future without the one lost to time. It is most apt, then, that a poet's lament at the death of a loved friend begins, "Stop all the clocks!" for "nothing now can ever come to any good" (Auden). This is a wound that has to heal in the process of mourning. For me in mine, words by a spouse for the lost partner suffices: "meanwhile thou hast [him] earth" (King, 1624).

The 'sense of an ending' that Kermode intuits in daily life subsequently percolated through my consciousness as I lived the tick-tock. This feels implicated in the business of meaning and purpose. What is life for? If it's going to end, why live it, we might well ask. Why surrender to a gripping novel if we know that it is going to end? Why suspend disbelief and sit through a play, knowing that it too will end. It will stop. In every ending we may be unconsciously aware of the final end. There is a sense of this as the analytical hour draws to its end. I felt this urgently working with an analyst who had a clock with Westminster chimes in the room. My emotion heightened at the three-quarter chime, ending was imminent, then irrevocable. How many analysands recall and blurt out a core issue resisted during the hour, only at its ending.

In these ways we are rehearsing the structure and the emotion of our dying. Surely there is some tantalizing delight in that eschatological intuition. Behind this haunts the eternal question, why live if we must die? Here I resonate with Jung's insistence on meaning, the element that makes life worth living and living healthily. He claims that without meaning, we become sick. Life has to mean something if it is to matter, and be not merely "full of sound and fury, signifying nothing."

The fictive powers that play with time celebrated by Steiner are active in the unconscious, most dynamically in our dreaming. Through this medium, our life's work and our death-work are revealed and enacted. In unconsciousness, we are released from the boundaries of time, place and space and can flourish in the quantum world of non-locality. But also, paradoxically, in absolute locality. In my last dream, I quoted the amplificatory site of Tasmania, which at that very time was crucial.

I can and do dream of deceased figures from the past, with whom there remains unfinished business. There is anger to be acknowledged, even expressed, perhaps envy to be recognized, hatred even, confrontations from outside of time. The process of withdrawing projections goes on in inner chambers of the soul. The dead live on in me. Some most healing encounters in which the hitherto unspoken can be expressed. One such powerful and recurrent dream meeting has been with someone from my youth who had been of tremendous help to me. In dream I met and was able to thank him for all he gave to me those many years ago when I would not have been able to articulate what his gift was. So our understanding of past selves goes on, with healing efficacy. No doubt this will go on until it ends in death, past deceased figures presenting unfinished business that still await completion. And strangers yet unmet. Making peace with those whom I could not be at peace in life because of my own or their issues. This was, is, especially powerful in relation to primary and primordial archetypal relationships, my own and in my analysands' experience. With a history of a very difficult relationship with my mother, I was able to spend hours with her in hospital before her sudden death. I was left with a bereft sense of never having known who she was and now it was too late. I had only the vaguest idea of her deprived childhood and early work life in service as a housemaid in the 1930's. Then I dreamed:

… seeing myself on the slab in a mortuary. I am killed, shot through the head. I am dead. I know I am dead but I am amazed that I can still be aware. Men come to take my body to a morgue. I am put on a stretcher, covered by a white sheet, strapped on and carried off. I am dead, but I am content and curious. Then they hose down my corpse, to wash it. It is cold water, a fast jet. It's like being on a powerful water-chute. I am carried by the gushing water … it is invigorating and exhilarating. I am jubilant. I have a strong feeling that "now I will know," I think, "This isn't a dream. This is it." Then I realize that before I can experience full rest, I must experience my mother's life. I am dead but I can experience her body, as a child, and feel her life. I am a child in a large kitchen. Everyone is in Edwardian dress. I am being pushed around and told off, not physically abused but taken advantage of by everyone. I'm chopping herbs on a wooden table. Mint, perhaps. It feels good, smells good. Then I have to re-experience my own childhood. I am me, as a child and I still know that I am dead. It is very different but it feels exactly the same. But I want to be dead and rest. Then I have to experience my daughter's life. It is very different but I can't remember it. I now know that I can be thoroughly dead. I am excited. But then I realize that I have to be born again. I have to be alive again. I am shattered. I want to stay dead. To rest. I come alive. Then I am in Zürich finishing my training. Everything is difficult at a practical level but I know that things can never be the same because

I have experienced death. I have a sense that my life in Zürich is fed by the River Liffey.

The dream tasks continue, history being alive and revised.

> … As we bury my mother she stirs in her coffin and begins to come alive. I am stunned, but time goes on reversing … she comes alive and ages backwards, getting younger and younger. It becomes awesome because she's gone back even beyond conception, almost to mere protoplasm. No more. I am left with a disturbingly odd sense of undoing history.

Jung commented that women extend backwards to mother and forwards to her daughter, the succession of feminine generation. It can be vital to heal the past to ensure the health of the future. Jung's commitment to the primacy of the value of meaning heightened my response to such apprehensions as Polanyi's to the whole reality of existence, even down to the ultimate atom. He suggested that "even protozoa have the faculty of learning; they respond to potential meaning" (Polanyi, p. 91).

So we sustain the link with life before birth and life beyond the grave, continuing to encounter people who still enter dreamlife, asking for attention. I am inclined to replace the word 'confrontation' with 'engagement' which for me feels more appropriate. But I have entered into confrontation, directly, in dreams.

> I know that I am 53 years old, but I've died at the age of 31. After death I'm aware that I'm still conscious in exactly the same way as before death. Central to my awareness is that 31 is very young to die. 53

would be more acceptable. I'm arguing with God,
though God is a huge awareness that I'm both part
of and apart from. I'm arguing that 31 is too young,
though my present age would be more appropriate
for death. The numbers were very important.

Such bargaining energy accompanied me into consciousness,
energizing my sense of lived life. But I had a keener sense of
confrontation in another dream.

I am at several funerals, but all I remember
experiencing were the corpses, heavy and waxen
and somehow luminous … transcendent. Lots more
happening but all that came with me from sleep
was a sense of evil, cruelty, power, darkness … all
somehow embodied in a huge, towering figure … I
can't really say, man. I am raised up somehow and
feel face-to-face with 'its' head. Aware of frightening
massiveness. What is most vivid is not even the
encounter with this figure but the complexity of
my experience 'exiting' the dream. By waking up,
I could escape. Then, partly conscious, a powerful
knowing that I had to go back and deal with 'him.'
He was, in some sense, death, but that felt secondary
to something larger and more paradoxical.

In both of the last two dreams I had a sense of my rather arrogant
'taking God on,' like Abraham (Genesis 18) bargaining for more
mercy for the sinful men of Sodom. But I was also aware of Isaiah's
experience of invitation to having it out with God: "Come let us

reason together, says the Lord" (Isaiah 1.18). I have often felt it necessary to do just this in dream and in waking.

Early Renaissance devotional literature cultivated the *ars moriendi*, the art of dying. Jeremy Taylor's resonant prose advocated the art of dying *well* (Taylor, 1650). Was there a choice in how one dealt with death, at least developing an attitude even if the hour and the place and the manner of death was out of my hands? Some years ago, I had an amazing experience of someone dying well. Having been called to say goodbye to an aged analyst with an indomitable spirit, I spent several hours reading poetry to her. She chose the poems and I found and read them aloud to her from her own library, all works that she had delighted in her rich literary life. At the end of the day, knowing her aversion to organized religion, I told her that I was going to read a Christian poem by an Anglican priest-poet. I knew that it was one of the divine poems unfamiliar to her. I had always been as unimpressed as she was by pious pictures of angels sitting on clouds with heavenly orchestra or choir. But in a poem in preparation for death, Donne's image was bolder. He imagines lying on his death bed attended by his physicians. In his dying body, they were searching for his south-west passage, straits … we might say symptoms … through which he must pass to death (Donne). He imagines his state of dying as being held in a waiting room, where he must tune his instrument so that the music will be in tune, in anticipation that he himself will become the music.

> Since I am coming to that holy room,
>> Where, with thy choir of saints for evermore,
> I shall be made thy music; as I come
>> I tune the instrument here at the door,
>> And what I must do then, think here before.

The idea of becoming music of the spheres touched us both; not the instrument or the player, but the sound, the music itself. Being an intrepid discoverer of psyche's depths, the cartographic image and the geo-enantiodromic fantasy delighted her.

> Whilst my physicians by their love are grown
> Cosmographers, and I their map, who lie
> Flat on this bed, that by them may be shown
> That this is my south-west discovery,
> *Per fretum febris*, by these straits to die,
>
> I joy, that in these straits I see my west;
> For, though their currents yield return to none,
> What shall my west hurt me? As west and east
> In all flat maps (and I am one) are one,
> So death doth touch the resurrection.

She listened intently with eyes closed and at the end, murmured, "Read that again." After a second hearing, she broke the ensuing silence with the exclamation ... "O Josephine, isn't that wonderful ... even as I am dying, I am learning something new!" Within a few days, she was dead. She, more than anyone I know, had indeed tuned her instrument in preparation for death. This, I knew in mind, heart and soul, constituted 'dying well.'

Though I had had this privilege of contributing something so rich to her dying, some time later, I had a dream about her, the end of which troubled me, which I nevertheless recorded as being a transfiguring dream and a transfiguring experience.

> I am in a huge, magnificent hall ... it feels ancient
> and sacred. Dozens and dozens of people are there.

> All for one reason. At the end of the hall, on a raised
> platform [that same analyst] lies dying. We are all
> attending her death. Perhaps she is in white. There is
> a radiance, a luminosity around her and throughout
> the room. But for some reason, I have to leave. This
> is very hard. I realize that it is not over yet.

I woke imagining that her spirit was not 'dead' but would live on. It was her unique path, not mine. I had to attend to death's business for myself.

Having dreamed of analysts dying, I have also dreamed of analysands' deaths. In one particular dream, I am carrying the analysand's dead body in my arms and cradling his corpse on my lap on a bus journey. We are being transported somewhere I know to be important but had no idea where that was. The dream gave me vital information about both transference and counter-transference experience, but also vividly reminding me that we also accompany those in our circle of therapeutic care to the ending of their lives as well as the necessary symbolic deaths that unconscious psyche sometimes requires of them. A colleague pointed out the visual and psychic echo of the Pietà. I did indeed feel great 'sorrow' as so much in this man's life and living had to die.

Working with analysands who actually die is challenging and humbling. Two women chose to go on working until the very end, one of them, until she was virtually comatose on the 'end of life pathway' in the hospice where I met with her. Her dreams were mostly vivid evocations of past experiences of people, both familiar and strange. The strangers felt intriguing, carrying a sense of futurity.

Most poignant for me has been accompanying analysands whose children die during our work. One woman in particular who lost a daughter. She had no formal religious knowledge, but after the death, her dreams brought specific Christian content. Angelic messengers seemed to affirm her own life as did several positive appearances of the daughter, as it were, from beyond the dreamer's life. She had died with her daughter and it took many months of grieving and remembering to come back to her own life, to feel that she had permission to live richly for herself. The same psychic territory was entered working with a woman in her fifties who had yet to come to terms with the trauma that her mother had died giving birth to her. Her life had cost her mother's. Guilt was embedded deeply, accessible only through dream pathways. Nowhere do death and life feel more closely bonded. Lines from a nativity poem hovered over our work: "I had seen birth and death, but had thought they were different" (Eliot). What an imponderable enigma!

My own continuing experience in recent bereavement is knowing myself in a strange psychic field of insipient movement between absence of presence and presence of absence, sounding different tones and semi-tones. I resonate with current theological talk of a 'second presence' as in Moltmann, "we experience their presence in our life as a kind of 'second presence.'" In this strange second presence "the dead do not bind the living to themselves, but let them go free, although the living know that there are still bound to those who are gone" (Moltmann, p.254). Saying 'goodnight' as I pass my husband's grave each evening when I go to lock up the church enlivens such intimations.

Over the last decades, my thinking and apprehending the reality of ending and death, personal, collective and cosmic, has culminated in my responses to the ideas of John Polkinghorne. His writing resonates with my own (what I can only call) potent intimations of futurity. His participation in the University of Heidelburg and Princeton seminars on eschatology have been both

271

rough sea and haven to my current believing, though now and always, in the same sense as Michael Polanyi, "a frame of mind in which I hold firmly to what I believe to be true, even though I know that it might conceivably be false" (Polkinghorne, 1998, p. 15).

Fred Hoyle (Nobel prize winning astronomer) remarked that his scientific work leads him to the conviction that "the universe in some sense must have known we were coming" (Polkinghorne, 1994, p. 76). In the same spirit of discovery, Polkinghorne's own response to his exploration is that the "most astonishing event in cosmic history known to us --- the emergence of persons by which the universe has become aware of itself" (ibid. p.32). What Jung communicated to me is the miracle of consciousness and the thrill of its relationship to psyche. It is this trust in human consciousness that makes me feel, intuit, that it can never be extinguished. That whatever the new Creation will be, it will be in another dimension but related to this field of psyche. Somehow. When I read the reflections of physicists in the collection of papers from the Heidelberg seminars, I am reminded of Jung in Africa, an experience that reverberated for me on first reading (Jung, 1961, p.255).

Jung is now my ancestor, joining all the poets, artists and thinkers who have enriched and enlarged me. He becomes one of my footnote community. How pertinent and impressive his claims about our "ancestral heritage, the collective unconscious contain[ing] the whole spiritual heritage of mankind's evolution, born anew in the brain structure of every individual" (Jung, 1927/31, §342).

In closing, I reflect on my own particular eschatological grammar. What prepositions associate me with death, my death. I live *towards* death. I arrive *at* death. Most charged is *through*. I will die through death, a passage like Donne's southwest discovery, through those straits to die. Ultimately *into* 'yonder' as dramatized in the poem I read at my husband's funeral, a poem we shared with solemn joy since our relationship began, "The Leaden Echo and the Golden Echo" where hope counters despair. The final lines float free. "Now we follow. Yonder, yes, yonder, yonder" (Hopkins).

On the wall in my office, the words so compelling for Jung as for me, *Vocatus at que non vocatus, Deus aderit.* I have called and still do call, but I am also called by an invisible and ineluctable voice. I have lived between laboratory and oratory, and I think I must add, library. I now feel that my cup has always run over. They say that at the moment of death, the whole of life flashes before one's eyes. My experience was rather like that as I buried my husband, so many of the foregoing thoughts and images flooding together in a moment that held all, the fulcrum of life lived as a mortal. Learning to become friend to death has replenished life itself, rendering it even more precious and joyful. I realize that I am now content to wait and see where and what yonder could be. I inhabit a strange pleromatic space with room enough to wait and see, in fullness and with no impatience. What I now realize is so crucial for me is trust in psyche that has evolved through eighty plus years of living, nearly half a century of those, working, imagining in psychic space in and with consciousness. I end as I began with the affirmation that ours is "a flame but borrow'd thence to light us thither," with firm knowing in an unknowing way, that God is both thence and thither, both source and terminus. In that spirit, I feel compelled to make my last word, Amen.

References

Berger, P. L. A. (1990) *Rumor of Angels,* N.Y.: Anchor Doubleday.

Hillman, James (1964/2013) *Suicide and the Soul*, U.S. Spring Publications.

Hillman, James (1996) *The Souls Code*: *In Search of Character and Calling*, New York: Random House.

Hillman, J. & Shamdasani S. (2013) *Lament from the Dead: Psychology After Jung's Red Book*, New York & London: Norton & Company.

Jung, C. G., (1961) *Memories, Dreams Reflections*, New York: Vintage Books. Revised 1989.

Jung, C. G. (1916/61) "Two Essays on Analytical Psychology: Adaptation, Individuation, Collectivity." *The Collected Works of C.G. Jung*. Trans. R.F.C. Hull. London: Routledge & Kegan Paul, 1974.

Jung, C.G. (1931) "The Structure of the Psyche," Vol. 8. *The Collected Works of C.G. Jung*. Trans. R.F.C. Hull. London: Routledge & Kegan Paul, 1974.

Jung, C.G. (1946) Preface and "Essays on Contemporary Events," Vol. 18. *The Collected Works of C.G. Jung*. Trans. R.F.C. Hull. London: Routledge & Kegan Paul, 1974.

Jung, C.G. (1930/31) "The Stages of Life." Vol. 8. *The Collected Works of C.G. Jung*. Trans. R.F.C. Hull. London: Routledge & Kegan Paul, 1974.

Jung, C.G. (1934) "The Soul and Death," Vol. 8. *The Collected Works of C.G. Jung*. Trans. R.F.C. Hull. London: Routledge & Kegan Paul, 1974.

Jung, C.G. (1935) "Tavistock Lecture 111." Vol. 18. *The Collected Works of C.G. Jung.* Trans. R.F.C. Hull. London: Routledge & Kegan Paul, 1974.

Jung, C.G. (1943) "Psychotherapy and a Philosophy of Life," Vol. 16. *The Collected Works of C.G. Jung.* Trans. R.F.C. Hull. London: Routledge & Kegan Paul, 1974.

Jung, C.G. (1946) Preface and "Essays on Contemporary Events," Vol. 10. *The Collected Works of C.G. Jung.* Trans. R.F.C. Hull. London: Routledge & Kegan Paul, 1974.

Kermode, Frank (1968) *The Sense of an Ending: Studies in the Theory of Fiction,* Oxford: Oxford University Press.

Marlowe, Christopher, 1604/1631, *The Tragical History of the Life and Death of Doctor Faustus.*

Moltmann, Jurgen (2000) "Is There Life After Death?" In Polkinghorne J. & Welker, M. *The End of the World and the Ends of God.* Harrisburg, PA, Trinity Press International.

Nelson D. & Giberson, Karl (2011) *Quantum Leap,* Oxford & Grand Rapids, MI: Monarch Books.

Polanyi, Michael (1966) *The Tacit Dimension,* Chicago: University of Chicago Press.

Polkinghorne, John (1994) *The Faith of a Physicist,* Princeton, NJ: Princeton Legacy Library. (Gifford Lectures)

Polkinghorne, John (1998) *Belief in God in an Age of Science,* New Haven, CT: Yale University Press. (Terry Lectures)

Polkinghorne, John & Welker, Stephen (2000) *The Ends of the World and the Ends of God: Science and Theology on Eschatology,* Harrisburg, PA: Trinity Press International.

Quarles, Francis (1638) *Hieroglyphikes of the Life of Man.* Facsimile editions of the Emblem books are available from the Scolar Press, Menston. UK

Shakespeare, William: *Hamlet* (c.1603) and *Measure for Measure.* (c. 1604)

Steiner, George (1997) *Errata: An Examined Life,* London: Wiedenfeld & Nicolson.

Taylor, Jeremy (1651) *Rule and Exercise of Holy Dying.*

Weber, Max (2015) *Science as a Vocation*, ed. Lassman et al. London, Routledge. (Originally published, 1919)

Poetry

Auden, W.H. (1936). "Stop all the clocks."

Donne, John, "Hymne to God my God in my sicknesse." *Divine Poems*, (1615)

Eliot, T.S. "Journey of the Magi." (1927)

Herbert, George, "The Forerunners." (1633)

Hopkins, Gerard M. "The Leaden Echo and the Golden Echo." (1882).

King, Henry, "Exequy." (c. 1624)

Patten, Brian, "Burying the dog in the garden." (1960's)

Tennyson, Alfred, Lord: "Tithonus." (c. 1858)

Vaughan, Henry: The are all gone into the world of light. *Silex Scintillans*, 1655

Wordsworth, William, "Ode: Intimations of Immortality from Reflections of Early Childhood." (1807)

My Appointment with Death

Ursula Wirtz

Contemplating the hermeneutics of death has been a long-standing pursuit for me. My beliefs, values, spiritual practices, and experiences in dealing with death have all been shaped in the crucible of suffering, stemming from the loss of loved ones and my immersion in understanding human suffering. I gained insights into death through my interactions with patients who had lost their children or spouses and those on the precipice of departing from the realm of the living. Profound lessons about death were also gleaned from my deep conversations with my Polish friend Halina, a survivor of Auschwitz, as well as my work with individuals who had endured torture in Chile's death chambers. Additionally, I garnered a profound understanding of death while traversing the harrowing killing fields of Cambodia and empathizing with mothers' agonizing journeys toward forgiveness during the truth and reconciliation hearings in South Africa. The encounter with death, whether in its literal or symbolic form, lies at the core of the trauma experience, and my comprehension of death was honed through my extensive work in the field of psychotraumatology and through my own losses.

Irvin Yalom (1980), writing about our major existential conflicts and the intricate interplay between suffering, love, and death, points to the paradox of death, quoting Forster:

"...the paradox became clearer and clearer. Death destroys a man: the idea of Death saves him. Behind the coffins and the skeletons that stay the vulgar mind lies something so immense that all that is great in us responds to it."

-*E. M. Forster (1910)*

Indeed, it is this paradox of death that I have wrestled with all my life. Fate compelled me from the outset to face death, a *mysterium tremendum* as a profound reality. This appointment with death was something beyond my ego concerns; I did not create it, it rather happened to me.

The archetype of death, this ineffable solemn mystery, has cast its awe-inspiring presence within me since early on. "Death transforms life into fate," André Malraux once wrote, and my fate seems intimately connected with death. I believe that already in the weeks prior to my birth, an unconscious matrix was constellated that initiated me into the mystery of dying and becoming, the existential continuum of life and death, or as Jung put it: *Waxing and waning make one curve.* (*Jung, CW 8, § 800*).

Jung emphasized the need for a myth about death, as rationality alone often plunges us only into a void, a dark pit of nothingness. He suggested that "*Myth, however, can conjure up other images for him, helpful and enriching pictures of life in the land of the dead.*" (MDR) My own myth finds expression through the tapestry woven by Clotho, the spinner, and Lachesis, the allotter, weaving the *Leitmotiv* of love and death into my life's fabric. Love, to me, is as enigmatic and miraculous as Atropos, the unturnable, a metaphor for death.

My personal myth traces its origins back to a house steeped in mourning, as my mother had just lost her husband and baby to a sudden, fatal illness. My earliest memory of being transported in a baby carriage was to the cemetery, where my mother introduced me to Karl, my departed father, and Karl Fred, my baby brother who had died so young.

I've frequently contemplated my personal myth, delving into its unconscious core of meaning, particularly in relation to the unfolding of my life's purpose. Living out this myth involves the continuous act of crafting significance, intricately weaving together the diverse threads of my existence, and uncovering the reason for my existence. I yearned to fathom the essence of death, to determine the appropriate attitude to adopt toward its inevitability and to grasp the profound sentiment expressed by John Donne: "and death shall be no more," a sentiment also echoed in Revelation 21:4.

From a young age, I sensed that I had been initiated into the realm of Hades, a realm that initiated a lifelong exploration of existential questions about the mystery of Being and why something exists rather than nothing. From Heidegger, I learned that life is a "Being-towards-Death" and death an integral part of the natural order.

I was just 8 years old when I stood by the deathbed of someone I knew well. He lay in a dimly lit room, with black-draped windows and numerous candles casting their flickering glow. It felt as though I were bearing witness to a profound mystery, enveloped in a hushed reverence. This poignant scene, along with its ethereal ambiance, left an indelible mark on me. I remain deeply appreciative of this tranquil introduction to my first conscious encounter with death.

The imprint of death on the canvas of my life, its "eminent imminence" as Heidegger described it, led to an early recognition of the dynamic unity between life and death. Goethe's words have granted me a profound understanding of this dynamic: "And so long as you haven't experienced this: to die and so to grow, you are only a troubled guest on the dark earth." This concept, encapsulated in my book on trauma titled *"Stirb und Werde"* (Die and Become), became the guiding mission of my life.

Death and life exist in an interdependent relationship, a wisdom elegantly encapsulated by Gibran Kahlil Gibran: *"For life and death are one, even as the river and the sea are one."* Despite insights from wisdom traditions, I am aware that there remains a gap between intellectual understanding and lived experience when it comes to the concepts of transience and impermanence.

In my current situation, as I stand on the precipice of losing my husband, this paradox of simultaneously having and not having as expressed in the Tao Te Ching—*"having and not having arise together"*—manifests as a delicate balance between letting go and holding on.

Rilke artfully grappled with death's paradox in a letter to Countess Margot Sizzo-Noris-Crouy, asserting: *"The great secret of death, and perhaps its deepest connection with us, is this: that, in taking from us a being we have loved and venerated, death does not wound us without, at the same time, lifting us toward a more perfect understanding of this being and of ourselves"* (Rilke 1923).

Although I comprehend that death is our friend and preparing for death and loss necessitates profound relinquishment, creating space for new beginnings, I still find myself not entirely ready for this formidable task. I am not yet prepared to fully accept that his precious life, because it has been full and beautiful, does not need to last forever. I detect a certain reluctance to embrace the notion of *"it is what it is,"* as beautifully expressed by Erich Fried in a poem about love.

Recollections of Freud's *"Reflections on War and Death"* (1918) come to mind, where he criticized our tendency to relegate death and exclude it from our daily lives. He believed that the fear of death exerts more control over us than we often realize. When we examine our death-phobic culture, it becomes evident that the fear of death is pervasive. We often seek to avoid facing the existential reality of death and the potential terror it holds. Nonetheless, research has offered compelling evidence of the profoundly positive and transformative impact that an encounter with death can have on individuals' lives. I am thinking of the paradigm of posttraumatic growth, highlighting the archetypal function of trauma, namely both destruction and also transformation, and renewal. (Calhoun/ Tedeschi 2006, 2013). To integrate death into life and release existential fear and self-alienation, one must cultivate an expanded consciousness, and this endeavor remains a lifelong journey.

Jung identified the fear of death as originating from our ego's attachment to the material world and our apprehension of losing our identity. Rather than dreading the void, he encouraged embracing death as an intrinsic facet of life. He likened death to *"a ripe fruit on the tree of life"* (Jung, CW 18, § 1705-7). Does the process of dying call upon us to maintain this perspective? Is it a sign of wisdom to accept death without fear as the ripe fruit of a fulfilled life? Such a commitment to wholeness in dying may not necessarily align with the medical profession's perspective.

An intriguing Swiss study on the fear of death (Meerwein, 1991) reveals that doctors often harbor a latent fear of death surpassing that of the general population; they frequently grapple with *thantophobia*. Among psychotherapists, the topic of death carries heightened significance, exemplified by the highest suicide rate among psychiatrists. This phenomenon might signify the undercurrents of the underworld, the contagion of trauma, and the risks entailed in our work's profound depths. According to J. Hillman (1979), death is a fundamental fear within our field, and the proliferation of optimistic, healing, and creative therapies could be seen as a manic defense against this dread.

Death anxiety and the fear of annihilation are pervasive, and the dread of dissolution can be so overwhelming that it is perceived as a psychic death to be avoided at all costs. While physical death might not be the primary fear, it is the specter of our existential limitations that haunts us. Cultural anthropologist Ernest Becker (1973; 1975) posited that we are all affected by the terror of death and are prone to deny our mortality to ward off this terror, a theory known as Terror Management Theory (TMT).

Freud's advice to acknowledge the reality of death and afford it its rightful place is epitomized by his motto *"si vis vitam, para mortem"* (if you want life, prepare for death). (Freud 1918).

My initial encounters with impermanence and life's transient nature steered me toward the realms of philosophy and literature. My *"thaumazein"*—my sense of wonder and amazement sprouted from a profound curiosity about why something exists rather than nothing. I yearned to unravel the mystery of existence itself, delve into the fundamental underpinnings of being, and explore the origin from which my life emerges, and to contemplate the destination into which it eventually dissolves.

Philosophy has deeply molded my perspective on mortality. Montaigne's wisdom, that engaging in philosophy is essentially a preparation for the inevitability of death (*philosopher, c'est apprendre à mourir*), has become a guiding light in my journey. Sages like Socrates, Schopenhauer, Nietzsche, Kierkegaard, Heidegger, Wittgenstein, and the Stoics have provided answers to my burning existential questions and broadened my comprehension of the enigmatic process of dying. The words inscribed on philosopher Ernst Bloch's tombstone—*"Thinking means transcending. The Principle of Hope."* (Denken heist überschreiten. Das Prinzip

Hoffnung)—have profoundly influenced my attitude toward death. Immersing myself in philosophical Thanatology, exploring Existentialism and Death, and contemplating Adorno and Marcuse's Ideology of Death, I have observed while Marcuse once saw death as a symbol of freedom, the contemporary medicalization of death, the sterile control and management of death in our culture seems emblematic of the ultimate deprivation of freedom and autonomy in our dying process.

Heidegger, in particular, has played a pivotal role in shaping my understanding, emphasizing the imperative of embracing our finitude to lead an authentic life. His perspective on death and dying issues a profound call to humanity—an invitation to recognize our limitations, affirm them, and internalize the concept of death itself. Only when we exist in a state of awareness regarding our mortality, when our existence embodies a "Being toward Death," do we attain a sense of completeness. Our existence, designed with an end in sight, finds fulfillment only through this consciousness.

> *Heidegger (1962): "If I take death into my life, acknowledge it, and face it squarely, I will free myself from the anxiety of death and the pettiness of life—and only then will I be free to become myself."*

The idea of attaining completeness through death is eloquently expressed by von Franz (1979). According to her, life cannot achieve its fullness without the experiences of suffering and death. In her work, she elucidates that as consciousness evolves, there is a division that occurs, leaving something behind, and it is only in death that this schism is reconciled, leading to a return to wholeness. From my perspective, ever since humanity partook of the fruit from the tree of knowledge, we've been ensnared in a dualistic consciousness. It is only in death that we transcend this divide and awaken to a nondual, holistic understanding.

I am convinced the manner in which we confront death and the courage displayed in facing adversity ultimately lead to a deeper sense of meaning.

Synchronicities have often played a significant role in my life, particularly at pivotal junctures. I understand Jung's visionary concept of acausal, meaningful connections between an internal, subjective state and an external event as a beckoning to become more conscious.

Synchronistic phenomena, little "miracles," have also occurred often in my trauma therapies, *Kairos* experiences and shared somatic phenomena manifested the underlying field of interdependencies extending beyond face-to-face encounters in space and time.

Therefore, it is not surprising that the opportunity to contribute to this book on confronting death aligns with the impending passing of my husband, a man with whom I've shared 43 years of life. The time is rich with meaningful coincidences promoting individuation. Yesterday a friend visited me and brought as a gift the tarot cards from Niki de Saint Phalle. Curious, I took one card from the series, and when I turned it, it was the Death card that I had drawn.

In our garden, a magnificent, large Japanese cherry tree typically beautifully blooms every May. As I sit outside composing this essay, the serene atmosphere is suddenly disrupted by a deafening crash. I witness, with a sense of horror, the thick trunk of the cherry tree splitting apart and collapsing, its weight burying the once-vibrant bamboo grove beneath it.

Inside our house, a magnificent Benjamin tree has graced us for 43 years. Its two trunks have grown together, symbolizing the depth of our bond. I think of these lines from *Captain Corelli's Mandolin* by Louis de Bernières:

> *"... Those that truly love, have roots that grow towards each other underground,*
> *And when all the pretty blossoms have fallen from their branches,*
> *They find that they are one tree and not two."*

Unexpectedly, for reasons unknown, the tree sheds all its leaves and appears to wither away, leaving us bewildered by its abrupt decline.

I often contemplate whether the grief and mourning that will follow my "Beloved's" impending loss, as I affectionately call him, will reveal deeper truths about love, death, and the human condition. At 90 years old, he is in the winter of his life, time slowing down, and soon his earthly journey will conclude, and I must bid him farewell. Will I have the capacity to unearth the meaning concealed within the process of dying once the veil has been lifted? Can I bear witness to his dying process without fear and the constraints of reason? Will I summon the courage to accompany him like a midwife and then release him to his soul's final voyage to the last of seas? Can I uphold the promise of love's immortality, like all lovers who seem to yearn for love's extension through space and time, a sense of continuity? Can I endure my own vulnerability and uncertainty at this juncture while still retaining trust in the unknown and the unknowable? Can I maintain faith in the awareness of "the invisible, which has no name, which has no matter and yet effect" (Paracelsus)? Will our connection penetrate these concealed depths and provide solace amid my sorrows? What consolation is possible in the face of the inconsolable pain of death?

What images of meaning, transformations, and promises can rise above the gloom of Hades?

We both understand the heightened preciousness and beauty of life, with death casting its ever-present shadow over our days. Art and music emerge as cherished treasures in this journey. Music becomes our refuge, soothing the soul when it yearns for solace—whether it is Brahms' exquisite German Requiem with its profound words, *"Lord, teach me that my life has a goal and I must go towards it,"* or the haunting melodies of Schubert or of Mahler in *Das Lied von der Erde* (Song of the Earth). I firmly believe that music serves as a conduit that connects us with the depths of our unconscious.

We share what sustains us, drawing us closer to transcendence. We read to one another, sharing moments of both laughter and tears. This paradox of surrendering to our inherent limitations empowers us to live more deeply. Time takes on a different rhythm, and the pressures of society lose their grip on us. An overwhelming sense of gratitude envelops our companionship during this time overshadowed by separation and impending loss. Life gently peels away, as a friend of mine eloquently put it. I observe how his attachment to the material world diminishes in significance. The immaterial realm, where dreams and imagination reside, unfolds like a portal—a sort of window into another dimension. As I watch him, lost in a reverie-like state while lying on the sunbed in the garden, entranced by the dance of two butterflies and delving into childhood memories, it becomes clear that his imagination and memory have melded into a retrospective understanding of the unfolding of his life. Perhaps it is a summation of the meaning he has discovered. Maybe preparing for death in this reverie means closing any gap between who he once envisioned becoming and who he ultimately became.

As his physical form weakens, his spirit seems to expand. Every morning, he dedicates himself to reading and writing about Wisdom. In the evenings, he taps into his innermost wellspring, playing the cello—a miraculous feat given his frail state. Listening to what he refers to as his musical "evening prayers," I hope he will depart from this world with serenity.

When his time has come and he takes his last breath, I want to recite the Mantra from the Heart Sutra, a mantra we both learned during our Zen retreats.

"*Gate, gate, paragate, parasamgate--- BODHI--- svaha!*" "*Gegangen, gegangen, ans andere Ufer gegangen, gänzlich hinüber gelangt---ERWACHEN---aaah!*" "*Gone gone, all the way over, gone to the other shore of enlightenment.*"

I've come to realize that death, with all its enigmatic qualities, serves as a profound teacher, inspiring my pursuit of a life rich with meaning. It has beckoned me to contemplate my own mortality, confront my fears, and delve into the profound mysteries of existence. I learned to perceive death as a catalyst, an agent that unveils a sacred truth about the constants of human existence.

Embracing a meaningful engagement with death's enigmatic presence has led me to heed the philosophical maxim Γνῶθι σαυτόν, "*Gnothi seauton,*" "Know thyself." Socrates taught that an unexamined life is not worth living. This commitment obliges me to scrutinize my own life in preparing for death. Unlike Freud, I firmly believe that the quest for meaning is a noble and worthwhile pursuit. Freud however wrote in a letter to Marie Bonaparte:

"*The moment a man questions the meaning and value of life, he is sick, since objectively neither has any existence; by asking this question one is merely admitting to a store of unsatisfied libido to which something else must have happened, a kind of fermentation leading to sadness and depression. I am afraid these explanations of mine are not very wonderful. Perhaps because I am too pessimistic. I have an advertisement floating about in my head which I consider the boldest and most successful piece of American publicity: 'Why live, if you can be buried for ten dollars'"* (Freud 1937).

Facing death is akin to confronting the truth of my existence—embracing the unchangeable past, the unknowable future, and the narrowing of possibilities. A profoundly moving narrative that encapsulates this encounter with the *"nigredo"* state of an unexamined life, and a profound shift in one's perception of life on the precipice of death, can be found in Tolstoy's novella "The Death of Ivan Ilyich." Tolstoy, grappling with his own existential crisis, delved into the question: What enduring significance does life hold that death cannot erase? Within the novella, the central character, Ivan Ilyich, also wrestles with whether his life possesses any intrinsic meaning. As he lies on his deathbed, he raises the haunting question, "Could it be that my entire conscious life had been mistaken? Perhaps I didn't live as I should have?" It is only at this juncture, as he confronts his inner darkness, that he begins to realize the absence of a genuine and enduring connection with his soul throughout his lifetime. He suffers most from the lie perpetuated by his family that he was not dying, but simply ill. Tolstoy emphasizes that such a deception at a person's deathbed diminishes the profound act of dying and taints the last precious moments of Ivan Ilych.

It is only in this face-off with mortality that he undergoes a profound awakening, feeling compassion and love that dissolve his fear of death. At this threshold, he senses a transformation: *"In the place of death, there was light,"* he whispers to himself, exclaiming, *"Death is finished ... it exists no more!"* And with that, he takes his last breath. It is akin to a radiant departure, as though he gains insight into the very essence of existence. His passing resembles that of an eagle soaring skyward, in stark contrast to Keats's imagery in "Elgin Marbles":

"My spirit is too weak—mortality
Weighs heavily on me like unwilling sleep,
And each imagined pinnacle and steep
Of godlike hardship tells me I must die
Like a sick eagle looking at the sky."

Enlightenment through compassion brings to mind the tale of Parsifal, the fool who attained wisdom through his compassion. Wagner's opera *Parsifal* delves into the cyclical nature of birth, suffering, death, and rebirth. This opera intricately weaves a tapestry of rich symbolic imagery, encapsulating the agony of the wounded Amfortas, who yearns for death but is denied it, while Kundry exists in a deathlike liminal state, desiring eternal sleep yet unable to attain it. Wagner's portrayal of death often carries nuanced dialectics. While generally viewed as tragic, for Kundry and Amfortas, death signifies redemption from unending suffering. In our contemporary world, many individuals find themselves trapped in a state where they are neither able to live nor die, largely due to the complexities of the advanced health care system. Although medical technology and palliative care extend the lifespans of the terminally ill, they also deny these individuals the right to choose when and how to end their lives. Some among them yearn to be released from a life they no longer find worth living, yet they are not permitted to make this choice. The debate surrounding assisted suicide has given rise to organizations like Exit, where membership grants individuals the autonomy to determine their final exit and prepare for death while they still cherish a life of value.

As a devoted opera enthusiast, I have frequently encountered the theme of the undead, cursed to endure eternal life, in works such as Monteverdi's *Orfeo*, Mozart's *Don Giovanni*, Hoffmann's *Undine*, and Wagner's *Flying Dutchman*.

Throughout my life, literature and poetry have been steadfast companions, echoing Hölderlin's wisdom: *"But what remains is the poet's gift—was aber bleibet stiften die Dichter."* I am continually amazed by the workings of my unconscious mind as I prepare for the impending death of my Beloved. During the quiet hours of the night, verses of forgotten poetry from Hofmannsthal, Rilke, and Rose Ausländer resurface in my mind.

Literature and the Arts have portrayed death as both a revealer and a destroyer of forms. How we visualize and mythologize death significantly influences our approach to it—whether as a friend or foe, an angel or a grim reaper, a messenger of the beyond, or an executioner. The Dance of Death has long held my fascination. In traditional pagan customs, people would dance naked over graves in cemeteries. Christian cemetery dances, rooted in the idea that death signifies life's renewal, advocated celebrating it with joy. The concept was that each person carries their own death, their transience, and dances alongside it through life in a macabre dance. Sadly, we seem to have lost this perspective on dancing with death as we navigate our lives today.

Rilke writes:

> *"Formerly one knew (or perhaps one guessed it) that one had one's death within one, as a fruit its kernel. The children had a little death within them and the grown-ups a big one. The women had it in their womb and the men in their breast. One had it, and that gave one a singular dignity and a quiet pride."*
> *(Rainer Maria Rilke 1949)*

Similarly, in *The Red Book*, Jung listened to the spirit of the depths, who conveyed that the profound mystery of emergence and passing away resides within us all and that this knowledge is an inherent part of our being.

My study of analytical psychology introduced me to the archetype of death as a primordial and universal pattern. Delving into the mythologies of the underworld, I discovered that they offer images and patterns that enriched my understanding of the realm of Hades. My imaginative resonance led me to explore further the archetypal representations of death and the afterlife. Across cultures, human imagination has long been captivated by the concept of the abode of the deceased. In mythological imagery, the awakening of a new consciousness is frequently depicted as the conquest of death and the reclamation of life. This journey symbolizes transformation and renewal, akin to Jung's *nekya*, which opened doors to the vast realms of the unconscious and laid the foundation for his psychology.

My engagement with the Books of the Dead and journeys to the afterlife has cultivated an understanding of the unfathomable. Furthermore, it has shed light on the significance of the symbolic realm in confronting death. I immersed myself in the *Odyssey*, familiarized myself with the *Tibetan Book of the Dead*, and, in preparation for my travels to Egypt, studied *The Egyptian Texts of the Dead* to grasp their interpretations of death and the afterlife. These Egyptian texts contain comforting messages about the potential for renewed life in death and provide spiritual guidance for the living. The profundity of these symbolic texts has expanded my consciousness regarding the enigma of life and death.

In my exploration of feminist anthropology and early goddess cultures, I found Marija Gimbutas's work to be enthralling. She documented the interconnectedness of life and death, emphasizing the seamless continuum and the nonlinear nature of time. I was drawn to the archaic geometrical patterns associated with death and rebirth, which are inherent in the cult of the magna mater. These patterns persist in archaic symbolism found in tribal textile artifacts from the Near East, as eloquently described by Terenzio del Grosso (1993).

Jung regarded symbols as "libido transformers," acting as focal points for psychic energies. Symbols possess the capacity to release and transform psychic energy as they become conscious. I have learned to pay attention to the emergence of spontaneous symbols during moments of profound crisis—symbols that resemble a saving hand or convey messages of wholeness. Psychoanalyst Igor Caruso regarded them as keys to human existence, capable of unlocking the meaning of life, and Edward C. Whitmont considers symbols among the most potent energy mediators, capable of moving mountains. When I confronted the deaths of loved ones and the ground beneath me turned unsteady, symbols assisted me in rediscovering my center.

My journeys to explore the mysteries and symbolism of death have taken me to diverse places, from the death camps of Auschwitz to the burning Ghats in India, the killing fields in Cambodia, and the Pyramids in Egypt and Mexico. While traveling in Bali, I marveled at their vibrant funeral rituals. I was equally intrigued by Tibetan funeral practices, the towers of silence, and the sky burial, all of which vividly exemplify life's impermanence while also embodying an act of generosity by providing sustenance to other sentient beings, specifically the vultures that feed on the flesh. It is considered a final act of charity to nourish other life forms, as these cultures recognize the profound mystery that something must end for something else to begin anew.

Analytical psychology, with its profound insights, and fairy tales serve as my guiding lights in comprehending the enigma of death. One such illuminating gem is the Grimm fairy tale "Godfather Death."

This tale imparts the notion that Death assumes the role of a godfather to a physician, establishing an intimate connection between the healer and mortality. It demands that the physician let go of attachments to status and possessions. This contrasts sharply with the prevailing attitude in modern medicine, where doctors often attempt to outwit death, a quest that frequently ends in failure. In contrast, by embracing their own vulnerabilities, physicians can become what Jung termed "wounded healers." This transformation enables them to empathize with patients and provide solace in times of grief. Moreover, as the "godson of death," they must possess the audacity, similar to the "wounded healer," to address patients' inner conflicts.

The fairy tale underscores the importance of physicians acknowledging death's presence and recognizing the limitations of medical prowess. Instead of adopting the arrogant stance of an all-powerful healer, doctors should accept their role as instruments wielded by death. Obedience and humility should guide their actions, following death's directive. The presence of death, standing vigil by the patient's bedside, determines the extent of the doctor's healing abilities. While doctors can employ their skills, conquering death remains an unattainable goal. Alignment with death's power allows for healing, whereas attempts to outsmart death lead to one's own demise.

In the narrative, Death leads the godson of death into an underground cavern illuminated by numerous candles of varying sizes—large, medium, and small. These flames symbolize the life lights of individuals, flickering with ephemeral existence. Some extinguish in a fleeting moment, while others rekindle, perpetuating a dance of fleeting vitality. When the physician inquired about his own life light, he was dismayed to observe its near depletion. He implored Death for a fresh light, driven by a desire to savor life, ascend to kingship, and wed the king's beautiful daughter. Death's response, however, was unwavering: "I cannot grant this, for a new light can only emerge after one has faded." The tale emphasizes the need to embrace death and forsake the illusion of control. Death remains a formidable force; its presence dictates a physician's capabilities.

Both philosophy and literature have paved the way for my subsequent work in the field of trauma. I've come to understand that severe illness, impending death, and traumatic experiences can lead to a radical rupture and disintegration of existing ego structures. This ego dissolution can resemble a form of dying. In these liminal states, something breaks open, allowing archetypal energy to flood the empty space, often with profound numinosity. The ego's surrender and deconstruction can lead to a spiritual void, akin to a death experience. Contact with the numinous, however, whether it brings a terrifying and trembling encounter or a sacred shudder—a *"tremendum"* or *"fascinosum"*—creates an awe-inspiring connection with the wholly other, the ultimate, and forcefully alters one's perspective.

Karl Jaspers termed such encounters with death "limit situations," revealing our true essence but also evoking *Angst*. Facing them with dignity and coming to terms with such limit situations, we achieve authenticity, leading to the fullness of life. For him, these borderline situations bring both suffering and a release of forces intertwined with the joy of existence, meaning, and growth. He believed that pleasure and sorrow were inextricably linked. I contend that these liminal situations can prepare us for a meaningful transition into death.

Karl Dürckheim has also eloquently captured this paradoxical mystery of being and nonbeing, of life and death. He explains that only at the limit are we close to what lies beyond the limit, and at the agonizing end of the finite, the infinite can find us, liberating us from all agonies.

Liminality possesses the power to birth new possibilities. This space between life and death harbors transformative potential, concealing the mystery of growth, the potential that nothing is set in stone, and one can experiment with who one is, was, and will be.

I personally encountered a liminal experience in the desert of Rajasthan following a near-fatal accident, which left me suspended in that stillness between life and death. Uncertain if I would bleed to death internally, it was a traumatic yet numinous experience that forever altered my relationship with mortality. This event stripped away some of my fear of dying, paving the way for a potential encounter with the angel of death with "a smiling knowledge of the eternal," as Thomas Mann aptly put it.

Encountering the archetype of death can lead to a numinous experience. Thus, it is not surprising that the confrontation with mortality holds the potential to initiate a transformative and healing process. Across various wisdom traditions, a common belief resonates: Mastering the art of dying is inseparable from mastering the art of living—*Ars Moriendi* and *Ars Vivendi* are intertwined. As seen through the lens of Thomas Mann, encountering death ultimately guides us toward a deeper understanding of life and our shared humanity. I perceive ancient myths and spiritual texts as preparatory tools for *Ars Vivendi*, inspiring readers to lead conscious lives and expand in wisdom. The most important function of myths and rituals is that they enable us to come into contact with the unfathomable mystery of being. Myths make us feel that our own being is connected with the being of others, that we are embedded in something greater, more comprehensive.

Analytical psychology offers a trove of psychospiritual insights into death and its paradoxical relationship with life. Jung eloquently articulates: *"Death is as psychologically important as birth; like birth, it is an integral part of life when viewed from the correct psychological perspective. Death is not an end but a goal."* (Jung, CW 13, par. 68).

Mark Twain had a similar welcoming psychological perspective on death:

> *"But death was sweet, death was gentle, death was kind; death healed the bruised spirit and the broken heart, and gave them rest and forgetfulness; death was man's best friend; when man could endure life no longer, death came and set him free."*

Once again, I find myself summoned to confront loss and death. Through the years, I've traversed the terrain of numerous deaths and existential losses, each one marked by the poignant English metaphor: "A part of me dies." Yet, amid these experiences that have shaken me to my core, I've learned to coexist with the physical absence of loved ones, moving through the pain of loss while preserving their existential presence within my soul.

In my personal mythos, death has been the catalyst for my individuation journey—a summons to become the person I was meant to be. This journey into the realms of spirituality has led me to the inner sanctum of the soul, where I've learned to surrender to the transient nature of all things. Embracing the unalterable and mining it for transformative prospects has become a lifelong pursuit. My spirituality revolves around connecting with the greater whole and comprehending the unity of existence. Rooted in a spiritual tradition, I've discovered it is easier to summon the strength to face death with dignity—a profound insight reinforced by my trauma research. My encounters with survivors of war and death camps have revealed how imminent death can trigger profound spiritual shifts. It is evident that living a life with dignity can lead to dying with dignity. A heightened awareness of death, rather than denial of it, might ultimately guide us toward more authentic lives.

One of my mentors, Karlfried Graf Dürckheim, considered his wartime ordeal pivotal in his spiritual awakening. He believed that confronting mortality propels us toward an authentic life. Dürckheim was convinced that only when confronted with death can something indestructible arise within us. Dying, he said, reveals the truth of the infinite while demanding the end of the finite. Approaching death, the ego might still cling to life, but the hour of truth cannot be avoided.

Once I lived and taught in Ireland, and an Irish friend introduced me to their unique perspective on death. In the Irish language, death is often referred to as departing "on the way of truth" or being "in the place of truth." This view suggests that death is a revelation of truth, a departure from falsehood and illusion. One frequently used expression for "to die" is *bás a fháil*, which means "to receive death" or, intriguingly, *bheith ag saothrú an bháis*, to earn (harvest) death by preparing for it.

Near-death experiences lend further credence to the idea of truth associated with death, often described as illuminating and revealing deeper truths. In these experiences, consciousness of another reality often shines forth, providing a sense of intense meaningfulness. Jung expressed something similar after his nearly fatal illness in a letter written to Kristine Mann:

The only difficulty is to get rid of the body, to get quite naked and void of the world and the ego-will. When you can give up the crazy will to live and when you seemingly fall into a bottomless mist, then the truly real life begins with everything which you were meant to be and never reached. It is something ineffably grand.

I once shared a panel with Pim Van Lommel, the author of *Endless Consciousness: A Scientific Approach to the Near-Death Experience.* As a Dutch cardiologist, his research provides validation for initiation and spiritual insights during cardiac arrest. From a Jungian perspective a near-death experience manifests the archetype of transformation giving rise to archetypal imagery and motives.

My exploration led me to the work of Peter Fenwick, a neuropsychiatrist, and his wife, who examined over 300 near-death experiences. They concluded that death initiates a profound expansion of consciousness. These experiences often involve encounters with a disc of living light, perceived after traversing a lengthy tunnel. Symbolism tied to light is significant among Quakers, who characterize death as a transition into the light. Ancient Egyptian funerary texts similarly capture this essence with their title: *The Book of the Dead: Book of Emerging Forth into the Light.*

Jung eloquently captured the yearning to embrace the light as a longing for consciousness, recognizing that the soul harbors an inherent desire for light and an irrepressible urge to rise out of primal darkness.

Common threads within near-death experiences encompass sensations of tranquility, out-of-body episodes, traversing through tunnels toward radiant light, encounters with luminous "beings," passage through barriers, and reunions with departed loved ones. People often report seeing a great light, a form that has no content but takes on meaning according to the individual's cultural roots. Upon returning, individuals frequently experience a renewed sense of life purpose and heightened psychic awareness. These experiences, rich with archetypal symbolism, echo ancient death-rebirth myths deeply embedded in our collective unconscious.

In my journey, I've also been drawn to Buddhism, which has prepared me for approaching death, particularly through meditation. Inner resources like self-awareness, acceptance, compassion, and forgiveness play vital roles in this preparation. Buddhism's principle of embracing both the 10,000 joys and the 10,000 sorrows as part of life deeply resonates with me. Within this framework, living means giving happiness and agony their rightful place, just as Rilke advises: *"Let everything happen to you, beauty and terror."* Rilke, in giving his exultant yes to life, did not shut out suffering and death. Adversity, in its essence, bestows the gifts of wisdom and compassion.

My engagement with insight meditation (Pali: vipassanā) and Zen has cultivated a more balanced mind and fostered deeper insights into phenomenal reality, with expanded self-awareness. Thich Nhat Hanh, the Vietnamese Zen monk, whose Vietnam monastery I have visited, employs the metaphor *No mud, no lotus* to emphasize that growth, maturity, and compassion emerge from loss and suffering much like the lotus flower taking root in dirt and blossoming from the mud.

On my journey, I've come to understand that transformation and destruction are two facets of the same life process. We are intrinsically connected to both the world of limited time and space and the unconditioned reality beyond such confines, as C. G.

Jung also believed. Our souls reach into realms that transcend the categories of space and time.

> *"This spectacle of old age would be unendurable did we not know that our psyche reaches into a region held captive neither by change in time nor by limitation of place. In that form of being our birth is a death and our death a birth. The scales of the whole hang balanced." (Letters, Vol.I, p. 569)*

My fascination with mystics led me to write my first symbol paper for Ian Baker, delving into the states of mystic consciousness. The mystics bear witness to a nontemporal state where past, present, and future intertwine into a timeless present—the *nunc stans*. As philosopher Ludwig Wittgenstein aptly remarked, *"If by eternity is understood not endless temporal duration but timelessness, then he lives eternally who lives in the present."* (Quoted in Holecek 2013). Adding to this concept, Holocek noted, *"Nowness, in other words, is the funnel into eternity."*

The insight of the mystics, *"If you die before you die, then when you die, you won't die,"* resonates deeply with me. It is a call to relinquish attachments and cravings, a process of untethering the mind, and an invitation to embrace the essential, all while preparing for death and aligning our lives with what truly matters.

Alchemy, drawing from its ancient philosophical and spiritual tradition, has been a guiding light in my work with trauma, elucidating the symbolic framework of transformation. In alchemy, death symbolizes transmutation—not just the cessation of the physical, but the dissolution of the old self. This archetypal symbolism underscores that genuine change arises from confronting darkness. The Black Sun, also known as the *nigredo,* marks the initial stage of the alchemical process, representing darkness and the raw material from which transformation springs. At the precipice of death, the soul confronts the challenge of self-transformation, heralding an enantiodromia. This mirrors my perception of death as the transmutation of energy, retaining its core even as its form shifts.

Ramana Maharshi posits that while the body may perish, the transcendent spirit remains untouched by death. This conviction underpins my belief in postmortem transformation. I've borne witness to such metanoia, seen the glow of the eternal on the face of my deceased friend. Yet, I've also witnessed the anguished struggle in the dying process of those who desperately cling to life. At the deathbed of my friends, I've often witnessed a process of emergence, where life and death, light and darkness, intricately intertwine and connect. In their profound existential queries, they wrestled to embrace and harmonize these apparent opposites, enduring their inherent tension.

These poignant moments have prompted me to contemplate the notion of a meaningful death or a "good death" —one imbued with value. For me, it would mean a death with full awareness and lucidity, acknowledging that I am dying. From a spiritual standpoint, a meaningful death involves embracing whatever unfolds.

I have asked myself: What mindset toward dying could facilitate a tranquil transition? When can I release myself peacefully, accepting the fading that follows blooming? Is death ripe for me when I've lived fully, acutely aware that life and death tread the same path? Am I prepared to depart when I've unearthed my destiny's answer and conscientiously and responsibly addressed life's inquiries? Will I recognize Hermes, my psychopomp, the guide who traverses boundaries, as the escort to the other realm, and will I willingly follow? Leonard Cohen's final song before his passing, where he sang "Hineni," Hebrew for "Here I am," followed by "I'm ready, my Lord," deeply moved me. What does it take to be "ready?"

In my work with patients grappling with profound suffering, I've witnessed that facing death shattered their identification with inauthentic self-images, allowing their true selves to emerge. Often, at this threshold, an imaginal realm, a *mundus imaginalis*, materializes, a domain of profound significance that stirs the unconscious with vibrant dreams. It is remarkable how an intensely charged energetic field takes shape on the deathbed.

I firmly believe in the potency of dreams and the transformative power of symbols and archetypes, particularly when facing existential crises like a cancer diagnosis. Many people have lost touch with the healing symbols and energies of our psyche that help us to cope with death and dying. A book like David Blum's is therefore of particular importance. His book *Appointment with the Wise Old Dog: A Bridge to the Transformative Power of Dreams* (Blum 2020) and the documentary film *Appointment with the Wise Old Dog: Dream Images in a Time of Crisis* resonated deeply with me. It was touching to see Blum's act of painting his dreams and adorning his room's walls with them, transforming the room into a sanctuary. This film magnificently captures the miraculous force of the unconscious and the human spirit, testifying to what I mean when I speak of a good death or dying wisely. I also learned about the skill of dying wisely from my Zen teacher, who suffered from cancer and confronted death courageously. To the Wise, death is not a downfall but a transition.

In the dreams of my patients, I've observed their psyche preparing for death, serving as bridges between the familiar and the unknown. Archetypal themes and images often arise like a journey to undertake, a beckoning to return home, a waiting train, a river to cross into another realm, and a gate or tunnel to traverse. Gibran Khalil Gibran invites us: *Trust in dreams, for in them is hidden the gate to eternity.*

One dream and the painting of it remains vivid, featuring a woman who sensed her imminent passing due to illness.

The dream commences with an extensive journey alongside numerous individuals through inhabited places and landscapes. A guide leads the group before they cross a road. The path descends through a lengthy tunnel into subterranean chambers where they assemble. Eventually, the dreamer finds herself outside, progressing toward a massive black lattice gate positioned amidst towering dark rocks. Lifeless human bodies lie to her right, frozen and undead, awaiting passage through the gate to true death. She's drawn to the captivating, indescribable light radiating beyond the gate. A voice from the light advises against entry, asserting she must return. A new path emerges to her left, leading her atop a hill overlooking the resplendent land—a dreamlike, unreal, beautiful landscape.

Similarly, this patient, endowed with profound imaginal capacity, experienced the subsequent dream:

> *"I enter a spacious basement with a group of people. It holds various rooms and a partially filled swimming pool, into which people fall from above and swim around. I'm now in an open-roofed, expansive room adjacent to others. A tunnel at the front connects these rooms, and within it, Thanatos rides an electric scooter, moving back and forth between rooms, escorting the deceased. Thanatos arrives at my room's entrance, locking eyes with me before continuing to the tunnel's end. Eager questions arise: will he return for me? He eventually*

> *comes back with a distinguished lady, and I realize*
> *that even the wealthy are guided this way."*

I'm a firm believer that the soul's voice speaks through dreams, occasionally even through uncanny encounters. The night before my mother died, I dreamt of water that had to be crossed to get to the other shore.

The night of her death I dreamed:

> *I am in a kind of seminar in which healers participate.*
> *A man of Arab maybe Egyptian origin chooses me*
> *to demonstrate something. He just touches me on*
> *the head, on the top of the skull, my fontanelle, and*
> *exclaims in amazement: Your arché is wide open!*

When will I receive the final call of the angel of death? These thoughts echo the verses of D. H. Lawrence's poignant poem "The Ship of Death": *"Have you built your ship of death, O, have you? Oh, build your ship of death, for you will need it."*

Now, at 77 years old, I find myself honing the art of letting go, embracing my mortality, and attuning my ear to the everlasting rhythm of impermanence that underpins life. I've come to view death as a threshold, potentially leading to heightened awareness—an expansion of consciousness, yet I anticipate with trepidation the loss of my Beloved, along with the painful realization of my own eventual departure.

As I gaze upon the myriad objects collected during my extensive travels, these soulful mementos evoke memories of days long past, and I wonder what will happen to them when I will cross the last threshold. They are imbued with energy and love and have special meaning for me. Musings and imaginings bestow joy, and I comprehend Jung's sense of kinship with objects. When my moment comes to cross the threshold of death, placing complete trust in the unknown, I aspire to do so with serenity.

My pursuit of establishing an unwavering connection between the ego and the Self, serving as a "window to eternity," is a preparation to face death. Death remains an inseparable companion on my life's journey, entwined with the moment of my birth. Though its arrival remains unpredictable and uncertain, without any foreknowledge of the time, place, or cause of my demise, I know that I am inevitably drawn toward death. A sense of solace emerges from the realization that the archetype of death binds us to all of humanity.

From my Buddhist mentors, I've encountered a poignant narrative of a young woman during the era of the historical Buddha. Grief-stricken by the death of her only child, she resorted to self-inflicted harm. With great hope and expectation, she went to the Buddha and asked him if he could bring her child back. Buddha didn't say yes or no. He said, "Before I can help, you have to find some white mustard seeds from a family untouched by death." Hearing this answer, her mood was lifted, and she went from house to house, village to village, and asked all the families, "Has anyone died in your family?" And every family said, "Yes, somebody died." So, she finally went back to the Buddha and told him that she couldn't find what he had asked for. At that moment, in front of the Buddha, she realized that death is a truth of life—and she became awakened, a person who has seen the truth. Her quest made her realize the universality of impermanence and mortality, expanding my perspective from my personal suffering toward evoking compassion for the suffering of all living beings.

Additionally, Ovid's *Metamorphoses* enriched my comprehension of life's impermanence:

*"I tell you Nothing is permanent in all the world.
...That which has been is not; that which was not,
Begins to be; motion and moment always In process
of renewal ... Nothing remains the same: the great
renewer, Nature, makes form from form, and, oh,
believe me, That nothing ever dies..."*

This core notion, that nothing truly perishes but instead changes its form, resonates with the teachings of Heraclitus. His concept of matter as energy and the cosmos as a perpetually regenerating entity underscores the constant cycle of change.

Buddhist teachings on Impermanence have shaped my understanding of our ephemeral existence in this world. We come and we go, arriving and departing belong together, all things in the world are impermanent, this is the nature of life, nothing is certain or everlasting.

These insights, however, do not imply that the experience of losing a loved one is easily processed. The understanding of impermanence and nonattachment doesn't shield me from grief and mourning. John Welwood recounted a tale where Chögyam Trungpa Rinpoche, during a memorial service for his dear friend Shunryu Suzuki, cried out loudly and openly wept. (Tricycle, Spring 2011).

It is crucial not to exploit Buddhist teachings for "spiritual bypassing," using them to evade the pain of loss and disregard our genuine needs and attachments, as highlighted by John Welwood, who coined the term. Spiritual bypassing involves evading unresolved emotional issues and avoiding uncompleted developmental tasks. Grieving and mourning are ways of loving and should have their place.

I'm reminded of a letter Freud sent to Ludwig Binswanger in 1929, on the birthday of his deceased daughter Sophie Halberstadt:

"Although we know after such a loss the acute state of mourning will subside, we also know we shall remain inconsolable and will never find a substitute. No matter what may fill the gap, even if it is filled completely, it nevertheless remains something else. And, actually this is how it should be, it is the only way of perpetuating that love which we do not want to relinquish." (Freud 1960)

I hold a deep belief that when the soul departs at death, it does not truly vanish. This perspective has been influenced by various cultures, where I have learned the practice of nurturing a symbolic connection with departed souls. I keep their legacy and values close, maintaining our ongoing bond. They continue to reside within my soul through memories and dreams.

In my garden, I have created a sacred space where I buried the ashes of my loved ones. At the entrance of my home, there stands a small abode for my ancestors, crafted by a friend in a style reminiscent of those we encountered during our travels in Asia. A statue of Guanyin sits in this shrine, protecting my loved ones. I pay homage to all my close friends who have passed away, acknowledging their presence in this shrine for my ancestors. I place flowers in a delicate vase within this shrine. To me, death severs the material connection but not the ethereal one with those I love. Their spirit is still with me; they are not totally gone, *"They are the source of all our conscious thoughts, and one of these primordial thoughts is the idea of life after death."* I forge a presence within absence, an enduring tie to the dead. I share this collective yearning to maintain an inner continuity between the past, present, and future even after death. My beloved and I reminisce together about where he would want me to leave some of his ashes, in our garden and in Venice, the city of love we both consider our second home.

The notion of individual immortality and perpetual significance is embedded in many myths and archaic beliefs about the afterlife. Jung articulated the necessity to remain attuned to these primordial images residing in the unconscious, from which springs the idea of life beyond death.

My understanding about symbolic immortality has been deepened by Robert Jay Lifton's *The Broken Connection* and *The Future of Immortality*. His foundational works on Thanatology and psychotraumatology profoundly shape the symbolic narrative surrounding death and symbolic immortality. He posits a universal impulse to combat oblivion and transcend death—surviving through memories, creativity, art, literature, music, scientific achievements, and benevolence. The pursuit of symbolic immortality echoes also in religious and spiritual depictions of mastery over death.

Similar to the Jungian approach to dissecting death anxiety, Lifton delves into imagery that counters denial and dread. His exploration of *"experiential transcendence"* strikes a chord, mirroring mystical encounters and near-death experiences where time and death dissolve. His emphasis on symbolic creativity and experiential transcendence relates to Jungian principles and aligns with my personal contemplation of mortality.

"The individual who is not anchored in God can offer no resistance on his own resources to the physical and moral blandishments of the world. For this he needs the evidence of inner, transcendent experience which alone can protect him from the otherwise inevitable submersion in the mass." (Jung, CW 10, § 511).

I think most of us share the desire to transcend the fragility of our human existence, trying to leave behind something valuable and meaningful that will last. *"The feeling* of immortality," Jung wrote, *"has its origin in a peculiar feeling of extension in space and time" (CW9I, §§248-49),* but there is also a shadow side of this symbolic immortality which we can observe in the rise of suicide bombers.

Sigmund Freud maintained a rather pessimistic stance toward immortality, as can be seen in his letter to Marie Bonaparte in 1937.

"To the writer immortality evidently means being loved by any number of anonymous people. Well, I know I won't mourn your death, for you will survive me by years, and over mine I hope you will quickly console yourself and let me live in your friendly memory—the only form of limited immortality I recognize."

My Beloved and I are endeavoring to creatively utilize the time remaining by coauthoring a book on *Wissenschaft und Weisheit* as two complementary ways of understanding the world. We recall Martin Walser, who recently passed at the age of 96, saying: *"Die deutlichste* Überwindung *von Tod und Sterben ist das Schreiben"*— "The clearest overcoming of death and dying is writing."

Our shared psychoanalytic writing carries perhaps the potential for symbolic immortality. We both, in preparing for death, would like to depart from this world in the spirit of Austrian composer Gottfried von Einem:

"Enden werde ich leise,
ins Licht entschwindend,
mit allem schwerelos verbunden.
Es wird erfüllte Stille sein."
"I shall end quietly,
fading into the light,
connected weightlessly with everything.
It will be a fulfilled silence."

References

Becker, E. (1973). *The denial of death*. New York: Free Press.

Becker, E. (1971). *The birth and death of meaning*. New York: Free Press.

Blum, D. (2020). *Appointment with the wise old dog: A bridge to the transformative power of dreams*. Chiron Publications.

Calhoun, L. G., & Tedeschi, R. G. (2006). *Handbook of posttraumatic growth: Research and practice*. New Jersey: Lawrence Erlbaum Ass.

Calhoun, L. G., & Tedeschi, R. G. (2013). *Posttraumatic growth in clinical practice*. New York: Routledge.

Collins, E. O. (2017). *Psychologically preparing for death: Facing your mortality and creating your symbolic immortality (Doctoral dissertation)*. Pacifica Graduate Institute, ProQuest.

Dürckheim, G. K. (1971). *The way of transformation: Daily life as spiritual exercise*. London: Allen & Unwin.

Fenwick, P., & Fenwick, E. (1997). *The truth in the light: An investigation of over 300 near-death experiences*. New York: Berkley Books.

von Franz, M.-L. (1979). *Alchemical active imagination: Revised edition (C. G. Jung foundation books)*. Boston: Shambhala.

Forster, E. M. (1910). *Howard's End*. London: Edward Arnold.

Freud, S. (1937). *Letter from Sigmund Freud to Marie Bonaparte, August 13, 1937. In E. L. Freud (Ed.), Letters of Sigmund Freud, 1873-1939 (pp. 436-437). New York: Basic Books. Retrieved from https://pepweb.org/browse/document/zbk.051.0436a*

Freud, S. (2011). *Reflections on war and death. The Project*

Gutenberg EBook. (A. A. Brill & A. B. Kuttner, Trans.).
Retrieved from https://www.gutenberg.org/ebooks/35875

Gibran, K. (1923). The prophet. New York: Knopf.

Heidegger, M. (1962). Being and time (J. MacQuarrie & E.
Robinson, Trans.). New York, NY: HarperCollins. (Original
work published 1927)

Hillman, J. (1979). The dream and the underworld. New York, NY:
Harper and Row.

Holecek, A. (2013). Preparing to die. Boston: Shambhala.

Jaspers, K. (1971). Philosophy, Volume 2 (E. B. Ashton, Trans.).
Chicago, IL: University of Chicago Press.

Jenkinson, S. (2015). Die wise: A manifesto for sanity and soul.
Berkeley: North Atlantic Books.

Jung, C. G. (1965). Memories, dreams, reflections. New York:
Vintage Books.

Jung, C. G. (1973). Letters, vol I, 1906-1950 (G. Adler, Ed., & R. F.
C. Hull, Trans.). Routledge.

Yates, J. (Ed.). (1999). Jung on death and immortality. Princeton,
NJ: Princeton UP.

Keats, J. (2006). In R. Longman (Ed.), The Longman anthology of
poetry. Palgrave.

Lawrence, D. H. (1933). Last poems (R. Aldington, Ed.). London:
Martin Secker.

Lifton, R. J. (1979). The broken connection: On death and the
continuity of life. New York: Simon & Schuster.

Lifton, R. J. (1987). The future of immortality and other essays for
a nuclear age. New York: Basic Books.

Meerwein, F. (1991). Die Arzt-Patienten-Beziehung des Krebs-
kranken. In F. Meerwein (Ed.), Einführung in die Psycho-
onkologie. Bern-Göttingen-Toronto.

de Montaigne, M. (n.d.). Essais I,20.

Oosthuizen, W. F. (2013). *Death: An archetypal education of the ego (Doctoral dissertation). Pacifica Graduate Institute, ProQuest.*

Ovid. (1993). *The metamorphoses (A. Mandelbaum, Trans.). San Diego: Harcourt.*

Rilke, R. M. (2018). *The dark interval: Letters on loss, grief, and transformation (U. Baer, Trans.). New York: Random House Modern Library.*

Rilke, R. M. (1949). *The notebooks of Malte Laurids Brigge (M. D. Herter Norton, Trans.). New York: Norton.*

Twain, M. (n.d.). *Letters from the Earth. Retrieved from https:// www.goodreads.com/book/show/37813.Letters_from_the_ Earth*

Tolstoy, L. (2020). *The death of Ivan Ilych (L. & A. Maude, Trans.). Retrieved from https://study.com/academy/lesson/the-death-of-ivan-ilych.html*

del Grosso, T. (1993). *Le trame della grande dea. Treviso: Marchi Artitessili.*

Trycycle. (2011). *Interview with John Welwood by Tina Fossella. The Buddhist Review, Spring.*

Yalom, I. (1980). *Existential psychotherapy. New York: Basic Books.*

Experience of Death from the Viewpoint of Modern Japanese Buddhism

Haruko Kuwabara

New tradition of death in Japan: "Enzeru-kea," or *after death care* in hospitals

Japan is said to be a highly modernized country. While this is true, when we face death, our old collective consciousness is actively stimulated. I started writing this essay while I was preparing my father's third memorial service, which means two years have passed since his day of death, *"Meinichi." Meinichi* originally means "Day of Life" in Chinese characters. Thus, in Japanese itself, the death anniversary also implies the anniversary of life. This essay is based on my personal experience of my father's death. Although I tried to refer to as many books and articles as possible, there are so many differences in mortuary customs among modern Japanese Buddhist sects that I cannot cover everything here.

My father passed away on April 9, 2021, when this world was still surrounded by so many deaths caused by the COVID-19 pandemic, most of which were "lonely deaths." The person dying had to depart without their family or friends around. Families and friends were not allowed to enter hospitals or nursing homes in Japan back then. This made the mourning process more difficult and hurtful for the family since many Japanese, consciously or unconsciously, have the idea that it is against *"Oya-Koko,"* or filial duty, to let the parent die alone. I have considered myself more westernized and not so-much-traditional-Japanese, as I studied in both Texas and Switzerland. But when it came to facing my father's death in reality, I realized that I was deeply rooted in this collective consciousness of "*Oya-Koko*," which was originally based on Confucianism. I felt so worried that I might not be able to be by his side when he would pass away, which would definitely lead to deep regret in the future.

However, my father fortunately passed away between the surges of COVID-19. His doctor also understood the needs of my family and let us stay with him for the last few days of his life, which was quite an unusual decision for a doctor to make those days. In Japan, a country of great conformity pressure, it would have been a much easier decision for the doctor to say no to the family to spend the last days with the dying, considering that there was a high chance of infection. Many hospitals only allowed 10 minutes of meeting time for families with maybe one or two members each time. Luckily, my father had a doctor who was willing to make a different decision than the standards back then.

All our family gathered for him in his last days, and he passed away in a peaceful manner surrounded by the words of "*arigato*" or "thank you." Not very many Japanese people, especially people above my age, would express the affection of "I love you" in words to their parents. Here, "thank you" also includes "I love you." When he passed away, the male nurse came and asked us if we wanted to join him to do "*Enzeru-kea*," meaning after-death care or end-of-life care. None of my family except me was interested in it, given that we were in deep sorrow due to his passing. I heard the word "*Enzeru-kea*" for the first time, and I was not sure if it was different from the traditional ceremony of "*Yukan*" in Japanese funerals. Yu means hot water, and Yukan means to bathe and purify the person before laying them into a coffin or casket. It is not clear exactly when this ritual of Yukan began in Japan. Yokoi (2016) discusses different cases of Yukan rituals in different regions of Japan. He suggests that Yukan was more related to archaic religious and magical attitudes to make the distinction between death and life clear before the introduction of Buddhism. People tried to differentiate between death and life using Japanese Sake, salt, or something white for purification from death. After Buddhism was introduced in Japan, Buddhist interpretation and meaning were added to Yukan (Yokoi, 2016). Yukan was a rite to lead the dead to the state of *"Jyobutsu,"* meaning attaining Buddhahood, or *"Oujyou,"* meaning birth into the Pure Land after one's death (Ohgi, 2018).

The idea of Yukan is probably based on idea of *"Kegare,"* or impurity, although Yokoi does not mention its influence on development of Yukan. Kegare is the idea of impurity both in Shintoism and Buddhism in Japan. Matsuo (2011) discusses the development of Funerary Buddhism in Medieval Japan. In ancient Japan, various kinds of Kegare were first defined in *"Engi-shiki,"* the ancient Japanese book of laws and regulations written in 927. Kegare included the death and birth of people or animal, eating meat, abortion, pregnancy, menstruation, fire, burial, and so on. Kegare caused by death of people, or *"Shie,"* was regarded as the worst and most powerful of Kegare. People who touched this Shie, or Kegare of death, were required to perform 30 days of penitence and were not allowed to participate in rituals or come to the palace or court. Kegare was basically infectious, so if a person met someone with Shie, then the person was also infected by it. Thus, death could influence the living person in a negative way, leading to fear and anxiety to avoid it.

Buddhism was introduced in Japan in sixth century. But in ancient Japan, Buddhist priests did not conduct funerals because of the idea of Shie (Matsuo, 2011). The dead, except the aristocrats, were discarded at the end of town or along the rivers without being buried nor cremated. It was called "*Fuso*," meaning wind burial. In Kyoto, there are some names of towns which used to be open-air burial sites, such as "*Toribeno.*" Most of them were located in the borderline surrounding the town. Tori means birds, since back then in Japan, birds or animals played the role of eating up the bodies of the deceased. The idea that death is Kegare is still active in today's Shintoism. Hence, people who have lost their family less than a year ago refrain from visiting the shrine, which is a sacred space, since they carry the Kegare of death. People need to do some kind of "*Misogi*," or purification bath, to get rid of Kegare. Water plays an important role in purification, so people wash their hands before entering the site of the shrine even today.

Thus, Yukan is itself rooted in the combination of Buddhism, Shintoism, and other archaic religious attitudes in premodern Japan. Japanese life events, especially rituals surrounding death, are deeply influenced by "*Shinbutsu Shugo*," or the syncretistic fusion of Shintoism and Buddhism (Matsuo, 2011), starting in the sixth century.

In Japanese funerals, "*Nokan*" is another ceremony done by a specialist called "*Nokan-shi*," which means a process of laying the dead into the coffin. It usually consists of dressing the dead, putting the makeup, and getting them ready for the departure to the life after death, or to the Pure Land. Yukan is done as the early part of Nokan, so both rituals are regarded as preparing the dead to be purified for their departure to the world after death.

Then, what is the difference between traditional Yukan and Enzeru-kea done in Japanese hospitals in 21st century? The nurse was a specialist of "Enzeru-kea." Enzeru-kea, or after-death care, is not "Angel care" and has no religious background. It started in

Japanese hospitals around 2000 (Inaha, 2002). Enzeru-kea consists of cleaning the body of the person, and dressing and getting ready them for departure. It is supposed to be for both the terminal care of the patient and grief care of the family. As I took part in my father's Enzeru-kea, I helped the nurse in cleaning him with a hand shower, shave the hair with a razor, and put a lot of moisturizing cream with nice aroma and dress him in Yukata, or a casual kimono. His body was cold and stiff, so I felt through all my senses that his soul had left his body. During the process, I was talking with the nurse about how he had chosen Enzeru-kea as his specialty. He told me that he made it a rule to talk to the person by name as a living person and make them as clean and beautiful as possible so that the person might say thank you to him should he someday meet the person in the life after death. I was deeply moved by his words as someone who met my father after his death paid so much respect to his departure to the life after death. My father was purified, shining and smelling like a flower, and even smiling thanks to the Enzeru-kea, free from all the pains he suffered at the end of his life. Everyone was relieved to see him with a smile and resting in peace and being free from suffering and the family no longer seeing him in the pain of dying. Enzeru-kea also gave me a sense of *"Oya-koko,"* or filial duty, that I had done everything I could do as a daughter for him, who was now in the transition of life. Thus, Enzeru-kea is the newest combination of old traditional Yukan, and the new Western ideas of terminal and grief care.

Process of Buddhist Funeral in Funerary Buddhism in Modern Japan

Religion does not play a major role in modern Japan. Still, many people, consciously or unconsciously, keep some religious attitudes in everyday life and life events, especially rituals related to death.

Hayao Kawai (1986) points out that "the most of what modern Japanese formally hold now as Buddhist rituals have been passed down rather because of intrinsic beliefs in Japan; even if the Japanese do not have 'religious faith' as the Westerners say, the religiosity, which has been underlying in the Japanese Unconscious since ancient time, has unexpectedly supported much of the Japanese' sense of stability" (p. 79. my translation).

Buddhism in Japan is often called Funerary Buddhism, meaning that Buddhism and Buddhist temples play their essential role only in funerals and mortuary services. Matsuo (2011) observes that Funerary Buddhism started in the Edo era in the 17th century, when the shogunate decided that all Japanese were Buddhists and that everyone should belong to a temple as parishioner. The system was to prohibit Christianity, which started to spread rapidly and threatened the government. This system led to the present-day situation whereby many Japanese say with a kind of hesitation that they were Buddhist and had funerals in a Buddhist manner. When my father passed away, we had to decide in a short time which sect of Buddhism his funerals should be based on. It usually depends on which sect your family belongs to. My father's side belonged to *Soutou-Zen* sect, and my mother's side belonged to *Jyodo-Shinshu,* or Shin Buddhism sect. So, what about my family's sect? We have never done funerals by ourselves as a nuclear family of parents and two daughters, and we were at a loss regarding what to do. Relatives on my father's side are all ancestors or the deceased, or too old to help us. We also heard of funerals of the Soutou-zen sect being quite pricey. If you want to have the highest rank of "*Kaimyo,*" a posthumous Buddhist name, you must pay more than 1 million yen or 8,000 U.S. dollars just for the name. A name in the afterlife costs that much. No, a rational modern Japanese could not find enough meaning on paying that much just for his name.

Shin Buddhism, on my mother's side, is the biggest sect of Buddhism in Japan, and almost 20 percent of the Buddhists in Japan today belong to this sect. It was founded by Shinran Shonin (1173–1263) in medieval Japan. Its teaching has several different ideas from the other sects. The deceased is immediately supposed to be born into "*Jyodo*," or the Pure Land, to be Buddha by "*Tariki*," or other power of Amida Buddha. The life in this world is the life before birth in the Pure Land. It does not require Kaimyo or a posthumous Buddhist name, but "Homyo," or a name in accordance with the teachings of Buddha. "*Kue-Issho*" is the key concept of Shin Buddhism, and its funerals and services, and it means "See you again in Amida's Pure Land" (Ohgi, 2018). Issho means one place, which is the Pure Land, where every deceased is supposed to go according to the teachings of Shin Buddhism. So, my father's death is the end of his life in this world, but we are supposed to see each other again in the Pure Land. This idea was probably one of the reasons why Shin Buddhism became so popular and widespread in Japan. Separation in this world is temporal, and there will be reunion in the future, which helps one in having a sense of relief and acceptance of death.

Jung talks about death as a goal and role of religions in understanding death:

> I am convinced that it is hygienic—if I may use the word—to discover in death a goal towards which one can strive, and that shrinking away from it is something unhealthy and abnormal which robs the second half of life of its purpose. I therefore consider that all religions with a supramundane goal are eminently reasonable from the point of view of psychic hygiene. ... From the standpoint

of psychotherapy it would therefore be desirable to think of death as only a transition, as part of a life process whose extent and duration are beyond our knowledge.

(Jung, 1933/1960, para. 792)

As Jung states here, telling the story or to "mythologize" (Jung, 1963, p. 353) about death as a transition and birth into the Pure Land seemed reasonable for psychic hygiene. So, our family decided to do my father's funeral according to Shin Buddhism.

Another problem to be solved was what to do with our family grave. A family grave is usually taken over by the oldest son, or sometimes by the oldest daughter if the family had only daughters. My father was the youngest son of the family, so he had to build his own family grave. His parents' grave was taken over by his oldest brother, who was already deceased and, in turn, was taken over by the oldest son of his oldest daughter. However, in the case of our family with two daughters, as my older sister and I had already been married, we could not take over our family grave even if my father should have built a new one. Rowe (2011) discusses the concept of "*Muen*," or to be without bonds, which is "a multivalent term that encapsulates the fears of Japanese who do not have graves, as well as those who lack relatives to maintain their graves into the future (p.44)." The idea of Muen has come into focus especially in the last 10 years because of the demographic, social, and economic shifts in Japan. Rowe (2011) discusses 21st-century Japan as "a society that not only is incapable of caring for its dead but also cannot even identify them (p.44)." In the society of Muen, what to do with the grave depends largely on individual preferences and choices. We did not wish this problem of Muen to come true in our family. Hence, we decided to do it in a more practical way, as we did with my father's name: We decided not to build a family grave altogether.

Recently, there are more people who decide not to build a family grave or who dismantle their family grave. The new ways to bury ashes of the deceased are community graves, mausoleums, and ossuaries in temples or towns, "*Sankotsu*," or scattering of ashes in nature like the ocean or mountains, "*Jumokuso*," or burial in which a tree is planted instead of a tomb (Rowe, 2011; Gamaike, 2022). Gamaike (2022) also points out that some of these "new" ways of burials, such as community graves and Jumokuso, were widespread in medieval Japan before "*Ie*," or the feudalistic family system was established in the Edo era. In Shin Buddhism, there is a custom of followers' remains being interred in the mausoleum, where the founder Shinran Shonin is said to rest. The mausoleum has beautiful temples and is full of beauty in the four seasons of Japan. My family decided to lay my father there to rest, since he loved to be surrounded by his friends and family and loved to take pictures of beautiful scenery and annual festivals of Kyoto. Kyoto was like our second hometown, my mother's hometown, and where I spent 15 years of university and began my career as psychotherapist. Now, everything was settled for my father's departure.

Synchronistic Experience Surrounding Death: Experience of Interconnected World

In "*On Life after Death*," Jung (1963) discusses many synchronistic phenomena surrounding the death of his family and friends. In an interview held in October 1959, Jung discusses that "there are these peculiar faculties of the psyche, that it isn't entirely confined to space and time." He says, "When the psyche is not under that obligation to live in time and space alone, and obviously it doesn't, then to the extent the psyche is not subjected to those laws, and that means a practical continuation of life, of a sort of psychical existence beyond time and space" (Jung, 1959/1978, p. 437). I also had a synchronistic experience beyond time and space in the process of my father's death.

My father was a person with green fingers and was really good at raising plants and flowers. Tree peonies were his favorite flowers, and he devoted himself so much to taking care of them. They used to come into full bloom in the beginning of May, which was during a week of holidays, so my family often gathered at his house and enjoyed the flowers together. A few years before his death, he was hospitalized in early spring, but he persuaded his doctor into discharging him from the hospital, saying he had to take care of the peonies. The life of the peonies came first for him before his own life.

Tree peonies are originally from China, and the story says *Kukai* or *Kobo Daishi*, the founder of *Shingon* sect or Esoteric Buddhism, brought the flower to Japan in ninth century. In Japan, tree peonies are depicted on the edges or frames of the Womb Realm Mandala or Garbhadhatu Mandala. Tree peonies, or "*Botan*" and "*Kara Jishi*," which are imaginary sacred animal similar to lions, are popular motifs in Buddhist temples and objects. The story of their relationship is as follows: Kara Jishi was invincible, but worms or parasites inside his own body were the only enemy. The dew collected inside tree peonies during the night was the only medicine to exterminate the parasites, so Kara Jishi always slept under tree peonies. Also, tree peonies have been widely raised in Buddhist temples and offered to Buddhist statues since the 13th century (Amemiya, 2015).

On the evening my father passed away, it was the beginning of April, so the tree peonies were far from coming into bloom. I was talking with my family that my father must be really sorry that he could not see the peony flowers this year, since he had put so much energy and time at the end of his life. We saw the picture of the tree peonies in "*Ikebana*," or the Japanese art of flower arrangement by my mother. He sent it to my older sister the year before. It was beautiful and reminded me of the Mandala. We all wished we could have had the flowers at his funeral, but we knew that it was too early. When I came home to my parents' house late that night, I checked the peonies. But of course I could not see any buds.

The next morning when I opened the curtain of the living room, I could not believe what I saw: Some of the tree peonies were in full bloom. I felt the spirit of the tree peonies knew my father, who loved them the most, passed away and that they were saying goodbye to him. I could see the image of him smiling surrounded by tree peonies in the garden, being so proud of them. I cried for the first time after my father's death; my dissociation between the body and feeling was connected again by experiencing the interconnected world of synchronicity.

We brought the peonies to my father and put them surrounding his face in the casket. Now, he looked like Buddha with a peaceful archaic smile on his face. We then had two different ceremonies, one in the evening called "*Tsuya*," or wake, and the next day "*Kokubetu-shiki*," or funeral. Since it was during the COVID-19 pandemic, many people had a small family wake and funeral instead of having a big ceremony. It was a small but cozy ceremony, full of the family's warmth and love. Other than Buddhist services, the funeral home prepared a small ceremony for the family to join. His granddaughters wrote a letter to their grandfather. We even saw a movie of his life from his childhood until the last days that was made by the funeral home. A movie of the deceased must be a new and popular standard of funeral, since it was included in the package of the funeral. I felt that showing the movie of life of the deceased was so similar to a typical Japanese wedding celebration, which reminded me of Jung's experience of "dance music, laughter, and jollity as though a wedding were being celebrated" on the night train after his mother's death (Jung, 1963, p. 368-369). If death is the goal, as Jung says, and if death is also the birth as Buddha into the Pure Land, as the teaching of Shin Buddhism says, then it is understandable to have the funeral as celebration in a way.

After the funeral service is over, the family of the deceased heads to the crematorium. We have a special ceremony after cremation: "*Kotsu-age*," or the bereaved family's putting the bones of a deceased person into an urn. Matsuo (2011) has conducted crosscultural research on funeral rites and memorial services, and suggests that the ceremony of Kotsu-age was only held in Japan, as even among Asian countries, cremation was the main choice of burial method. It is surely shocking to see your beloved one being only bones and ashes after cremation for the first time, so in most families, young children do not participate in the ceremony. My daughter was 10 years old, and she decided not to participate in Kotsu-age, since she was in great shock to see her beloved grandpa passing. I was in my mid-20s when I first participated in the ceremony for my great-aunt, who was like a grandmotherly figure to me. I felt a numinous feeling (Otto, 1917), a great awe and attraction at the same time, and strong feeling of "*Mujo*," anicca or transience. The view of Mujo or anicca has played a major role in Japanese world view and culture since the medieval times, especially for understanding death. Even today's children in the fifth grade learn to recite the first parts of "*Heike Monogatari*," or The Tale of the Heike, the most famous passages of Mujo, or ever-changing world:

The sound of the bells of Gion Monastery echo with the ever-changing nature of all things. The fading hues on the blossoms of the sala tree signify that all that flourishes must fade. The arrogant do not prevail for long, nothing but a spring night's dream. The mighty in time succumb, dust before the wind.

(translation by MacMillan, 2020, p. 195)

In Kotsu-age, we observe the entire process of transformation from life to death, or the birth to the next world. You see bones or ashes as remains, but you know clearly that the soul of your loved one is no longer there, having been freed from the body. It reminded me of "*Kuso-zu*," the Japanese Buddhist art that depicted the nine stages of the decaying corpse, especially that of the beautiful noble lady's transformation. The drawing was to help people meditate on "*Mujo*," or anicca (Gamaike, 2022). Every family member attending the ceremony put the bones, from the legs to the head from the bottom of the urn to its top so that the bones would line up inside the urn in the order as the deceased person used to live in this world. The last bone to be put in the urn is "*Nodo-Botoke.*" Botoke means "*Hotoke*," or Buddha. Nodo is throat. That is, it is the thyroid cartilage, or Adam's apple. In Japan, the shape of Nodo-Botoke is said to be identical to meditating Buddha, so it symbolizes Buddhahood in the dead. We use special chopsticks, usually one made of wood and another made of bamboo or different ingredient, to make a clear distinction between the chopsticks of everyday life and those of the Kotsu-age ceremony after death.

In my father's Kotsu-age, there was another surprise for me: Some parts of his skull turned out to be pink after cremation. We put several red and purple tree peonies around my father's face so that he could depart surrounded by the flowers he loved the most in his life. I was deeply moved to see the connection between my father and the tree peonies. I was thankful to the synchronistic event that they came into full bloom.

Buddhist Memorial Services after Funeral: How the Dead Will Go to the Life after Death?

After the funeral, it depends on Buddhist sects how often one should hold Buddhist services for the dead. Regardless of the sects, memorial services are influenced by the story of the 10 kings (Matsuo, 2011). The 10 Kings are considered to judge if the dead should go either to the Pure Land or to Hell every seven days after his/her death until the seventh seven days, which is called "Shijuku-nichi," or 49th-day memorial, when we hold a big memorial service. After that service, many families bury the urn of the beloved family member. Then, the 100th-day memorial, first-year memorial, and third-year memorial are occasions when the dead will be judged by the 10 kings. The story of the 10 kings was originally introduced from China, and it became popular at the end of Heian period around the 10th-11th centuries based on the idea of "*Mappo*," or the latter-day of laws. According to Buddhist teachings, Mappo was a period when Buddhist law would fall into decline, bringing chaos and disorder to the world. Hence, many people back then had great fear and anxiety, and they hoped to be saved by faith in the Pure Land. The 10 kings' story was related to "manifestation theory," holding that gods in Shintoism were manifestations of Buddhas in Japan. In the Kamakura era, or medieval Japan, each of the 10 kings was connected to different kinds of Buddhas. The first seven-days memorial was judged by Acala, and the last, third memorial was judged by Amitabha. The 10 kings' story was deeply woven into the ideas of Japanese Buddhism, especially in the Jodo or Pure Land sects, whose founder *Honen* was the master of Shinran Shonin, who founded Shin Buddhism. The bereaved family holds Buddhist services when the 10 kings judge the dead to help accumulating good deeds so that the dead could go into the Pure Land. Thus, Buddhist memorial services in Japan combine various aspects of Buddhism, some of which are deeply influenced by Shintoism, Chinese Confucianism, and Daoism. In Shin Buddhism, the deceased are said to be born in the Pure Land immediately as Buddha by the power of Amitabha, so the story of the 10 kings does not apply. Therefore, memorial services are not for the deceased person but for the bereaved family in Shin Buddhism to get in touch with the Buddhist teaching and feel gratitude to the Other Power of Amida. We have to be flexible and adjust to different patterns of funerals and Buddhist memorial services. However, the 49th-day memorial has a special meaning and is a must to do as a custom and manner, regardless of the sect.

After the 49th-day memorial, we brought the urn to the mausoleum to bury it there. In the process of Buddhist service of burying his ashes, I realized that now my father belonged to the Buddhas. His Buddha name consists of three Chinese characters, the first one meaning Buddha, one Chinese character from his first name meaning superior, and the last Chinese character, *"kokoro,"* meaning psyche. The last Chinese character was chosen by the Buddhist priest who conducted the funeral service after he listened to the family's explanation of my father's life and personality. I found it meaningful that the priest chose kokoro as his Buddha name, since I am literally a psychotherapist and teach clinical psychology. Now, the 49th-day memorial was over, so we should wait for the first-year memorial.

Dream of My Father after His Death

When I started to get depressed after all the hassles of the legal processes related to his death were over, I had this one dream.

Dream on July 13: I'm with my father and a young woman who is in her 20s, maybe a college student. She is making a bonfire on the beach, and she is putting a huge turtle, which is bigger than a human being, onto the fire. I think the turtle is dying, burned in the fire, but she says, "No, she/he's OK, just look at her/him well!" She/he looks [like she is] enjoying the warmth of [the] fire and [being] happy. Now, the girl pours water onto the fire, and the water wets the turtle too. Now, the turtle stretches her/his body, and she/he looks at me with a joyful look in her/his eyes. Her/his eyes are big and jet black. Then, she/he slowly starts to move. The girl says in a joyful manner, "See, now she/he is OK!" My father holds up his camera and says, "Let's take a picture together, all of us. It's such a precious opportunity for us to be able to take a picture with such a huge turtle." The turtle is really huge, and she/he looks full of vital power to live through the time of eternity. I also feel very lucky to meet her/ him, such a precious animal. My father looks really happy and joyful, taking pictures of the turtle.

Waking up from this dream, I felt relieved that he is really having a great life now in the world after death. The turtle in this dream reminded me of the tortoise Cassiopeia in the story "*Momo*" by Michael Ende (1973). Cassiopeia can communicate through writing on her shell and can see 30 minutes into the future. The turtle also reminded me of the sea turtle in the story of the Japanese folk tale "*Urashima Taro*." The sea turtle takes Urashima Taro, who saved her life from the bullying children, to the world underwater, where Urashima met beautiful Oto Hime or the princess of the Dragon

Palace. He lived happily there for three years when he missed his home and decided to go home. Oto Hime gave him a box and told him never to open it. When he got back home, everything was totally changed, since three years underwater meant 300 years in this world. Urashima opened the box in despair and transformed into an old man. The turtle in this story is regarded to symbolize a bodily aspect of the feminineness of the timeless Unconscious (Kawai, 1982). The turtle also symbolized longevity in Japan, as the old proverb says "Crane lives for 1,000 years, and Turtle lives for 10,000 years," meaning to celebrate the longevity.

Jung discusses the "experience of the evolution of the soul after death." About a year after his wife Emma's death, he awoke one night and knew that he had been with her. She was engaged on studies of the Grail, which was her unfinished work:

> Interpretation on the subjective level—that my anima had not yet finished with the work she had to do— yielded nothing of interest; I know quite well that I am not yet finished with that. But the thought that my wife was continuing after death to work on her further spiritual development—however that may be conceived—struck me as meaningful and held a measure of reassurance for me.
>
> (Jung, 1963, p. 364)

In the dream of my father, I felt that he was continuing to pursue his work on his spiritual development even after his death, to take pictures of the precious, as Jung points out here.

Toshio Kawai (2022) also discusses the nonsymbolic and direct appearance of image in synchronistic visions and dreams, and he suggests that there are two aspects of the nonsymbolic:

literal and synchronistic (p. 625). He regards Jung's vision about Wilhelm R. before his death as an example of the synchronistic meaning of the nonsymbolic. It happened as a real fact and real presence of Wilhelm's soul and its farewell. I saw this dream of my father right before "*Hyakkanichi*," or the 100th-day memorial for him, when the soul of the deceased is supposed to be judged again by "*Byoudou-ou*," or Equal King, the eighth of the 10 kings. The 100th-day memorial is also called "*Sokkokuki*," meaning graduation from mourning, so it is the timing of transition after death both for the dead and bereaved family. I actually forgot about Hyakkanichi before I had this dream. Not very many people today have a memorial service for Hyakkanichi. So, it was a great surprise for me to see my father in the dream around the 100th-day memorial.

The dream was so real and nonsymbolic, as Kawai (2022) discusses. It was not a symbol of my father at a subjective level but of my father as himself. It was literal but also synchronistic: My father in the dream seems really happy and well, free from all the physical pains and suffering. He is enjoying his lifetime work, taking pictures joyfully in the world after death. This dream helped me go through mourning and accept separation in this world with reassurance. Since then, I have my father's dream once in a while. In every dream he is so lively, and I take my dreams seriously to remember him. I learned this attitude of taking dreams of the dead seriously from Jung and analytical psychology.

The Ancestors as a Deity Returning to This World

Regarding the Buddhist services after the third Memorial, people usually have Buddhist memorial services commemorating the seventh (after 6 years), 13th, 17th, 23rd, and 27th Memorials. The last memorial, or death anniversary, is the 33rd Memorial, which is called "*Tomurai-age*," meaning completion of mourning. Some families continue services until the 50th memorial. However, most direct descendants except grandchildren may no longer be alive for the 50th memorial, so ordinary people stop at the 33rd memorial. The story of 10 kings was developed into the story of 13 kings in the Kamakura era, adding the seventh, 13th, and 33rd memorials as further occasions for the dead to be judged about their future (Matsuo 2011). I could not find literature about the specific reason for the 17th, 23rd, and 27th memorials, but fewer people have memorial services for these three anniversaries.

As Kawai (2012) suggests, the ancestors in the Japanese worldview are supposed to be gods who return to the world regularly (p. 586). The equinoctial day in Spring and Autumn, and the Bon festival in summer are usually occasions of their returning home. Shin Buddhism has a different understanding from other sects about the ancestors' returning, saying that the ancestors returned to this world as Buddha to teach important Buddhist teaching to many people living in this world (Ohgi, 2018); thus, the ancestors as Buddha are supposed to be always in this world. We have various kinds of annual events relating to Buddhism and Shintoism. I have experienced these events so many times since childhood without considering their religious backgrounds. So, I feel that the Bon festival is the period when my ancestors return to this world and that they go back to the afterlife at *"Gozan no Okuribi"* in Kyoto on August 16. It is a day when huge bonfires are burned on the five mountains surrounding Kyoto in the shapes of some Chinese characters, ship, and "Torii," or shrine gate. The bonfire is a means to send the spirits of the ancestors back to the afterlife.

Even though we have special memorial services and some annual events, "people live in touch with the dead, or the dead continue to live in touch with living people" (Kawai, 2012, p. 386) in everyday life too. Whenever I go to Kyoto for work, I pay a visit to the mausoleum for my father and my ancestors. As we decided not to have a family grave of our own, instead of going to the family grave and getting in touch with the dead, I do so by visiting the temple. Many Japanese families have a Buddhist altar at home, even if they are not enthusiastic believers of Buddhism, and the size of altar is much smaller than the former days. My mother has a small altar for my father, and she places flowers and fruits, sweets, or whatever my father used to love and burns incense sticks for him. When I visit my parents' house, the first thing to do is to go to the altar, bring something he liked, burn incense sticks for him, and tell him, "I'm home, Dad." I never thought I was a kind of person who would do it before, but I started doing it after my father's death. The altar itself is not for the deceased ancestors but for the Amida Buddha, and burning incense is regarded as an act to reflect on the workings of Amida Buddha in Shin Buddhism (Ohgi, 2018). But psychologically speaking, it is a moment of getting in touch with the dead. A combination of all these acts, such as praying and burning incense at the altar in everyday life, visiting the gravesite, the annual rites, and memorial services have "hygienic" (Jung, 1933/1960) meaning for the living to feel connected with the dead or ancestors, who will protect the descendants if they get proper respect and "devotion" (Kawai, 2012).

Acceptance of Death in Psychotherapy: The Death of a Client

Has my experience of my father's death, as mentioned above, changed my attitude toward death? After my father's death, I came across one of the most difficult aspects of psychotherapy. My client suddenly passed away. It was not suicide, but her heart just stopped one morning. She had a long history of eating disorder and was also suicidal. She cut herself or tried to choke herself up when she was stressed out. She hurt her body, hoping to be freed from this world.

> A wrong functioning of the psyche can do much to
> injure the body, just as conversely a bodily illness

can affect the psyche; for psyche and body are not separate entities but one and the same life.

(Jung, 1917/1953, para. 194)

Jung states here the oneness of the psyche and body. He also points out the importance of equilibrium between the two, the life of the body and the life of the spirit:

So the relation between the life of the spirit and the life of the body is very critical. Too much of the body and the spirit dies; too much of the spirit and the body dies. There is a sort of changing equilibrium between the two factors, and a bit too much of one means the destruction of the other.

(Jung, 1934/1988, p. 177)

My patient's situation was starting to lose the equilibrium between the two, as her conscious wish to die had hurt her body all the time and she could not feel the pain of the life of the body. Then, it reached the condition Jung discusses below:

Those people who are completely identical with consciousness are often so unaware of the body that the head walks away with them, so they lose control of the body and anything can happen to it: the whole system becomes upset.

(Jung, 1935/1988, p. 750)

She had talked about her wish to die in every session, how hard life had been for her entire life. She had a difficult family history. I felt her whole being was attracted to the image of death as peaceful final rest, and I was afraid suicide could happen anytime. In the last session, she smiled beautifully, telling me the memory of being loved by her grandmother. Then her death came, not as suicide, but her heart just stopped.

When I heard the news of her death, the first thing that came to my mind was that she was now free from her suffering. Her body, or her "somatic unconscious" (Jung, 1935/1988, p. 441), must have taken control of her life and released her soul now. I thought that her body responded to her unconscious by saying, "It's too much for her to endure." The body released her spirit so that it could go on. Her soul continues to go on, or in a Buddhist sense, she is now born in the Pure Land as Buddha, where there is no suffering, only beauty and purity. Jung's (1933/1960) idea that death is a "goal" and that the soul continues to develop after death (Jung, 1963) was reassuring for me. I accompanied her only for a part of her journey, but I am thankful that I could meet her in this world.

My experience of my father's death, Jung's writings, and studying and training to be a Jungian analyst all helped me to accept her death. My journey still goes on, regardless of how long it will last, but I will keep in mind Jung's words on life after death and prepare for my own death:

> A man should be able to say he has done his best to form a conception of life after death, or to create some image of it—even if he must confess his failure. Not to have done so is a vital loss. For the question that is posed to him is the age-old heritage of humanity: an archetype, rich in secret life, which seeks to add itself to our own individual life in order to make it whole.
>
> (Jung, 1963, p. 356)

This essay is my trial to "mythologize" (Jung, 1963) about death in my second half of life to make it whole. I would like to send a heartfelt "thank-you" to my analyst and the editors of the books to have afforded me this *"Goen,"* or meeting, led by *"Engi,"* or dependent co-arising.

References

Amemiya, K. (2015). Nihon ni okeru Botan to Shisi bunka no Keisei to Youkyoku "Ishibashi" (Formation of culture of tree peonies and Shishi, Noh song "Stone Bridge" in Japan). *Kokusaikankeikenkyu: Research of international relations*, 36, 67-78.

Ende, M. (1973). *Momo*. London: Puffin Books.

Gamaike, S. (2022). *Shinshu to Gendai Sougi. (Shin Buddhism and modern Funerals)*. Kyoto:Hozokan.

Inaha, S. (2002). *Kanjya no shibo ji kara omiokuri made: Shigo no kea or Enzeru kea*. (The time of death until the departure— Care after death). *Nursing: the Japanese nursing journal*, 22 (11), 34-40.

Jung, C. G. (1917/1953). *On the psychology of the unconscious. CW. Vol.7*. Princeton, NJ: Princeton University Press.

_____. (1926/1960). *Spirit and life. CW. Vol.8*. Princeton, NJ: Princeton University Press.

_____. (1933/1960). *The stages of life. CW. Vol.8*. Princeton, NJ: Princeton University Press.

_____. (1934-39/1988). *Nietzsche's Zarathustra: Notes of the Seminar given in 1934-1939 by C. G. Jung*. Princeton, NJ: Princeton University Press.

_____. (1959/1978). *C.G. Jung Speaking: An Autobiography*. Princeton, NJ: Princeton University Press.

_____. (1963/2019). *Memories, Dreams, Reflections*. London: William Collins Publisher.

Kawai, H. (1982). *Mukashi Banashi to Nihonjin no Kokoro*. (The Japanese Psyche: Major Motifs in the Fairy Tales of Japan). Tokyo: Iwanami Shoten.

_____. (1986). *Shukyo to Kagaku no Setten*. (Meeting point of religion and science). Tokyo: Iwanami Shoten.

Kawai, T. (2012). The Red Book from a pre-modern perspective: the position of the ego, sacrifice and the dead. *Journal of Analytical Psychology*, 57, 378-389.

_____. (2022). The symbolic and non-symbolic aspect of image: clinical and cultural reflections. *Journal of Analytical Psychology*, 67, 621-634.

Matsuo, K. (2011). *Soushiki Bukkyo no Tanjo. (The birth of funerary Buddhism)*. Tokyo: Heibonsha.

McMillan, P. (2020). *Nihon no Koten wo Eigo de Yomu. (Reading Japanese classics in English)*. Tokyo: Shodensha.

Ohgi, S. (2018). *Shin-Buddhism in simple English*. Kyoto:Hozokan.

Otto, R. (1917/1968). *Das Heillge: Ueber das Irrationale in der Idee des Goettlichen und sein Verhaeltnis zum Rationalen*. (Seinaru Mono.) Tokyo: Iwanami Shoten.

Rowe, M. (2011). *Bonds of the dead: Temples, Burials, and the Transformation of Contemporary Japanese Buddhism*. Chicago and London: The University of Chicago Press.

Yokoi, K. (2016). *Yukan ni kansuru ichi kosatsu*. (A study on Yukan). *Bukkyo Keizai Kenkyu*, 45, 175-204.

How I Confronted Death and How Death Confronted Me[1]

Henry Abramovitch

During my life, I have had many encounters with death. These had profound aspect on me as a person, but also in guiding my journey toward becoming a Jungian analyst as well as becoming a specialist in the anthropology of death. In the later part, I will discuss two Jungian texts which were extremely helpful in dealing with clinical aspects of difficult issues such as the death of a patient or the death of an analyst.

My Grandfather

My first encounter with death happened long before I was born but cast a significant shadow over my life. My grandfather, for whom I am named, comes home from hospital after a pointless surgery revealing death-bringing stomach cancer. He arrives home, weak, disheveled. He groans at each step as his climbs to the cramped living quarters above his small country store. Somehow, he makes it to his bed, where he flops down exhausted. But gathering his strength, he calls out to his wife, my grandmother, Sura. He asks for all his five young children to join him in bed.

---

[1] This chapter is based in part on Abramovitch (1975; 1984;1991; 2000; 2001; 2005; 2010; 2015; 2020).

They jump in and snuggle up next to him. He then turns to his wife and with a massive smile says: "Am I not a lucky man?" A week later he is dead. My mother, only 4 years old, is one of those children, the middle of five. She grows up without a father. Nevertheless, my mother embodies and transmits my grandfather's message: The proper response to the reality of death is to live all the more intensely. Confronting death is designed to bring us all the more fully back into life.

How to Die

My next experience confronting death occurred when I was a little more than 4 years old. We lived with my grandmother Sura, who had been widowed so long before. A vital, energizing woman, she had suffered a paralyzing stroke. In my eyes, she was a very old woman with wild hair who lived in the room next to ours, unable to get out of bed. She would call us her "doctors and nurses." She was friendly but also scary. My main job was to bring her a glass of water. One night, her breathing slowed. My uncles and aunts began arriving. The atmosphere was numinous, imminent. Something was happening, but no one told me what. When she died, there was an emptiness in the room she had lived in. My mother, her brothers, and sister sat "shiva." Sitting on low chairs, eating a boiled egg, remaining inside while relative and friends came to sit with them. After a week, they arose and went to the cemetery. A year later, there was a gray stone above her body. I wondered whether she was cold there deep inside the earth. Later, I understood that this is the natural way to die: at home, in bed, surrounded by those you love best, saying *shma' Israel*[2].

---

[2] Shma' Israel, *Hear Oh Israel, the Lord Our God, the Lord is One. (Deutoronomy 6:4)* is a central prayer in Judaism, recited in synagogue, at bedtime before sleep,

His Heart Stopped Working

My third encounter with death was more intense. I remember well, waking up in the middle of the night, walking over to my parents' bedroom and saying, "Mommy, my head hurts." Then I collapsed and started convulsing on the floor. This was in the mid-1950s. There was no intensive care unit, nor even emergency rooms as we know them today. My mother called our family doctor, who rushed over with his car, took one look at my condition, and swept me up in his arms and rushed to the Neurological Institute. When my parents arrived there, they were told to wait … and wait … and wait …, not knowing whether their child was alive or dead. Finally, a neurosurgeon emerged. She brushed up against my mother and said, "Well, his heart stopped working … but we got it going again." And walked away. A pediatrician followed. Before he spoke, he took her hand in his. Then he said, "Pray for him. Speak to him. Maybe you can bring him back." I lay in a coma, between living and dying, for many, many days. My mother was speaking to me. I remained unconscious, unresponsive. Until one day, I suddenly opened my eyes and blurted out, "My brother stole me toy!" She reacted by laughing and crying at the same time. I had suffered a near-death inflammation of the entire brain, encephalitis. Later when I was training at Hadassah University Hospital in Jerusalem, I would meet people who had serious psychiatric *sequelae* as a result of the encephalitis. In retrospect, I understood there had been two miracles: one that I came back to life at all, and the other that I did so without damage. I would tell only closest friends "my secret." I was really a ghost that had died and came back to life.

---

and is traditional last words of a Jew. Shma' is incorporated in certain Christian Prayers and occurs in Sura 112.

One Day in September

My next encounter with death was even more shocking. One day in September, visiting home in the liminal time between undergrad and graduate school, I walked into my parent's master bedroom. My mother has had a cold, perhaps a flu, and I am looking after her as she had looked after me in childhood. I walk inside and see my mother, lying turned around on the bed, her exquisitely beautiful blue eyes staring up at the corner of the ceiling. Strange, I thought. Then I realized she was not breathing. Using my water safety training, I tried to give her the kiss of life, but her entire passageway was clogged with vomitus. Using an alternative form of artificial respiration, I held her flaccid hands together with mine and pressed down hard on her diaphragm. From out of her mouth came a fountain of vomit. My brother was with me and said, "She's gone." "No!" I screamed back. But she was. Dead. In one moment, I became a hero crushed down by failure to save my mother and by my inability to make sense of her senseless, sudden death. I was barely 21. I remember feeling how lucky I was to have had her for 20 full years, when she herself had her own father for barely four. Part of me wanted to jump into the grave with her; but another part knew she had set me on a journey to find answers to the place of life in death, like Gilgamesh.

Madagascar

Still bearing the weight of an enormous mother complex, I looked for ways to come to terms with her loss. As an anthropologist-psychologist, I searched for a society that knew how to make peace with the dead. I stumbled across Madagascar, the island continent off the east coast of Africa. How I got there is a story in itself, but once I found my place on a small island, I became immersed in spirit possession healing and rituals surrounding death. The island is today called *Ile Sainte-Marie de Madagascar,* but you can understand my synchronicity when an Abramovitch, "Son of Abraham," discovered that the original name of the island was *Nosy Ibrahim,* the Island of Abraham.

In this culture, burial at the time of death is a relatively simple affair, but years later, the entire extended family and clan gather in the cemetery for the *fahamadiana* or "second burial." The white bones of the deceased are dug up from the earth and laid out on a woven reed mat. The head of the lineage goes down on one knee and speaks to the soul of the dead relative, saying, "See, we have not forgotten you; look how many people are here; look how much ancestors' beer we have made ready in your honor." After he makes his peace with the spirit of the deceased, he turns to call on all the great ancestors, the *razabe,* to receive this "fresh soul" in the midst of the family as a junior ancestor. Then everyone—young men and old men, young women and old women—start drinking and dancing ecstatically in the cemetery. Some may even dance with the bones, rewrapped in the white cloth and the reed mat. The bones are placed in a wooden or cement sarcophagus that resembles their huts, so that the cemetery looks like a miniature village for the dead. Infertile women prize the reed mat upon which the bones had lain for its fertility powers, so much so that contact with the dead is seen as a source of living vitality. I had always associated graveyards with separation and sadness. Yet this ritual of becoming an ancestor remains the most joyous event I ever witnessed. I am still struck, many years later, by how the most important event in their life cycle occurs years after they are dead, when they become ancestors.

The ancestors remain ever present through dreams, illness, prophesy, sacrifices, and spirit possession. As Roger Bastide has noted, such communities live within an ongoing dialogue of the dead with the living. In the West, social life involves a monologue, a monologue of the dead.

A Resurrection Experience

The Malagasy are wonderfully friendly and open people but have a dark xenophobic shadow. Naively, I did not realize that I was entering deeply into cultural secrets that certain people did not want me to know. One day, following a terrible bout of diarrhea, I became confused and found myself drinking salt water, wandering aimlessly, unable to concentrate, and thinking that I was going to die. Passing out, I had a vivid vision: I had indeed died and was buried, and the process of bodily disintegration had begun. My dead body was being pulled apart by worms, moles, and insects. Suddenly, a voice called out, "Stop!" The process was halted and then reversed. My decomposed body was reconstituted, revived, and resurrected, rather like in a shamanistic initiation. I had other intense psychoticlike visions and eventually found my way to a clinic and then to a hospital. I was told that I might have been poisoned. Because I was a foreigner, the culprit had given me enough poison to get rid of me but not to kill me. Whatever actually happened, I was deeply traumatized and recovered very slowly. My persona had been stripped away. I could not travel by myself, and my sister had to come and take me home. I had left Madagascar, but my soul had not yet caught up.

When I finally managed to return to my university and told the story of my experiences and visions to one of my professors, he said, "You would be a good candidate for Jungian analysis." One of my doctoral supervisors, Daniel Levinson, had discovered Jung via his own midlife crisis and had done pioneering work on adult development published in the best-selling *The Seasons of a Man's Life*. He suggested that I see a Jungian colleague who was part of his research team, Ray Walker, who had trained at the C. G. Jung Institute of New York. We started working on my dreams, and I felt I had arrived back "home" at last.

When I finished my doctoral studies, I decided I needed to take a moratorium. What followed was an important year that included a trip to my ancestral roots in Romania and hitchhiking around Eastern Europe with my sister. I remember the moment at which I actually decided to become a Jungian analyst. I was in Rome, staying with my friends in The Living Theatre, an international political theatre group. I found Jung's *Memories, Dreams, Reflections* (1989), opened it at random, and read that ancestors represented the realm of the collective unconscious (p. 216). It was a eureka moment for me: "Yes, that's it!" That was the reality I had been living. My voyage continued eastward through Greece, Cyprus, and Israel. When I arrived in Jerusalem, I felt once again this is home and I have lived there ever since.

My Experience with Illness

While I was doing my Jungian training, I continued my personal encounter with death in an ethnographic way, by joining *hevra kadish,* a Jerusalem burial society. Members perceived themselves as doing the "highest form of loving-kindness," since the dead could never repay their kindness.

Jewish burials are unique in the cross-cultural landscape in that they are done very rapidly, often within hours after the death and, in Jerusalem, even at night. There are traditionally no coffins, but only cloth burial garments covered by a winding sheet, so the contours of the deceased are visible, as is the smell often. There is no contouring, no embalming, no "open casket." The body is laid out on simple stretcher. Despite the strong, historic tradition for eulogies, there are numerous days in the Hebrew calendar when eulogies are forbidden. At the graveside, forgiveness is asked from the deceased, and sometimes the deceased gives forgiveness to the mourners. Then one of the Hevra Kadisha enters the grave to receive the body, lay it out in the grave and undo the last slip knots holding the body together, symbolizing the breaking of ties between the dead and the living. At the end of a traditional funeral, the mourners walk between two lines of people and are ritually comforted. From the funeral they go directly home for a seven-day mourning period, called shiva, meaning "seven" (days). By Jewish tradition, the visitors, called "comforters," are urged not to speak until the mourner speaks. This allows a genuine dialogue to unfold. It is highly likely that Freud drew on this tradition in the creation of psychoanalysis. The most important ritual connected to mourning is the saying of the *kaddish*, traditionally by eldest son, but now commonly by all children, including daughters. Not to have someone say kaddish after you is seen as an almost unbearable tragedy, severing the continuity between the living and the dead. The Kaddish prayer is paradoxical. It is not in Hebrew but Aramaic, and as a result, most people do not understand the words or their meaning. It says nothing about deceased or mourning but is a short extract with the daily prayer that praises God and wishes for peace on earth as in heaven. How the iconic prayer began is also a mystery, although recent research suggests it may have originated in Renaissance Italy. It must be said with a *minyam*, a quorum of 10 people, highlighting the principle that one cannot mourn alone. Yet it is a haunting chant, with the call-and-response rhythm of mourner and community that is part Greek chorus, part symbolic containment. Saying kaddish at my mother's funeral helped me accept what ever I wanted to accept: the reality of death, its inevitability and universality. Saying kaddish, this ancient, chanting, connected me to all my ancestors who had said it before me. Yes, I was weeping, sobbing, but there was a cultural message which reverberated with my mother's refrain: Don't waste your money on the dead; money is for the living my mother. She was echoing Moses's farewell speech: "I put before you life and death … therefore choose life."

Being a student of the anthropology of death led me to surprising insights. I will share just a few: Death, an intensely emotional and often taboo subject in West, is considered as occurring at a specific, identifiable moment, symbolized by the "time of death" on the death certificate. This "punctual view of death" (Bloch 1988) in which a person is thus either alive or dead is not shared by many cultures. Cultures express the degree of alive/dead using different metaphors. The Merina of Madagascar, for example, use the image of wet/dry to indicate degrees of alive/dead. A newborn infant is very wet and thus very alive; in contrast, a shriveled elderly person, almost totally dry, is mostly dead. The process of drying, and hence dying, will be only completed long after biological death when the bones are dug up and placed in communal tombs (Bloch and Parry 1982). Among Sa'dan Toraja of Indonesia, a dying person has the ability to "see everything" but is not considered dead until the first sacrifice of mortuary rites has taken place, months or even years later (Tsintjilonis 2007).

In many societies, the occurrence of a death disrupts social life severely, so that "it is stricken in the very principle of its life in the faith it has in itself" (Hertz 1960, p. 78). Cultures and their rituals must provide an answer to the meaning of life for the community at a time when it is most threatened. The wandering spirits, for whom no rites were performed, may return as hungry ghosts. That is why we say, "Rest in peace." These ghosts yearn to be reincorporated into the world of the living. Since they cannot be, they behave like hostile strangers and consequently must find sustenance at the expense of the living. Many cultures use elaborate strategies to confuse the spirit of the deceased so that it will not return to the realm of the living. Illness, misfortune, and associated healing rituals are often attempts to incorporate these lost souls. The "tomb of the Unknown Soldier" in modern states, provides a resting place for unincorporated spirits of the war dead.

Cultures inevitably speak of a "good death" and "bad death." The Talmud compares a good death to the ease of plucking a hair from a bowl of milk and a bad death to the interminable agony of pulling wool from off a thorn bush. An Indian Hindu ideally should die in the open air, as an act of self-sacrifice, abandoning life to the sound of the chanting of the names of God, for his thoughts at that moment may determine his subsequent fate and rebirth. A reluctance to die at the appropriate time may lead to the death of a young relative in his place (Parry 1994). In the West, most individuals say they prefer to die in their sleep, not knowing they are going to die. But Jews and Christians, historically, saw just such a death as a very bad death, because you arrive at this crucial rite of passage, unprepared.

What's wrong with your eye?

My most recent encounter with death was no less powerful but began insidiously.

I discovered my left eyelid was drooping. I felt no pain, no discomfort, and only knew of it when a neighbor said, "What is wrong with your eye?" Overcoming a natural tendency to ignore health issues, I went to numerous doctors—ophthalmologists, neurologists. and internists—and underwent many tests, none of which uncovered the cause. At the same time, I began losing weight, eating less, and feeling without my usual bounce. Sleeping became painful from what I later discovered was a hugely swollen spleen and liver. One day I became breathless. I couldn't even walk up a flight of stairs when I used to zip up nine flights to my office at the university. Still, I felt it would pass; it was nothing to be worried about. Later, I sat with the hematologist in a deserted cancer institute. She explained what a lymph node was—I barely knew. For a whole month I had almost daily tests to discover what had been brewing in my body. CT revealed suspicious sightings in the soft tissue, near the spine, behind the kidneys, in the abdomen. Finally, my breathing got so bad—the lymphoma was blocking the drainage of the pleura, the sack around my right lung, compressing and compromising my oxygen supply—that they started treating me even before they had a definitive diagnosis. Hematologists love histology. They need to see how the cell looks like as an individual and how it grows in culture into a community. It sounds very Jungian, the individual and the collective. But since they do not know for sure what I have got or whether I am truly dying, they treat me for the worst with the strongest possible treatment.

Now in a more poetic mode:

Toward evening, my breathing becomes even worse, and pain stalks each sitting position. I do not know what to do with myself. For the first time, I feel really miserable.

I cannot face another unslept night. I have my first scary dream: I am driving in a car in a city street with my wife. We are going down a gentle incline, and I want to slow the car down but I cannot move my foot from pedal to brake momentarily, and immobilized, I cry out for help. Lying awake in dark's early light, I think of yesterday's "I will laugh this lymphoma under the table" and start sobbing.

Lymphoma also in the bone marrow, in clumps and more: an infected pelvic lymph node hidden and inaccessible, but the real shock comes when I ask about staging. Naively I had thought since there were no obvious lymph nodes, I might be Stage I or II. My doctor hesitates, and I know it is bad. In Hebrew, I say, "dugri"— "Tell me straight." I have been strong staring death down but I am not prepared for her reply: "Stage IV."

Today, there are no tests. I am not a patient but take care of my own patients. I think I must construct an up-to-date patient list in the event of my death, and suddenly I am sobbing for the first time since I heard. Alone in the bath, I go to my office and make that list and prepare copies to give to colleagues in case sessions need to be canceled when I have chemo or worse. The rest of the day, I sit and listen to other people. One lady, a senior mental health professional, recalls the brutal abuses of her father and then of the men in her life. She sobs, "I am damaged, so damaged." Later I want to transfer her to another analyst, but she cries again, saying, "Don't you understand, I cannot go to another analyst. I just cannot." Another younger man is about to be married. Every moment of joy brings the anguish of a missing father, murdered in a terrorist attack. He says he will never be happy again, not even on his wedding day. I am suddenly terrified that this will also be my children's fate. "To be well is a hobby; to be sick is a full-time job." One of the central experiences of illness is loss. In English, the word for illness is "Dis-ease" The loss of ease—the ease not to know when your next treatment or blood test is coming. The loss of ease that each sensation, pain, sweaty night, each ache, does not signal another medical earthquake. The loss of a future spreading out before you like a set table. Above all, for every cancer person, there is the loss of "my body as I knew it." For me, the bodily change was not weight loss, a half-closed eye, massively swollen spleen which stole sleep or even panicking white blood cells but one day after chemo, touching my chin to see my beard fall like fresh snow. Since I was 19, I have had a beard. No one in Israel had seen my naked face: not my wife, my children, my students or my patients. People did not recognize me; I did not recognize myself. I would look in the mirror and say, "Who stole my face?" I would walk up to old friends and start speaking only to be told, "Excuse me, sir, who are you?" "Who am I, indeed?" I was another Henry: Henry the sick.

Finally, a specific diagnosis is confirmed. It is "marginal zone" lymphoma. In those days, I was surely in the margins. I am given CHOP-R, a combination of treatments that include four types of chemo and one new biological agent:

Chemo is like an artillery barrage.
Biological treatments are more like a targeted assassination.

The assassination to C24 lymph receptor sites worked.
My splendid hematologist tells me with luck, I will die of something else.

The Dying Patient

Religious traditions see preparation for dying as a necessary part of the spiritual journey. In the Jewish tradition, it is sometimes expressed in phrase, "Return [to the way], a day before you die." But because you cannot never know the time of your death, one must be always ready to die. Joy Schaverein (2020), an English Jungian analyst and art therapist, received a middle-age man into treatment because of long-standing issues of isolation, emotional stuckness, and his unlived life. However, after three months in the analysis, he was diagnosed with a fatal disease. The book with profound clarity and sensitivity describes the journey of both the man and the analyst working together in psychotherapy, through chemotherapy, hospice, and the funeral. More recently, Schaverein shared the drawings she made during the time of their work together, and these are truly moving in their own right. (Schaverein 2020b). Her pioneering work helped prepare me for what was my worst experience as an analyst. I was treating a young, idealistic International Peace Worker of mixed Scandanavian and Latin American Heritage. We met in person while she was working in Jerusalem. After she was transferred to the Democratic Republic of Congo, we decided to continue working on Zoom. Our work was deep and fruitful. We continued until one day, she did not show up for our online session. All my attempts to communicate through email and text went unanswered. I hoped there were problems with Wi-Fi or that she had gone working in a more remote area. I lived a life of not knowing. Her absence was all around me, but I was going on "as if" normal, in a kind of gray zone. Then the following week, I learned the bitter truth from a shocking press release. She had strayed into unprotected "rebel" areas, where she and a companion were seized, murdered, and then decapitated. I often think we are often protected from the harrowing stories of our patients because we have heard worse. This was a horror and a death beyond my worst imagination. I needed to mourn, but there was no one to mourn with. I was alone in my solitary grief. Helplessness danced all round me. I felt as if evil done to her had entered my own soul.

But with time, the help of colleagues, and dreams, I came to see my role not only as a bereft father-analyst but as someone who had been privileged to accompany her on her journey until it was time to part. At some point, I was forced to let her continue on her journey by herself. In Hebrew, at the funeral, we say the dead person has "gone to their world," *halach leolamo,* a world created just for them, as if in the ultimate stage of individuation.

Death of Two Analysts

Another unique document is Pamela Power's *Death of the Analyst* (2005), in which she describes the death of not one, but two of her analysts! One of her analysts was a very well-known Jungian analyst and she writes:

> I went to my regularly scheduled appointment in early May of 1998. My former analyst began the session by telling me he had been diagnosed with wide-spread metastatic cancer in the lungs. He told me that it was the bladder cancer he had lived with for over twenty years that had metastatized. He further informed me that the doctors gave him 9 months to a year to live. Hardly able to speak, he answered my unformed question: "You are probably wondering what impact this will have on our work. I plan to continue to see you as long as I feel well enough." When I returned to my next session, two weeks later, he began by telling me he was "going downhill fast" and this would be our last session. At the end of the session he invited me to contact him if I had any wish to do so. Almost two months to the day he was dead.

With negative synchronicity, around this time, Pamela, discovered an enlarged lymph node; after intense diagnostic investigations, it turned out to be lymphoma, cancer of the lymph—the system of white blood cells which serves to protect the body. When finally diagnosed, she became a difficult patient "in emotional turmoil" and adds: "I was distraught, confused and desperately missed my dead analyst. I felt he could give me the larger psychological perspective and help I needed which I was getting from no one. I thought about the course of <u>his</u> cancer. He was diagnosed with a slow growing bladder cancer in the early 1970's. He received no treatment except to have it scraped out when it caused symptoms. He refused radiation treatment which the doctors tried to insist upon. I wanted to learn more about how he thought about his illness so that I could learn from him and perhaps follow his course. After all, he lived 26 years after his initial diagnosis. I was full of regret that I had not asked him more about his condition and especially his attitude toward it. I felt very alone. … I felt stuck in my grief over the loss of my analyst, I felt stuck in my physical condition, endlessly trying to make meaning of my situation, trying to find a way to move on."

Her vulnerability was clearly related to the fact that her own father died suddenly a few months after her sixth birthday. With devastating synchronicity, a previous analysis begun at age 27 ended after four years with the illness and death of <u>that</u> analyst. In the sparse literature, Pamela's case is far from unique to have not one but two analysts die while in treatment! We often think of synchronicity in positive terms but clearly it is not always so. Pamela Power goes on:

> In spite of a lengthy analysis, the death of my analyst felt abrupt and premature. It precipitated a

period of inner turbulence that lasted several years. … When the analyst dies suddenly, before these [a release of creative energy and … resolution of transference] have been accomplished, a precarious and dangerous situation can result. A premature end can bring about a state of "negative creativity", a "transference chaos" expressed in somatic and psychological disturbances.

Pamela Power's brave essay helped me think more deeply about how illness and dying impacts analysts and patients. It helped me understand the tragic situation of a fellow training candidate who died of breast cancer while still seeing patients. I had the unenviable duty of informing her patients that their beloved analyst had died. On follow-up, 25 years later, one former patient said, "It was the worst thing that ever happen to me." When I became sick with lymphoma, I felt more prepared to deal with the issues. Later, I began to give workshops on "Illness and death in the analyst," using active imagination, professional literature, experience of Freud and Jung as well as mine, which had raised awareness of this crucial issue.

The World to Come

In our new play, *My Lunch with Thomas,* Murray Stein asks me: "What do you think about life after death?" I respond: "I think that we come into consciousness through our body. When our body ceases to function, we lose the ability to perceive, to reflect or to understand. … What can I say then about life after death, or as we say in Hebrew, *olam haba,* 'the world to come'? Perhaps I can only cite Wittgenstein's famous insight, 'Of that which we cannot speak clearly, we must pass over in silence.'"

Death will always remain a mystery; nevertheless, the cross-cultural and depth psychology investigation of death will continue to provide unexpected insights into how humans cope with that mystery and give it meaning.

References

Abramovitch, H. (1974). "A Spirit Possession cult in ile Sainte-Marie de Madagascar." pp.13-23. *Revue du Musée d'art et d'archéologie.* Taloha 6.

_____. (1991). 'The Jerusalem Funeral As a Microcosm of the "Mismeeting" between Religious and Secular Israelis.' In Z. Sobol & B. Beit-Hallachmi (Eds.), *Tradition, Innovation, Conflict: Judiasm and Jewishness in Contemporary Israel.* SUNY.

_____. (2000). 'The Jerusalem Funeral: An Anthro-pological Perspective.' In R. Malkinson, S. S. Rubin & E. Witztum (Eds.), *Traumatic and Nontraumatic Loss and Bereavement* Madison, CT. pp. 255-72. Psychosocial Press.

_____. (2005). 'Where are the Dead? Bad Death, the Missing, and the Inability to Mourn' *Death, Bereavement and Mourning.* In Samuel Heilman (Ed.), pp. 53-68.. New Brunswick, N.J. & London: Transaction Publishers.

_____. (2011). 'Illness in the Analyst' *Facing Multiplicity: Psyche nature culture Proceedings of 16th International Congress of Analytical Psychology.* In Pramila Bennett (Ed.). Daimon Verlag.

_____. (2012). "Into the Marginal Zone." In N. Lowinsky & P. Damerypp. (Eds.) *Marked By Fire: Personal Stories of the Jungian Way*, pp. 94-109. Fisher King Press.

_____. (2015). 'Anthropology of Death.' In J. Wright (ed.) *International Encyclopedia of the Social & Behavioral Sciences,* 2nd edition, pp. 870–873, Vol 5. Elsevier.

_____. (2020). Who is my Jung? *Jung Journal: Symbol & Culture,* 14, pp. 137-148. Routledge/Taylor and Francis.

Bloch, M. (1988). "Death and the concept of person." In S. Cederroth, C. Corlin, & J. Lindstrom (Eds.), *On the Meaning of Death: Essays on Mortuary Rituals and Eschatological Beliefs.* Uppsala.

Bloch, M., & Parry, J. (Eds.), (1982). *Death and the Regeneration of Life.* Cambridge University Press.

Huntingdon, R., & Metcalf, P. (1991*). Celebrations of Death: The Anthropology of Mortuary Ritual.* (2nd edn.). Cambridge University Press.

Hertz, R. (1960). "Contributions sur la representation collective de la mort." In *Annee Sociologique.* (trans. Needham, R. & Needham, C.) Free Press.

Jung, C. G. (1989). *Dreams, Memories, Reflections,* In Aniela. Jaffe (Ed.). Vintage Books.

Palgi, P., & Abramovitch, H. (1984). "Death: A cross-cultural perspective." In *Annual Review of Anthropology*, 13, pp. 385–417.

Park, C. W. (2010). *Cultural blending in Korean death rites: New interpretive approaches.* Continuum.

Parkes, C., Laungani, P., & Young, B. (Eds.), (1997). *Death and Bereavement Across Cultures.* Routledge.

Parry, J. (1994). *Death in Benares.* Cambridge University Press.

Power, P. (2005). "Death of the analyst." *Journal of Jungian Theory and Practice,* 7(2), 35–46.

Robben, C.G.M. Antonius (ed.) (2004). *Death, mourning and burial: A cross-cultural reader.* Blackwell.

Schaverein, J. (2020). *The Dying Patient in Psychotherapy: Erotic Transference and Boarding School Syndrome.* Routledge.

Schaverein, J. (2020). 'Spectral Houses: the Analyst's Drawings: Postscript to The Dying Patient in Psychotherapy' ATOL: Art Therapy On Line, Volume 11 (1) April. http://journals.gold.ac.uk/index.php/atol

Tsinntjilonis, D. (2007). *The death-bearing senses in Tana Toraja,* 72: pp. 173-194. Ethos.

Love, Death, and The Infernal Machine

Ladson Hinton

Tyger, Tyger burning bright,
In the forests of the night:
What immortal hand or eye
Dare frame thy fearful symmetry?
(William Blake, 1794)

Introduction

Death exceeds all efforts to escape it and defies our capacity to understand. And yet we continually reflect and wonder about it, in fear, or in shame at our vulnerability, peering into that abyss. We are creatures who must live within the parameter of time, transient creatures who are time-bound, who die.

Death remains something whose nature is inapparent. Why is human life so transient? We do our thing, and are good and foolish, and sometimes evil. Then life ends. No religion or mythology, or mystical revelation has provided a satisfactory final answer.

However, amid the failures of our efforts to understand, something draws us back to death, something hidden or inapparent. That is part of its phenomenology. We want to understand, but the subject is endlessly elusive. Death itself is a fact, and that fact invokes a penumbra of uncanniness, invoking an urgent passion to know more or to flee. A meditation on the penumbra, the experiential surround of death in multiple situations, can perhaps expand our knowledge in a subtle way that has its own kind of truth. Such a phenomenology of death may provide a more nuanced sort of knowledge and have more "depth" than a gross facticity (Inverso, 2022).

We human beings endlessly return to questions of life and death. That is part of its phenomenology. Death pulls us, provokes us, seduces us to endlessly fear and wonder about it. Religions all have their deep and thoughtful reflections, mythologies, and promises. Tyrants and criminals try to project death into subgroups of others, declaring them, among other things, "unworthy life." Ritual killings—in war or otherwise—seem all too common in human history. In the 20th century, Nazism and the Cambodian Khmer Rouge provided vivid examples. Cults of death bring forth the most terrible dimensions of human beings. It is important to try and understand such phenomena, rather than merely recoil in horror. That is true of personal experience of death as well as social violence, Death as an "Infernal Machine" of horror, and mystery is always potentially present in our personal and social lives.

The interconnection of psychoanalysis and death is so strong that some have suggested that *hauntology* should replace the term *psychoanalysis* (Gunn, 2006). Amid this gargantuan history, I can only offer my own experiences of death and the torments of being a timebound creature (Hinton, 2015). Such sharing can be deeply gratifying, as we go along our paths in the world. There is a penumbra around Death that often brings us closer to others as well as ourselves. I hope that my own narrative of death will contribute a small amount to that endeavor. I have not indulged in conclusions about the subject and will leave that to the imagination and intellect of my readers.

I will begin by describing some early childhood experiences of death, then proceeding toward the present.

Death Core

I am now 89, and my first conscious memory of death was at age 8, when I viewed the dead body of my great-grandfather on my father's side. Augustus "Papa" Reichert had died at age 88 of "old age." His parents were German immigrants from Saxony who had settled in Fort Smith, Arkansas, in the mid-19th century. Papa's father was a shoemaker, and Papa had become a Master Plumber at a time when indoor plumbing was all the rage. The Reichert family was prosperous, with a large home near the center of town—a small city of 34,000 when I was born in 1934. The Reichert family was Lutheran, and Papa's body was laid out in an open coffin in the large dining room, which was lighted by a colorful Tiffany chandelier that I liked. I can still recall my sense of boredom and restlessness when visiting there as a child, perhaps echoing the mood of my mother when she was around that side of the family. Mother was a divorcee—a somewhat taboo situation at that time, in that culture. She had felt they were judgmental.

I remember surveying the open coffin across the dining room. My younger female cousins were playing on the floor near it. A mood came over me, as if I were frozen or suspended. I think I saw some adults come by and kiss Papa on the forehead. That seemed to be the expected behavior, but I felt totally incapable of even approaching the casket, much less kissing him, (Actually, I have no memory of ever kissing him!) The cousins were all younger girls, and they seemed to have no problem with being around dead Papa. My shame was great.

My usual "escape" from the family gatherings at that old house was to go to the large glass-front bookcase in the living room and look through the books. That's what I did that day. It was a refuge, and I could let my shame subside. The books were often interesting, and I was a precocious reader.

I can still feel my paralyzing anxiety regarding the coffin and Papa's dead body, along with the strong sense of shame. As I sit now at the desk in my study, writing this remembrance of death, that same bookcase is at my right hand, full of favorite tomes! The Hinton Coat of Arms is on the wall to my upper right, and a reproduction of Klee's painting the *Angel of History*—so beloved by Walter Benjamin—is on my upper left. Continuity with the past is quite apparent!

****

World War II for the United States began in 1941, and the outbreak of war was very frightening to me. I clearly recall the first news of the Japanese attack on Pearl Harbor and how scary it felt. President Franklin Roosevelt's radio speech announcing a Declaration of War on Germany and Japan impacted me greatly, and I feared the Japanese might bomb our house, although we lived in the middle of the United States, far from both the Atlantic and Pacific oceans. I recall crying, feeling very fearful of death and destruction, as I played with my toy soldiers on the floor near the large radio. I asked my dad whether "they" would bomb our house, and he kindly reassured me. Nevertheless, war and death were strongly in the air. The world no longer seemed safe.

When the war ended in 1945, I was 11 and had another memorable experience concerning death. My Uncle Ken, who was married to my favorite aunt, returned home from service in the U.S. Army Medical Corps. He was a strong early influence on me, a gregarious masculine presence who was a contrast to my more reticent father. After World War II began, he volunteered for military service because he was the youngest physician in the clinic where he practiced internal medicine. He felt it was his duty, and I deeply admired that.

When my uncle left for military service, he gave me his young dog, a fierce Airedale Terrier. "Frankie"—short for Frankenstein—became my faithful companion for the next dozen years of my life. I intermittently sent simple letters to Ken while he was in Europe and faithfully followed the progression of the war in the newspaper. Often there were maps, including specific units like my uncle's, marking the progress of the American army in Europe.

When he returned after the war, I didn't see much of him at first and heard that he was in a strange state, maybe a bit "shell-shocked." A few weeks after his return, my aunt asked me to stop by and say hello, and I was happy to comply. I biked to their home a few blocks from mine, and we sat down in the living room. He gave me a German helmet that he had transported back. Then he offered to show me some photos. I was, of course, extremely curious.

He was an excellent amateur photographer and had managed to get film to photograph a lot of his experiences. There were photos of meeting the advance units of the Russian army coming from the East. He said the Russians were generally friendly toward him but "uncivilized" toward German civilians. He said he had several times witnessed them "attacking" German women and throwing them in the river, where the American soldiers would often try to rescue them.

What struck me most strongly were photos of the concentration camps his units had liberated. There were stacks of skeletal bodies, as well as a few tattered figures in ragged, striped clothes—that looked to me like pajamas—walking around. I must have looked upset because he gave a little clarification. He told me, "Laddie, that's what Hitler did to the Jews." He said very little more. It was a powerful shock. Our family had Jewish friends, and I had Jewish pals. Those photos and that experience with my uncle could have happened yesterday. The impact has never left my mind and has affected me in many ways. The world contains death-makers who might kill anyone for no reason.

Many years later, when I was a young psychiatrist in practice, married with family, my uncle and I had a long conversation that was special and moving. He was probably in his late 80s. I was visiting at his home with my wife and children and saw a brochure from a veterans organization lying on a table. I asked him whether he was still active in that group. He said he wasn't, but it set off a long conversation, which led to more memories of World War II. He especially focused on the Battle of the Bulge in the Ardennes Forest in France, a last desperate German attempt to turn back the Allies before they reached the homeland. There was extensive fog for days, and the U.S. and Allies could not use their rule of the air. The German artillery ('88s') had a longer range than the Americans', who had to hunker down and survive until the weather changed. My uncle described the endless shelling and feeling terribly helpless. He had to take care of the many wounded, whom it was difficult to evacuate. Ken broke down in sobs when describing the experience, including a close friend who was blown up, standing just beside him. Death had clearly been his companion throughout the rest of his life. I have never forgotten his stories and those photos—further evidence of death and horror in the world.

***

When I was a junior in college, I had a powerful "inner" experience with death that dramatically changed the course of my life. I was feeling aimless and uncertain about the future. Because of my uncle, I had considered becoming a physician. However, I had never much liked the sciences but enjoyed my studies in literature and history. Graduate studies were mildly appealing but not engaging. My teachers seemed OK, but not inspiring. In that context, a fateful sequence of inner and outer events disrupted my life.

I was barely 20 and had transferred to Southern Methodist University in Dallas, Texas, to be near an "older woman" of 24! I was in love! She was an artist, teaching at a private school. I still recall one of her paintings of a beautiful young woman who had a tear coursing down her cheek. We had lively and engrossing conversations, often losing track of time. Erotic feelings were in the air but minimally expressed. Her level of maturity in relationship was greater than mine, but I was persistent. This pattern continued for several weeks, and then one day she said that we had to talk about something important. It turned out that she had a strong barrier in our relationship because she and her family were traditional Roman Catholics, and I was from a Protestant background. She couldn't consider a deep relationship unless I converted. I was totally shocked but also proud and stubborn and angry. I broke off the relationship. In retrospect, I think that her stand was at least partially an excuse because she realized how immature I was. In any case, I felt deeply wounded, dejected, and lost.

Soon after that, I was alone during the late afternoon in my little apartment in Dallas, reading *The Brothers Karamazov*. I fell asleep and had a dream/vision of death that changed the course of my life: In the dream, I was lying in the gutter of a golden road in a deep forest, clearly dying. A deep male voice, absolute and powerful, pronounced, "*You will go to medical school!*" I awakened in a panic, terrified.

A simple dream in structure, but the affective punch was powerful, and pervaded my being. Warned of death along the road of life! It is difficult to convey in writing the absolute certainty of that voice, that time when I was alone and bereft in my little apartment. I was terrified. The message was simple, and I had no doubt that *the choice was life or death.* It felt like an absolute commandment and radically changed the course of my life.

My immediate sense of urgency was unequivocal. I was quite literally unable to attend classes that didn't relate to a pre-med course of studies and received a lot of incompletes. I couldn't even walk through the entrance to a classroom or lecture hall if it didn't relate to my goal. I meditated a lot and became more ascetic. At times I feared I was crazy, but I had a profoundly clear sense of what I had to do. It was live or die. I had my orders. No choice at all! I soon told my parents that I was "changing my major," and they were emotionally and financially supportive. Recalling now their accepting love and kindness, I feel a deep sense of gratitude.

Once during that time, I saw a sign at the student infirmary about a psychiatrist being available at certain hours and impulsively went back later. However, the psychiatrist was not there at the hour advertised. Years later, my analyst remarked that I was lucky! The likelihood of my experience being misunderstood would have been great, and I could easily have been medicalized.

I didn't share my experience with anyone until four years later, when I told the story to my wife-to-be. She was the first person. Her understanding was a part of the early, basic cement for our 60 years of marriage. We sometimes had differences over the years, but whatever the turbulence, a level of deeper trust and bonding was always there.

My experience of death helped ground me and provided discipline and fostered a supply of energy and focus that generally persists to this day. I can feel it as I write. It has often given me at least a grain of confidence, whatever the turbulence. The encounter with death opened many authentic gateways to life and enabled me to be who I am. It provided a standard that has served me well, a sense of what is authentic and what is B.S. Death is a wise but demanding teacher!

***

To return to the earlier thread of my story: I married and graduated from Washington University (in St. Louis) Medical School in 1961. At that time, the U.S. military was expanding in size due to tensions with the Soviet Union, and I was drafted into the Amy Medical Corps in 1962, during my internal medicine internship at Georgetown University Hospital in Washington, D.C. (At that time, a year of clinical/medical internship was required before entering training in psychiatry.) I was offered the option of entering the Army in 1962 as a general medical officer or entering three years later, after both the internship and a subsequent three-year residency in psychiatry at Stanford University Hospital. The Medical Corps had a shortage of psychiatrists, so they were willing to wait!

My medical internship itself was demanding, scary, and deeply gratifying. We had two small children at the time, and I was on call every other night at the hospital. My wife was extraordinarily hardworking and loving, and I remain eternally grateful to her for that. It was a time of deep initiation for her as well as for me.

Georgetown Hospital was a large general hospital, sharing responsibilities for medical emergencies with District of Columbia General Hospital. The university was administered by the Jesuit Religious Order, and the hospital was administered by Roman

Catholic Sisters. It was not sectarian in spirit, and I, with my Protestant background, felt a congenial welcome there. I liked the religious aura in the background and the Jesuit respect for learning.

The maelstrom of emergency care and recovery—or death—was intense. During most of my rotations, I was on call for 36 hours and off 12 with, as I recall, a two-week vacation. The experience was demanding and sometimes scary. Georgetown was an acute care hospital, and severe illness and death were common. It was a core role of the medical interns to draw blood samples for testing very early each morning before rounds and daily routines began.

Among the many responsibilities, a core role was to break the news of deaths to families and to request permission for an autopsy. Often, the interns were the ones who pronounced the people dead. I discovered that it is often difficult to know when someone is dead! Perhaps there is now a more precise measure. I know that most of the interns mentioned a nightmare of having made an error, of corpses arising ghoulishly from their coffins and the like. It was an unforgettable initiation into both the deep grief of families and rituals of death that go back to the origins of the human culture. Funeral/burial objects are perhaps the earliest cultural artifacts (Knight, Power & Watts, 1995). *Homo Sapiens* seems to be the creature that most fully knows of its own mortality.

At the graduation banquet at the end of training, I received a small verbal recognition for having had the fewest deaths on my services during my year at Georgetown. As I recall, the number was 26. It was totally unexpected. I had not been forewarned. It was evidently a customary thing among other, more major, awards that were given with large custom plaques. I was deeply gratified because I had sometimes felt inferior to other interns who were major scientific intellects, many of whom went on to careers in academia. I later joked that my own fear of death had motivated me, and that is clearly part of the truth!

***

After my year at Georgetown, I crossed the country with my young family to begin three years of psychiatric training at Stanford University Hospital in Palo Alto, California. I had had a difficult time deciding between a residency at Massachusetts General Hospital in Boston and Stanford. I had really enjoyed my interviews at Mass General. The faculty was very open and dynamic, although a bit more on the traditional side. California was at the core of a new horizon in America and a world center of the "New Age."

Indeed new and exciting things filled the air at Stanford, as well the whole Bay Area. I quickly caught the scent of the spirit that was beginning to emerge. At Stanford, David Hamburg had just begun as Chair of Psychiatry, and new beginnings were in the air. Hamburg had psychiatry residents designated as "Fellows of the University," and that appealed to me. We were encouraged to take advantage of the possibilities of the larger university and not remain ensconced within a narrow medical enclave. Irv Yalom, the Existentialist, soon became one of my clinical supervisors. William Dement, the co-discoverer of REM sleep, arrived and was an active teacher. Karl Pribram, a pioneer in the neuropsychology of brain processing, had his monkey lab not far from my office at Stanford Medical Center. Don Jackson, who had trained under Harry Stack Sullivan, was an early and influential supervisor. My training group of seven psychiatric residents was lively and diverse. One of them was Tom Kirsch, who added an important part among all the eclectic influences whirling around me.

The informal learning was lively and intense. I recall long discussions of the Case of Ellen West, a key chapter in Rollo May's pioneering, early work on *Existential Psychotherapy* (Binswanger, 1958). It was the story of a woman who chose death by suicide after unsuccessfully trying multiple forms of therapy, over many years, for her extremely disabling symptoms. Ludwig Binswanger, the pioneer of *Daseinanalysis,* was her psychiatrist, and agreed with her decision to die. Carl Rogers later disagreed with Binswanger's conclusions. I recall many intense discussions about this case, and I ended by siding with Rogers! This experience stimulated thoughts and questions about death and is a sample of the dimensions of my psychiatric education at Stanford. I feel grateful for that.

During my last year of my residency, we were encouraged to undertake special studies in some area that had stimulated us during training. Tom Kirsch and I chose a yearlong period of studies with Kurt Reinhardt, a Professor Emeritus at Stanford who was still actively writing and teaching. He was born and educated in Germany, and was the author of *The Existential Revolt*, as well as a monumental study of German history (Reinhardt, 1960). It was a fateful decision for me because I had also seriously considered working in the Dream Lab of William Dement. I went with my heart and took the less conventional course. Perhaps my decision was affected by the earlier death experiences, to take and trust the less known path. Death and freedom do often seem connected!

Reinhardt had been at the University of Freiberg as a young student and attended Martin Heidegger's lectures. Tom Kirsch and I met with Kurt for two hours every other week, slowly reading and reflecting together. He suggested we begin with *Being and Time*, which had recently been released in its first English translation (Heidegger, 1962). It was a transformative experience to study with this revered teacher and philosopher for a year. Life as being-toward-death was at the center of my studies!

Is the basic being of the human indeed Temporality? This reversed the ancient tradition that privileged, eternal iterations of (Platonic) Ideas that were atemporal, beyond time, deathless. In contrast, under the Heideggerian aegis of being-towards-death, temporality is our fundamental reality, and Death is the most profound manifestation of our boundedness by temporality. We know that we are creatures who die. Temporality is our core being, our core humanity. This is the insight that Kurt Reinhardt powerfully reinforced in my worldview, and I will always be grateful to him.

***

After finishing my residency, at least two years of military service were required. I had originally been drafted into military service as a general practitioner while I was at Georgetown but instead agreed to go into military service later, after completing my specialty training in psychiatry. I, like many others at that time, considered it a primal duty to serve the country—and there was often some travel and adventure involved!

The military allowed doctors to state their preferred geographical area for service, and I had chosen Europe. Family housing and transport were to be provided. There was a large contingent of American military forces in Germany, as well as many American families, for whom housing, schooling for children, and commissaries for groceries and other general needs were available. Indeed, there was an entire American subcommunity in Europe at that time, mainly in Germany.

Especially with the example of my uncle, I saw military service as part of my duty as a citizen and had no resentment about being drafted. To my mind, the Soviet Union was an aggressive threat to Western culture, and Communism was an ideology that had gone terribly wrong and was a threat to freedom of the citizenry. In addition, my uncle had had some significant interactions with Soviet military people at the end of the war and had a very strong reaction to the atrocities that he thought were perpetrated on German civilians.

The Russian officers did not seem to control acts of revenge on civilians. He thought this reflected basic cultural differences.

The German civilians largely welcomed the Americans, even as they continued rebuilding their bombed-out cities. There was a strong fear of the Russians and often a sense of shame about being betrayed and misled into horrible crimes by Nazi leaders. This was the cultural surround that greeted me and my family in West Germany. Once we were settled in an apartment in a pleasant, small area of housing for military families near downtown Munich, I could turn toward my military/professional duties.

My unit, the 24th Infantry Division had small clinics in Munich and Augsburg. As a Captain and physician, I was the chief psychiatric medical officer for all military personnel and their families in Southwest Germany. There were thousands at that time. As my administrator, I had a military-trained, psychiatric social worker who was also an officer, as well as 10 or so college graduates, enlisted men who had been trained in interviewing, along with a modicum of diagnostic knowledge.

In addition, I discovered that I was responsible for a military stockade (small prison) in Dachau, not far from Munich. The jail had been one part of the infamous concentration camp, where "people of special interest" to the Nazi regime had been held: political prisoners, Russian officers, and the like. After the war it was administered by U.S. Army Military Police, and it was used as a prison for members of the military.

This was not the camp that was liberated by my uncle's unit during the war but was the first "concentration camp," built prior to World War II, originally for political prisoners. Munich, nearby, had been a hotbed of the Nazi movement. After the war, the Dachau prison had become a U.S. Army stockade, administered by the Military Police. Not surprisingly, this assignment immediately aroused my curiosity. One of the experienced enlisted men who worked in one of my clinics volunteered to drive me to Dachau to see the premises and meet the Commanding Officer.

It was an hour or so drive through Munich suburbia. Then the camp came into view. I caught sight of the famous sign typical of all the camps, an immensely ironic and iconic wrought iron sign over the gate reading *Arbeit Macht Frei*! (Work makes you free!). It was notorious and it was a shock. The Nazi propaganda had framed the camps as a place where "unworthy" or "lazy" elements of society could learn how to be honest, hardworking "real Germans." What began as a jail soon had become a place of torturous human experimentation and extermination.

We entered the gates and parked, then walked toward the jail building that was the core of the prison compound. My guide pointed out the "shooting wall," where prisoners were regularly executed before the later installation of large human gas chambers for more massive killings. We approached the jail building and showed our IDs. We went through one gate, and I shuddered as it clanged shut behind me.[3] Then a second gate and a brief perusal by the MPs, who were friendly and efficient. We met with the Commander of the prison, and he was professional in a friendly way. I think he knew the effect the prison had on people. He was pleased when I proposed that I would try to arrange group therapy for interested prisoners.

There was much to think about when I made my biweekly visits to Dachau. I soon realized that my main job would be to process

---

[3] In more recent times I visited the Holocaust Museum in Berlin, and part of the effect in one area was achieved by the clanging of an iron gate behind you as you entered. Then you walk on crunchy material in the semidarkness, and that turns out to be replicas of splintered bones. Eisenman did great job of re-creating a feeling of total uncanniness. This indoor museum affected me even more than the famous outdoor memorial.

people out of the Army, and only very limited psychotherapy would be possible due to the brief time most of the inmates stayed in the prison. However, the effect of those visits to the prison will stay with me forever.

Then something very shocking occurred. A substantial part of the main concentration camp had been preserved as a museum and memorial. The prison where I consulted was a smaller, separate entity. A couple my wife and I had known at Stanford were in Europe and stopped in Munich to visit us. He was Jewish, and they were both eager to visit the museum at the Dachau Camp. My wife and I had not visited the larger camp area and its museum.

We went there together. It was a shocking experience. Indeed, beyond shocking! There were photos of prisoners being frozen as "experiments" to test for "treatments" to be used "for the benefit of the troops in cold climates." I recall another in which the top of the skull of a prisoner was sawed off, to expose the brain. Then the medical experimenters could create very careful brain mapping, using electrical stimulation to the exposed brain of the prisoners. Some of these mappings were so accurate that they were used later in medical schools when I was a student.[4]

As we left the camp with our friends, I felt a terrible pain in my right ankle. I could hardly walk! It was red and swollen and exquisitely painful. We drove to the U.S. Army Hospital in Munich, and I was hospitalized for tests. It turned out to be acute gout, a very treatable but extremely painful condition.

I had often thought of the wounded state of the world, especially the Western world, after Nazism and the Holocaust. This was my wound too! Indeed, a deep collective wound.

---

[4] Before the lectures, there were extensive discussions with Jewish and other organizations about the ethics of using such material in teaching. They decided to use them in teaching, because it could symbolically honor the death and terrible suffering involved. It might, at least, now save human lives.

Being within these remnants of such a gigantic human horror, had exceeded my capacity to assimilate. It was clearly and dramatically psychophysiological, the scream of my body, or the *Weltschmerz,* a blow of the world that was too much for my psyche.

I quickly responded to medical treatment and remained on preventive medication for many years. Later, I had two very minor attacks in other joints, nothing like the first. Some years ago, my physician took me off all gout medication, and I have not had any further problem. Hopefully that is a sign of progress!

My family and I had many wonderful experiences in larger Europe, as well as in Germany, touring around in our Volkswagen bus. The German people were very hospitable to us, especially considering that we were occupiers.

***

Another notable experience of death and horror came to my door in Germany. I was the only U.S. Army psychiatrist in Bavaria, and military attorneys asked me to evaluate two soldiers who were being tried for the murder of a German woman in Augsburg. The accused men were at the stockade in Dachau. I received a packet of evidence for the trial to come. I vividly recall the many autopsy pictures of the victim, with descriptions by the pathologist. The victim had been brutalized and ravaged, killed by blows to the head. There were large gouges in her body, especially her breasts, made by human teeth. The cause of death, as I recall, was trauma to the brain. It was unbelievably bloody and brutal. It was very difficult to make myself view the reality of the sadistic brutality inflicted upon her.

The next day, I went to the Dachau prison to interview the accused. I was told by the administrator that the defense attorneys knew that guilt was not an issue. There was abundant evidence.

However, because of the grisly nature of the murder, they hoped that an insanity defense might be possible. Were the perpetrators insane? The attorneys told the accused men to be totally honest with me, to tell all. The evidence was so strong that a plea of "diminished capacity" seemed to be their only chance.

I interviewed the men, who were in full uniform, in a private room at the prison. The first was a hulking young man from the rural South. His speech was flat and unexpressive, and his powers of description were poor. He seemed almost illiterate and readily admitted the crime. Details were hard to clarify. I was a bit flummoxed. He was able to know what they had done but showed no scintilla of remorse. The victim was just a "German whore" to him, who had resisted sex and "pissed them off."

Then, I interviewed the other man. He was a somewhat handsome young man, whose uniform was embellished by a variety of medals for marksmanship and good conduct. He was verbal and seemed intelligent. It quickly became clear that he wanted to blame the other guy. They had been drinking with the woman in a local pub and intended to rape and rob her, but things went wrong when she strongly resisted. He smiled with a kind of pleasure as he described the other soldier. "He was really violent and crazy," he said with a strange smile as he recalled the violent murder. After she was unconscious and likely dead, they had taken her money and left the scene. He also told me with a smirk that they had methodically beaten several drunken soldiers in the past, after they had left a pub alone. "Crazy shit, huh?" the soldier said, obviously hoping that I would support a plea of insanity. He seemed to especially enjoy detailing the violent frenzy of his fellow soldier.

From a traditional psychiatric point of view, they were not psychotic, and their capacity for judgment was not legally impaired. I left the prison, shaken by the tales of cruel, sadistic violence, basically without remorse. Some days later, I felt a bit frightened when I later testified at their trial. They stared at me as I recited my opinion that they were sane in the light of the law. They were found guilty and then were sent back to the United States, where their attorneys, without much hope, planned to appeal.

This was a major experience for me, as a young psychiatrist who had just finished his residency training. What was the most shocking, most disturbing, was the sheer pleasure they seemed to take in their sadistic crime. No awareness of morality at all, no sense of what they had done to another human being, no regret. This experience of raw darkness was forever imprinted in my memory. I maintained my professional demeanor and reasoning, but down deep I hoped that they would never walk the streets again. This event brought me severely down to earth. The look of pleasure on the faces of brutal murderers shattered any remnants of my naive idealism!

***

The 1980s were a time of restless exploration for Darlene and me. The details of that period would require a book of their own! We traveled and wondered, and eventually decided to launch a new life in Seattle in 1990. A part of that restless energy was amplified by a monthlong stay in Bali in 1987.

The psychic background of my interest in Bali was partly due to a memorable experience during my residency training, a film that Gregory Bateson showed and discussed in 1963.[5] It was titled *Trance*

---

[5] **Gregory Bateson** (9 May 1904 – 4 July 1980) was an English anthropologist, social scientist, linguist, visual anthropologist, semiotician, and cyberneticist whose work intersected that of many other fields. His writings include *Steps to an Ecology of Mind* (1972) and *Mind and Nature* (1979). In Palo Alto, California, Bateson and colleagues developed the double-bind theory of schizophrenia. (Wikipedia)

and Dance in Bali. He made the film there with Margaret Mead during the 1930s (see *YouTube*). It conveyed the reality of a true dance of life and death. In the ritual, a group of men are put into a trance by the witch Rangda, who then commands them to kill themselves with their swords. They are entranced and terrified but resist. The ritual music and dance accompanying this enacted struggle between life and death is potent and unforgettable. At last, a helpful dragon, the *Barong*, arrives and drives Rangda away. The families and friends in the surroundings rush to the aid of the exhausted, still half-entranced men. The healing Barong music and energy continue as they revive. I was later told that some men would kill themselves during the ritual in the old days. A dance of death, for sure!

With this background and an underlying desire to deepen my knowledge of the culture that had produced that trance and dance of life and death, my wife and I planned a month's stay in Bali. Coincidentally, I heard from friends about a rental house available near Ubud, the cultural center of the island. Within a few weeks, we made plans for a three-week stay. I was a bit possessed by the excitement of the trip and studied the history and culture of the island, learned some Malay, the national language of Indonesia, as well as a small amount of "Old Bali," a Sanskrit-based language that was originally the primary language of the island. Those preparations were very important to my later experiences.

After the journey via Garuda Airlines, we settled in a small house that was half Balinese and half California style, in a beautiful setting on a small hill overlooking a valley and a small river, with the outskirts of Ubud town visible on the low hill on the other side of the river. It was quite beautiful. The population of the core city is now about 11,900, and of the larger Ubud region about 74,000. At the time we were there during the '80s, I suspect the population was lower.

Our domicile was a medium-sized house, sort of California-Balinese style, two bedrooms on the first floor, along with dining and kitchen; we mostly ate outdoors, on a large patio. Upstairs there was a long, covered porch looking across the valley toward the town. The kitchen had a propane stove, with a very limited electrical supply from a small generator. At night, there was an array of kerosene lamps ("lampu"), always lighted and hanging from a roof ledge, above the outdoor porch. It was all quite beautiful and functional. We were taken care of by a young Balinese family: Mahdi, Ketut, and Wayan. Mahdi was the father, our driver and chief adviser, Ketut was our cook and personal adviser, and Wayan was their brightly precocious son, about 6 years old.

Many things from that experience are worth discussion, but I will focus on two experiences related to death. The milieu is crucial to know.

One day Mahdi and I took a walk together to pick up some supplies in Ubud. He knew some shortcuts, and I noted we were walking through the grounds of a large, brownish building, perhaps two or three stories high, spread out over a couple of hundred feet. It looked dark and old, and the grounds we were walking through were extensive. There were a lot of trees and shrubs. I asked him what kind of structure it was, and he said (to the best of my memory) "Temple of Siwa." I was confused and asked him to clarify, and he said, "The Lord of Death," I assumed that he was referring to Shiva, but with a different accent.[6]

I asked him whether they cremated all the dead, and he said, "Yes, but not always right away! Lots of people don't have

---

[6] The Hinduism of Bali is apparently quite different from that on the Indian subcontinent, and the Balinese tend to take pride in that difference. There also seems to be a connection with Buddhism because there is a Bodhi tree in the courtyards of all their temples.

the money, and they wait for a rich person to have a big ceremony, and they dig them up and throw them on the fire!" Since Balinese don't, to my knowledge, use an embalming process, I asked him to clarify. He said yes, I had it right. Then I sort of reactively asked him whether the bodies smelled bad after all that time, and he grinned and said, "Yes, pretty bad!"

Mahdi may have been pulling my leg, and he did have a great sense of humor, but somehow it felt like the truth. He had a very different view of the raw smell of death and decay than I was accustomed to in the U.S. It stopped me and made me more aware of my own culturally restricted attitudes toward death. It put me more fully into a liminal space, a space of the unknowable, and tested my defenses against what seemed uncanny and enigmatic.

A more dramatic experience around death occurred 10 days into our stay. Mahdi had carefully instructed us to bar the door to our bedroom, which faced onto the porch. One night I was awakened by the sound of the door being violently shaken. I leapt up and grabbed a flashlight, The shaking stopped, and I jumped up and thought I saw, in the light of the lampu, two small figures running away. I shouted, awakening Mahdi and his family next door. He came quickly with more flashlights and listened carefully to my description. He was very concerned. I told him that the best I could see, the intruders were small, like children. He said, "Yes, or old people!"

I had already gleaned that old people were looked upon with some suspicion in their culture. Both men and women kept their hair dyed very black, even in very old age.

For the next few nights, Mahdi or some extended family slept on the grounds outside to guard us. They must have believed there was something amiss on a serious level. Then one day Mahdi told me that a special person was coming the next morning and that meeting with her was very important.

We were mystified but of course agreed. The next day, Mahdi gently summoned us to come with him. At the side of the house, a woman awaited us. She appeared middle-aged and emanated a sense of presence I have rarely encountered in my life. I understood that she was a sort of spiritual leader in Mahdi's home community. She brought a few simple things and asked permission to perform a small ceremony. (Chills always go down my spine when I remember this experience). She performed a simple ritual, using air, fire, earth and water. I must have evinced a bit of reflex reaction about sipping the sacred water because Mahdi, with his usual humor, interjected, "Don't worry Doctor Hinton, it's holy water!" The woman smiled too and shook both our hands firmly, and took her leave with our abundant thanks. My wife and I always remembered that meeting with reverence and thanks for the gift she gave us and the deep loving-kindness that came from both her and Mahdi. They wanted to protect us from danger on more than one level.

Later in our stay, we learned from Mahdi that the land where the house was built had also been a matter of contention for several decades. The family of the rich man who had died had to sell the land against his professed wishes to pay for a munificent public cremation in which all the people of the area could participate after his death. His "evil spirit" still lurked around, and my hosts feared we could be in deadly danger from it.

These experiences of death in Bali remain clear in my mind at age 89! The effects were subtly profound rather than dramatic. It enhanced the depth of my respect for the depth and kindness of spirit that can unexpectedly come your way in the face of possible death and evil.

***

I will now move on to discuss another experience later and closer to home. My wife, Darlene, died in 2017, after an acute deterioration from several chronic conditions. The final stage lasted about 10 days, and she died a week short of our 60th wedding anniversary. She had suffered from a multiplicity of medical problems, the prognosis was hopeless, and we had extensively, tearfully, and painfully discussed the details of care and when she wanted to let go of life. Maintaining a mere semblance of life when there was no hope seemed degrading to her. We had once had long discussions about such a heartrending subject with our friend, Donald Sandner, who chose not to be "medicalized" at the end of his own life. Hospice care is excellent in Seattle, and our three sons had time to come from out of town to say their goodbyes. They were deeply present to her, as was our daughter-in-law. Our own goodbye was wrenching, and we had our final kiss in the last seconds of her life.

There were the usual rituals as we mourned together with friends and families. My old friends Tom and Jean Kirsch came for the memorial, bearing some very moving photos taken by Tom's father, James, in 1963, when we were all spending a weekend at the senior Kirsches' home in Los Angeles and Darlene was pregnant with our third son. Those pictures are haunting and still bring tears to my eyes. I am grateful to Tom for preserving them, and to James, his father, for taking them.

Darlene and I had never been apart more than a day or two during almost 60 years of marriage. Of course, there were ups and downs, although rarely significant longer-term. I would say, overall, we had a close and long marriage, and were very much in synch as parents. Our love was deep and real. After everyone had left town following the memorial, I felt like a ghost myself! I wondered how I could go on. My grief was beyond tears.

Then I had a wrenching, unforgettable dream. In the dream, Darlene and I were in Mendocino, California, a small town on the Northern California Coast that we had, in earlier years, loved for special times away. In the dream, we had just finished lunch at a small restaurant, and as we left, I paused to give some advice to a young couple who were just arriving. Darlene wandered away as we talked, and then I turned to find her. There was a small street fair outside, and I thought she might be stopping to look at some arts and crafts. Then I saw that she was walking rapidly away on the other side of the crowd. I went to catch up to her and called out, but she didn't seem to hear me. It felt like she was in a sort of spell. She reached a set of low, adobe buildings and went into one. I neared the building she had entered, but before I could enter, I heard a loud, horrible sound like grinding, clanging mechanical gears. I awakened in shock, with the words "The Infernal Machine!" emblazoned like a headline in my mind.

This dream filled me with horror. Was Death eating up my gentle, beautiful, kind wife? The grinding, clattering gears felt inexorable, a horrible inevitability. Not just death, but antilife in its essence! The dream vision continually assaulted me from within. I was intermittently disoriented for days, and ordinary functioning was ofttimes difficult.

However, as my mind settled down somewhat in the following weeks, I slowly recalled that she had, in fact, "left" me in a peaceful way that was gentle, as was her nature. After some days, I came to more fully realize that it was *my* dream, *my* experience, not hers. Her loss was a horrible event for *me*, not necessarily a mediumistic knowledge of *her* experience. This perspective felt true and eventually calmed me somewhat, so that I could reflect more and not just react in anger and anguish at my loss. I began to accept the experience as my own.

"Infernal Machine" felt vaguely familiar to me and was immensely evocative, but I had no conscious memory of what it meant or where it came from. The voice still echoes in my mind, along with the gruesome sound of the grinding, merciless gears of inevitability. Even now, I can feel it, like a sucking quicksand that could engulf me.

However, life beckons, and the call is still strong to live my life, to be with those whom I love, my loving family and friends, and be the best I can be in our needy, troubled world. That would, I am very sure, please Darlene.

The term "Infernal Machine" has many connections with warfare. There was an attempt on Napoleon's life using a hidden bomb, which he later referred to as an "infernal machine." Hidden land mines and booby traps, which may threaten every step a soldier takes, are often referred to as "Infernal Machines." The hidden death that can occur anytime.

In Celan's *Death Fugue*, the very rhythm of the verse conveys the relentless clicking of the wheels of the trains heading to Auschwitz, loaded with those to be exterminated. This powerfully conveys the sense of the truth of inevitable death to come—the camp as an "Infernal Machine" of hatred and genocide.

My most significant, personal association was a scene from a movie named *Mondo Cane* ("Dog's World") that I had seen in 1962, during my first year at Stanford. It was done in erratic, shocking, kaleidoscopic style—sort of a parody of a "nice, entertaining" travelogue. It shows scenes of cultural practice from around the world in a way that created shock or surprise. One scene is a junkyard in Los Angeles, where a giant machine, clanking loudly and with indomitable intent, and loud clanging and mechanical crunches, reduces the huge pile of junked cars, one by one, into a small ball of bare metal. A cube from the crushed car metal was later sold as art in a Los Angeles gallery!

That scene had provoked many intense discussions among the residents and young faculty. We all remarked on the visceral effect of the scene. It felt as if *our* bodies were being smashed and reduced. This "shock" movie indeed shocked us all. It has stuck with me for all these years. It powerfully captures the truth that our bodies are temporary (temporal) constructs in a very direct way. I have carried this memory for 60 years!

The ending seemed to also say that everything is ultimately for sale, after being "processed" by the linear, mechanical world.

It often seems that the Infernal Machine is around us again, both individually and collectively, in a world that all too frequently feels mechanical and indifferent to human cares or sentiments. We see it daily in the news and on the streets: racism, drugs, brutal crimes, rampant suicide rates, and wars and threats of dictators to use hydrogen bombs, the ultimate Infernal Machines, on our cities. COVID underlines the dread we already feel every day, acknowledged or not. It is urgent not to forget that our lives are now substantially being run by the new "Infernal Machines" of high technology! "Shock" movies can be very useful tools in waking us up to the underlying realities of our times.

My core dream/vision also raises the question of freedom versus unfreedom, at least on a personal level. The beginning scene included a young couple just setting out to explore a new place. In contrast, the uncanny, mechanical sounds came across like an inexorable force that often seems to live our lives and do its will, despite our conscious intentions. How much freedom do we ultimately have? The final monstrosity that appeared in my dream was death. My love, our love, could not defeat it. That, it seems to me, is our human fate. We do what we can.

Conclusion

Death pervades human life from the beginning. We evolve from an original, small clump of cells that must survive a life-and-death crisis in the uterus before it can become firmly implanted. The mother's immune system strongly resists the intruder. Most clumps of cells don't make it. There is a crisis of survival, which is resolved when maternal immune cells are converted to helper cells by a hormone secreted by the intruder. The majority of possible conceptions pass in the guise of a heavy menstrual period (Bassat, 2021). Uncertainty exists from the moment of conception.

The specter of death seems to underlie our specieswide concerns about conception. Children are our most primal way of continuing into the future. As I recall, the birth rate accelerates after wars.

Death has vast psychological, cultural, and historical contexts. Where is it not, whether hidden or blatant?! I could have written more about other dimensions than I have, or in more theoretical ways, but my intent was not political or sociological, but rather to reflect upon some of my experiences with death in the context of my own life. In the face of the deepest of enigmas, I wanted to speak from my core, as best I could, and especially to shun comfortable platitudes. That process has not always been easy.

I hope that the reader will find my effort of some value to others. My goal, in sympathy with the purpose of this volume, was to expand awareness of death and underline its elemental presence in every moment of life, amid the human drama of creation and destruction. The challenge has moved me deeply, and I want to thank Luis and Murray for inviting me to contribute.

References

Bassat, S.B. (2021). "War in a Time of Love"-Prenatal cell relations as a prototype of autistic anxieties, defenses, and object relations. *Tustin Memorial Prize.*

Binswanger, L. (1958). "The Case of Ellen West." in *Existence*, ed. Rollo May. *Basic Books*, 1958.

Gunn, J. (2006) "Review Essay: Mourning Humanism, or, the Idiom of Haunting." *Quarterly Journal of Speech*, Vol. 92, No. 1, February 2006, pp. 77-102. Taylor & Francis.

Heidegger, M. (1962}. *Being and Time.* Harper & Row.

Hinton, L. (2015). "Temporality and the Torments of Time." *Journal of Analytical Psychology,* 2015, 60, 353-370.

Inverso, H. (2022). "Phenomenology of the Inapparent: a methodological approach to the New Realism," in A. Schnell *et al.* (Eds.), Phenomenology *and Speculative Realism*, Würzburg: Königshausen & Neumann.

Knight, Power, & Watts (1995). "The Human Symbolic Revolution: A Darwinian Account," Cambridge Archeological Journal 5-1 (1995), pp. 75-114. Cambridge Core.

Reinhardt, K. (1960). *The Existentialist Revolt: The Main Themes and Phases of Existentialism: Kierkegaard, Nietzsche, Heidegger, Jaspers, Sartre.* Marcel.

Taking the Anima Along

John Beebe

A paradox of a long life is that those of us who are granted one have usually thought more about death when we were young than we do when we are old. At 84, I find that death is rarely the topic of conversation with my fellow survivors. Friendship over many decades has erased many taboos as to what can belong to our conversations, so it is not that we're politely avoiding the subject. It's that life is more what remains interesting to us. With his introverted focus on individuation, which included what he could see in the dreams of his patients, Jung, when he was himself 84, commented:

> I have treated many old people and it's quite interesting to watch what the unconscious is doing with the fact that it is threatened with a complete end. It disregards it. Life behaves as if it were going on, and so I think it is better for an old person to live on, to look forward to the next day, as if he had to spend centuries, and then he lives properly. (Jung 1977, p. 438)

When I was in my 20s, though, my friends and I could not seem to stop talking about death. I had become such a maestro of that conversation that it entered the pages of the first book I wrote, right out of psychiatric residency, which had chapters about suicide and homicide that echoed veterans at crisis intervention who were deft at the prevention of psychologically motivated deaths. At that stage, I viewed death as something to be counteracted: Its destructive dynamics needed to be pulled apart and put back together in a less lethal way. It took the arrival of the AIDS epidemic that decimated San Francisco's gay community and claimed several of my first analytic patients, people who had already taught me to listen to conscious bouts of emotion and unconscious bursts of dream without trying to change what I heard, to get me to see that death too is something that needs an attentive audience. It was one of these patients who, once the time for heroic resistance had passed, was kind enough to allow me to witness his surrender to death. I was privileged to observe, without drama, a dying process that was so beautiful to everyone that he shared it with that it took away my own fear of death.

But where had that fear originated? Long before I was witness to the frequent, mass death of my gay brothers—including many who were dear to my analysands—I had been aware of how easy it is for a young person, bright with potential and attractiveness, to attract an early death. Between the time I was 20 and 35, six of my closest friends from high school and college years—three women and three men—lost their lives, variously to a concealed congenital abnormality, to suicide, to what may have been murder, and to an auto accident.

Each of them fit the pattern described by Marie-Louise von Franz in her seminal lectures on *The Problem of the Puer Aeternus*, which I read in 1970 when I was still 30. In the ninth lecture, discussing the character of Melchior in Bruno Goetz's novel, *Das Reich ohne Raum* (The Kingdom without Space), published in 1919 followed by a second edition in 1925, von Franz points out that he belonged to a circle of young people whose lives were shortened by a "pull toward death" which seemed to mirror the difficulty Melchior was experiencing in staying connected to life. Behind the death trend surrounding him, von Franz sensed a negative mother complex that was too strong. Von Franz suggests that this aspect of the mother has so much power over a young person who has already grown up that it can attract early death. That this could become the case, she thinks, reflects a failure on the part of the *puer-* or *puella*-identified young person to have integrated the chthonic, earth-hugging shadow that defends the survival instinct. One of my analysts, Joseph Henderson, who had read the same passage in von Franz, similarly interpreted the presence of this pattern of friends dying young in my own life. Von Franz and Hillman had often regarded such grim coincidences as "generational," reflecting a "time problem" in which puer psychology was omnipresent, as in the troubled decade in Germany before Hitler's rise to absolute power, or the 1960s in Europe and America, when there was even, in 1968, a "puer revolution." But for Dr. Henderson and me, the death trend that I had noted in my immediate circle of well-educated young people interested in their own creativity led us to think that I must have an individual puer problem that needed to be addressed in analysis.

I did not resist the interpretation, or the implicit recommendation to let it guide my use of analysis, because I had long since, without any analyst's help, realized how much I was at risk of being a casualty of my own youth. I date this awakening from my visit to the New York World's Fair in 1964 with my mother, with whom I viewed the *Pietà* made by Michelangelo when he was a young man. Here's how Wikipedia describes it:

The sculpture captures the moment when Jesus, taken down from the cross, is given to his mother Mary. Mary looks younger than Jesus; art historians believe Michelangelo was inspired by a passage in Dante Alighieri's *Divine Comedy*: "O virgin mother, daughter of your Son ... your merit so ennobled human nature that its divine Creator did not hesitate to become your creature" (Paradiso, Canto XXXIII). Michelangelo's aesthetic interpretation of the *Pietà* is unprecedented in Italian sculpture because it balances the Renaissance ideals of classical beauty with naturalism.

At the Expo, the sculpture was by itself in a tent, on a dark blue cloth. As soon as she saw it, my mother, who was not a religious person, teared up. The meaning of her reaction, to me, was unmistakable. Like the Virgin, as depicted by Michelangelo, my mother had been young when I was born, just a few weeks before her 21st birthday. I had been welcomed as a divine child; my mother had never been able to let go of that stage of her motherhood. On the positive side, her veneration had been a symbolic impetus to my realization of my value and had enabled me to become, for a time, a Wunderkind with legendary academic status and a stint as a student panelist on a national quiz show, *Twenty Questions*, which gave me an opportunity to show off what my intuition could do. I was 14 then. Now, more than 10 years later, with my mother finally starting to look more middle-aged, my 25-year-old self, had no problem recognizing "this terrible impersonal pattern" (von Franz, 1970, Lec. 1, p. 20) that was ready to have me dead young, and my mother holding my memory as a kind of widow of the marriage that only worked if I remained a child. It was a chilling realization, one that galvanized me to seek to prevent it from happening. The danger I felt would have been part of a kind of cultural mass murder of the young to satisfy the religious needs of the "Greatest Generation" in America, of which my mother had become a passionate part. She had lived the first years of my life watching the United States win World War II and did not want to let go of that memory of victory through sacrifice. It could be continued if the young of my generation died too, and then the Greatest Generation could go on forever in the eternal memory of their parental grief, a way of staying connected to their own youth. It was there that I first confronted death as fate and determined not to let it happen.

As an analyst, Joe Henderson had made a specialty out of enabling the archetype of initiation to do its work of carrying his analysands past their mother and father complexes rather than simply letting them fly over or tunnel below this necessary work, as *pueri aeterni* and *puellae aeternae* tend to do. My work with Joe has allowed me to live 60 years past the moment of seeing Michelangelo's *Pietà* for the first time at the age of 25. As a man in his late 40s, I saw the *Pietà* again, in Rome. By that time, settled down both at work and at home, I was able to recognize that the dead Jesus my mother might have cried at seeing might not really, to her, have meant me, but rather the early death of a redemptive animus she had had when she was 25, the loss of which had produced a long depression. Her depression followed the failure of a love affair she had divorced my father to pursue, as a planned second marriage that she had imagined would give her a real life. Troubles intervened, and the second marriage never took place. Knowing as an adult who is also an analyst that this abandonment by the possibilities of life was her problem, and that it had permanently wounded her animus when she was young, has helped me to qualify any pride I might have taken in my heroic refusal to accept an early death and to begin to have some genuine compassion for the fact that the spirit of my eternally young mother had suffered a cruel injury from which it could not recover.

But it is only now, as I start to conclude my 85th year of life, that I have the curiosity to ask myself what I would have learned if I *had* had to go through the early death I once resisted so vigorously. What could I have discovered if I had not been so determined, in my heroic refusal to allow my mother to become my widow, to learn something from the puer about death, which is what the Pieta meant to Michelangelo as a realized religious symbol? To contemplate that possibility seems necessary for confronting my inevitable death now that I am old. Therefore, it is to artists like Michelangelo, who realized the puer and his death in their work, rather than to the wise old analyst Dr. Henderson had become, that I am turning for my example as to how to die well. It is not my mature old age that can teach me how to die. It is the puer who was already ready, whom I did not want to have to listen to too early, that I really must find a way to hear now.

As always when I have this kind of problem, I turn to films, a lifelong pleasure that my mother initiated me into very young. I invite you, reader, to come with me, as I went with her, even before I was ready to face the life-freezing gaze of auteur cinema, to see a film whose making accompanied a young filmmaker's death. This director was the 29-year-old Jean Vigo. His precocious cinematic achievement in the face of a preposterously short life (1905-1934) has long been recognized. And yet, even to those who have found *Zero de Conduite* and *L'Atalante* impressive enough to agree with the film critics who have placed one or the other on a *Sight and Sound's* list of the best films of all time, he remains for many an obscure figure. This was what the meticulous film historian David Thomson wondered about in his succinct but complete account of the director's short but prodigious career, which I will quote from here, but unpack a bit for those who don't have access to the fourth edition of his *New Biographical Dictionary of Film*, in which Thomson's references are presented with concise accuracy and cross-referenced elsewhere in his book:

> ... It is still mysterious that the poignancy of Vigo's career has been treated lightly. He is the first young martyr to cinema. ... Vigo needed film and died in its pursuit.
>
> Biography, therefore, is worth spelling out. ... Vigo was the son of the French anarchist known as "Miguel Almereyda." That led him into politics and the first potent sense of outrage when Almereyda died in mysterious circumstances in Fresnes prison [in Paris] in 1917. ... Vigo [who was twelve that year] was taken south to be educated. He returned to Paris at age nineteen, to study at the Sorbonne, but soon succumbed to an illness that was to hinder him for the rest of his life. It was while in a tubercular clinic that he met his future wife, "Lydou," Elizabeth Lozinska. He had already been encouraged by [the successful French director Claude] Autant-Lara and worked as an assistant to the [also well-established silent film cinematographer] Léonce-Henri Burel. But in 1929 his father-in-law loaned or gave him money with which he bought a camera and made *A Propos de Nice* [*Concerning Nice,* a short documentary that delivered a satirical critique of the *haut bourgeoisie* continuing to sun themselves on the French Riviera in 1930, at the outset of the

Great Depression. This was made] with the aid of Boris Kaufman, younger brother of Dziga Vertov [the director of the pioneering 1929 Russian documentary about filmmaking itself, *The Man with a Movie Camera*].

Vigo now had four years to live, and he spent them in beleaguered communion with Lydou, Kaufman, and his camera. He and his wife had bouts of illness: he was forced to sell the camera for money to live on; none of his films prospered. Germaine Dulac [a feminist pioneer as a seminal director in the French avant-garde] helped him to set up *Taris*. [The full title, when translated, is *Swimming with Jean Taris: Champion of France*, and it is a nine-minute film which features, alongside the fluent over and underwater movements of the then national hero of competitive French swimming, Jean Taris, whose legs move him forward as flexibly as a fish, Vigo and Kaufman's uncanny ability to make the wet wildness of the water that surrounds the swimmer as cinematic as film itself. Acting as his producer, a friend,] Jacques-Louis Nounez financed *Zero de Conduite* [*Zero for Conduct,* again directed by Vigo and filmed by Kaufman], which caused such a controversy that it was banned. Finally, Vigo made his only feature, *L'Atalante* [*The Atalanta*], again with Nounez's support, and Gaumont's backing [a coup, since this was the oldest film studio in the world; Kaufman was again the buoyant cinematographer, and the team was doing well]. But the distributor took fright at its intensity and released

a "popularized" version. Vigo was too ill to contest
the matter actively and within months he was dead.
(Thomson, 2002, p. 808-809)

For those who have not seen the film (and I urge you to do so),
L'Atalante is the name of a river barge of the type that is sometimes
called a canal boat. It is long and narrow and picks up and delivers
goods at ports along the river Seine between Le Havre and Paris.
Not really a swift vessel, it is ironically named for the Atalanta,
who in Greek mythology, was so outstanding a female foot-racer
that she could outrun any man. *L'Atalante*, however, is sluggishly
patriarchal in the way it goes about as a cargo ship that is managed
by an entirely male crew who must deal with an unfriendly
environment to be able to do their work.

Acting like the barge's manly and still healthy young skipper,
who has brought his bride, Juliette, along into what will be her
maiden voyage as a live-on-the-ship captain's wife, Vigo, knowing
his tuberculosis was advancing, chose to work outdoors in the cold
near even colder water to do the filming, and this occurred over 11
icy weeks in the harsh winter of 1933-1934. Vigo, at the time, said,
"I am killing myself with *L'Atalante*." Michael McDunnah, who
supplies this quote, along with the most complete account of the
film has said, "he was right" (2017). But the statement that he was
killing *himself* can also be heard by us now as the creative auteur's
inversion of an understanding, often attributed to so-called primitive
people, that there is always a soul murder involved in taking
someone's picture. That idea was taken up also by modernism, and
it has since been codified by the postmodernist suspicion of how art
made by a camera can be commodified in an age of absurdly easy
mechanical reproduction. Susan Sontag, within the opening essay of
her book *On Photography* (1977), pointedly states, "To photograph

is to appropriate the thing photographed." William Rothman, at the end of his seminal book of film theory, *The Murderous Gaze*, which shows the many ways Hitchcock's camera not only nails the furtive expressions of people but robs them of independent autonomy by locating them within a social scheme that dominates and orders the picture in which the auteur has placed them, goes so far as to say that "Every film image is a death mask of the world. ... The camera fixes its living subjects, possesses their life. They are reborn on the screen, creatures of the film's author and us. But life is not fully breathed back into them. They are immortal, but they are always already dead" (Rothman, 1982, p. 341). What Vigo, as an independent filmmaker, epitomizes in *L'Atalante* is a different ruthlessness, however, for it is not directed toward his subjects, who remain autonomously ensouled, and as alive as the swimmer Taris, but toward himself. He has taken the life of his soul and put it in this picture so that it can accompany its final documentation of how an artist lives when he is dying.

That his masterpiece has endured, despite taking his life, and that we can now see it as he thought it should be presented, is thanks to four generations of cineastes devoted to film restoration, the final result being the 2011 Criterion BluRay edition of *The Complete Jean Vigo* (four films totaling two hours and 41 minutes of running time) of which 87 minutes are occupied by *L'Atalante*, the longest of his films. *L'Atalante* is the return on the investment the director made in getting progressively vivified image sequences of his love of life onto celluloid. This is not just a grandiose exhibition of a creative anima. It is also a therapeutic achievement, a contribution to the soul of the world by demonstrating that the anima can accompany a dying person and doesn't have to be left behind when a life is ending.

What keeps the creative anima alive in Vigo's *L'Atalante* is the reality of the psyche that made the film. Personally oriented active imagination is at the heart of auteur cinema (Beebe, 2008, p. 19; Sarris, 1968, p.19). I realize now, after 50 years of watching Vigo's *L'Atalante,* that all along the way it has been helping me to see and therefore discover the soulful spirit that can accompany dying itself when the anima, which Jung had called the archetype of life, is willing to include herself in the dying process. My hope is that my effort to follow the symbolism of the movie will allow Vigo's culminating masterpiece to be recognized by others for what it has become for me, a one-off imaginal guide to dying ensouled. For I have come to see *L'Atalante* as a cinematic Book of the Dead for modern people who do not know how to die. For me, this is the mystery at the heart of a film that so many cineastes have found so indelible in its imaginal life that it has not only survived, but, as I will argue, has become for those of us who need such actively imaginative texts one of the "continuingly valid documents of the soul, especially in unusual individuals [that] tell us more about how the processes of the psyche work on its objective timeless level" (Hillman, 1968, p. 2).

To be sure, most critical opinion has stopped short of seeing *L'Atalante* as about Vigo's dying, even when recognizing fully the impact that must have had on making his final film as fully realized as it is. As Marina Warner has written in her lyrical appreciation of the youthful erotic spirit with which the film proceeds to consummate itself, *"L'Atalante* is a romance."* She explains with her customary erudition and recognition of our culture's story pattern that "Romance, in its earliest surviving form was called 'erotika pathemata' by the Greeks—tales of erotic suffering. After initial bliss and consummation, the lovers passed through a period of trials; temptations, as well as ordeals, tested their love, until at last they were reunited and their love was free to begin as the story came to a traditional happy ending" (Warner 1993, p. 9-10). David Thomson, who named it 'No. 3 Arthouse film of all time' in *The Guardian*, adds an important idea to that of "a romance." He says that "Marriage is the film's subject, and it is most moving in its cinematic grasp of a deeper bond than that permitted by the lovers' temporary misalliance." Truffaut, one of the heirs to the many innovations in cinematic storytelling that Vigo pioneered for both French and world film with *L'Atalante*, famously said (Warner quotes him) that *L'Atalante* is one of those films "whose feet smell," and this would seem to be appropriate in a romance that survives courtship and wedding into marriage itself. Everyone recognizes, for instance, (and again Warner is best at conveying the trope) that during the wedding party of the couple (the film starts as they emerge from the church, followed by the villagers who have lost the bride to her groom, who is the pilot of the river barge ironically named for the fleetfooted heroine of Greek myth, Atalanta), "The entire atmosphere evokes a funeral, not a wedding—the shadowy lighting, the coffin-like box of the barge, the expressionless guests, and the drowned bouquet" (Warner 1993, p. 20). She will have to live aboard the ship he captains, along with his first mate, an old sailor encrusted with layers of dirt, speaking with an equally thick Swiss accent. Père Jules has been all over the world and lives surrounded by trophies and cats. Outside the church where the wedding has taken place, he is accompanied by *L'Atalante*'s version of cabin boy, a deckhand who is older (and smarter) than he at first looks, but through the childlike demeanor he affects, plays "kid" to the sea goat Père Jules, who holds his hand to keep him from wandering off and in other ways reminds him he is there to assist. But the *gosse* (kid) is a cabin boy without a cabin and seems to be on the barge mostly for the ride up and down the Seine as a foil for the side of Père Jules that likes to entertain and needs a partner, just as Chaplin did in *The Kid* (1921). And like The Kid, the *gosse's* antique puerishness cannot be contained. Everyone else besides this comedic pair of *senex et puer* out of a Roman farce seems beyond grim. Walking through the town after the couple leave the church and start heading toward the barge, the bride looks old at first and only seems to begin to be going somewhere that might interest her when she is levered aboard the barge by Père Jules, who drapes her over a boom that he swings toward the deck of the boat while her mother, mourning the loss of her, looks on, verifying that the wedding has indeed been a funeral. It was not a surprise when the boy and the old salt, starting to dance to a hornpipe to cheer themselves up, managed to lose the flowers they have bought to greet the bride when she boards. Just in time to meet her and the captain, her solemn groom, the boy, like a figure from the antique imagination goes off and comes back with gobs of freshly picked clematis vine (Marina Warner identifies it as "Traveler's Joy" but it is also known by the name of Old Man's Beard). Having it wrapped around himself in a slightly cruciform but also pagan way summons the cultural memory of the child god Iacchus in the Eleusinian mysteries whose image led Ovid to write in his *Metamorphoses* (1964, 4/28-29): "Behold puer aeternus with his angel seeming face, But oh, those invisible horns!" Having that face appear suddenly here wrapped in what might be a funeral wreath is a surreal touch that allows Vigo to make the already ancient-looking *gosse* into a frozen stand of mortuary-bound blooms. Later, after the barge starts to move with the groom at the helm, while the bride tries to find her bearings, a woman on the bank with no relation to the wedding party crosses herself beside the child she has with her who is too young to understand what is happening, but she does: A life is being left behind for an unknown voyage.

To the best of my knowledge, however, no critic has considered that the voyage that follows is also funerary, so I'll be breaking some new ground by claiming that here. Warner was exceptionally careful not to front-load her analysis of the film by sharing her knowledge of Vigo's life (which was less widely known when the first edition of her British Film Institute monograph came out than when her monograph was given a revised, second edition in 2015) before she'd discussed the film on its own terms, but though she tells us that she has "purposely left out" her short account of Vigo's mortal background "till the end of the essay on *L'Atalante* because it's so extraordinarily dramatic that. ... it can overwhelm his work and shape the critical response." It's nonetheless true that Vigo knew he was dying of tuberculosis when he made the film, and that his real-life wife, whom he'd met in a sanitarium, was suffering from the disease as well. He died of septicemia of the lungs in 1934 before the then final print had been screened, and she "who had to be restrained from throwing herself out the window of their apartment at the time, survived him by four years before dying of tuberculosis herself on what would have been Vigo's 34th birthday" (Warner 1993, p. 75).

Since leading my first public seminar in 1979, showing a movie in the morning and then discussing it with the seminar audience for an entire afternoon at the C. G. Jung Institute of San Francisco, which I did with the title "Film as Active Imagination," I have imagined the kind of cinema Vigo is pioneering with this film as a dialogue between the director of a script and the elements of it that speak to him or her personally. The term *auteur* for this kind of sublimely supraordinate imaginal focus on a director's part, beyond his usual job as the "*metteur en scene*" (the one who stages the film and supervises all the film technology), would not be originated by critics and filmmakers in France for a quarter of century after

Vigo's death. At first, when so many of the auteurs were men, and often young men, not unlike Vigo, the medium was particularly suited to letting the anima of the director take the lead in giving life to the finished product. The anima, as an archetype, is peculiarly positioned in the psyche between ego and Self. The frontispiece to Edward Edinger's *Ego and Archetype*, for example, is a woodcut by the Renaissance Paracelsan physician Robert Fludd, titled "The World Soul," in which the anima figure is a woman standing naked with a corona of stars firmly positioned beyond the navel of the world. Edinger tells us that "The anima as personification of the ego-Self axis transmits guidance and support to the ego from the archetypal psyche" (1973). The anima is in that sense a mediatrix who stands amid any truly active imagination, a figure of fantasy that is also engaged in guiding the fantasy in a meaningful direction. This is the essence of *auteur* direction as well.

In *L'Atalante,* the bride brought aboard the barge also guides the film in what is magically ahead in the race among early French auteurs (we could name, for instance Jean Renoir and René Clair) to use film as active imagination. As played by Dita Parlo, she is the surest representative onscreen of what I have called "The Anima in Film." In an essay with that title, found in revised form in my book with Virginia Apperson, *The Presence of the Feminine in Film* [2008, pp 187-204]), I describe nine characteristics that define this figure when she appears in a film that has her kind of imaginal life. These are: 1) unusual radiance; 2) a desire to make emotional connection; 3) having come from some quite other place; 4) the character as a feminine mirror of traits we have already witnessed in the attitude or behavior of another, usually male character; 5) unusual capacity for life; 6) the will to offer a piece of advice, frequently couched in in the form of a rebuke that is almost unacceptable to a male hero; 7) a protective and almost therapeutic effect on someone else; 8) the ability to get another character to recognize a problem in living that is insoluble; and 9) the fact that the loss of this character is associated with the loss of purposive life itself. In *L'Atalante,* Dita Parlo's Juliette either is or does all these things.

Marina Warner recognized how Vigo's way of using Dita Parlo enabled him to move beyond the puerility of the cinema he was finding his way into at the height of the French surrealist movement, which he had appreciated in an early favorable critique when Cocteau and Buñuel came together to make *Un Chien Andalou.* That film is famous for the trick photography that allows a razor seemingly to split a woman's eyeball. (This was done using a grape to tantalize us with a sadism that Hitchcock would later make more real with his understanding in *Psycho* of the camera's ability to preempt human vision with a gaze that is compulsively if passively murderous). About Vigo, however, Warner notes that "Though he was a passionate admirer of *Un Chien Andalou,* introducing his own first film, *A Propos de Nice*, with a eulogy of Dali and Buñuel, he never emulated their provocative callousness." Rather, Juliette is a fully embodied anima figure who remains so, so much that she is to Warner's informed critical eye a tutelary figure in replacing his early fascination with the possibilities of surrealism with his own early version of a poetic realism and thus "is able to give the portrait of Juliette an individuality most surrealist images of women do not even attempt" (Warner, p. 43). She agrees with the great American film critic of the 1940s, James Agee, who, arguing for an archetypal scheme to the characters when *L'Atalante* first became available to contemplate after World War II on a New York movie screen, had written that Dita Parlo's Juliette is

the fullest embodiment of subarticulate sex that I have ever seen; the trinket salesman with whom she

flirts is an astonishing cross-breed of slapstick with
a kind of jail-bird Ariel; and Michel Simon, as a pre-
mental old man, is even more wonderfully realized
as a poetic figure, a twentieth century Caliban.
(Agee, 1969, p. 265)

Recognizing that she is a *femme-enfant* (or child woman, what a
Jungian might call a *puella aeterna),* Warner feels that Agee "put his
finger here on Dita Parlo's childishness, her Miranda-like qualities
of discovery and innocence and acceptance" (p. 43).

I would say that in embodying the anima in film for Vigo
(whom actors loved to work with, partly because he was himself
young and beautiful), Parlo was guiding his directorial hand into
the poetic realism that became the French style of the '30s and
'40s, reaching its apogee in *Les Enfants du Paradis* (1945). What
Juliette, whose vision stays intact, brings to the slight story is its
anima quality, which is with psychological daring put into direct
competition with the just as archetypal fascination Michel Simon's
Père Jules can command and manipulate. Père Jules is for many
viewers the most important figure in the film, not least because the
character thinks so himself. Simon, who had already distinguished
himself as a renegade holdout to any kind of capitalist conformity
to usual patriarchal values in Jean Renoir's *Boudu Saved from
Drowning* (1932), about a homeless man who crashes a bourgeois
suburb, plays in *L'Atalante* a kind of wise old man of voyage who
has nevertheless either lost something or left something out by
surrounding himself with cats and their litters, who crawl around
his artifacts and memories while he tries to get a phonograph
repaired that will at least bring living music to his world. The
interactions between Juliette and Père Jules, the bride and the old
first mate, let us see anima and senex in effect competing as to

which of them is the figure that best understands the unconscious purpose of voyaging itself, and thus are best positioned to take care of the young Captain's soul. In this film Jean Dasté plays the barge Captain as body itself; he fully embodies both the Captain's sexual need for Juliette and the angry, jealous temperament that leads him once he senses a bit too much attachment on her part to Père Jules and his memories, to destroy many of the artifacts that Père Jules has managed to collect. He also tries to postpone her first encounter with the city of Paris. The Captain is Juliette's groom and Père Jules' boss, but both have dibs on his body, and the question of which most can empower the captain's voyage and make it meaningful is at the heart of the film. This a tension Jung recognized as between the anima as the archetype of life, and the wise old man, the archetype of meaning (Jung 1934/1959), p. 32, para. 66 and p. 37, para. 79), and this couple—Juliette and Père Jules—dramatize the eternal tension between soul and spirit that is at the heart of so many psychological conflicts that Jungian analysts are called upon to solve. Vigo makes sure to show us, however, that simply knowing and holding the tension of these opposites is not enough, they must deal with and include the body, and in this film that is the body of the Captain. His body is an immediate subject of the film. Père Jules, keeps in a jar the hands of a former shipmate, which shocks Juliette until he tells her "that is all I have left of him" and she realizes the force of a love like her own, since she has just discovered sex on her honeymoon. Père Jules is clearly bisexual, and the fate of the Captain's body becomes the obscure object of desire for both Juliette and Père Jules. This keeps their own flirtation from being merely what Jung later in life (1963, Part Six) came to regard as an incomplete stage of the union of psychic opposites, a *unio mentalis* of spirit and soul that does not really include the body. That the body is included between Jules and Juliette, and emphasized by Captain Jean, gets us close to what *L'Atalante* is about, because in the scenario as mapped out by Vigo, there must be a way to include the body of the Captain itself in what spirit (Père Jules) and soul (Juliette) are playing with as they start to come together or the Captain will simply have to shut the funeral ship down. Indeed, when he himself tries to do that, he becomes depressed in a way that only spirit and soul can figure out how to resolve.

To proceed further would be what is called in contemporary film writing a "spoiler" of the reader's chance to appreciate this film by viewing it free of preconceptions, so I'm going to stop retelling the story and say instead that the reader of this essay needs to watch *L'Atalante* to discover that the interpretation I'm giving it is not reductive of the impact of the film as a whole. Fortunately, as *L'Atalante* has often been nominated as one of the 10 best films of all time, it is readily available, both on a magnificently restored Criterion Collection BluRay that can be purchased, or on YouTube, where it can be watched well enough for free. And these days, it can easily be streamed. It is only 87 minutes long, so the time demand is not great.

What I want to say here is that the key to the meaning of the film seems to me to be, not whether Juliette is an anima figure, but rather what figure Jules represents when contemplated archetypally. James Agee called him a Caliban, and that fits the quality of Shakespeare's *The Tempest* that Marina Warner summons. I have seen other archetypal figures summoned by other critics, but it surprises me that it has not occurred to anyone that Père Jules is an image of Charon, and that in the background is the Roman God Saturn, who likes to acquire interesting possessions, is sometimes associated with cats, and who becomes the god of Death. It's Pére Jules, not the Captain, whom I regard as the man directing the voyage and who knows that the barge is a death boat bearing the body of the captain to its destiny. But Père Jules' knowing is aesthetic and intuitive—in Agee's term, "pre-mental." And the change that takes place in this modern version of the Charon story is that he must take the anima, the archetype of life, along on this voyage of death. The film depends upon Père Jules recognizing that this is essential. From this perspective, there is an allegorical level: The Captain is thus the dying Vigo, and *L'Atalante* the swift forward motion of his own tuberculosis. The final shot of the film would have made sense to Vigo, who spent time working in a medical lab and knew what the tubercle bacillus looked like when viewed through a microscope. That is exactly what the final image of the boat moving through the water resembles.

As the newlyweds in the film quarrel, it falls to Père Jules to recognize that Juliette is necessary to the Captain's well-being on this journey. She needs to be aboard. It is this image of what it might be like to die well that I think only a young person, thinking about death, could have generated. Even Charon did not know the anima needs to come along. Nor does the story of Orpheus tell us exactly what's wrong about trying to bring Eurydice out of the underworld, and what looking back to see if she's really going lifeward leaves out. *L'Atalante* is a mythic miracle that gives us the right picture, even if, like Osiris, it has had to be assembled properly after the death of the genius who envisioned it. What *L'Atalante* can show us is that the anima, though the archetype of life itself, (Jung, 1934/1958, para. 66), is not something to be left behind by our dying. She needs to be allowed to be part of it. This was a gift of the pioneering work of Elizabeth Kubler-Ross, who broke the deal of silence about death that was being dispensed to patients who were not even told by the doctors of the 1950s that they were dying, since that was deemed sadistic. But it also is what the Jungian analysis of death and dying needs to take aboard. The return of the soul to accompany someone who is dying, enables the soul to exercise its immortality. *L'Atalante*, like the Egyptian and the Tibetan Books of the Dead, should be a document for the ages. The dying body wants to be with the anima that has loved and ensouled it in life, and the anima wants to be with the dying body. It is up to the person's remaining spirit to recognize this, for the spirit is the Charon that guides the voyage from below. The anima must face death and give up the illusory pleasures of material existence, but this the anima finds relatively easy to do, as seen in the details of Juliette's story. Her need is to be wanted, to be desired, and to be recognized as the soulmate she is even during dying itself. She takes the happy memories of life with her to comfort her dying husband. They are the song of life, represented in the film as mechanical reproductions on record, echoed in the unforgettable soundtrack, and in the images the film records. All of that can accompany the dying person who is taking the anima along.

In this essay, I am writing about a film by a young man with a creative anima that he insisted on exercising while he was dying and produced an enduring cinematic masterpiece. The question arises as to whether the role of the anima in the dying process applies to people who are not men, not geniuses, and not working on an artistic opus. My answer would be that at times all people who die are geniuses, and the archetype of life as lived (the French have a short, lovely word for this, *vecu)* applies to all of us. But it is worth asking about what it would be like for a woman who is not an artist but a patient in analysis who has a wise woman guiding her voyage out of this life. Fortunately, Jane Hollister Wheelwright, a Jungian analyst who was herself analyzed by Jung before she helped to organize the Society of Jungian Analysts in Northern California that formed the C. G. Jung Institute of San Francisco, has supplied an answer in her book, *The Death of a Woman: How a Life became Complete*. Jane was her patient's old wise woman, and the patient's goal seemed to be "completion," a value that is important to Chinese philosophy. The *I Ching* says to the person who is not destined to be famous, "Hidden lines. One is able to be persevering. If by chance you are in the service of a king, seek not works, but bring to completion." Completion can be the anima of a woman seeking the meaning of her life while dying. Just before Wheelwright's analytic patient "Sally" died of cancer, she recorded a final dream: "I was a palm tree, the middle one of three trees. An earthquake was about to occur that would destroy all life, and I didn't want to be killed by the quake" (1981, p. 269). I think that dream suggests that the archetype of life, the anima, should be allowed to accompany someone into death, whether there is any promise of an earthly future.

Who can say what the soul does after it has finished accompanying the dying body on the voyage to the next world? I suspect she lives in immortality, but all we know for sure is that the body of this somehow indestructible, since miraculously preserved, film has been, especially in the most recent Criterion Collection BluRay edition, as carefully wrapped as any Egyptian mummy, dressed for a living future. As an artifact of a high culture, it similarly encodes the character of engaged soul, and the spirit of the Wise Young Man who guided that soul's ambition in an uncannily embodied way. An old fan like me, born five years after Vigo had to leave his final film behind for the world to make of it what it can, continues to learn from his example.

References

Agee, J. (1969). *Agee on Film, Volume 1.* Grossets Universal Library.

Beebe, J. (2008). Jungian Illumination of Film. In V. Apperson & J. Beebe, *The Presence of the Feminine in Film* (pp. 17-28). Cambridge Scholars Publishing.

Edinger, E. (1973). *Ego and Archetype.* Penguin Books.

Hillman, J. (1968). Editor's Preface. In *Timeless Documents of the Soul* (American ed.). Northwestern University Press.

Jung, C. G. (1934/1959). *Archetypes of the Collective Unconscious.* In *The Collected Works of C. G. Jung*, vol. 9i. Princeton University Press.

Jung, C. G. (1963). *Mysterium Coniunctionis.* In *The Collected Works of C.G. Jung*, Vol. 14. Bollingen Foundation/ Pantheon Books.

Jung, C. G. (1977). The "Face to Face" Interview with John Freeman, BBC Television, Oct. 22, 1959. In *C. G. Jung Speaking*, W. McGuire, W. & R. F. C. Hull (eds.), pp. 424-439. Princeton University Press.

McDunnah, M. G. (2017). *L'Atalante.* The Unaffiliated Critic: Independent Study of World Cinema (https:// unaffiliatedcritic.com/2017/01/latalante-1934 consulted January 15, 2024)

Ovid (1964) *The Metamorphoses.* (R. Humphries (trans.). Indiana University Press.

Rothman, W. (1982). *Hitchcock: The Murderous Gaze.* Harvard University Press.

Sarris, A. (1968, May 12). Directors, how personal can you get? *The New York Times*, Section D.

Sontag, S. (1977). *On Photography.* Farrar, Straus & Giroux.

Thomson, David (2002). *The New Biographical Dictionary of Film* (4th ed.). Knopf.

Vigo, J. (Director) (2011). *The Complete Jean Vigo* (Blu-ray discs). Criterion.

Von Franz, M.L. (1970). *The Problem of the Puer Aeternus.* Spring Publications.

Warner, M. (1993). *L'Atalante*. Palgrave/British Film Institute.

Wheelwright, J. (1981). *Death of a Woman: How a Life Became Complete.* St. Martin's Press.

Wikipedia. "*Pietà* (Michelangelo)." en.wikipedia.org/wiki/Pietà_ (Michelangelo), accessed 3/10/2024.

About the Contributors

Henry Abramovitch is Founding President and senior training analyst, Israel Institute of Jungian Psychology in Honor of Erich Neumann, Professor Emeritus at Tel Aviv University, Past President of Israel Anthropological Association who studies mourning cross-culturally. His books include *Brothers and Sisters*, *Why Odysseus Came Home as a Stranger...* and a novel, *Panic Attacks in Pistachio: A Psychological Detective Story*. With Murray Stein, he coauthored plays, including *The Analyst and the Rabbi* and *Speaking of Friends*, available on YouTube. Email: henry.abramovitch@gmail.com

John Beebe, a past president of the C. G. Jung Institute of San Francisco, is the creator of the eight-function, eight-archetype model of psychological types and has often used type and archetype to explore developments in film, culture, and politics. He was founding editor of *The San Francisco Jung Institute Library Journal,* now called *Jung Journal: Culture & Psyche,* and the first American co-editor of *The Journal of Analytical Psychology.* He is the author of *Integrity in Depth.*

Paul Bishop is William Jacks Chair of Modern Languages at the University of Glasgow. His research is focused on the intellectual background to psychoanalysis and analytical psychology. His books include *Reading Goethe at Midlife: Ancient Wisdom, German Classicism & Jung* (2011; 2nd edn., 2020), *On the Blissful Islands with Nietzsche & Jung: In the Shadow of the Superman* (2017), and *Reading Plato through Jung: Why must the Third become the Fourth?* (2022).

Joseph Cambray, Ph.D. is a Jungian analyst now living in the Santa Barbara area of California. He is Past-President/CEO of Pacifica Graduate Institute; Past-President of the International Association for Analytical Psychology; and has served as the U.S. Editor for The Journal of Analytical Psychology. He was a faculty member at Harvard Medical School in the Department of Psychiatry at Massachusetts General Hospital, Center for Psychoanalytic Studies. He has numerous publications and regularly lectures internationally.

Professor Ann Casement (UK) is a senior member of the British Jungian Analytic Association, associate of the Jungian Psychoanalytic Association (New York), founding member of the International Neuropsychoanalytic Association, and New York State-licensed psychoanalyst. She served on the IAAP's Executive Committee from 2001-2007; its Ethics Committee from 2007-2016, becoming the Chair in 2010. She also served on the 2013 Gradiva Awards Committee (New York); has published widely, including articles and reviews for *The Economist* and professional journals. Email: adecasement@gmail.com

Claire Costello, Ph.D., RN, PMHCNS-BC, adult and child analyst, teaching member C. G. Jung Institute of San Francisco, works in private practice and Bay Area clinics serving a lifelong devotion to mind/body healing. Papers and presentations include: Born Through Grief and Awe During the Early AIDS Crisis (2020); Religion, Spirituality, and AIDS-Related Bereavement: Early AIDS Crisis As Initiation Into Personal, Collective, Cultural, and Global Individuation IAAP and IAJS 2008; IAJS 2012; Integrative Imagery: Engaging Psyche, Soma for Self-Healing (2015); Sandplay Within The Context of Relationship (2008). Email: clcostello7@icloud.com

416

Josephine Evetts-Secker graduated from the University of London and the Jung Institute, Zürich. She was in psychoanalytic practice in Canada while teaching at the University of Calgary. She is now in private practice in England. She has worked with the IGAP training program (London) and the International School of Analytical Psychology (ISAP) Zürich. She has lectured for Jung societies in the UK, Canada, the USA, and Russia. She has published poetry, articles, lectures, and book chapters, and edited collections of fairy tales. She serves as semiretired priest in the Anglican church.

Ladson Hinton, M.A., M.D., is a psychoanalyst who lives, practices, and teaches in Seattle. He is a founding member of the New School for Analytical Psychology and coeditor of two award-winning books, *Temporality and Shame: Perspectives from Psychoanalysis and Philosophy* (Routledge, 2018) and *Shame, Temporality and Social Change: Ominous Transitions* (Routledge, 2021).

Haruko Kuwabara, Ph.D., is a professor of psychology at the Shujitsu University, Japan, and Director of the Center for Counselling and Psychotherapy. She is a clinical psychologist who trained at Kyoto University. In 2017, she studied at ISAP-Zürich, and she is currently a diploma candidate at the AJAJ (Association of Jungian Analysts, Japan).

Luis Moris, M.A., is a Jungian analyst and lecturer at the International School of Analytical Psychology (ISAP-Zürich). He is the editor of *A Jungian Legacy, Tom Kirsch* (Chiron Publications, 2019). He has directed and produced numerous films about analytical psychology, and is the founder of Blue Salamandra, a film production house dedicated to creating artistic works related to Jungian thought. He is currently doing a Ph.D. at the University of Essex, UK, under the supervision of Dr. Roderick Main. The title of his thesis is *The Interplay Between the Here and the Hereafter: Life After Death in the Psychotherapy of C. G. Jung.* He lives and has a private practice in Zürich.

Susan Olson, M.A., M.S.W., graduated from the C. G. Jung Institute (Zürich) in 1992. She is a member of the International Association for Analytical Psychology, the Association of Graduates in Analytical Psychology, and the Memphis/Atlanta Jungian Seminar, an affiliate of the Inter-Regional Society of Jungian Analysts. Her publications include *By Grief Transformed: Dreams and the Mourning Process* (Spring Journal Books, 2010) and *Images of the Dead in Grief Dreams: A Jungian View of Mourning* (Routledge, 2020).

Murray Stein, Ph.D., was born in Canada and educated in the United States at Yale University (B.A. and M.Div.) and the University of Chicago (Ph.D.). He is a graduate of the C. G. Jung Institute of Zürich (1973) and is currently a Training and Supervising Analyst at the International School of Analytical Psychology Zürich (ISAP-ZÜRICH). He has been president of the Chicago Society of Jungian Analysts (1980-1985), the International Association for Analytical Psychology (2001-2004) and ISAP-ZÜRICH (2008-2012). He is the author of *Jung's Treatment of Christianity, Jung's Map of the Soul, Outside Inside and All Around*, and many other books and articles. His newly published Collected Writings so far contain eight volumes, among them *Psychology and Spirituality* (Volume 8). He lives in Switzerland and has a private practice in Zürich and from his home in Goldiwil (Thun).

Stephani Stephens, Ph.D., is a Jungian-oriented psychotherapist and a lecturer in Counselling at the University of Canberra, Australia. She holds a Ph.D. from the University of Kent, Canterbury, UK in Jungian psychology. She is the author of *C.G. Jung and the Dead; Visions, Active Imagination and the Unconscious Terrain* by Routledge. Her areas of research include the unconscious, transgenerational inheritance, cultural broaching, and the self in therapeutic practice. She teaches and maintains a small therapy practice.

Ann Belford Ulanov, M.Div. Ph.D. L.H.D., is a Jungian analyst practicing in New York City, Professor Emerita of Psychology and Religion at Union Theological Seminary, member of Jungian Psychoanalytic Association, IAAP, and its Editorial Advisory Board for the *Journal of Analytical Psychology*. She lectures here and abroad. She is author of many books with her late husband, Barry Ulanov, among which are *The Envied and the Envying: Cinderella and Her Sisters* and *The Healing Imagination*. She is author of many books of her own, among which are *Madness and Creativity, The Psychoid, Soul and Psyche: Piercing Space/Time Barriers, and Back to Basics*.

Ursula Wirtz, Ph.D., holds a doctorate in literature and philosophy, and trained as a clinical and anthropological psychologist as well as a Jungian psychoanalyst. She serves as training and supervising analyst on the faculty of ISAPZÜRICH. She has been internationally engaged in training Jungian analysts in Russia, Czech Republic, the Baltic States, China, and Taiwan. Her most recent book *Trauma and Beyond: The Mystery of Transformation* has been translated into multiple languages, including German, Russian, Polish, Czech, Chinese, and Ukrainian.

www.ingramcontent.com/pod-product-compliance
Lightning Source LLC
Chambersburg PA
CBHW020331270326
41926CB00007B/135